Lecture Notes in Computer Science   5453

Commenced Publication in 1973
Founding and Former Series Editors:
Gerhard Goos, Juris Hartmanis, and Jan van Leeuwen

Editorial Board

David Hutchison
  Lancaster University, UK
Takeo Kanade
  Carnegie Mellon University, Pittsbu. ఎ
Josef Kittler
  University of Surrey, Guildford, UK
Jon M. Kleinberg
  Cornell University, Ithaca, NY, USA
Alfred Kobsa
  University of California, Irvine, CA, USA
Friedemann Mattern
  ETH Zurich, Switzerland
John C. Mitchell
  Stanford University, CA, USA
Moni Naor
  Weizmann Institute of Science, Rehovot, Israel
Oscar Nierstrasz
  University of Bern, Switzerland
C. Pandu Rangan
  Indian Institute of Technology, Madras, India
Bernhard Steffen
  University of Dortmund, Germany
Madhu Sudan
  Massachusetts Institute of Technology, MA, USA
Demetri Terzopoulos
  University of California, Los Angeles, CA, USA
Doug Tygar
  University of California, Berkeley, CA, USA
Gerhard Weikum
  Max-Planck Institute of Computer Science, Saarbruecken, Germany

Jürgen Becker   Roger Woods
Peter Athanas   Fearghal Morgan (Eds.)

Reconfigurable Computing: Architectures, Tools and Applications

5th International Workshop, ARC 2009
Karlsruhe, Germany, March 16-18, 2009
Proceedings

 Springer

Volume Editors

Jürgen Becker
Universität Karlsruhe (TH)
Institut für Technik der Informationsverarbeitung (ITIV)
76128 Karlsruhe, Germany
E-mail: becker@itiv.uni-karlsruhe.de

Roger Woods
Queen's University Belfast, ECIT Institute
Queen's Road, Queen's Island, Belfast, BT3 9DT, UK
E-mail: r.woods@qub.ac.uk

Peter Athanas
Virginia Tech, Bradley Department of Electrical and Electronic Engineering
302 Whittemore (0111), Blacksburg, VA 24061, USA
E-mail: athanas@vt.edu

Fearghal Morgan
National University of Ireland, Department of Electronic Engineering
Galway, Ireland
E-mail: fearghal.morgan@nuigalway.ie

Library of Congress Control Number: Applied for

CR Subject Classification (1998): C, B, I.4, E.3

LNCS Sublibrary: SL 1 – Theoretical Computer Science and General Issues

ISSN   0302-9743
ISBN-10   3-642-00640-X Springer Berlin Heidelberg New York
ISBN-13   978-3-642-00640-1 Springer Berlin Heidelberg New York

This work is subject to copyright. All rights are reserved, whether the whole or part of the material is
concerned, specifically the rights of translation, reprinting, re-use of illustrations, recitation, broadcasting,
reproduction on microfilms or in any other way, and storage in data banks. Duplication of this publication
or parts thereof is permitted only under the provisions of the German Copyright Law of September 9, 1965,
in its current version, and permission for use must always be obtained from Springer. Violations are liable
to prosecution under the German Copyright Law.

springer.com

© Springer-Verlag Berlin Heidelberg 2009
Printed in Germany

Typesetting: Camera-ready by author, data conversion by Scientific Publishing Services, Chennai, India
Printed on acid-free paper   SPIN: 12637379   06/3180   5 4 3 2 1 0

In memory of Stamatis Vassiliadis (1957–2007), Steering Committee Member for ARC 2006 and 2007

Preface

Reconfigurable computing (RC) technologies offer the promise of substantial performance gains over traditional architectures by customizing, sometimes at run-time, the topology of the underlying architecture to match the specific needs of a given application. Contemporary configurable architectures allow for the definition of architectures with functional and storage units that match the specific needs of a given computation, in terms of function, bit-width and control structures. Compared to standard microprocessor architectures, advantages are possible in terms of power consumption on a broad range of different application fields. Moreover, the flexibility enabled by reconfiguration is also seen as a basic technique for overcoming transient failures in emerging device structures.

Techniques for achieving reconfigurable systems are numerous and require the joint development of reconfigurable hardware systems to support the dynamic behavior, e.g., suitable programming models, tools and languages, to support the reconfiguration process during run-time as well as during design-time. This includes verification techniques that can demonstrate formally correct reconfiguration sequences at each stage. While there are many problems, the existence and development of technologies such as recent multi- and many-core processor architectures, dynamically reconfigurable and multi-grain computing architectures, as well as application-specific processors suggest that there is a very strong need for adaptive and reconfigurable systems.

The International Workshop of Applied Reconfigurable Computing (ARC) aims to bring together researchers and practitioners of reconfigurable computing with an emphasis on practical applications of this promising technology. This year's workshop was accompanied by selected international invited speakers with strong views on the future of reconfigurable technology. This LNCS volume includes papers selected for the fifth edition of the workshop (ARC 2009), held at the Karlsruhe Institute of Technology (KIT), Germany during March 16-18, 2009. The ARC 2009 workshop attracted a large number of high-quality papers, describing interesting work on research related to applied reconfigurable computing. A total of 65 papers were submitted to the workshop from 22 countries: Japan (9), Germany (8), UK (7), Spain (5), Ireland (4), Republic of South Korea (3), Italy (3), France (3), The Netherlands (3), Poland (2), USA (2), Republic of China (2), Portugal (2), Thailand (2), Brazil (2), Mexico (2), Greece (1), India (1), Iran (1), Romania (1), Pakistan (1), and Finland (1). This distribution is reflective of the international engagement in the disciplines related to reconfigurable systems.

In all cases, submitted papers were evaluated by three members of the Program Committee. After careful selection, 21 papers were accepted as full papers (acceptance rate of 32.3%) and 21 as short papers (global acceptance rate of 64.6%). The accepted papers led to a very interesting workshop program, which we consider to constitute a representative overview of on-going research efforts in applied reconfigurable computing, a rapidly evolving and maturing field.

The workshop was distinguished by a strong focus on interdisciplinary applications of reconfigurable systems. Of the 21 papers selected for presentation, and of the nine presentation sessions, one-third were directly devoted to reconfigurable systems applications. Closely related to the application theme, other sessions at the workshop included resource allocation and scheduling, FPGA security and bitstream analysis, architectures, cryptography, and placement and routing strategies. As reflected by the diverse program, the application domains that are impacted by reconfigurable computing continue to expand. ARC continues to serve the international community by providing a forum for the intellectual exchange of technologies, methodologies and thought.

We would like to thank all the authors for submitting their first versions of the papers and the final versions of the accepted papers. We would like to acknowledge the support of all the members of this year's Steering and Program Committees in reviewing papers, in helping the paper selection and in giving valuable suggestions. We would also like to thank the members of the Organizing Committee for their competent guidance and work in the last month, as well as Springer for their continuous support of this event. Special thanks are dedicated to the distinguished invited speakers and their contribution to the technical program.

January 2009

Jürgen Becker
Roger Woods
Peter Athanas
Fearghal Morgan

Organization

Organizing Committee

General Chairs	Jürgen Becker (Karlsruhe Institute of Technology (KIT), Germany)
	Roger Woods (Queen's University of Belfast, UK)
Program Chairs	Peter Athanas (Virginia Tech, USA)
	Fearghal Morgan (National University of Ireland, Galway, Ireland)
Proceedings Chair	Alastair Smith (Imperial College London, UK)
Local Chair	Michael Hübner (Karlsruhe Institute of Technology (KIT), Germany)
Publicity	Pete Sedcole (Imperial College London, UK)
	Philip Leong (Chinese University of Hong Kong, China)

Steering Committee

Hideharu Amano	Keio University, Japan
Jürgen Becker	Universität Karlsruhe (TH), Germany
Mladen Berekovic	Braunschweig University of Technology, Germany
Koen Bertels	Delft University of Technology, The Netherlands
João M.P. Cardoso	IST/INESC-ID, Portugal
Katherine Compton	University of Wisconsin-Madison, USA
George Constantinides	Imperial College London, UK
Pedro C. Diniz	Instituto Superior Técnico, Portugal
Philip H.W. Leong	Chinese University of Hong Kong, China
Walid Najjar	University of California Riverside, USA
Roger Woods	Queen's University of Belfast, UK

Program Committee

Peter Athanas	Virginia Tech, USA
Michael Attig	Xilinx Research Labs, San Jose, USA
Nader Bagherzadeh	University of California, Irvine, USA
Jürgen Becker	University of Karlsruhe (TH), Germany
Mladen Berekovic	Braunschweig University of Technology, Germany
Neil Bergmann	University of Queensland, Australia
Koen Bertels	Delft University of Technology, The Netherlands
Christos-Savvas Bouganis	Imperial College London, UK
Mihai Budiu	Microsoft Research, USA

João M.P. Cardoso	IST/INESC-ID, Portugal
Mark Chang	Olin College, USA
Paul Chow	University of Toronto, Canada
Katherine Compton	University of Wisconsin-Madison, USA
George Constantinides	Imperial College London, UK
Oliver Diessel	University of New South Wales, Australia
Pedro C. Diniz	Instituto Superior Técnico, Portugal
Tarek El-Ghazawi	George Washington University, USA
Robert Esser	Xilinx Corp., Ireland
Suhaib Fahmy	Trinity College Dublin, Ireland
Antonio Ferrari	University of Aveiro, Portugal
Guy Gogniat	Université de Bretagne Sud, France
Jim Harkin	University of Ulster, Magee, UK
Reiner Hartenstein	University of Kaiserslautern, Germany
Christoph Heer	Infineon Technologies AG, Germany
Román Hermida	Complutense University of Madrid, Spain
Michael Hübner	Karlsruhe Institute of Technology (KIT), Germany
Ryan Kastner	University of California, Santa Barbara, USA
Andreas Koch	Darmstadt University of Technology, Germany
Philip Leong	Chinese University of Hong Kong, China
Wayne Luk	Imperial College London, UK
Maria-Cristina Marinescu	IBM T.J. Watson Research Center, USA
Liam Marnane	University College Cork, Ireland
Eduardo Marques	University of São Paulo, Brazil
Konstantinos Masselos	University of the Peloponnese, Greece
John McAllister	Queen's University Belfast, UK
Seda Ö. Memik	Northwestern University, USA
Fearghal Morgan	National University of Ireland, Galway, Ireland
Robert Mullins	University of Cambridge, UK
Walid Najjar	University of California Riverside, USA
Horácio Neto	INESC-ID/IST, Portugal
Joon-seok Park	Inha University, Seoul, South Korea
Andy Pimentel	University of Amsterdam, The Netherlands
Joachim Pistorius	Altera Corp., USA
Marco Platzner	University of Paderborn, Germany
Bernard Pottier	University of Bretagne, France
Tsutomu Sasao	Kyushu Institute of Technology, Japan
Pete Sedcole	Imperial College London, UK
Lesley Shannon	Simon Fraser University, USA
Alastair Smith	Imperial College London, UK
Hayden So	Hong Kong University, Hong Kong
Thilo Streichert	Daimler AG, Germany
Srikanthan Thambipillai	Nanyang Technological University, Singapore
Pedro Trancoso	University of Cyprus, Cyprus
Ranga Vemuri	University of Cincinnati, USA
Markus Weinhardt	PACT Informationstechnologie AG, Germany
Stephan Wong	Delft University of Technology, The Netherlands
Roger Woods	Queen's University Belfast, UK

Table of Contents

Resource Allocation and Scheduling

Applications 3

Posters

FPGA Design Productivity - A Discussion of the State of the Art and a Research Agenda

Brent Nelson

Department of Electrical and Computer Engineering,
Brigham Young University, Utah, USA

Abstract. As we near 20 years of history with reconfigurable computing there is continued (and even increasing) interest in design productivity for RC. Configurable computing machines (CCMs) based on FPGAs
are touted as re-usable, re-configurable platforms for accelerated computing, but the fact remains that FPGAs are simply not that easy to
"program", even after all this time. Why? The usual list of suspects is
familiar to most, and includes challenges with timing closure, gate-level
design, fixed-point arithmetic analysis, communication management, and
clock cycle level control of design resources, to name a few.

To address these problems there continues to be much research in the
community on higher-level languages, reusable core libraries, improved
CAD tools, debug infrastructure, etc. While these research activities focus almost exclusively on CAD, there are other interesting and often
overlooked pieces of the productivity puzzle. One such puzzle piece is
circuit and architectural support for design productivity. Another puzzle
piece poses the question: how is the RC landscape changing with the
introduction of new devices (many/multi-core and coarse grain)? A final
consideration is to look at the entire design productivity picture — if
all the puzzle pieces were fit together into a comprehensive approach for
improving productivity, is a 10× increase feasible? 20×? If so, at what
cost?

This talk will focus on the above questions in the context of design productivity for FPGA application development, introducing the
productivity problem, and identifying select issues which are key to providing radical design productivity improvements. It will then drill down
on those key issues, showing the range of improvements possible using
recently published and unpublished research results from a variety of
venues.

J. Becker et al. (Eds.): ARC 2009, LNCS 5453, p. 1, 2009.
© Springer-Verlag Berlin Heidelberg 2009

Resiliency in Elemental Computing

Joseph Hassoun

Director of Hardware Engineering and chip design, Element CXI

Abstract. This presentation describes a new reconfigurable architecture that lends itself to parallelizable applications such as Software-Defined Radio, while providing a new level of reliability, called resiliency. The architecture is called an Elemental Computing Array (ECA). At run time, code is dynamically placed into the ECA elements to work around defects on a device whether they were fabrication defects or came about later due to device wear out. Resiliency extends the useful lifetime of products and allows for graceful system degradation instead of catastrophic failure. The ECA combines four computational styles: sequential, data-flow, message-passing, and DMA in a rapidly-reconfigurable distributed system on a chip.

Also covered will be a description of the implementation of key algorithms of Orthogonal Frequency-Division Multiplexing (OFDM) on the new ECA reconfigurable architecture. OFDM is an essential technology for current and next generation standards such as 3G/4G, WiMax, and digital broadcasting standards. The implementation of these kinds of standards on the ECA architecture will be covered, as well as implementation of compute-intensive smart antenna techniques such as beamforming, MIMO, and maximum likelihood (ML) detection.

J. Becker et al. (Eds.): ARC 2009, LNCS 5453, p. 2, 2009.
© Springer-Verlag Berlin Heidelberg 2009

The Colour of Embedded Computation

Ian Phillips

ARM, Cambridge, UK

Abstract. Categories and classifications, like acronyms, are useful shortcuts to facilitate discussion and decision. Yet their use is frequently subsumed by business interests to become objects or objectives in their own right. So used, they subtly mislead and constrain the thought process: Not only of the many who can afford to be be enticed by the bejewelled shell; but of greater import, of the scientists whose role is to create the viable technology within. In this presentation the author will explore some of the common shortcuts prevalent in the area of microelectronic systems, to identify limitations caused by their commercial adoption, and in consequence the research avenues and business opportunities in danger of being overlooked.

J. Becker et al. (Eds.): ARC 2009, LNCS 5453, p. 3, 2009.
© Springer-Verlag Berlin Heidelberg 2009

A HyperTransport 3 Physical Layer Interface for FPGAs

Heiner Litz, Holger Froening, and Ulrich Bruening

University of Heidelberg, Computer Architecture Group, ZITI,
B6 26, 68131 Mannheim, Germany
{heiner.litz,holger.froening,
ulrich.bruening}@ziti.uni-heidelberg.de

Abstract. This paper presents the very first implementation of a HyperTransport 3 physical layer interface for Field Programmable Gate Arrays. HyperTransport is a low latency, high bandwidth point-to-point interconnect technology that can be used to directly connect hardware accelerators to AMD's Opteron CPUs. Providing support for HyperTransport 3 on FPGAs is highly relevant for increasing the performance of accelerators based on reconfigurable logic. This paper shows the challenges of such an implementation and novel ideas to solve them successfully. A new architecture is presented that uses Fast Serializer Logic to keep up with the increasing speeds of current host interface protocols. A solid evaluation is provided using a specially developed FPGA board as a verification platform.

1 Introduction

HyperTransport 2.x (HT2) [1][2] is an established technology for chip-to-chip connections offering a very low latency and a high bandwidth. It is used in all major AMD processors, including the Opteron [3]. The most recent development in the area of HyperTransport is the availability of the HyperTransport 3.1 (HT3) [4] and the HyperTransport Extension 3 (HTX3) [5] specification. The first allows for very high operating frequencies (3.2GBit/s per lane), the second defines a connector for add-in cards with direct HT3 connection to one of the CPUs.

HT3 will be mainly used by AMD processors. HT3 units can either be located on the mainboard, in the CPU socket or on an HTX3 add-in card. In all cases HT units are directly connected to the CPU(s) without any intermediate bridges or any kind of protocol conversion. The high performance of HT3 in terms of extremely high bandwidth of up to 25.6 GByte/s[1] and low latency due to the direct connection makes it highly suitable for high performance applications. Additionally, the direct connection allows to participate in the cache coherency protocol of the CPUs [6]. Typical applications are accelerated computing [7][8] and fine grain communication [9][10].

In order to leverage the advantages of Field Programmable Gate Array (FPGA) technologies some obstacles have to be overcome, because typical FPGA technology is not designed for the use in HT3 applications. In this paper we present an HT3 Physical Layer (PHY) as a major component of an HT3 unit implementation. The PHY together with the HT3 Core as an technology-independent module enables the

---

[1] Maximum theoretical bandwidth for a 16 bit wide HT 3.1 link.

J. Becker et al. (Eds.): ARC 2009, LNCS 5453, pp. 4–14, 2009.
© Springer-Verlag Berlin Heidelberg 2009

use of HT3 in FPGAs. This allows to leverage the FPGA's advantages in terms of re-configurability and high performance in a verification platform, rapid prototyping station or in applications like accelerated computing and fine grain communication. To the best of our knowledge there is currently no HyperTransport 3 implementation for FPGAs available. This paper presents a novel approach to use Fast Serializer Logic (FSL) for HyperTransport 3 interfaces leading to much higher supported bandwidths than any other existing implementations. Our proposed solution provides up to 12.8 GByte/s bidirectional host interface bandwidth, which is more than twice as much as the fastest PCI-Express 8x implementation for Xilinx FPGAs which offers 5 GByte/s.

The Physical Layer (PHY) is the first of seven layers in the Open Systems Interconnection (OSI) model of computer networking. Usually, it is the most complex one due to the large amount of different technologies. The PHY interfaces with the Medium Access Control (MAC) sublayer. Typical tasks for the PHY layer are media-dependent encoding and decoding and transmission and reception.

In the application here the PHY is responsible for: packet delivery, synchronization, data serialization and de-serialization, bit slip and clock/data recovery. It is not responsible for: flow control, error detection or correction and link configuration. These tasks are performed by the MAC sublayer, which is layered on top of the PHY layer. In this case, the MAC is the HT3 Core, which is based on an open source available HT2 Core [11]. An overview of the system in which the PHY is being used is provided in figure 1.

1.1 Contributions

This paper presents some novel ideas that allow to implement a high performance architecture for next generation's host interface technologies. The results of our research are highly relevant for upcoming high performance applications in the area of

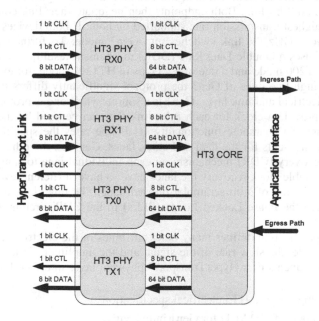

Fig. 1. System Overview

accelerated computing, coprocessors and interconnection networks. Our major contributions include:

- First HyperTransport 3 implementation for FPGAs
- First HyperTransport implementation using FSL
- Highest host interface bandwidth for FPGAs (12.8 GB)
- Manual oversampling technique for FSL
- Real world FPGA implementation

The rest of this paper is organized as follows: We will provide background information in the following section. Section 3 describes the architecture which was developed to solve the various problems occurring within a HT3 PHY implementation for FPGAs. Section 4 is dedicated to a concrete implementation thereof, which is evaluated in Section 5. Section 6 provides the conclusion and outlook.

2   Background

Within the HyperTransport 3.1 specification several new features were introduced that pose a challenge on FPGA implementations. The high line rates of 2.4 - 6.4 Gbps together with the demanding electrical characteristics of HT3 make FPGA implementations difficult. To our best knowledge there is currently no FPGA vendor that naturally supports HT3.

HyperTransport defines two different operating modes. The first one is the Gen1 mode which refers to HT1 and HT2 implementations, the second one is called Gen3 and refers to HT3. HT3 is downwards compatible which means that Gen3 devices have to support Gen1 as well. The link initialization always begins in Gen1 mode at 200 MHz with an 8 bit link. Both endpoints then negotiate their link connection and switch to the highest transmission rate supported by both. If both devices support frequencies above 1 GHz the link switches into Gen3 mode. To further increase link bandwidth HT uses a Double Data Rate (DDR) mechanism resulting in a line rate of 400 Mbps in HT200 mode and a rate of 2.4 Gbps in HT1200 mode, for example.

Due to the high line rates of Gen3 the protocol significantly differs from Gen1 in terms of the electrical and link layer. Gen1 is a source synchronous protocol requiring the sender to provide a clock for each 8 bit link that can be used by the receiver to sample the data. To guarantee functionality at all line rates the specification poses strict skew requirements for the data and clock lanes. Gen3 on the other hand uses a Clock Data Recovery (CDR) mechanism on each individual lane to sample the data. To allow for reliable clock recovery the lanes have to have sufficient level transitions which requires the use of a bit scrambler on each lane. The link clock is still used in Gen3 to provide the Phase Locked Loops (PLLs) in the CDR circuits with a stable reference clock.

The HT3 specification defines many other attributes of the electrical interface like the common mode, the slew rate of the signal and the amplitude. In a summary, the minimum requirements of a HyperTransport3 physical layer interface for FPGAs are the following.

- Compliance to HT3 electrical specification
- Support of 200 MHz for Gen1 initialization

- Support of source synchronous sampling mechanism
- Support of 1.2 GHz and above for Gen3
- Support of CDR data sampling mechanism
- Capability to switch between Gen1 and Gen3

3 Architecture

The high line rates of HT3 prohibit the use of regular IO cells for the PHY. A basic PHY has been implemented with regular IO cells. Measurements have been performed at the pins with an oscilloscope, the results are shown in figure 2.

It should be obvious that successful operation is not possible with the eye diagram shown above. The only solution, therefore, seems to be the use of Fast Serializer Logic (FSL) blocks provided by many FPGAs. They are capable of driving data rates of 3 Gbps and above however pose various limitations. At first, each FPGA only contains a very limited number of these FSL blocks. Low speed operation is a priori not supported, as a minimum line rate of 640 Mbps is required. Electrical parameters like the common mode are not flexibly adjustable but imposed by the FSL. This paper proposes a new architecture that solves these problems and that allows for successful HyperTransport 3 implementations in Xilinx FPGAs.

3.1 Electrical Compliance

The Xilinx FSL used in our implementation are not electrically compliant due to their supported common mode voltages. Various HSpice simulations have been performed to determine whether the common mode offset is critical. The simulations show successful operation, however, have to be approved in a real prototype.

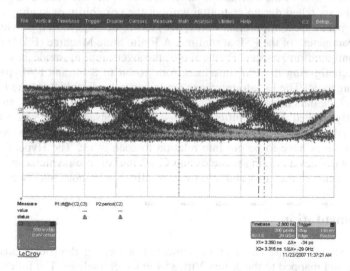

Fig. 2. Two Gbps line rate with regular IO

3.2 Gen1 Operation

For the HyperTransport initialization phase support of Gen1 mode at HT200 speed is required. However, the FSL blocks in Xilinx devices operate at a minimum line rate of 640 Mbps. To overcome this problem a manual oversampling mode has been developed. A reference clock of 200 MHz is provided together with a PLL multiplier value of 4 to generate the external 800 MHz link frequency. Internally, instead of implementing a 1:8 serialization rate in the PHY as required, a 1:16 ratio is used. If the 16 bit parallel data is provided to the PHY at the same speed of the 8 bit interface, the resulting line rate is doubled to 800 Mbps. Mapping the 8 bit data to the 16 bit interface is done by assigning it to the even bit positions of the 16 bit interface and a copy to the odd bit positions. The result of this mechanism is that adjacent odd/even tuples like 0/1 or 2/3 carry the same data value. This mechanism is transparent to the link and therefore it appears as a 400 Mbps interface to the other link endpoint. Oversampling is used on both the receive (RX) and transmit (TX) path with the exception of the TX link clock. This clock has to be phase shifted by 90 degrees in regard to the data. To achieve this behaviour the oversampling is deactivated for the clock lane and a static bit pattern is assigned to the serializer. This pattern is a sequence of alternating pairs of zeros and ones. The sequence is then shifted by a phase offset of a single bit time.

In Gen1 mode the link is not scrambled which may result in idle phases of the link where no signal transitions occur for a long period in time. The PLLs in the CDR circuits therefore lose their lock rendering the clock recovery impossible. As a solution the GTPs are operated in lock to reference mode using the RX link clock.

3.3 Gen3 Operation

For Gen3 operation the interface has to be run at a line rate of 2.4 Gbps. This is achieved by providing a 300 MHz clock with a multiplier factor for the PLLs of 8. The multiplier factor of the PLL is normally set at compile time. However, as the line rate has to be switched during operation without the possibility of loading a new design, the Dynamic Reconfiguration Port (DRP) has to be used, which provides access to several parameters of the FSL at runtime. A Finite State Machine (FSM) takes care of the reconfiguration process. Furthermore, the oversampling mode has to be disabled by reconfiguring the FSL interface from 16 bit to 8 bit and by bypassing the oversampling logic. The lock to reference mode has to be disabled and the FSLs have to perform clock data recovery. Each lane is sampled with its own clock, so the lanes are inherently skewed. Elastic buffers are used to compensate for the phase mismatch and synchronize the different lanes into a unified clock domain. To remove multiple bit skew the lanes have to be put into relation to each other. The HyperTransport 3 specification defines a training phase during Gen3 initialization which can be utilized to adjust the delay of the lanes and to provide a fully synchronous interface.

4 Implementation

The proposed architecture has been implemented in Verilog Register Transfer Level (RTL) code and mapped to the Xilinx Virtex5 FPGA technology. The following paragraphs present a detailed overview of the implemented logic, clocking scheme and IO cells.

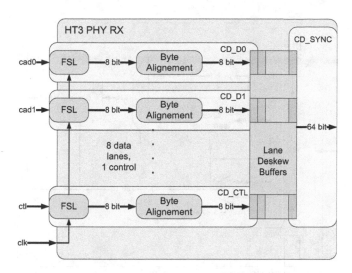

Fig. 3. RX PHY Toplevel Diagram

4.1 HT3 RX PHY

The HT3 PHY's purpose on the receive side is to deserialize the incoming link data, and to compensate for bit and byte skew by performing bitslip functionality. A toplevel block diagram with the different clock domains of the RX PHY is shown in figure 3.

The PHY comprises 10 different clock domains which are the 8 clock regions for control and data lanes, CD_D0 through CD_D7, another one for the CTL signal (CD_CTL) and the CD_SYNC domain. All domains run at the same clock frequency however have different phases. As in Gen1 mode a single reference clock is used to sample the data the CD_D domains can be regarded as synchronous. In Gen3 mode, however, the sample clock is provided by the FSL and, therefore, the lane deskew buffer is needed to synchronize the lanes so they can be accessed with single clock. The RX link clock is only needed in Gen1 mode as in Gen3 the FSL's are provided with a reference clock and perform CDR.

A detailed view of a per lane clock domain is given in figure 4. The functionality of the components again vary depending on Gen1 or Gen3 operation. In Gen1 mode the FSL provides a deserialized data stream of 16 bits width. Due to the manual over-sampling technique only every second bit of this interface is extracted by the over-sampling module. In both modes the bitslip module is provided with 8 bits of data each clock cycle. This module's purpose is to perform byte alignement. As the FSL is not aware of the position of the byte inside the serial data stream there are 8 possible ways of deserializing the same data stream. The bitslip module is responsible for compensating this misalignment and shift the bits accordingly. Therefore, it uses specific training patters which are send during initialization of both Gen1 and Gen3 and which determine the exact position of the byte in the serial stream.

Another task that has to be performed, while switching the operation mode, is to provide the correct clock. In Gen1 mode the 200 MHz RX link clock is used to sample the data. When switching to Gen3 the RX link clock changes to 1.2 GHz. The internal PLLs of the FSL, however, require a clock of 300 MHz in this mode which

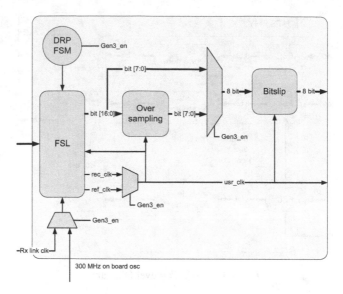

Fig. 4. Per Lane Clock Domain

has to be provided through an external clock source, e.g. an oscillator. Concurrently with the switch of the input clock the user clock has to be adjusted correctly. In Gen1 mode the FSL provides a reference clock which is the feed through receive link clock. In Gen3 the CDR circuit provides a recovered clock that must be used to drive the clock domain and which is used to push the date into the lane deskew buffers.

The final task is to switch between lock to reference mode and clock data recovery in between the Gen1 to Gen3 transition. This is realized through an FSM that writes the correct values into the configuration registers of the FSL using the dynamic reconfiguration port. The DRP is also used to adjust some analog parameters that control the PLLs. As soon as all modules are in Gen3 mode the FSL block and all its internal blocks are resetted. After reset, the CDR mechanism waits for valid scrambled data on the lanes to be able to lock and to recover a clock. If the complete initialization process including the training phase is successful the HT core connected to the PHY is notified and can start to process incoming data.

4.2 HT3 TX PHY

The transmit side of PHY is responsible for deserializing the data and driving it onto the lanes. The main functionality is already provided by the FSL, which allows for a straight forward implementation. An overview of the transmit side of the PHY is given in figure 5.

It can be seen that the transmit path also uses several clock domains, one for each outgoing link and a synchronous source clock domain. In Gen1 mode all TX domains can be regarded as synchronous as they are provided with the same reference clock, in Gen3, however, the transmit PLLs provide their dedicated clocks per output lane. The transmit clock requires special attention. In Gen1 mode it has to possess a defined phase of exactly 90 degree relative to the CAD and CTL lanes. This behaviour can be achieved with the following technique. A static bit pattern of alternating ones and zeros is provided to the serializer with the reference clock frequency. As manual oversampling is used on the TX side, each value has to be duplicated. The 90 degree phase shift can now be achieved by starting with a single digit followed up by the duplicate values, as shown in figure 5. In Gen3 mode no oversampling is used and therefore the phase shifted clock cannot be generated in this way. As in Gen3 no skew requirements for the lanes exist, it is sufficient to provide a clock with the correct frequency of 1.2 GHz.

The transmit clock domains CD_D0 through CD_D7 implementations are similar to the ones of the receive side. An oversampling circuit is used in Gen1 which duplicates the tx data to produce the desired manual oversampling effect. It is bypassed in Gen3 mode. As the PLL of an FSL is shared between the rx and tx side no other modifications through the DRP are necessary. The parallel transmit clock for each specific FSL domain is already provided by the PLL.

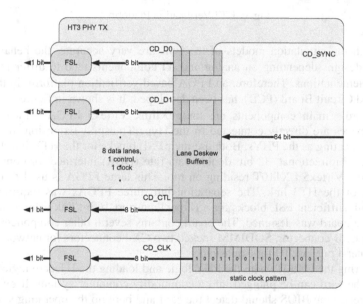

Fig. 5. TX PHY Toplevel Diagram

5 Evaluation

The PHY implementation has been evaluated by simulations and in a real world test design. For the simulation, the PHY is connected to a HyperTransport bus functional model on the host interface side and to a HT3 core on the parallel side. The implementation of the HT3 core is out of scope of this paper. The complete system has been embedded into a System Verilog based verification environment to be able to provide the best possible test coverage. The PHY was tested under different operating conditions using randomly constrained and corner case test patterns. Especially the Gen1 to Gen3 switch has been tested precisely showing the desired behaviour for both modes.

Fig. 6. HT3 Verification Platform

Although the simulation models of the FSL are very accurate, the behaviour of simulated designs depending on analog and IO components tend to differ from real world implementations. Therefore, an FPGA based verification platform, in the form of a Printed Circuit Board (PCB), has been developed. It is shown in figure 6.

The board's main components are three Xilinx Virtex5 FPGAs. Two Virtex5 LX50T devices are directly connected to the HyperTransport Extension link on the bottom side, acting as the PHYs. Both use their FSL blocks for the HTX interface and implement a bidirectional, 32 bit, double data rate (DDR) interface for communication with the Virtex5 LX110T residing on top. This large FPGA is used to hold the core logic of the HT3 link. The separation into three FPGAs was required as no FPGAs with sufficient FSL blocks for a HyperTransport 16 bit link were available at the time the board was designed. The board contains several other components which include an USB connector, SODIMM socket, two CX4 connectors for networking and several general purpose IO for extensions.

Configuring the LX50Ts with the PHY logic and loading the HT core logic into the LX110T, the card can be plugged into a commodity computer system. If everything works correctly the BIOS should detect the card and boot up the operating system. In the first basic test the card was configure to support only Gen1 operation at the HyperTransport initialization frequency of 200 MHz. In this mode the PHYs operate in lock to reference mode as described above. The critical issues which are checked in this configuration are the compliance to the electrical specification, the functionality of the data sampling mechanism, the oversampling and the bitslip mechanism. Electrical compliance has been tested by measuring eye diagrams of the link interface, see figure 7, and by checking the internal registers of the Opteron CPU which is connected to the FPGA board. While proceeding the boot process in single step mode it can be seen that the HT3 PHY is correctly detected and that the link initialization process passes successfully. Long-run tests haven't shown any problems regarding signal integrity or the common mode. A Linux Operating System has been successfully booted on the system showing the HT device in its device tree. To perform further testing, a device driver and an application interface (API) has been developed

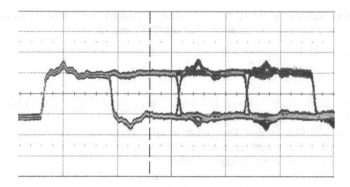

Fig. 7. Eye diagram of the FSL based HT link

which provides access to the verification platform from software. Various tests have been performed that write to and read data from the memory mapped device.

The successful tests for HyperTransport speeds of 200 MHz prove the correct functionality of the PHY at low clock rates that use the lock to reference mode and manual oversampling. This is an important result already, as in general, the fast serializer logic is built for transmitting data at frequencies of 640 Mbps and above.

The remaining task is to test the complete system at higher speeds and especially the in system switch from low speed to high speed operation. We have therefore configured the HT core to support higher frequencies like 800 and 1600 Mbps. In this case the system again boots in Gen1 mode at 200 MHz, then determines the capabilities of the HT device and then ramps up the link frequency. The PHY has to detect the switch, disable oversampling, change to clock data recovery mode and adjust the frequency of the PLLs through the DRP as explained above.

The card has been successfully booted in both high frequency modes and the same tests have been performed. This is an excellent proof of our HyperTransport 3 PHY architecture. It furthermore shows that fast serializer logic can be used for Hyper-Transport implementation despite their different electrical specification. The system already provides exceptional performance with 16 lanes at 1600 Mbps per lane. Further testing will show how far the frequency can be increased and which HyperTransport speeds can be supported at a maximum with our PHY.

6 Conclusion

To the best of our knowledge this paper presents the first fully functional HyperTransport 3 physical layer interface for FPGAs. It furthermore shows the first successful utilization of fast serializer logic for HyperTransport. The result is an architecture that offers high flexibility and great performance. To prove the quality of our work the design has been implemented in hardware description language code and mapped to a Xilinx FPGA. The verification of this design has been performed in a real world system. Therefore, an FPGA based rapid prototyping station has been designed which is comprised of three Xilinx Virtex5 devices. A device driver and API has been written to fully test the HyperTransport 3 PHY implementation. The current implementation has been tested with link speeds of up to 1600 Mbps. We believe that our implementation can scale up to 3200 Mbps, so future work will focus on increasing the frequency to the maximum of what our PHY can support.

References

[1] Anderson, D., Trodden, J.: HyperTransport System Architecture. Addison-Wesley, Reading (2003)

[2] Hypertransport Consortium, The Future of High-Performance Computing: Direct Low Latency CPU-to-Subsystem Interconnect (2008),
http://www.hypertransport.org

[3] Keltcher, C.N., McGrath, K.J., Ahmed, A., Conway, P.: The AMD Opteron proc¬essor for multiprocessor servers. IEEE Micro. 23(2), 66–67 (2003)

[4] Hypertransport Consortium. HyperTransport^{TM} I/O Link Specification Revision 3.10 (2008), http://www.hypertransport.org

[5] HyperTransport Consortium. HTX3^{TM} Specification for HyperTransport^{TM} 3.0 Daughtercards and ATX/EATX Motherboards (2008), http://www.hypertransport.org

[6] Conway, P., Hughes, B.: The AMD Opteron Northbridge Architecture. IEEE Micro. 27(2), 10–21 (2007)

[7] Gothandaraman, A., Peterson, G.D., Warren, G.L., Hinde, R.J., Harrison, R.J.: FPGA acceleration of a quantum Monte Carlo application. Parallel Computing 34, 4–5 (2008)

[8] Zhuo, L., Prasanna, V.K.: High Performance Linear Algebra Operations on Reconfigurable Systems. In: Proceedings of the 2005 ACM/IEEE Conference on Supercomputing (2005)

[9] Litz, H., Froening, H., Nuessle, M., Bruening, U.: VELO: A Novel Com¬munication Engine for Ultra-low Latency Message Transfers. In: 37th International Conference on Parallel Processing (ICPP 2008), Portland, Oregon, USA, September 08 - 12 (2008)

[10] El-Ghazawi, T., Carlson, W., Sterling, T., Yelick, K.: UPC: Distributed Sharend Memory Programming. Wiley Series on Parallel and Distributed Computing. John Wiley and Sons, Inc., Hoboken (2005)

[11] Slogsnat, D., Giese, A., Nuessle, M., Bruening, U.: An Open-Source HyperTransport Core. ACM Transactions on Reconfigurable Technology and Systems (TRETS) 1(3), 1–21 (2008)

Parametric Design for Reconfigurable Software-Defined Radio

Tobias Becker[1], Wayne Luk[1], and Peter Y.K. Cheung[2]

[1] Department of Computing, Imperial College London, UK
[2] Department of Electrical and Electronic Engineering, Imperial College London, UK

Abstract. Run-time reconfigurable FPGAs are powerful platforms for realising software-defined radio systems. This paper introduces a parametric approach to designing such systems based on application and device parameters. We analyse the potential for reconfiguration in several software-defined radio components and demonstrate how the degree of parallelism in a reconfigurable module influences reconfiguration time and performance. In a case study with a reconfigurable FIR filter, our method increases the performance by a factor of 2.4.

1 Introduction

Software-defined radio is an emerging technology that involves processing digital radio signals by means of software techniques. Today's mobile applications feature an abundance of radio standards with ever increasing bandwidth. This leads to a demand in both increased design productivity and flexibility after device deployment. Software techniques are seen as a solution to quickly design flexible mobile applications. In this paper we consider the implementation of the physical radio interface on reconfigurable hardware devices, such as FPGAs, which combine hardware-like performance and efficiency with software-like flexibility.

FPGAs are powerful computing devices that deliver performance through parallelism and can be more efficient than DSPs or general-purpose processors. Combining reprogrammability and performance, they are displacing ASICs in telecom equipment such as mobile base stations. SRAM-based FPGAs can also be reconfigured at run-time, a feature that has been subject to much research [1]. Run-time reconfiguration has also been proposed for software-defined radio applications [2] and successfully demonstrated [3].

This paper focuses on a structured design approach based on application and device parameters. Most importantly, this includes analysing how the degree of parallelism in a reconfigurable application affects reconfiguration time and global performance. We further consider application data buffering and configuration storage. Using an example of software-defined radio, we show how our method can be used to explore the design space and optimise the reconfigurable system.

The rest of the paper is organised as follows. Section 2 explains the background of software-defined radio and outlines four basic reconfiguration scenarios. In section 3, we analyse the potential for reconfiguration in several components

J. Becker et al. (Eds.): ARC 2009, LNCS 5453, pp. 15–26, 2009.
© Springer-Verlag Berlin Heidelberg 2009

of a digital receiver. In section 4, we introduce our parametric approach and show that choosing between a serial or parallel implementation can be used to optimise performance and area. In section 5, we illustrate our approach on the example of a reconfigurable FIR filter. Finally, section 6 concludes the paper.

2   Background

Software-defined radio was first motivated by moving from analogue to digital technology in radio systems [4]. Because of the exponential increase in performance and productivity of digital technology compared to slow advances in analogue circuits, digital technology will continue to move closer to the antenna and replace much of the analogue front end.

Figure 1 shows a receiver where the signal is digitised directly after being mixed to an intermediate frequency (IF). A digital radio however is not synonymous with a software-defined radio. In current mobile phones, digital baseband processing is usually performed by inflexible but power-efficient ASICs. In order to support multiple standards, multiple pieces of IP have to be assembled into a complex system, that subsequently needs to be tested and manufactured. In contrast, a software-defined radio performs the same task by employing software-programmable and flexible DSPs or general-purpose processors in order to support multiple radio standards [5].

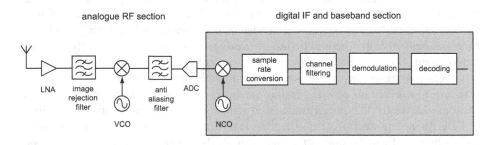

Fig. 1. Receiver architecture of a software-defined radio

However, classic software-programmable architectures such as DSPs or processors are often too inefficient to satisfy the power and performance constraints of communication devices. FPGAs are considered as a solution to this because they can deliver the flexibility of programmable architectures with power efficiency and performance much closer to ASICs. But despite successful demonstration of run-time reconfiguration for software-defined radios [3], we find a lack of systematic methodology in designing and optimising such systems. We therefore propose a more structured approach. Table 1 identifies different opportunities for reconfiguration in software-defined radio.

Although reconfigurability has promising aspects in all four scenarios, we mainly consider the latter two because they are the most challenging to realise.

Table 1. Scenarios showing opportunities for reconfiguration in software-defined radio

1. *Pre-deployment.* The programmability of the target architecture is used to make changes late in the design process before the device is deployed. Generic programmable devices also simplify the design by reducing the number of components needed.
2. *In-field upgrade.* The device is updated to support a new standard or feature that was not included at deployment. In this case, the device will be rebooted and downtime during reconfiguration does not matter.
3. *Reconfiguration per call or session.* The device is reconfigured at the beginning of a call or data transfer session e.g. to select the most efficient or cheapest service available at the moment. In this case, the reconfiguration downtime has to be short, preferably below the level of human perception but no data need to be buffered.
4. *Reconfiguration during a call or session.* The device is reconfigured during a call or data session e.g. to hand over from one service to another. Reconfiguration downtime time has to be very short and streaming data has to be buffered during reconfiguration.

3 Software-Defined Radio

Table 2 gives an overview of some of the most important communication standards that are currently being employed. These standards vary widely in their technical details and satisfy different needs. We now analyse how the components of a digital receiver as illustrated in figure 1 can benefit from reconfiguration.

As the first digital processing step, the real signal is down-converted into a complex baseband signal. This is done by multiplying the IF signal with sine and cosine signals from a numerically controlled oscillator (NCO). One common method of generating sine and cosine functions in digital hardware is the

Table 2. Comparison of different mobile communication standards

	GSM	EDGE	DECT	UMTS TDD	UMTS FDD	Bluetooth
Frequency band	900, 1800, 1900 MHz	900, 1800, 1900 MHz	1.9 GHz	1.9, 2 GHz	1.9, 2.1 GHZ	2.4 GHz
Channel bandwidth	200 kHz	200 kHz	1728 kHz	1.6 or 5 MHz	5 MHz	1 MHz
Channel access	FDMA/TDMA	FDMA/TDMA	FDMA/TDMA	TD-CDMA	DS-CDMA	TDMA
Duplex	FDD	FDD	TDD	TDD	FDD	TDD
Modulation	GMSK	GMSK, 8-PSK	GMSK	QPSK	QPSK	GFSK
Pulse shaping	Gauss ($BT = 0.3$)	Linear. Gaussian	Gauss ($BT = 0.5$)	Root-raised cos ($\beta = 0.22$)	Root-raised cos ($\beta = 0.22$)	Gauss ($BT = 0.5$)
Error correction	convolutional, CRC	convolutional CRC	CRC	convolutional, turbo, CRC	convolutional, turbo, CRC	-
Slot duration	0.577 ms	0.577 ms	0.417 ms	0.667 ms	0.667 ms	0.625 ms
Bit or chip rate	270.83 kbit/s	270.83 kbit/s	1152 kbit/s	1.28 or 3.84 Mchip/s	3.84 Mchip/s	1 Mbit/s
Net bit rate	13 kbit/s	up to 473.6 kbit/s	32 kbits/s	up to 2 Mbit/s	up to 2 Mbit/s	1Mbit/s

CORDIC algorithm. Since CORDIC is an iterative algorithm, a pipelined version would most likely be used to provide sufficient throughput. It is also possible to use an optimised, reconfigurable CORDIC processor to achieve higher performance and less area requirements [6]. The down-converter must be able to adapt quickly to different frequencies in order to support a change of channel between transmission slots (see table 2). This corresponds to scenario 4 in table 1.

Filters are applied at multiple stages of the receiver. In order to select the channel of interest, all other signals have to be removed. In practise, this is done by combining multiple stages of filtering and decimation. IIR filters are usually avoided due to instability issues and their non-linear phase. FIR filters are used instead, but in wideband architectures they can require a high order to filter narrowband-signal at high sample rate. Filters can be reconfigured between changing communication standards (scenario 3) or during a call or data session (scenario 4).

The last step in the receiver chain is decoding and error correction. Different methods of cyclic redundancy checks (CRC), convolutional codes and turbo codes are employed. GSM for example uses CRC for the most important bits and a convolutional decoder for less important bits. UMTS also uses turbo codes for error correction. Again, the reconfigurability can categorised as scenario 3 if the error correction is changed between standards. However, it is also possible to change an error correction to adapt to different channel conditions during a call or data session [7]. This case corresponds to scenario 4.

Finally there could be an additional encryption scheme such as AES at the end of the receiver chain. This is completely independent from any particular radio standard and could be reconfigured during or between sessions.

4   Design Parameters in Software-Defined Radio

Many run-time reconfigurable systems are designed in an ad-hoc manner. During the design process it is often unclear how the final implementation will perform. We propose a structured design approach that identifies design parameters and maps these onto the reconfigurable device. In the following, we consider three implementation attributes: performance, area and storage. First, we identify parameters of a reconfigurable module:

- Area requirement A
- Processing time t_p for one packet or datum
- Reconfiguration time t_r
- Configuration storage size Ψ
- The number of processing steps s in the algorithm
- The amount of parallelism p in the implementation

We can also identify parameters of the application that employs a reconfigurable module:

- Required data throughput ϕ_{app}
- The number of packets or items of data n that are processed between reconfigurations

The reconfigurable device is characterised by the following parameters:

- The available area A_{max}
- The data throughput of the configuration interface ϕ_{config}
- The configuration size per resource or unit of area Θ

4.1   Storage Requirements and Reconfiguration Time

All designs on volatile FPGAs require external storage for the initial configuration bitstream. Designs using partial run-time reconfiguration also need additional storage for the pre-compiled configuration bitstreams of the reconfigurable modules. The partial bitstream size and storage requirement Ψ (in bytes) of a reconfigurable module is directly related to its area A:

$$\Psi = A \cdot \Theta + h \approx A \cdot \Theta \tag{1}$$

A is the size of a reconfigurable module in FPGA tiles (e.g. CLBs) and Θ is a device specific parameter that specifies the number of bytes required to configure one tile. Configuration bitstreams often contain a header h. In most cases, this can be neglected because the header size is very small.

The time overhead of run-time reconfiguration can consist of multiple components, such as scheduling, context save and restore as well as the configuration process itself. In our case there is no scheduling overhead as modules are loaded directly as needed. There is also no context that needs to be saved or restored since signal processing components do not contain a meaningful state once a dataset has passed through. The reconfiguration time is proportional to the size of the partial bitstream and can be calculated as follows:

$$t_r = \frac{\Psi}{\phi_{config}} \approx \frac{A \cdot \Theta}{\phi_{config}} \tag{2}$$

ϕ_{config} is the configuration data rate and measured in $bytes/s$. This parameter not only depends on the native speed of the configuration interface but also on the configuration controller and the data rate of the memory where the configuration data are stored.

4.2   Buffering

As outlined in table 1, we can distinguish between run-time reconfigurable scenarios where data do not have to be buffered during reconfiguration, and scenarios where data buffering is needed during reconfiguration. For the latter case we can calculate the buffer size B depending on reconfiguration time t_r and the application data throughput ϕ_{app}:

$$B = \phi_{app} \cdot t_r = \frac{\phi_{app}}{\phi_{config}} \cdot \Psi \tag{3}$$

Table 3 outlines the buffer size for several receiver functions and a range of reconfiguration times. We can observe that the data rate is reduced through

Table 3. Buffersize for various functions and reconfiguration times

function	data throughput	buffer size for a given reconfiguration time		
		100 ms	10 ms	1 ms
down-conversion (16 bit)	800 Mbit/s	80 Mbit	8 Mbit	800 kbit
down-conversion (14 bit)	700 Mbit/s	70 Mbit	7 Mbit	700 kbit
demodulation UMTS	107.52 Mbit/s	10.75 Mbit	1.07 Mbit	107 kbit
demodulation GSM	7.58 Mbit/s	758 kbit	75.8 kbit	7.58 kbit
error correction UMTS	6 Mbit/s	600 kbit	60 kbit	6 kbit
error correction GSM	22.8 kbit/s	2.28 kbit	228 bit	22.8 bit
decryption UMTS	2 Mbits/s	200 kbit	20 kbit	2 kbit
decryption GSM	13 kbit/s	1.3 kbit	130 bit	13 bit

all stages of the receiver. Hence, a reconfiguration-during-call scenario becomes easier to implement towards the end of the receiver chain. Obviously, the buffer size also increases with the bandwidth of the communication standard and the duration of the reconfiguration time.

A buffer can be implemented with on-chip or off-chip resources. Most modern FPGAs provide fast, embedded RAM blocks that can be used to implement FIFO buffers. For example, Xilinx Virtex-5 FPGAs contain between 1 to 10 Mbit of RAM blocks [8]. Larger buffers have to be realised with off-chip memories.

4.3   Performance

The performance of a run-time reconfigurable system is dictated by the reconfiguration downtime. If reconfigurable hardware is used as an accelerator for software functions, overall performance is usually improved despite the configuration overhead [9]. In our case we use reconfiguration to support multiple hardware functions in order to improve flexibility and reduce area requirements. In this case, the reconfigurable version of a design will have a performance penalty over a design that does not use reconfiguration. The reconfiguration of hardware usually takes much longer than a context switch on a processor. This is due to the relatively large amount of configuration data that need to be loaded into the device. Early research on run-time reconfiguration showed that a reconfigurable design becomes more efficient the more data items n are processed between reconfigurations [10]. The efficiency I of a reconfigurable design compared to a static design can be expressed as:

$$I = \frac{t_{static}}{t_{reconf}} = \frac{n \cdot t_p}{n \cdot t_p + t_r} = \frac{n}{n + \frac{t_r}{t_p}} \tag{4}$$

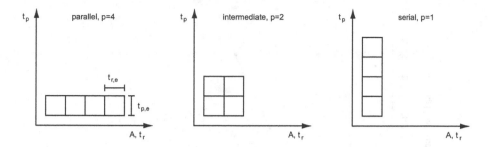

Fig. 2. Different spatial and temporal mappings of an algorithm with $s = 4$ steps

The reconfigurable system becomes more efficient by processing more data between configurations and by improving the ratio of configuration time to processing time. We propose a more detailed analysis where we consider the effect of parallelism on processing time and configuration time. Many applications can be scaled between a small and slow serial implementation, and a large and fast parallel or pipelined implementation. FIR filter, AES encryption or CORDIC are examples of such algorithms.

Figure 2 illustrates the different spatial and temporal mappings of an algorithm with regard to processing time, area and reconfiguration time. The processing time per datum t_p is inversely proportional to the degree of parallelism p. It can be calculated based on $t_{p,e}$, the basic processing time of one processing element, s, the number of steps or iterations in the algorithm, and p, the degree of parallelism:

$$t_p = \frac{t_{p,e} \cdot s}{p} \tag{5}$$

Parallelism speeds up the processing of data but slows down reconfiguration. This is because a parallel implementation is larger than a sequential one, and the reconfiguration time is directly proportional to the area as shown in equation 2. The reconfiguration time t_r is directly proportional to the degree of parallelism p, where $t_{r,e}$ is the basic reconfiguration time for one processing element:

$$t_r = t_{r,e} \cdot p \tag{6}$$

We can now calculate the total processing time for a workload of n data items:

$$t_{total} = n \cdot t_p + t_r = \frac{t_{p,e} \cdot s \cdot n}{p} + t_{r,e} \cdot p \tag{7}$$

Figure 3 illustrates how parallelism can affect the optimality of the processing time. We consider an algorithm with $s = 256$ steps which is inspired by the observation that filters can have orders of 200 or higher. The plots are normalised to processing time per datum and we assume that the reconfiguration time $t_{r,e}$ of one processing element is 5000 times the processing time $t_{p,e}$ of one processing element. This value can vary depending on the application and target device but we estimate that at least the order of magnitude is realistic for current

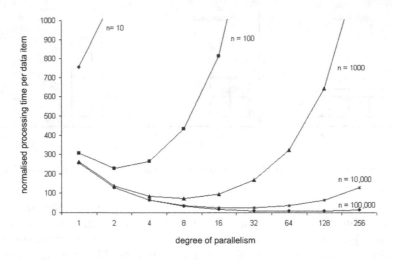

Fig. 3. Normalised processing times for a range of workload sizes n and different levels of parallelism p. The number of steps s is set to 256 and we assume $t_{r,e} = 5000 t_{p,e}$.

devices. We can observe that fully sequential implementations are beneficial for small workloads. In this case, the short configuration time outweighs the longer processing time. However, the overall time is still high due to the large influence of the configuration time. Large workloads benefit from a fully parallel implementations since the processing time is more dominant than reconfiguration time. In case of medium workloads, the degree of parallelism can be tuned to optimise the processing time. An analysis of how different configuration speeds can influence the optimal implementation is shown in section 5.

In order to find the optimal degree of parallelism, we calculate the partial derivative of the function given in equation 7 with respect to p:

$$\frac{\partial t_{total}}{\partial p} = -\frac{t_{p,e} \cdot s \cdot n}{p^2} + t_{r,e} \tag{8}$$

To find the minimum, we set equation 8 to 0 and solve for p:

$$p_{opt} = \sqrt{\frac{s \cdot n \cdot t_{p,e}}{t_{r,e}}} \tag{9}$$

The result p_{opt} is usually a real number which is not a feasible value to specify parallelism. In order to determine a practical value for p, p_{opt} can be interpreted according to table 4.

After determining the optimal degree of parallelism that reduces the overall processing time per workload and hence maximises performance, it is still necessary to check if the implementation meets the throughput requirements of the application Φ_{app}:

$$\frac{n}{t(p)_{total}} = \Phi_{hw} \geq \Phi_{app} \tag{10}$$

Table 4. Interpretatipn of p_{opt} to determine a practical value for p

$0 < p_{opt} \leq 1$	fully serial implementation, $p = 1$
$1 < p_{opt} < s$	choose p such that $s/p \in \mathbb{Z}$ and $\|p_{opt} - p\|$ minimal
$s \leq p_{opt}$	fully parallel implementation, $p = s$

The resulting area requirement A also has to be feasible within the total available area A_{max}. In summary, to implement an optimised design according to our model, the following steps have to be carried out:

1. Derive Φ_{app}, s and n from application.
2. Obtain Φ_{config} for target technology.
3. Develop one design and determine t_p and A.
4. Calculate t_r, $t_{p,e}$ and $t_{r,e}$ using equations 2, 5 and 6.
5. Find p_{opt} from equation 9 and find a feasible value according to table 4.
6. Calculate t_{total} using equation 7 and verify throughput using equation 10.
7. Implement design with p from step 5 and verify if its actual throughput satisfies the requirement.
8. Calculate buffer size B using equation 3 and check $A \leq A_{max}$.

The above methodology can be adopted for a wide variety of applications and target technologies; it will find the highest performing version of the design. In order to find the smallest design that satisfies a given throughput requirement, one can try smaller values for p while checking equation 10.

5   Case Study: Channelisation Filter for GSM

We now demonstrate our method on the example of a channelisation FIR filter for GSM. As *step 1*, we determine the application parameters ϕ_{app}, s and n. The sample rate f_s in our example is $2.167MHz$ which corresponds to 8 times the baseband bit rate. This is a realistic scenario after a first round of filtering and decimation. With 16-bit samples, the application throughput Φ_{app} is $34.672MBit/s$. We filter a 200 kHz wide GSM channel and suppresses neighbouring channels with an attenuation of at least $-80dB$. The filter coefficients are calculated with the MATLAB Simulink Digital Filter Design blockset. This results in a filter with 112 coefficients. The number of processing steps s is therefore 112. We consider a scenario where the filter needs to be reconfigured between GSM frames. One GSM frame has a duration of $4.615ms$ and produces $10,000$ samples at the given sample rate. Hence, the workload size $n = 10,000$.

Step 2. We use a Xilinx Virtex-4 LX25 FPGA as target device for the implementation of our filter. Virtex-4 FPGAs provide an internal configuration access port (ICAP) that is 32 bit wide and runs at $100MHz$. This corresponds to a theoretical maximal configuration throughput $\Phi_{config} = 400MB/s$. However, when using the HWICAP core [11] in combination with a MicroBlaze processor we only measure a throughput of $5MB/s$. But Claus et.al. recently presented an improved version with a throughput of approximately $300MB/s$ [12]. We therefore compare two scenarios of slow reconfiguration based on our measurement with $\Phi_{config} = 5MB/s$ and fast reconfiguration based on $\Phi_{config} = 300MB/s$.

Step 3. We first implement a fully parallel version of our filter as illustrated in the first row of table 5. The filter is created with Xilinx CORE Generator and implemented with ISE 9.2. The filter requires 6921 slices and is implemented in an area A of 1792 CLBs. In Virtex-4 FPGAs, the configuration size per CLB is $225.5bytes/CLB$. Hence, its corresponding partial bitstream has a size of $\Psi = 404.1kB$ (note: we use $1kB = 1000$ bytes).

Step 4. The processing time per datum t_p is $4ns$. Since this is a fully parallel version, the processing time per element $t_{p,e}$ is also $4ns$. With HWICAP, the filter can be reconfigured in $t_r = 81ms$ and $t_{r,e}$ is $0.72ms$. When using the fast ICAP version we estimate that $t_r = 1.35ms$ and $t_{r,e} = 0.012ms$.

Step 5. For slow configuration, the optimal value for $p_{opt} = 2.49$ and feasible values are 2 and 4. With fast reconfiguration, $p_{opt} = 19.3$ and feasible values are 14 and 28.

Step 6. For slow reconfiguration we expect processing times of $t_{total} = 3.68ms$ for $p = 2$ and $t_{total} = 4.01ms$ for $p = 4$ and for fast reconfiguration we expect t_{total} to be $0.49ms$ for $p = 14$ and $0.50ms$ for $p = 28$. All of these satisfy our requirement of processing one frame in $4.615ms$.

Step 7. Our previous results are projections based on a fully parallel version. We now verify these results by comparing them to attributes of real implementations. Table 5 shows six different versions of the filter with p ranging from 112 to 4. Smaller, more serial versions could not be created with CORE Generator. We observe that $t_{p,e}$ and $t_{r,e}$ are not constant as previously assumed. Especially configuration size and reconfiguration time do not scale linearly with the degree of parallelism. This is because serialising a design introduces an overhead for the implementation. For $p = 4$ and with slow reconfiguration, the filter has an actual t_{total} of $6.8ms$ which violates our requirement. We therefore have to consider that projections with low degrees of parallelism and operating close to the limit of the application requirement can fail. With fast reconfiguration, our projection is correct in finding the highest performing versions. The actual t_{total} is $0.57ms$ in both cases which is 2.4 times faster than the fully parallel version.

Step 8. The buffer size for $p = 14$ is $9.2kbit$ and the storage size is $79.4kB$. Since all versions with fast reconfiguration meet the application requirement of $t_{total} < 4.615ms$, we could also choose the smallest version with $p = 4$. The buffer size for this version is $3.3kbit$ and the storage size is $28.9kB$. All versions of the filter fit into the device which provides $A_{max} = 2688$ CLBs.

Figure 4 illustrates the performance of our filters for different levels of parallelism based on the two different configuration speeds. We observe that slow configuration speeds lead to more serial implementations. Slow processing carries almost no weight compared to penalty of reconfiguration time. For faster configuration speeds, the optimum is a solution with an intermediate degree of

Table 5. Parameters of the FIR filter with different degrees of parallelism p when implemented on a Xilinx Virtex-4 LX25 FPGA

p	slices	size [kB]	f_{max} [MHz]	$t_{p,e}$ [ns]	t_p [ns]	slow reconfiguration: HWICAP [11]			fast reconfiguration: ICAP by Claus et.al. [12]		
						t_r [ms]	$t_{r,e}$ [ms]	t_{total} [ms]	t_r [ms]	$t_{r,e}$ [ms]	t_{total} [ms]
112	6921	404.1	250	4.0	4.00	80.8	0.72	80.9	1.347	0.012	1.39
56	3719	216.5	251	3.99	7.97	43.3	0.77	43.4	0.722	0.013	0.80
28	2111	122.7	256	3.91	15.63	24.5	0.88	24.7	0.409	0.015	0.57
14	1326	79.4	260	3.85	30.77	15.9	1.13	16.2	0.265	0.019	0.57
8	873	50.5	264	3.79	53.03	10.1	1.26	10.6	0.168	0.021	0.70
4	462	28.9	263	3.80	106.56	5.8	1.44	6.8	0.096	0.024	1.16

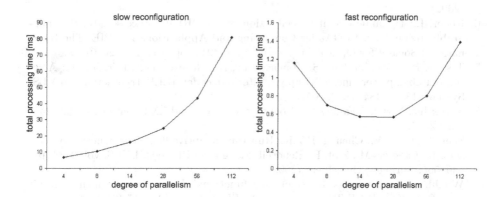

Fig. 4. Total processing time of our reconfigurable FIR filter when processing 10,000 data items between reconfigurations

parallelism. Increasing configuration speeds shift the optimal solution to more parallel implementations.

6 Conclusion and Future Work

This paper introduces a quantitative approach for developing run-time reconfigurable designs for software-defined radio applications. This approach is based on a simple model relating application-oriented parameters such as desired throughput, and implementation attributes such as area, processing time and reconfiguration time. It enables systematic development and optimisation of designs, which is illustrated in a case study involving a channelisation filter for GSM. Current and future work includes extending our approach to support a large variety of software-defined radio applications, and developing tools that automate our approach.

Acknowledgement. The support of Xilinx and UK EPSRC is gratefully acknowledged.

References

1. Compton, K., Hauck, S.: Reconfigurable computing: a survey of systems and software. ACM Computing Surveys 34(2), 171–210 (2002)
2. Cummings, M., Haruyama, S.: FPGA in the software radio. Communications Magazine 37(2), 108–112 (1999)
3. Uhm, M.: Software-defined radio: The new architectural paradigm. Xilinx DSP Magazin, 40–42 (October 2005)
4. Mitola, J.: The software radio architecture. Communications Magazine 33(5), 26–38 (1995)
5. Tuttlebee, W.: Software Defined Radio: Enabling Technologies. Wiley, Chichester (2002)
6. Keller, E.: Dynamic circuit specialization of a CORDIC processor. In: Reconfigurable Technology: FPGAs for Computing and Applications II. SPIE. The International Society for Optical Engineering, vol. 4212, pp. 134–141 (2000)
7. Tessier, R., Swaminathan, S., Ramaswamy, R., Goeckel, D., Burleson, W.: A reconfigurable, power-efficient adaptive Viterbi decoder. IEEE Transactions on VLSI Systems 13(4), 484–488 (2005)
8. Xilinx Inc. Virtex-5 Family Platfrom Overview LX and LXT Platforms v2.2 (January 2007)
9. Seng, S., Luk, W., Cheung, P.Y.K.: Run-time adaptive flexible instruction processors. In: Glesner, M., Zipf, P., Renovell, M. (eds.) FPL 2002. LNCS, vol. 2438, pp. 545–555. Springer, Heidelberg (2002)
10. Wirthlin, M., Hutchings, B.: Improving functional density using run-time circuit reconfiguration. IEEE Transactions on VLSI Systems 6(2), 247–256 (1998)
11. Xilinx Inc. Xilinx Logic Core: OPB HWICAP v1.3 (March 2004)
12. Claus, C., Zhang, B., Stechele, W., Braun, L., Hübner, M., Becker, J.: A multi-platform controller allowing for maximum dynamic partial reconfiguration throughput. In: Field Programmable Logic and Applications, pp. 535–538. IEEE, Los Alamitos (2008)

Hardware/Software FPGA Architecture for Robotics Applications

Juan Carlos Moctezuma Eugenio and Miguel Arias Estrada

National Institute for Astrophysics Optics and Electronics, INAOE
Street Luis Enrique Erro no.1, Puebla-Mexico
jcmoctezuma@inaoep.mx
http://ccc.inaoep.mx

Abstract. This work presents a Hardware/Software FPGA Robotics Architecture for applications on Mobile Robotics. A test mobile robot was built and it is based in a commercial programmable robot called Create from iRobot, also the test platform has additional components like sonars, infrared sensors and a robotic arm, these components are used to increase robot's functionality and to show that it is feasible to build any kind of hybrid robot. The Hardware/Software Architecture is a complete Embedded System (ES). Hardware side includes processor, buses, memory and peripherals like co-processors, sensors, robotic arm, controllers, UARTs, etc., Software side includes a Linux OS with a set of libraries that performs different functionalities and to control all components in FPGA, these functions are easy-understanding for robotic programmers. The main purpose of this work is to show the advantages of using FPGAs to implement Robotics Platforms. Some of these advantages are parallelism, flexibility and scalability. Finally some experiments was performed to show these advantages

1 Introduction

Mobile Robotics works with robots that are ables to navigate in their environment with certain grade of intelligence. A mobile robot is a set of subsystems for locomotion, sensing, decision making and communication between components [1]. Since movement and behavior of these kind of robots are based on what they are sensing, a systems development that can manipulate many hardware components, communicate between them, support real-time responses and have software support for user programs are very important.

On the other hand, an ES is a computer for specific purpose, these systems can be optimized since they are focus to perform special functions, reducing cost and size of the final product. The four major components of an ES are: Processor, Buses, Memory and Peripherals [2, 4]. Embedded Systems have some special features like: performance specific task, real-time requirements, interacting with its environment (re-actives), dedicated hardware, which be optimized, among others. These features make an ES a suitable option to implement Robotic Platforms.

J. Becker et al. (Eds.): ARC 2009, LNCS 5453, pp. 27–38, 2009.
© Springer-Verlag Berlin Heidelberg 2009

This work presents the design and implementation of a FPGA-based Robotics Platform for applications on Mobile Robotics, showing the significant advantages that this devices offers to improve the performance in a Mobile Robot. This paper is organized as follows: in Section II Robotics Platforms are defined. Section III describes FPGA platform proposed and its design, both Hardware and Software sides. Section IV describes platform implementation and the test robot that was built for this work. Section V presents the experiments that were done and the results obtained. Finally, in Section VI the conclusions are presented.

2   Mobile Robotics Platforms

A robotic platform can be considered the robot itself, both hardware and software components. These Robotics platforms are used in research projects to test and to validate control architectures, navigation and vision algorithms, or testing sensor protocols. There are robotic platforms based on microcontrollers or microprocessors. So a FPGA platform is a robotic platform based on FPGA, the 'brain' of the robot is a FPGA board, which has implemented an embedded system that control all peripherals (e.g. memory, sensors, actuators, etc.).

One of the reasons why research centers decide to develop their own robot prototypes is to propose new architectures that can be more interesting (i.e. flexible, more power computation, etc.) compared with the existing ones.

One efficient way of building a robotic platform is join pre-built robot parts, for example acquire a mobile robot with desired locomotion, pre-built sensors with specific interface, robotics arms, cameras, etc. In this way, we can build a complex robot as we desire. But this is not possible if it does not have a system that controls and supports all parts and puts them together; this system must be modular, scalable and flexible. So it is necessary a device that accomplish these requirements. FPGAs are a good choice, because they can implement a processor-based system or a microcontroller-based system or combination of both, moreover they can implement complete embedded systems on a chip, co-processors, custom user logic, communication protocols or multi-processor systems.

3   FPGA Platform Design

3.1   Hardware Platform

Like most ES, they are divided in two parts: Hardware and Software. Fig 1 shows functional diagram of hardware platform and all the components interconnected to form whole system.

FPGA hardware platform proposed is designed to support any kind of mobile robot that has a low-level command interface, like serial protocol. Also hardware platform must support any additional element to increase its functionality, as sensors, robotics arms, cameras or a hardware component in general, regardless

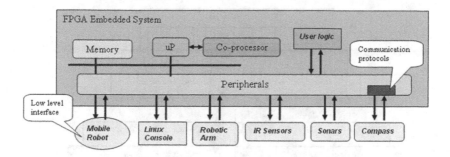

Fig. 1. Complete diagram of Hardware platform

interface communication that they use; since any protocol can be implemented with FPGA logic.

Other important feature of this hardware platform are co-processors, they can accelerate software execution of some specific task, taking advantage of parallelism in hardware.

In this case, an image processing co-processor was added to perform convolution task. This core improves convolution processing through a series of parallel modules working in different places of image at the same time. In general, co-processors can be used to implement any kind of hardware accelerator to improve performance of some algorithms.

Custom logic are another feature that helps with data processing. For example in this work, it implements a hardware module that makes distance conversion of a sonar, this is done in hardware, letting processor free to execute another tasks.

Also custom logic can be used to implement protocols, in this case an I2C protocol was implemented in FPGA to communicate with some sensors. In general, FPGA allows implementation of any kind of communication protocol.

3.2 Software Platform

To control and to manage all hardware elements a software platform is required, also microprocessor are used to run user programs. Fig. 2 shows software architecture proposed, this platform is organized in abstraction layers, at bottom layer there is sensors and actuators hardware. Upper Drivers and OS layer has all drivers needed to low-level communication with the hardware elements, also these drivers are working over a Linux OS that runs on FPGA.The General Case: Nontriviality.

Next layer is Basic Functions, this layer converts peripheral language into robotic programmers language, e.g. for mobile robot, it has functions like move forward, move backwards, stop, turn, etc. They are functions that a robotic programmer understand, but their functionality is basic.

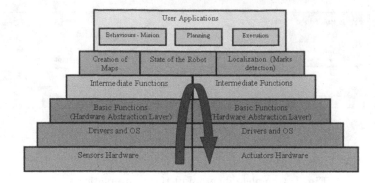

Fig. 2. Functional diagram of Software platform

In Intermediate Functions layer, it has functions with a higher level of abstraction, functions that perform behaviors like avoiding obstacles, position movements for robotic arm, following a line, etc.

Next two layers are more complex, they have specific functions that helps to creation of maps, localization, state of robot, vision algorithms, etc. In addition, in top layer, it has user applications, in this layer user can take basic and intermediate functions to develop his programs. This work focus only in first four low layers, but software platform are open to construct a more elaborated software architecture.

The details of implementation are describe in next section, also it presents specific hardware components and software libraries used on FPGA platform.

4   FPGA Platform Implementation

4.1   Development Tools

Embedded systems are complex. Getting the hardware and software portions of an embedded design to work are projects in themselves. Merging the two design components so they function as one system creates additional challenges. Add an FPGA design project to the mix, makes that situation has the potential to become very confusing indeed. To simplify the design process Xilinx offers several sets of tools [5, 9]:

EDK (Embedded Develpment Kit). EDK is a suite of tools and IP cores that enables you to design a complete embedded processor system for implementation in FPGA.

ISE (Integrated Software Enviroment). ISE is the foundation for FPGA logic design, its utilities allow constraints entry, timing analysis, code synthesis, logic placement and routing, FPGA programming, and more.

Another companies have similar tools to work with ES, like Altera. The difference is that these tools are focus to work with their own FPGAs. So this work can be done with tools of other FPGAs companies.

4.2   Test Robot Platform

Our Test Robot Platform consist of the following components:

Create Mobile robot. Create [10] is a programmable robot that makes transparent low-level mechanism for actuators and sensors, this robot has a differential-pair locomotion with a caster wheel.

Sonars. This FPGA platform supports three different types of sonars: two channels for burst and entry echo (SRF05), one channel for both burst and entry echo (PING Ultrasonic), and a sonar that works with I2C protocol (SRF02).

Compass. The CMPS03 compass operates with I2C protocol and has been specifically designed for use in robots as an aid to navigation.

Infrared sensors. A proximity sensor and a line tracking sensor were used for this work. They have digital outputs.

Robotic Arm. AX-12 Smart Robotic Arm was used [12]. This arm has seven servo motors called dynamixels, they are connected in daisy chain and work with half-duplex serial protocol.

Image Processing Co-processor. This is an internal component of FPGA platform. This module performs the convolution process of an image.

All these elements conform whole robotic test platform used in this work. Although it is possible to construct another different robot with any kind of extra elements. FPGA platform has enough hardware/software resources to do that.

4.3   Implementation Process

The implementation process consists in four principal steps: a) Hardware platform development, b) Software Libraries development, c) Mounting Linux OS on FPGA and d) Co-processor development.

a) Hardware Platform Development. The Hardware Platform development is done in EDK and it is a Microblaze-based system. Microblaze is a RISC soft processor optimized and implemented with FPGA resources. This processor is highly configurable, it allows having a flexible architecture, and it balances execution performance against implementation size. By integrating one or more MicroBlaze processors along with the right mix or peripherals on an FPGA, you can reduce component count as well as board design complexity, reducing overall product cost [8]. The general process of construction in EDK is as follows:

1. Putting all hardware components (IP cores) needed for system (e.g. Processor, Memory, Controllers, UARTs, Timers, General Purpose IO, etc.).
2. Connect Buses to hardware components in general level.
3. Connect every signal of each component as design required and assigns I/O signals for the system.
4. Assign memory space for each peripheral, so that processor can communicate with them.

b) Software Libraries Development. Once systems hardware has been created, next step is to create systems software (i.e. drivers, libraries, users applications, etc.). Before creating any user program it is necessary generate a software infrastructure to communicate with hardware. This bridge between software and hardware is called Board Support Package (BSP). BSP is a collection of files that contain drivers for each peripheral, libraries, I/O standard devices and other software elements. Also BSP allows Linux OS mounting in hardware platform.

With respect to user applications, they can be done using BSP, i.e. using drivers to communicate with peripherals. In this way, it is possible to make Libraries to control each element of test robot, building Basic and Intermediate layers of fig. 2. For example, for Create robot, functions as drive forward/backward, to turn certain degrees, to stop robot, sensing bumpers, etc. For robotic arm, functions as tracking object to take it, move to an initial position, move to pick up an object, etc. And so on for remainder elements of the robot.

In total, software platform has more than 80 functions in Drivers layer and more than 50 functions in Basic and Intermediate layers. These last 50 functions are available to programmers to develop robotic applications.

c) Mounting Linux OS on FPGA. Linux Distribution used for this work is Petalinux [11]. PetaLinux is an uClinux port, source-based hardware and software distribution which has been developed specifically for using Embedded Linux on reconfigurable logic devices. The PetaLinux distribution includes everything needed to easily create Linux systems running on Xilinx FPGAs. In general, to mount a Linux OS on FPGA, it needs four things:

1. Hardware platform running on FPGA.
2. The BSP for hardware platform.
3. The Linux Distribution (Petalinux).
4. GCC Microblaze tool-chain, that includes all necessary to build uClinux kernel on a Linux host.

d) Co-processor Development. This core was implemented on Xilinx System Generator (XSG) tool [13] and the core is configurable by user through a user graphical interface (GUI), i.e. user can choice size of image entry, size of mask convolution and mask coefficients with an arbitrary fixed point representation. So it is possible represents any kind of mask convolution.

Two important Simulink techniques were used to implement this core: Dynamic Blocks Generation and Masking Subsystems. So with aid of these techniques it is possible that the model was automatically generated when GUI parameters changes.

5   Experiments and Results

Four main experiments was development in a test environment of 3x3 meters. Fig. 3 shows test robot platform built for this work and its additional

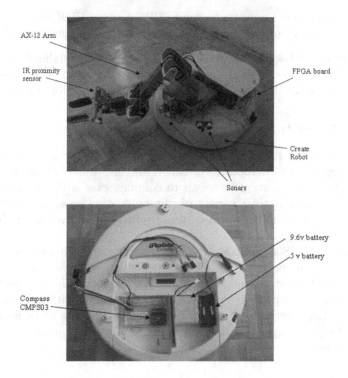

Fig. 3. Test robot built with a FPGA board, a programmable robot and additional sensors/actuators

elements. FPGA board used for this work is Spartan 3E 1600. This board has a XC3S1600EFG320 Spartan-3E FPGA and 64 MByte of DDR SDRAM, among others features.

5.1 FPGA Platform Functionallity

The hardware part of the system and the Linux OS with some examples applications are store in Flash memory of FPGA board. So when FPGA board is turn on, FPGA is automatically cofigured with the hardware platform and after that, a bootloader program automatically download Linux OS image into RAM memory. The application program can execute immediately after Linux OS boots, or execute through the petalinux console.

If user wants to implement another application program, he needs to have EDK tools and follows next steps:

1. Develop C code application in a Linux host
2. Crosscompile application with petalinux tools
3. Generate a new Linux OS image with the new user applications

4. Download the new Linux OS image to FPGA using EDK tools
5. Now user can execute its new applications on the petalinux console

To change or add some hardware module, it needs a qualified person that can work with EDK tools. FPGA platform is still in development phase, so in a future this platform will be totally functional and easy-use for the user.

5.2 Experiment 1: Protocol Implementation

CMPS03 works with I2C protocol. In this experiment, we implement an I2C protocol and glue it to Microblaze system. With this, it shows that it is possible to implement communication protocols to communicate with sensors or actuators. EDK tools have a great variety of communication protocols, but the user also has the option of implement a custom protocol, this gives flexibility to the system.

In addition, CMPS03 compass was used to improve turn task of the robot, since it only has an encoders mechanism to calculate degrees of turn, this turn sometimes is not exact for many factors: type of floor, slip of wheels, decay of wheels, etc. But with this encoders mechanism and with compass aid, it is possible to improve turn of robot. Table 1 shows results of turn correction with and without compass. Although the main contribution was the protocol implementation.

Table 1. Results of turn correction experiment

Turn (degrees)	Error (degrees)	
	Without Compass	Using Compass
45	4.5	1.2
90	5.2	1.0
135	6.4	1.5
180	7.7	1.5
225	6.8	1.2
270	7.6	1.3
315	7.2	1.4
360	6.5	1.0
60	4.3	1.4
120	3.4	1.3

5.3 Experiment 2: Sonars Working with Parallel Hardware

This experiment consist in showing difference between software and hardware implementation of the sonars conversion process, i.e. convert pulse width to centimeters. This process can be done in software or hardware. Table 2 shows results of both implementations.

The problem of implementing conversion process in software is that it is sequential. If it takes x seconds for conversion of one sonar, then it will take Nx

Table 2. Results of Sonars conversion Process

Distance to object (cm)	Number of sonars	Software Time (ms)	Hardware Time (ms)
10	1	1.4	1.4
	4	5.48	
20	1	1.97	1.97
	4	7.72	
35	1	2.8	2.8
	4	11.3	
60	1	4.25	4.25
	4	17.0	
100	1	6.57	6.63
	4	26.4	
150	1	9.5	9.4
	4	38.8	

seconds for N sonars. Unlike if we use parallel hardware to implement conversion process, it only takes x seconds for N sonars, since each sonar has its own hardware module that implement its own conversion process, and all these modules are working in parallel. Moreover, processor is free to execute another tasks.

5.4 Experiment 3: Image Co-processor

This experiment consists in compare software versus hardware implementation of convolution process. Software implementation was done in Microblaze processor and all process was performed by software functions. Hardware implementation was done with image co-processor, so Microblaze only request use of this co-processor. Again, processor is free to execute another tasks while co-processor is working. For this experiment it is supposed that entry image is stored on RAM memory. Table 3 shows results obtained.

Since hardware co-processor is based in fixed point representation, and software in floating point representation; then results of output image can vary. A correlation coefficient (CC) was defined to compare SW versus HW output image. This coefficient is defined as:

$$CC = number\ of\ equal\ pixels/number\ of\ total pixels \qquad (1)$$

With this experiment, it demonstrates that co-processor is a very flexible way to accelerate several programs execution, taking advantage of inherent FPGA parallelism.

5.5 Experiment 4: General Tests

Two general test was made: 1) wall following and 2) transporting objects. These two tests are to probe correct general performance of the FPGA robot platform.

Wall following test consists in putting robot in an initial position and then robot has to follow the wall until a final position, maintaining certain distance from the wall (e.g. 10cm), this test used Create robot and sonars.

Table 3. Resuslts of SW vs HW convolution process

Image size	Filter	SW execution (seg)	HW execution (seg)	Correlation coefficient
200 x 200	Gaussian (3x3)	4.4	0.55	0.96 (UFix_8_8)
	Gaussian (9x9)	6.4	0.88	0.94 (UFix_10_10)
	Unsharp (3x3)	3.3	0.46	0.99 (Fix_10_6)
	Laplacian (3x3)	2.1	0.29	0.98 (Fix_10_7)
	Sobel (3x3)	1.9	0.16	1 (UFix_10_10)
300 x 500	Gaussian (3x3)	7.5	0.81	0.96 (UFix_8_8)
	Gaussian (9x9)	10.9	1.20	0.94 (UFix_10_10)
	Unsharp (3x3)	6.3	0.69	0.99 (Fix_10_6)
	Laplacian (3x3)	4.3	0.55	0.98 (Fix_10_7)
	Sobel (3x3)	3.9	0.36	1 (UFix_10_10)
480 x 600	Gaussian (3x3)	9.1	1.19	0.96 (UFix_8_8)
	Gaussian (9x9)	15.2	1.74	0.94 (UFix_10_10)
	Unsharp (3x3)	8.1	0.86	0.99 (Fix_10_6)
	Laplacian (3x3)	6.2	0.80	0.98 (Fix_10_7)
	Sobel (3x3)	5.8	0.73	1 (UFix_10_10)

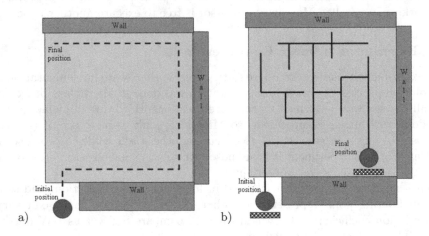

Fig. 4. Two test scenarios: a) Wall following, b) Transporting objects

Transporting objects test consists in transport small objetcs from one place to another, but through a labyrinth of lines, so robot has to find the Exit by itself. This test used Create robot, both infrared sensors and robotic arm. Fig 4 shows these two tests scenarios, where robot is represent with a circle.

With this two test, it probed that it is possible to develop several robotic applications with our FPGA robotic platform, and using functions available for user. Also it probed that it is feasible to construct any kind of hybrid robot, merging all elements into a FPGA platform.

Finally in Table 4, it presents pros and cons of using FPGAs to implement Robotics Platforms.

Table 4. Comparative Table of pros and cons of using FPGAs as Robotic Platforms

Pros	Cons
• Flexibility to implement any kind of user logic • Capacity of reconfiguration • Power of Parallelism • Implementation of only necessary resources, i.e. build custom-system. (performance/cost trade-off) • Hundreds of I/O pins • Software tools that facilitate embedded development systems • Pre-built and optimized IP cores available to user • Development of custom IP to implement any kind of protocol or user logic in general • Avoids processor obsolesce • Different Embedded Linux solutions from third party distributors • Implementation of multi-processors systems	• Power consumption • Communication protocols not included, they have to be implemented • Complexity to design embedded project • Difficulty to change platform's functionality, needs specialized people • Tools system dependency

6   Conclusions

FPGA represents a flexible solution to implement Robotic Platforms, since a great variety of IP cores are integrated in a single chip. This allows development different kind of architectures, communication protocols, components interconnection, adding custom logic, etc. Also this platform is flexible in software level, that is, it allows mounting different Linux OS according with project requirements.

FPGA Platform is scalable, it provides enough resources to add more hardware devices (e.g. sensors, actuators, device interfaces, processors, cameras, etc.) without to modify entire system. Also in software level, platform provides a low level infrastructure to increase software architecture.

This platform is open to be used with any kind of mobile robot, sensor, actuator or any robotic device in general. Different kind of protocols can be implemented on FPGA (e.g. I2C, UART, SPI, CAN bus, USB, etc.). Also many memory controllers are available to user (e.g. DDR, DDR2, BRAM, SRAM, SDRAM, etc.).

Parallelism on FPGA and using of co-processors allows to accelerate algorithms execution to improve overall performance, this is possible because multiples hardware modules can work at the same time, distributing tasks between hardware and software.

Using embedded Linux OS is a good choice, since this kind of OS provides well-known features like reliable, efficiency and stability. Moreover, it is a familiar environment for Linux programmers.

Reconfiguration on FPGA is a good feature because it allow to implement different kind of hardware/software architectures on the same chip for a wide variety of mobile robots, sensors and actuators. Also dynamic reconfiguration allows re-programming FPGA in execution time. So we can implement different hardware depending of what robot is sensing, all this when robot is running.

Programmability of FPGA platform with software tools reduce development time of the system and facilities modification of platform if user has a good knowledge of the tools.

References

1. Gregory, D., Michael, J.: Computacional Principles of Mobile Robotics, 1st edn. Cambridge University Press, Cambridge (2000)
2. Thomas, B.: Embedded Robotics: Mobile Robot Design and Applications with Embedded Systems, 2nd edn. Springer, Heidelberg (2006)
3. Qing, L., Carolyn, L.: Real Time Concepts for Embedded Systems. CMP Books (2003)
4. Caas Jose, M., Vicente, M., Rodrigo, M.: Programacion de Robots Moviles, Universidad Rey Juan Carlos, Espana, Instituto Nacional de Astrofisica Optica y Electronica, Mexico (2004)
5. Xilinx Company: EDK Concepts, Tools and Techniques: A Hands-on Guide to Effective Embedded System Design, Version 9.1i (2007)
6. Davis, D., Beeravolu, S., Jaganathan, R.: Hardware/Software Codesign for platforms FPGA, Xilinx Inc. (2005)
7. Xilinx Company, XAPP529: Connecting Customized IP to the Microblaze Soft Processor Using the Fast Simplex Link (FSL) Channel (2004)
8. Xilinx Company: MicroBlaze Processor Reference Guide, UG081 ver 7.0 (2007)
9. Xilinx website (July 2008), http://www.xilinx.com
10. Creates from iRobot website (March 2008), http://www.irobot.com/create
11. Petalinux from Petalogix website (March 2008), http://www.petalogix.com
12. AX-12 Smart Robotic Arm from CrustCrawler website (March 2008), http://www.crustcrawler.com
13. Xilinx System Generator Design Tool website (May 2008), http://www.xilinx.com/ise/optionalprod/systemgenerator.htm

Reconfigurable Operator Based Multimedia Embedded Processor

Daniel Menard[1], Emmanuel Casseau[1], Shafqat Khan[1], Olivier Sentieys[1],
Stéphane Chevobbe[2], Stéphane Guyetant[2], and Raphael David[2]

[1] INRIA/IRISA, CAIRN, 22100 Lannion, France
daniel.menard@irisa.fr
[2] CEA, LIST, 91191 Gif-Sur-Yvette, France

Abstract. Image processing applications need embedded devices that can integrate evolutionary standards or various standards, that is to say devices have to be flexible to implement different algorithms at different times. In other respects these devices are constrained with stringent power requirements as well as high performance. Reconfigurable processor can address these points. However, previous reconfigurable architectures suffer from their interconnect cost and do not meet low power constraints. In this paper preliminary work about the design of a reconfigurable processor based on a coarse-grain granularity tailored for multimedia applications is presented. The architecture is flexible and scalable. Coarse-grain operators can be optimized in term of the function they implement, the data word-length and the parallelism speed-up. The processor is designed to limit interconnection overhead.

1 Introduction

In multimedia applications, image processing is one of the major challenges embedded systems have to face. Image processing at pixel level, like image filtering, edge detection, pixel correlation or at block level such as motion estimation have to be considered. Such applications are typically computationally intensive with control statements and designers have to cope with power and performance stringent requirements when embedded system integration is investigated.

Focusing on the applicative domain permits some simplifications on the architecture, for instance on the choice of operators, the sizing of memories and the interconnect patterns. Moreover, the multimedia domain allows the use of subword parallelism SWP operators and fixed point arithmetic.

For that goal, we propose to develop a reconfigurable processor able to adapt its computing structure to image processing applications. The processor is built around a pipeline of coarse-grain reconfigurable operators exhibiting efficient power and performance features. On the contrary of previous attempts to design reconfigurable processors which have focused on the definition of complex interconnection networks between operators, we propose a pipeline-based of evolved coarse-grain reconfigurable operators to avoid traditional overhead, in reconfigurable devices, related to the interconnection network.

J. Becker et al. (Eds.): ARC 2009, LNCS 5453, pp. 39–49, 2009.
© Springer-Verlag Berlin Heidelberg 2009

The reconfigurable processor presented hereafter is associated with a software framework currently on progress [1]. Roughly, from the high-level applicative specification, frequently executed code fragments, such as kernel loops, are extracted. A dependency graph-based internal representation is used to perform this pattern extraction. Pattern code transformation is then performed to exhibit features that the reconfigurable processor can efficiently implement [2]. A compilation step then generates the control code as well as the configurations of the operators.

The paper is organized as follow. Section 2 presents related work around reconfigurable processors. The organization of our reconfigurable processor is presented in section 3. Subword-based multimedia operator design is presented in section 4 as well as first implementation results. Finally conclusions are presented in section 5.

2   Related Work

The model of an ASIP processor with instruction-set extensions dedicated to a given application domain, such as Tensilica[3] or [4] can be pushed further with reconfigurable functional units inside the processor pipeline. In this design space, different trade-offs were explored such as DREAM[5] with a multi-context fine grain extension, or the Stretch processors [6] with a coarse-grain reconfigurable extension. These two solutions try to take advantage of the flexibility of the reconfigurable area to speed-up kernel loops throughout the application. Their drawbacks are mainly due to the sequentiality of the execution model based on the Von Neumann paradigm.

To decrease the constraints of the previous execution model on the intrinsic parallelism of the multimedia applications, processors based on coarse-grain arrays have been intensively explored, with roughly two approaches based on the data access. On the one hand, each processing element (PE) has a local register file, filled from external caches or data banks, global for the whole array. CRISP (Coarse-grained Reconfigurable Instruction-Set Processor)[7] clusterizes PEs into slices; ADRES [8] has a hybrid structure with either VLIW mode or an acceleration mode on the array; ASERP[9] is a recent proposal of such array with mixed SIMD/MIMD modes. The memory access and the size of the register file inside the PEs become a limitation when the application requires a high computational load combined with a high data bandwith.

On the other hand, several reconfigurable processors are based on computing patterns mapped on the array, that receive data from memory banks with address generators or fifos to cross over the previous memory access limitation. Thus this kind of processing is more oriented towards data streaming. The XPP, from PACT[10], is a standalone platform, that integrates a coarse grain streaming matrix with RAMs and small VLIW processors. The matrix by itself is a coprocessor, just as other proposals, as [11] which has a hierarchical structure, or [12] with complex address generators.

A last model derives from the processing-in-memory (PIM) concept: in this case, the reconfigurable PE's are associated with small memory cuts, as in the

MORA (Multimedia Oriented Reconfigurable Array)[13]. Each PE has its own micro-code; although similar to the ADRES array mode, the processing is here applied on larger data sets and the control is distributed. This solution takes advantage of the data locality of the application but pays it by a none negligible cost on the communication network.

Besides, as technology scales, gate delays become negligible in comparison with signal propagation in wires. Thus, lot of the previously defined reconfigurable architectures face the problem of keeping under control the communication delays in reconfigurable devices designed in advance technologies. Finally, together with algorithmic and technological evolutions, reconfigurable architectures have to face another challenge related to their energy efficiency. If reconfiguration paradigm has been intensively explored to demonstrate its interest on a performance or silicon density, very few projects have considered the optimization of dynamic and even more static power.

Power saving, as well as performance enhancement, can be addressed taking special care about the operators used to implement the computations. For example, power consumption is linked to data-word-length [14]. Thus, each operation word-length has to be adapted according to its contribution in the global system accuracy. Fixed architectures can not address this kind of optimizations when various applications or accuracy constraints are concerned. On the contrary, reconfigurable architectures can be specifically configured depending on the particular piece of code fragment to be implemented which leads to interesting power consumption gains.

3 Processor Design

3.1 Processor Design Flow

The processor described hereafter is a framework to define applicative-domain specific reconfigurable processors, targeting computing efficiency (expressed in GOPS/W) and flexibility inside the domain, expressed subjectively by the coverage of the application domain.

The design flow consists first in selecting the applicative domain, and defining the kind of computations that are typically found into the loop kernels and frequently executed code fragments. At this point, creating a bench representative of the targeted application domain can greatly facilitate the design space exploration by further refinements of the architecture. Selecting operations at a too low level, such as sum of absolute differences in image and video processing, or selecting an insufficient number of functions for the bench will lead to optimize only the peak performance of the architecture, but this will prove to be not representative enough of a real applicative behavior, in particular because control statements have a great impact on the overall performance.

After the complexity analysis of the algorithms, the operators can be extracted and optimized separately (cf. section 4). The operator is constrained only by the operator interfaces, and must be left complete freedom for the internal design,

provided that the operator behavior is respected. At this level the latency of
the operators is not constrained, as it is considered as a performance issue, but
is not mandatory for synchronization; moreover, data dependent processing will
lead to unpredictable execution time inside the operators.

The usual chaining between the operators is also identified and the union of
these patterns serves to create the operator interconnect scheme, simplified from
the costly full crossbar, in order to mitigate the area cost.

A parameterizable number M of memories feed the operators; this number
and their size are also decided according to applicative requirements, taking into
account data dependencies, for example image lines or blocks.

Setting all these parameters defines an implementation of the processor that
can be synthesized in order to conduct performance evaluation. The application
is ported to the structure with the help of a toolchain that compiles the control
code and prepares the configuration bitstreams for the operators. For further
details on the toolchain, one can refer to [2].

3.2   Processor Description

A more detailed view of the processor template is depicted in figure 1. The high-
level control and the datapath are separated. To face the increasing amount of
control statements multimedia processing exhibits, data dependent processing
for example, they are tightly coupled, so that an intermediate result from any
operator can raise an interrupt at any time to the control sequence. A configuration interface allows the controller to feed the operators with configuration data.
As the design of the processor started with the goal to avoid the classical area
overhead due to reconfigurable interconnects in reconfigurable processors, with
the flexibility reported inside the operator design, the interconnect is separated
in two parts: one is the interconnect towards the memories, and the other is a
low latency interconnect used for chaining the operators together.

The operator interconnect maps the high-level patterns that chain the operators; possibly all patterns are implementable at design time: some examples
are SIMD patterns, where all operators do the same processing on independent
data flows, up to the pipeline that chains all operators and that processes only
one data stream, and all possible variants, with various Y-shaped patterns, with
multiple inputs and one output.

The operators are configured by a bus interface: the configuration interface
is memory mapped, but broadcast modes are provided to accelerate the loading
of the operator configuration. In order to avoid reconfiguration overhead at run
time, the size of the reconfiguration data is kept low, typically under a hundred
bytes. It can consist of operator configuration and/or selection, internal simple routing data, constant parameters, functional look-up-tables, adaptive filter
coefficients, or even a short microcode for a programmable finite state machine.

Address generators are used to create the streams from all memories, in order
to relieve the control processor with the task of fetching data; the generators
should provide at least the following access modes: base address and horizontal
or vertical scan with a step, in both directions.

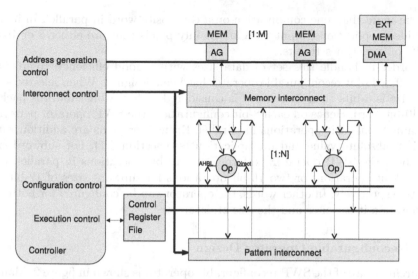

Fig. 1. Reconfigurable processor template architecture

3.3 Execution Model

The control code contains explicit operator reconfiguration commands, that are dynamically loaded before a function can start executing. Every function mapped on the processor follows the same steps: first the context has to be loaded; it is comprised of operator's configuration data, interconnect patterns, selection of involved memories, and program for address generators.

The execution of the function can then start with a control signal on the execution control interface with data that come from the external DMA or are already stored into memories from previous computations. To save time, unused operators or data memories can possibly be loaded during this step in preparation for the next computation. The processing step is finished as soon as the write-back address generator has completed its program. The status of the different operators can be checked, else the processor can step forward.

4 Reconfigurable Operators

The processor is made of reconfigurable operators operating concurrently. Computing efficiency and flexibility inside the multimedia domain drove the operator design. Both parallelism rate and efficiency can be increased if data-level parallelism is also implemented. Subword parallelism SWP [15] particularly suits image processing. With SWP each operand is partitioned into multiple lower precision operands, called subwords. Such as with SIMD, a single SWP instruction performs the same operation on multiple sets of subwords in parallel using SWP enabled operators. As a result, same datapath and operator can be used to perform more than one computation on a composite word in parallel. In image and video applications, input data are mainly pixels thus are either 8 or 10 or 12-bits or sometimes 16-bits.

In order to handle this set of data sizes with a good efficiency/complexity trade-off, a 40-bit reconfigurable operator has been designed. When selected subword size is 8-bits then each input is considered as five 8-bit subwords packed in a 40-bit word. Hence on each 8-bit configuration, the SWP operator performs five same 8-bit basic operations in parallel. Basic operations are addition, subtraction, absolute value and multiplication (see section 4.1). For subword size of 10-bits, the SWP operator performs four 10-bit operations in parallel, and three 12-bit operations or two 16-bit operations for subword sizes of 12-bits or 16-bits respectively. In other words, the operator can be configured for both the computation it executes and the size of data.

4.1 Reconfigurable Operator Design

The architecture of the SWP reconfigurable operator is shown in figure 2. Mainly the SWP operator consists of SWP basic arithmetic units, SWP subwords adders units and accumulator unit. These units are connected in such a way that a variety of multimedia oriented basic and complex SWP operations can be performed, such as sum of absolute differences SAD for motion estimation algorithm, sum of products for discrete cosine transform DCT algorithm... Multiplexers are used to provide appropriate data to arithmetic units. Control signals for the multiplexers and enable signals for registers (not shown in figure 2) are provided externally by the controller based upon the selected operation. The subword size is selected by control bits which are communicated to all SWP units (not shown in figure 2). To reduce the switching activity, all operators are guarded, so that unused units can be disabled.

Basic SWP arithmetic units are used to perform basic arithmetic operations on the selected subword size data. These operations include SWP $(a \pm b)$ signed, SWP (abs) signed, SWP $(a \times b)$ signed/unsigned, SWP $|a - b|$ unsigned, SWP (a + b) unsigned. SWP $(a \pm b)$ operator is used to perform addition or subtraction of signed subwords data. Its architecture is based upon the breaking of carry chain at subwords boundaries. SWP (abs) signed unit is used to perform the absolute operation on signed subwords data. Operator abs takes the two's complement of subwords depending upon the value of most significant bit.

SWP $(a \times b)$ signed/unsigned unit is used to perform SWP multiplication of signed as well as unsigned data. Because multiplication hardware implementation is area and delay costly, particular care was taken for the design of the multiplier. Its implementation is based upon an extension of the SWP multiplier proposed in [16] which supports only classical subword sizes (8, 16 and 32-bit). Here the multimedia oriented subword sizes of 8, 10, 12 and 16-bits are considered which do not have any uniform arithmetic relation with the word size (40-bit) of the SWP operator. Partial product bits are generated in such a way that they remain valid for all subwords size multiplications. Hence no suppression and detection of carries is required at subword boundaries.

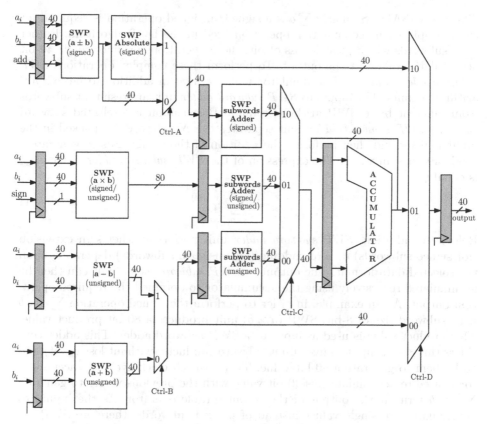

Fig. 2. Reconfigurable Multimedia SWP Operator

SWP $|a - b|$ unsigned unit is used to perform absolute difference of unsigned subwords. This unit is required because usually the pixels are stored as unsigned data. To avoid the absolute operation, this unit either calculates $a - b$ (when $a > b$) or $b - a$ (when $b > a$).

Like the inputs, the output data of all the basic SWP units consist of 40-bits except for the SWP multiplier whose output consists of 80-bits. The basic arithmetic units produce outputs in the form of resultant subwords packed in a register. As per the requirement, these packed subwords can be obtained at the output of the reconfigurable operator through the use of appropriate control bits. As a single multiplication is not usually required in multimedia applications, and also because the output of the SWP operator is 40-bits wide, the multiplier unit output is not directly routed to the output of the reconfigurable operator. However the accumulation of products can be obtained at the output of the operator through the *SWP subword adder*.

For certain multimedia applications more complex operations are required. For instance ($\sum |a - b|$) operation is required in the calculation of sum of absolute differences (SAD). Similarly $\sum a \times b$ signed/unsigned operation is required for the multiplication-accumulation operation used in the DCT algorithm. Rather than subwords which provide loss of bit, these operations produce single 40-bit accumulated values at the output. To perform these complex operations *SWP subword adder* units and accumulator unit are used in addition to basic SWP arithmetic units. The inputs to *SWP subword adder* unit are resultant subwords from different basic SWP arithmetic units. Based upon the selected subword size, the *SWP subword adder* unit separates the N subwords x_i packed in the input register and then performs the addition of these subwords to generate a single 40-bit sum value. The expression of the *SWP subword adder* output z_{sa} is equal to

$$z_{sa} = \sum_{i=0}^{N-1} x_i \tag{1}$$

Before the addition, *SWP subword adder* unit performs either sign extension (for signed subwords) or zero padding (for unsigned subwords) depending upon the selected data format. The output of *SWP subword adder* unit can then be accumulated recursively using the accumulator to obtained the required operation output. As an example, in order to perform the signed operation $\sum a \times b$ with subword size of 8-bit, SWP $(a \times b)$ unit produces a 80-bit product value. This product value is used as input to a SWP subword adder. This adder considers this 80-bit input as five 16-bit subword products (without loss of bit) and adds them to generate a 40-bit value. Then at each clock cycle the accumulator is used to accumulate this 40-bit value with the previous values to generate $\sum a \times b$ term at the output of the reconfigurable operator. As the inputs to accumulator are single values instead of packed subwords, therefore SWP capability is not required for the accumulator unit implementation. Likewise the accumulator generates the single output without loss of bit.

The other complex SWP operations which can be performed using this SWP operator are $\sum a \pm b$ signed, $\sum |a \pm b|$ signed, $\sum |a - b|$ unsigned, $\sum a + b$ unsigned. Based upon the requirements, any combination of these operations can also be obtained such as $\sum a \times b + \sum |a \pm b|$ signed etc. For the complex operations which involve the accumulation of results generated by basic units, the output word-length depends upon the number of values need to be accumulated. In the worst case when performing $\sum a \times b$ operation on 16-bit subwords, the output of the SWP $(a \times b)$ unit consists of two 32-bit subwords. As the accumulator is 40-bits wide, the extra eight bits are used as guard bits to avoid any overflow. Therefore this operator can perform at least 256 (2^8) accumulations of worst data length product terms. For other smaller subword data sizes, the numbers of guard bits are greater and thus the number of accumulations which can be performed increases further without any overflow.

4.2 Synthesis Results

To analyze the area, speed and power consumption, overall reconfigurable operator design is synthesized to ASIC standard cell HCMOS9GP 130nm

Table 1. Synthesis results on ASIC technologies

Technology	NAND Gates	Critical Path (ns)	Gates × CP	Dynamic Power (mW)	Leakage Power (μW)
90nm CMOS	24063	7.7	185285	2.5	534
130nm CMOS	25379	7.6	192880	4.1	48

(CORE9GPLL 4.1 low leakage standard cell library from ST Microelectronics) and 90nm (fsd0t_a standard performance low voltage threshold cell library from UMC) technology using Synopsys Design Vision and to FPGA (Xilinx Virtex II) using Mentor Graphics Precision RTL tool. The area, critical path (CP) and power consumption have been measured. Table 1 shows the results obtained for the two ASIC technologies. To analyze the overall efficiency, product of gates and critical path (CP) is also computed. Smaller value of this product term indicates higher efficiency. On ASIC technologies, implementations are made for a clock period of 8ns. When clock frequency is decreased, the area reduces accordingly but the overall efficiency reduces because the throughput of SWP operator reduces with the decrease in clock frequency. On the FPGA Virtex II platform, 2793 CLBs are required and the critical path is equal to 17.2 ns. Actually area and CP overheads for implementing SWP capability are less on ASIC technology compared to FPGA technology. The reason is that in FPGA implementation resources are CLBs rather than gates as in ASIC. Therefore ASIC resources better suits the SWP designs.

4.3   Results Analysis

The unit which consumes maximum design resources is the SWP multiplier. Although the multiplier architecture is based on [16] which is known to be for far more efficient for SWP implementation than conventional multiplier architectures, it consumes almost 60% of total SWP operator area. The other blocks like signed arithmetic units, unsigned arithmetic units, subwords adder units and register units consumes respectively 8%, 9%, 14% and 6% of total area. Similarly power consumption of the SWP multiplier is also more compared to other units. SWP multiplier unit consumes almost 50% of total power. The other blocks like signed arithmetic units, unsigned arithmetic units and subwords adder units consumes respectively 9%, 19% and 15% of total power.

At present time, reconfigurable operators have been synthesized, and first performance assessment can be given at the operator level. The sum of absolute difference kernel used in motion estimation algorithms is a good candidate at this granularity level. For comparison, state-of-the-art Texas Instruments (TI) TMS320C64x DSP architecture is used. The processing unit of the TI DSP is made-up of two clusters. Each cluster consists of four functional units among with one multiplier and two arithmetic and logic units. This architecture provides SWP capabilities based on 8, 16 and 32 bit data word-lengths. For a fair comparison, one reconfigurable operator is considered for our processor and one cluster is considered for the TI DSP. For 16-bit pixels, the number of cycles

N_{cycles} required to compute the SAD applied to 16 by 16 image blocks is 128 for both implementations. N_{cycles} is 60 and 64 for our operator and TI DSP based solution respectively when 8-bit pixels are considered. For 10 and 12 bit pixels, the granularity in term of data size of our operator allows the number of cycles to be reduced. N_{cycles} is reduced by 50% and 25% for 10 and 12 bit pixels respectively. In practice, processing is spread on two clusters with TI DSP so N_{cycles} is divided by two.

5 Conclusion

In this paper the design of a reconfigurable processor tailored for multimedia processing is introduced. The architecture is designed to provide a good trade-off between performance and power consumption targeting embedded devices. The processor is based on pipelined coarse-grain reconfigurable operators that have flexibility and scalability properties.

Future work will consist in porting real applicative cases with the help of the software framework on a FPGA-based demonstrator for validation purpose. The scalability of the processor template allows to explore the design space in order to extract performance and power consumption metrics. For instance, each operator can be configured to complete a SAD on a particular image block, and performance assessment of the motion estimation part of a video codec will be performed with various number of operators.

Acknowledgment

This work is supported by the french *Architectures du Futur* ANR program ANR-06-ARFU-004.

References

1. http://roma.irisa.fr
2. Wolinski, C., Kuchcinski, K.: Automatic Selection of Application-Specific Reconfigurable Processor Extensions. In: DATE 2008: Proc. of the Conf. on Design, automation and test in Europe, pp. 1214–1219 (2008)
3. http://www.tensilica.com
4. Mingche, L., Jianjun, G., Zhuxi, Z., Zhiying, W.: Using an Automated Approach to Explore and Design a High-Efficiency Processor Element for the Multimedia Domain. In: CISIS 2008: International Conference on Complex, Intelligent and Software Intensive Systems, pp. 613–618 (2008)
5. Campi, F., Deledda, A., Pizzotti, M., Ciccarelli, L., Rolandi, P., Mucci, C., Lodi, A., Vitkovski, A., Vanzolini, L.: A dynamically adaptive DSP for heterogeneous reconfigurable platforms. In: DATE 2007: Proc. of the Conf. on Design, automation and test in Europe, pp. 9–14 (2007)
6. http://www.stretchinc.com

7. Barat, F., Jayapala, M., Aa, T.V., Deconinck, G., Lauwereins, R., Corporaal, H.: Low power coarse-grained reconfigurable instruction set processor. In: Y. K. Cheung, P., Constantinides, G.A. (eds.) FPL 2003. LNCS, vol. 2778, pp. 230–239. Springer, Heidelberg (2003)
8. Veredas, F.J., Scheppler, M., Moffat, W., Mei, B.: Custom implementation of the coarse-grained reconfigurable ADRES architecture for multimedia purposes. In: FPL 2005, Int. Conf. on Field Programmable Logic and Applications, pp. 106–111 (2005)
9. Yeo, S., Lyuh, C., Roh, T., Kim, J.: High Energy Efficient Reconfigurable Processor for Mobile Multimedia. In: ISSCC 2008: Int. Conf. on Circuits and Systems for Communications, pp. 618–622 (2008)
10. http://www.pactxpp.com
11. Yazdani, S., Cambonie, J., Pottier, B.: Reconfigurable Multimedia Accelerator for Mobile Systems. In: SOCC 2008: 21st Annual IEEE Int. SOC Conference (2008)
12. Carta, S.M., Pani, D., Raffo, L.: Reconfigurable Coprocessor for Multimedia Application Domain. J. of VLSI Signal Processing 44, 135–152 (2006)
13. Lanuzza, M., Perri, S., Corsonello, P., Margala, M.: A New Reconfigurable Coarse-Grain Architecture for Multimedia Applications. In: AHS 2007: Second NASA/ESA Conf. on Adaptive Hardware and Systems (2007)
14. Yasuura, H., Tomiyama, H.: Power optimization by datapath width adjustment. In: Pedram, M., Rabaey, J.M. (eds.) Power aware design methodologies. Kluwer, Dordrecht (2002)
15. Fridman, J.: Sub-Word Parallelism in Digital Signal Processing. IEEE Signal Processing Magazine 17(2), 27–35 (2000)
16. Krithivasan, S., Schulte, M.J.: Multiplier Architectures for Media Processing. In: Thirty seventh Asilomar Conf. on Signals, Systems and Computers, vol. 2, pp. 2193–2197 (2003)

A Protocol for Secure Remote Updates of FPGA Configurations

Saar Drimer and Markus G. Kuhn

Computer Laboratory, University of Cambridge
http://www.cl.cam.ac.uk/users/{sd410,mgk25}

Abstract. We present a security protocol for the remote update of volatile FPGA configurations stored in non-volatile memory. Our approach can be implemented on existing FPGAs, as it sits entirely in user logic. Our protocol provides for remote attestation of the running configuration and the status of the upload process. It authenticates the uploading party both before initiating the upload and before completing it, to both limit a denial-of-service attack and protect the integrity of the bitstream. Encryption protects bitstream confidentiality in transit; we either decrypt it before non-volatile storage, or pass on ciphertext if the configuration logic can decrypt it. We discuss how tamper-proofing the connection between the FPGA and the non-volatile memory, as well as space for multiple bitstreams in the latter, can improve resilience against downgrading and denial-of-service attacks.

1 Introduction

Networked FPGA-based systems gain particular flexibility if remote configuration updates are possible. The question of how to secure such updates against malicious interference may seem easily answered at first glance: many existing cryptographic authentication protocols protect the confidentiality, integrity and authenticity of transactions, such as overwriting a file (e.g., an FPGA bitstream) in a remote computer. They can be applied easily if the FPGA is merely a peripheral device and the remote update of its configuration bitstream can be handled entirely by software running on the system's main processor. Here, however, we consider designs that lack a separate trustworthy main CPU, where the FPGA configuration itself becomes fully responsible for securing its own update.

Two constraints of volatile FPGAs pose particular problems here: they lack memory for storing more than a single configuration at any time, and they retain no state between power-cycles. These, in turn, have two main implications. Firstly, FPGAs have no notion of the "freshness" of received configuration data, so they have no mechanism for rejecting old or revoked configuration content. Secondly, unless a trusted path is established with devices around the FPGA (such as non-volatile memory), they have no temporary memory to store the bitstream while it is being authenticated or decrypted before being loaded into configuration memory cells. In other words, merely initiating a reconfiguration will destroy the current state.

J. Becker et al. (Eds.): ARC 2009, LNCS 5453, pp. 50–61, 2009.
© Springer-Verlag Berlin Heidelberg 2009

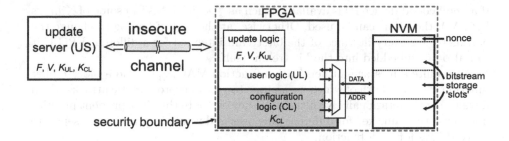

Fig. 1. An update server (US) installs a new bitstream in a system's NVM over an insecure channel by passing it through update logic in the FPGA's user logic (UL). After reset, the hard-wired configuration logic (CL) loads the new bitstream.

The key observation we make is that the FPGA's user logic can be used to perform security operations on the bitstream before it is stored in external non-volatile memory (NVM) and loaded into the FPGA's configuration cells. We then rely on system-level properties, such as tamper proofing and remote attestation, to compensate for the lack of cryptographic capabilities and non-volatile memory in the FPGA's configuration logic. Our solution does not require that FPGA vendors add any hard-wired circuits to their devices' configuration logic, and therefore can be implemented with existing products.

We first list our assumptions (Section 2.1) and then present our secure remote update protocol (Section 2.2), which meets the following goals as far as possible: no additions to the configuration logic; use of the user logic; bitstream confidentiality and authenticity (Section 2.3); prevention of denial-of-service attacks; no reliance on bitstream-encoding obscurity; and, finally, prevention of replay of older, revoked bitstream versions. We then outline a more robust variant of the protocol for systems where the NVM can hold multiple bitstreams (Section 2.4). Finally, we discuss the security properties of our protocol (Section 3) and place it into the context of related work (Section 4).

2   Secure Remote Update Protocol

Our secure update protocol defines an interactive exchange between an *update server* (US), the entity in charge of distributing new bitstreams to FPGA systems in the field, and an *update logic*, the receiving end, implemented in the *user logic* (UL) of each FPGA (Figure 1). Bitstreams are loaded into configuration memory cells by the *configuration logic* (CL), which is hard-wired into the device by the FPGA vendor.

2.1   Assumptions

We require a unique, non-secret, FPGA identifier F, which the authentication process will use to ensure that messages cannot be forwarded to other FPGAs.

If an embedded device ID is available (such as "Device DNA" in some of Xilinx's FPGAs), then that can be used. Otherwise, at the cost of having to change the parameter for every instance of the bitstream intended for a different FPGA, it can also be embedded into the bitstream itself.

We require a message-authentication function $\mathrm{MAC}_{K_{\mathrm{UL}}}(\cdot)$ and a block cipher function $E_{K_{\mathrm{UL}}}(\cdot)$, both of which we assume to resist cryptoanalytic attacks. Even if we use both notationally with the same key, we note that it is prudent practice not to use the same key for different purposes and would in practice use separate derived keys for each function.

The secret key K_{UL} is stored in the bitstream. It should be individual to each device, such that its successful extraction from one device does not help in attacking others.

Device-specific keys can be managed in several ways. For example, K_{UL} can be independently generated and stored in a device database by the update server. Or it could be calculated as $K_{\mathrm{UL}} = E_{K_{\mathrm{M}}}(F)$ from the device identifier F using a master key K_{M} known only to the update server. As a third example, F could contain a public-key certificate that the update server uses to securely exchange the secret key K_{UL} with the update logic.

Where the configuration logic also holds a secret key, K_{CL}, it could be stored in battery-backed volatile or in non-volatile memory, as long as it cannot be discovered through physical attacks or side channel analysis.

We assume that each FPGA of a given model and size loads only bitstreams of fixed length $L \times b$ bits, where b bits is the capacity of the memory block B that the update logic uses to buffer an incoming new bitstream before writing it to NVM. The size b must be large enough to guarantee that the FPGA configuration logic will not load a bitstream from NVM if its last block of b bits is missing. This is normally ensured if any checksum that the FPGA's configuration logic verifies is entirely contained in the last b bits of the loaded bitstream. (In practice, b might also be the minimum amount of data that can be written efficiently to NVM.)

The system needs to be on-line on demand or within a reasonable amount of time, for both update and/or remote attestation. Our protocol handles both malicious and accidental (transmission errors, packet losses, etc.) corruption of data. However, it merely aborts and restarts the entire session if it detects a violation of data integrity, rather than trying to retransmit individual lost data packets. Therefore, for best performance on unreliable channels, it should be run over an error-correcting protocol layer (TCP, HDLC, LAPM, etc.), which does not have to be implemented inside the security boundary.

2.2 The Protocol

Algorithm 1 shows the implementation of the update-logic side of our protocol, which forms a part of the application that resides in the FPGA's user logic. We focus our discussion here on the FPGA side, as this is the half of the protocol that runs on the more constrained device. It supports a number of different policies that an update server might choose to implement.

Algorithm 1. Update-logic state machine

Constants:

K_{UL}	key shared with update server	L	length of bitstream (blocks)
V	version ID of operating bitstream	F	FPGA chip unique ID

Variables:

V_{NVM}	version ID of NVM bitstream	V_e, F_e	expected value of V, F
V_u	version ID of uploaded bitstream	N_{NVM}	NVM counter value
N_{US}	nonce generated by update server	N_{max}	upper bound for N_{NVM}
B	b-bit buffer for a bitstream block	M, M'	MAC values

1: $V_{NVM} := V$
2: Receive($C, V_e, F_e, N_{max}, N_{US}, M_0$)
3: **if** $C \neq$ "GetStatus" **then** Send("Abort"); **goto** 2
4: ReadNVM$_N(N_{NVM})$
5: $S := [M_0 = \text{MAC}_{K_{UL}}(C, V_e, F_e, N_{max}, N_{US})] \wedge (V_e = V) \wedge (F_e = F) \wedge$
     $(N_{NVM} < N_{max})$
6: **if** S **then**
7:     $N_{NVM} := N_{NVM} + 1$
8:     WriteNVM$_N(N_{NVM})$
9: **end if**
10: $R := ($"RespondStatus"$, V, F, N_{NVM}, V_{NVM})$
11: $M_1 := \text{MAC}_{K_{UL}}(M_0, R)$;   Send($R, M_1$)
12: **if** $\neg S$ **then goto** 2
13: Receive(C, M_0')
14: **if** $M_0' \neq \text{MAC}_{K_{UL}}(M_1, C)$ **then goto** 2
15: **if** $C =$ "Update" **then**
16:     $V_{NVM} := 0$
17:     WriteNVM$_{B[1...L]}(0)$
18:     **for** $i := 1$ to L **do**
19:         Receive(B_i)
20:         $M_i' := \text{MAC}_{K_{UL}}(M_{i-1}', B_i)$
21:         **if** $i < L$ **then** WriteNVM$_{B[i]}(B_i)$
22:     **end for**
23:     Receive(V_u, M_2)
24:     **if** $M_2 = \text{MAC}_{K_{UL}}(M_L', V_u)$ **then**
25:         WriteNVM$_{B[L]}(B_L)$
26:         $V_{NVM} := V_u$
27:         $R := ($"UpdateConfirm"$)$
28:     **else**
29:         $R := ($"UpdateFail"$)$
30:     **end if**
31:     $M_3 := \text{MAC}_{K_{UL}}(M_2, R)$;   Send($R, M_3$)
32: **else if** $C =$ "Reset" **then**
33:     $M_2 := \text{MAC}_{K_{UL}}(M_0', $"ResetConfirm"$)$;   Send("ResetConfirm"$, M_2)$
34:     ResetFPGA()
35: **end if**
36: **goto** 2

In addition to the unique FPGA identifier F, the update logic also contains, as compiled-in constants, the version identifier $V \neq 0$ of the application bitstream of which it is a part, and a secret key K_{UL} that is only known to the update server and update logic.

Each protocol session starts with an initial "GetStatus" message from the update server and a "RespondStatus" reply from the update logic in the FPGA. This exchange serves two functions. Firstly, both parties exchange numbers that are only ever used once ("nonces", e.g. counters, timestamps, random numbers). Their reception is cryptographically confirmed by the other party in subsequent messages. Such challenge-response round trips enable each party to verify the freshness of any subsequent data packet received, and thus protect against replay attacks. The nonce N_{US} generated by the update server must be an unpredictable random number that has a negligible chance of ever repeating. This prevents attackers prefetching a matching reply from the FPGA. The nonce N_{NVM} contributed by the update logic is a monotonic counter maintained in NVM (avoiding the difficulties of implementing a reliable and trusted source of randomness or time within the security boundary). To protect this counter against attempts to overflow it, and also to protect against attempts to wear out NVM that only lasts a limited number of write cycles, the update logic will only increment it when authorized to do so by the update server. For this reason, the update server includes in the "GetStatus" message an upper bound N_{max} (of the same unsigned integer type as N_{NVM}) beyond which the NVM counter must not be incremented in response to this message. The protocol cannot proceed past the "RespondStatus" message unless the NVM counter is incremented.

The second purpose of the initial exchange is to ensure that both parties agree on values of F and V. The update server sends its expected values V_e and F_e, and the update logic will not proceed beyond the "RespondStatus" message unless these values match its own V and F. This ensures that an attacker cannot reuse any "GetStatus" message intended for one particular FPGA chip F and installed bitstream version V on any other such combination. The update server might know V and F already in advance from a database that holds the state of all fielded systems. If this information is not available, the update server can gain it in a prior "GetStatus"/"RespondStatus" exchange, because both values are reported and authenticated in the "RespondStatus" reply.

All protocol messages are authenticated using a message-authentication code (MAC) computed with the shared secret key K_{UL}. This is done in order to ensure that an attacker cannot generate any message that has not been issued by the update server or update logic. In addition, with the exception of the initial "GetStatus" message, the calculation of the MAC for each message in a protocol session incorporates not only all data bits of the message, but also the MAC of the previously received message. This way, the MAC ensures at any step of the protocol that both parties agree not only on the content of the current message, but also on the content of the entire protocol session so far. This mechanism makes it unnecessary to repeat in messages any data (nonces, version identifiers, etc.) that has been transmitted before, because their values are implicitly carried forward in each message by the MAC chain. In the presentation of Algorithm 1, M, M' and B are registers, not arrays, and their indices merely indicate different values that they store during the execution of one protocol session.

Note that any "GetStatus" request results in a "RespondStatus" reply, even without a correct MAC. This is to allow update servers to query F even before knowing which K_{UL} to apply. However, an incorrect MAC in a "GetStatus" will prevent the session from proceeding beyond the "RespondStatus" reply. This means that anyone can easily query the bitstream version identifier V from the device. If this is of concern because, for example, it might allow an attacker to quickly scan for vulnerable old versions in the field, then the value V used in the protocol can be an individually encrypted version of the actual version number $\hat{V}$, as in $V = E_{K_{\mathrm{UL}}}(\hat{V})$. Whether this option is chosen or not does not affect the update-logic implementation of the protocol, which treats V just as an opaque identifier bitstring.

The protocol can only proceed beyond the "RespondStatus" message ($S = $ true) if the update-logic nonce has been incremented and both sides agree on which FPGA and bitstream version is being updated. If the update server decides to proceed, it will continue the session with a command that instructs the update logic either to begin programming a new bitstream into NVM ("Update"), or to reset the FPGA and reload the bitstream from NVM ("Reset"). The MAC M'_0 that comes with this command will depend on the MAC M_1 of the preceding "RespondStatus" message, which in turn depends on the freshly incremented user-logic nonce N_{NVM}, as well as V and F. Therefore, the verification of M'_0 ensures the user-logic of both the authenticity and the freshness of this command, and the same applies to all MAC verifications in the rest of the session.

The successful authentication of the "Update" command leads to erasing the entire bitstream from the NVM. From this point on, until all blocks B_1 to B_L have been written, the NVM will contain an invalid bitstream. Therefore, there is no benefit in authenticating each received bitstream data block B_i individually before writing it into NVM. Instead, we postpone the writing of the last bitstream block B_L into NVM until the message authentication code M'_L that covers the entire bitstream has been verified. This step is finally confirmed by the update logic in an "UpdateConfirm" message.

Since a system that can store only a single bitstream in its NVM must not be reset before all blocks of the bitstream have been uploaded, our protocol also provides an authenticated status indicator V_{NVM} intended to help recover from protocol sessions that were aborted due to loss or corruption of messages. After a successful reset, the update logic sets $V_{\mathrm{NVM}} := V$ to indicate the version identifier of the bitstream stored in NVM. Before the process of erasing and rewriting the NVM begins, it sets V_{NVM} to the reserved value 0, to indicate the absence of a valid bitstream in NVM. After the last block B_L was written, the update logic receives from the update server the version identifier V_{u} of the bitstream that has just been uploaded into NVM, and sets register V_{NVM} accordingly. Should the update session be aborted in any way, then the update server can always initiate a new session with a new "GetStatus"/"RespondStatus" exchange, where it will

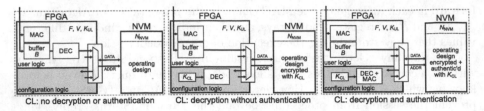

Fig. 2. Scenarios for different configuration logic capabilities

learn from the V_{NVM} value in the "RespondStatus" message the current status of the NVM, that is, whether the old bitstream is still intact, the new bitstream has been uploaded completely, or it contains no valid bitstream. It can then decide whether to restart the upload or perform a reset.

If no messages were lost, the update server will automatically receive an authenticated confirmation. "UpdateConfirm" indicates that the "Update" command has been processed, and its MAC M_3 confirms each received data byte, as well as the old and new version identifiers, FPGA ID, nonces, and any other data exchanged during the session. The "ResetConfirm" command can only confirm that the reset of the FPGA is about to take place; any attestation of the successful completion of the reset must be left to the new bitstream.

The initial "GetStatus"/"RespondStatus" exchange can, besides for initiating a new session or restarting after an aborted one, also be used for remote attestation of a system. For this purpose, "GetStatus" is simply sent with $N_{\mathrm{max}} = 0$ and the values of V_e and F_e do not matter. This will not affect the NVM counter, but results in authenticated fresh values of V, F, and V_{NVM} in "RespondStatus".

2.3   Bitstream Encryption and Authentication

Some FPGAs can decrypt bitstreams in their configuration logic, using embedded (or battery-backed) keys, while others lack this capability. Parelkar and Gaj [1] and Drimer [2] have also proposed adding bitstream authentication. Algorithm 1 can be used with FPGAs that support any combination of these functions (three are shown in Figure 2), provided that the user logic compensates for those that are missing.

For confidentiality, bitstreams should always be transmitted encrypted between the update server and update logic. Where the configuration logic is able to decrypt a bitstream while loading it from NVM, the update server can encrypt the bitstream under a secret key K_{CL} shared with the configuration logic, leaving the update logic and NVM merely handling ciphertext. If the configuration logic cannot decrypt, the update server has to encrypt the bitstream under a key derived from K_{UL} and the user logic has to decrypt each block B_i before writing it to NVM (using some standard file encryption method, such as cipher-block chaining). If the configuration logic also performs authentication, the requirements above do not change; the authentication in the update logic is still necessary to prevent denial-of-service attacks that attempt unauthorized overwriting of NVM content. Again, the last buffered block B_L must contain the MAC of the bitstream that the configuration logic will verify, such that the bitstream will not load without the successful verification of M_2.

2.4 Multiple NVM Slots

NVM that provides only a single memory location ("slot") for storing a bitstream can seriously limit the reliability of the system. There will be no valid bitstream stored in the NVM from when the update logic starts erasing the NVM until it has completed writing the new bitstream. A malicious or accidental interruption, such as a power failure or a long delay in the transmission of the remaining bitstream, can leave the system in an unrecoverable state. Such single-slot systems are, therefore, only advisable where loss of communications or power is unlikely, such as with local updates with a secure and reliable power source.

Otherwise, the NVM should provide at least two slots, such that it can hold both the old and the new bitstream simultaneously. The FPGA's configuration logic will then have to scan through these NVM slots until it encounters a valid bitstream. It will start loading a bitstream from the first slot. If the bitstream is invalid (i.e., has an incorrect checksum or MAC), it will load another bitstream from the next slot, and so on, until all slots have been tried or a valid one has been found.

The additional slot is then used during the update as a temporary store, in order to preserve the currently operating design in case of an update failure. The role of the two slots – upload area and operating bitstream store – can alternate between updates, depending on how multiple slots are supported by the configuration logic. The update process may be modified as follows.

At manufacturing, slot 1 is loaded with an initial design whose update logic can only write new bitstreams into the address space of slot 2. Before the $V_{\text{NVM}} := V_{\text{u}}$ changeover is made (line 26), the update logic erases slot 1, which then allows the configuration logic to find the new bitstream in slot 2 at the next power-up. The new bitstream, now in slot 2, will write its next bitstream into slot 1, and erases slot 2 when that update is complete, and so on. If an update is aborted by reset, one slot may remain with a partially uploaded bitstream. If this is slot 1, the configuration logic will fail to find a correct checksum there and move on to load the old bitstream from slot 2, from where the update process can then be restarted. If the partial content is in slot 2, then the configuration logic will never get there because the bitstream in slot 1 will be loaded first.

If the configuration logic tells the user logic which slot it came from (through status registers), then the user logic can simply pick the respective other slot and there is no need to compile one bitstream for each slot. If not, then the update server must ensure, through remote attestation, that each newly updated bitstream is compiled to write the next bitstream to the respective other slot. This might be aided by encoding in V which slot a bitstream was intended for. A third slot might be provided with a fallback bitstream that is never overwritten, and only loaded if something goes wrong during the NVM write process without the update logic noticing (e.g. data corruption between the FPGA and the NVM). This could leave both slot 1 and 2 without a valid bitstream and cause the fallback bitstream to be loaded from slot 3. Alternatively, the FPGA may always load, as a first configuration, a bootloader bitstream that controls from which slot the next bitstream is loaded from.

Recent FPGAs, such as Virtex-5 [3, UG191, Chap. 8, "Fallback MultiBoot"] or LatticeECP2/M [4, TN1148, "SPIm Mode"], implement a multi-slot scan in the configuration logic. Some, including Stratix IV [5, SIV51010-2.0, "Remote System Upgrade Mode"] or Virtex-5 [3, UG191, Chap. 8, "IPROG Reconfiguration"], provide a "reload bitstream from address X" command register, so that a user-designed bootloader bitstream can implement a multi-slot scan and checksum verification (but such a bootloader itself cannot necessarily be updated remotely). Alternatively, external configuration logic could be added to do the same.

3   Analysis

Algorithm 1 alone does not prevent the configuration logic from loading old bitstreams from NVM. In order to maintain our security objective of preventing attackers from operating older, outdated FPGA configurations, we also need to rely on either tamper proofing or binding the provision of online services to remote attestation. With Algorithm 1, if attackers can either feed the FPGA with N_{NVM} values of previously recorded sessions, or have access to its configuration port, they can replay older bitstreams. Therefore, these interfaces must be protected: the FPGA, NVM and the interface between them (configuration and read/write) must be contained within a tamper-proof enclosure. Manufacturing effective tamper-proof enclosures can be challenging, although there are now a number of strong off-the-shelf solutions available, such as tamper-sensing membranes that trigger zeroization of keys stored in battery-backed SRAM when penetrated. But protection against highly capable attackers is not necessary for all applications. Sometimes, it may suffice to deter attackers by using ball-grid array packages and routing security-critical signals entirely in internal printed circuit board layers without accessible vias. Some manufacturers may not be concerned if a few of their systems are maliciously downgraded with great effort in a laboratory environment, as long as the financial damage of the attack remains limited and it is impractical to scale it up by creating a commercial low-cost kit that allows everyone to repeat the attack with ease. For example, in consumer electronics, an attractive attack cannot require risky precision drilling into a printed circuit board or desoldering a fine-pitch ball-grid array. New stacked-die products, where the NVM is attached to the top of the FPGA die inside the same package (such as the Xilinx Spartan-3AN family) also make tamper proofing easier.

In some applications (e.g., online entertainment set-top boxes), the device's only use is to provide a service by interacting with a central server. Here, the provision of the service can be made conditional to a periodic successful remote attestation of the currently operating bitstream, in order to render the device inoperable unless it has an up-to-date bitstream loaded in the NVM. The remote attestation facility can provide the service provider authenticity assurances even where no tamper proofing exists, though the system must be on-line at short intervals.

If the bitstream is kept in the NVM encrypted under an FPGA-specific key (K_{CL}), then neither bitstream reverse engineering nor cloning will be possible, even if the tamper proofing of the NVM link fails. We already assume that such ciphertext can be observed in transit between the update server and update logic. If the plaintext bitstream is kept in NVM, because the configuration logic lacks decryption capability, we rely on NVM tamper-resistance to protect against cloning and the risk of bitstream reverse engineering. Projects for the latter, such as "ULogic" by Note and Rannaud [6], illustrate the risk of merely relying on the obscurity of the bitstream's syntax for security.

3.1 Parameter Sizes

As the NVM counter is well protected against overflow attacks by the N_{max} parameter (controlled by the update server), a size of 32 bits appears more than sufficient for most applications. Since an attacker can keep asking for a response for any value of N_{US} during remote attestation, N_{US} should be large enough to make the creation of a dictionary of responses that can be replayed impractical. For instance, using a uniformly distributed 64-bit word for N_{US} will ensure that an attacker who performs 10^3 queries per second will fill less than 10^{-7} of the dictionary within a decade. MAC values (M, M') of 64-bit length provide an equally generous safety margin to brute-force upload attempts.

4   Related Work

The Xilinx "Internet Reconfigurable Logic" initiative from the late 1990s discussed how remote updates can be performed, though the program was short lived [3, App. Note 412]. Remote reconfiguration using embedded processors has also been proposed [3, App. Note 441]. A patent by Trimberger and Conn [7] describes a remote update through a modem, an FPGA controller (in addition to the main FPGA) and "shadow PROMs" for recovery from failed writes. Altera describes how field updates can be performed for Stratix and Cyclone devices using a soft processor in the user logic and a hard logic interface using a non-volatile memory device, with the ability to revert to a "factory bitstream" stored in the NVM [5, User Guides SII52008, SIII51012, SIV51010, CIII51012]. However, the security aspects of remote update are not considered in any of the above.

Castillo et al. [8] propose a solution based on an OpenRISC1200 processor implemented in the user logic, together with an RSA engine for remote configuration on every start-up. However, the cryptographic key on which its security depends is obfuscated in a non-encrypted bitstream stored in the local NVM. Fong et al. [9] propose a security controller based on the Blowfish block cipher for encryption and CRC for data correctness. Attached to a "Media Interface", the FPGA is able to receive updates that are programmed into the configuration logic through the internal configuration port. The authors point out the vulnerabilities of their scheme: key obfuscation within the bootstrap bitstream, but more significantly, lack of data authentication with freshness, opening the system to replay attacks. Both the above schemes require an on-line connection at start-up to receive the operating design, while ours performs a secure remote update once, stores the bitstream locally, and loads it into the FPGA at start-up without on-line connectivity.

Replay attacks despite bitstream encryption and authentication were described by Drimer [10, p. 21], who suggested adding a non-volatile counter as nonce for bitstream authentication, or remote attestation in user logic as countermeasures. Motivated by this, Badrignans et al. [11] proposed additions to the hard-coded configuration logic in order to prevent replay of old bitstreams. They use a nonce in the authentication process, in addition to a mechanism for alerting the developer of its failure. Our solution of using user-logic resources instead of adding hard-wired configuration logic functionality is more flexible: our update logic can also update itself in the field. More importantly, our approach can be used with existing FPGAs, although it can equally benefit from additional security features in future ones. We also discuss denial-of-service attacks and failed updates, how the system can recover, and specify the detailed behaviour of our update logic, ready for implementation.

5   Conclusions

We have proposed a secure remote update protocol that maintains the confidentiality, integrity and freshness of bitstreams to the extent possible. In contrast to other proposals, our solution requires no additions to the configuration logic of existing FPGAs and uses the user logic for most security functions. The required cryptographic primitives consume some user-logic resources, but they can be reused by the application. Even local attackers can be deterred from restoring old and outdated bitstreams, which the update server may want to suppress (e.g., due to known vulnerabilities), by tamper proofing the NVM connection.

The update logic proposed here can be implemented either in software on a soft processor, or as a logic circuit. The design and presentation of our protocol was influenced by our experience with an ongoing logic-circuit implementation on a Virtex-5 evaluation board, using the publicly available AES design by Drimer et al. [12].

Possible extensions for the protocol presented here include role- and identity-based access control (beyond the current single role of "update server"), as well as receiving on-line partial configuration content at start-up, to be programmed into memory cells using an internal configuration port.

Acknowledgments

Saar Drimer's research is funded Xilinx, Inc. We thank Steven J. Murdoch, Sergei Skorobogatov and the anonymous reviewers for valuable comments and suggestions.

References

1. Parelkar, M.M., Gaj, K.: Implementation of EAX mode of operation for FPGA bitstream encryption and authentication. In: Field Programmable Technology, pp. 335–336 (December 2005)
2. Drimer, S.: Authentication of FPGA bitstreams: why and how. In: Diniz, P.C., Marques, E., Bertels, K., Fernandes, M.M., Cardoso, J.M.P. (eds.) ARCS 2007. LNCS, vol. 4419, pp. 73–84. Springer, Heidelberg (2007)
3. Xilinx Inc., http://www.xilinx.com
4. Lattice Semiconductor Corp., http://www.latticesemi.com
5. Altera Corp., http://www.altera.com
6. Note, J.B., Rannaud, É.: From the bitstream to the netlist. In: ACM/SIGDA Symposium on Field Programmable Gate Arrays, pp. 264–264. ACM, New York (2008)
7. Trimberger, S.M., Conn, R.O.: Remote field upgrading of programmable logic device configuration data via adapter connected to target memory socket. United States Patent 7, 269, 724 (September 2007)
8. Castillo, J., Huerta, P., Martínez, J.I.: Secure IP downloading for SRAM FPGAs. Microprocessors and Microsystems 31(2), 77–86 (2007)
9. Fong, R.J., Harper, S.J., Athanas, P.M.: A versatile framework for FPGA field updates: an application of partial self-reconfiguration. In: IEEE International Workshop on Rapid Systems Prototyping, pp. 117–123 (2003)
10. Drimer, S.: Volatile FPGA design security – a survey (v0.96) (April 2008), http://www.cl.cam.ac.uk/~sd410/papers/fpga_security.pdf
11. Benoît, B., Reouven, E., Lionel, T.: Secure FPGA configuration architecture preventing system downgrade. In: Field Programmable Logic, pp. 317–322 (September 2008)
12. Drimer, S., Güneysu, T., Paar, C.: DSPs, BRAMs and a pinch of logic: new recipes for AES on FPGAs. In: IEEE Symposium on Field-Programmable Custom Computing Machines. IEEE, Los Alamitos (2008)

FPGA Analysis Tool: High-Level Flows for Low-Level Design Analysis in Reconfigurable Computing

Krzysztof Kępa[1], Fearghal Morgan[1], Krzysztof Kościuszkiewicz[1], Lars Braun[2], Michael Hübner[2], and Jürgen Becker[2]

[1] Bio-Inspired Electronics and Reconfigurable Computing Group,
Dept. of Electronic Engineering, National University of Ireland, Galway, Ireland
Krzysztof.Kepa@poczta.fm, Fearghal.Morgan@nuigalway.ie,
K.Kosciuszkiewicz@gmail.com
[2] Universität Karlsruhe (TH), Germany,
Institut für Technik der Informationsverarbeitung (ITIV)
{braun,huebner,becker}@itiv.uni-karlsruhe.de

Abstract. The growth of the reconfigurable systems community exposes diverse requirements with regard to functionality of Electronic Design Automation (EDA) tools. Those targeting reconfigurable design analysis and manipulation require low-level design tools for bitstream debugging and IP core design assurance. While tools for low-level analysis of design netlists do exist there is a need for a low-level, open-source, extended tool support.

This paper reports a Field Programmable Gate Array (FPGA) Analysis Tool (FAT) being a versatile, modular and open-source tools framework for low-level analysis and verification of FPGA designs. The analysis performed by FAT is based on available Xilinx FPGA device specification data. FAT provides a set of standalone, high-level Application Programming Interfaces (APIs) abstracting the Xilinx FPGA fabric, the placed and routed design netlist and the related bitstream. The operation of FAT is governed by "recipe" scripts. A lightweight graphic front-end allows visualisation of the design within the FPGA fabric. The paper illustrates the application of FAT for bit-pattern analysis of the Virtex-II Pro intertile routing and verification of the spatial isolation between designs.

Keywords: FPGA, Reconfigurable Computing, EDA tools, design assurance, design verification, bitstream debugging, security.

1 Introduction

Reconfigurable hardware provides a cost-attractive alternative to ASIC implementation for small- to mid-volume applications. We are now seeing an explosion in the number of designs which use reconfigurable hardware, with applications ranging from embedded systems [1] to super-computers [2]. Although FPGAs are often fielded in critical applications, the development of design assurance tools for FPGA design is relatively new. Reconfigurable systems are often composed of several modules (IP cores), incorporated on a single FPGA device. Shrinking time-to-market and cost-pressure stimulates design reuse. Thus, a typical embedded system incorporates IP cores developed by various (e.g. third party) vendors. Companies must be confident in

J. Becker et al. (Eds.): ARC 2009, LNCS 5453, pp. 62–73, 2009.
© Springer-Verlag Berlin Heidelberg 2009

the quality of externally developed designs. Any design error or imperfection in the IP core might result in inadequate performance, or even failure of the final application. This issue grows in importance as organisations increasingly rely on incorporating commercial off-the-shelf (COTS) hardware or software into critical projects.

In order to provide reliability in reconfigurable systems in this multi-party environment it is vital to ensure design correctness down to the lowest-level, e.g. FPGA configuration files (bitstreams) [3], [4], [5] and [6]. This requirement results in an increasing demand for low level design analysis EDA tool support. While tools for low level analysis of placed and routed FPGA design netlists do exist there is a need for an open-source, extended tool support which provides unrestricted design analysis and bitstream manipulation. This would find application in design assurance, e.g., design security and IP protection.

The aim of this work is to develop an open-source tool framework for low level FPGA design analysis. The proposed FPGA Analysis Tool (FAT) framework facilitates design assurance within the Partial Reconfiguration (PR) design flow and also bitstream-level design analysis. FAT can therefore support secure IP core management in self-reconfigurable systems [5]. FAT enables automated access to the FPGA design netlist, related FPGA configuration bitstream and FPGA fabric resources description. FAT includes a Graphical User Interface (GUI) in order to provide visualisation of design analysis results. The FAT framework uses Xilinx published datasheets and documentation. All assumptions regarding the unpublished FPGA architectures and file formats are left to be evaluated by the user.

The major contribution of this paper is an open-source extension of the FPGA design flow for low level analysis of designs targeting the range of Xilinx devices. FAT provides a number of APIs which enable access to the placed-and-routed design, the Xilinx FPGA configuration bitstream, and the standardised Xilinx FPGA platform description (which is common to all FPGA device families). The paper illustrates the application of FAT for bit-pattern analysis of the Virtex-II Pro inter-tile routing and verification of the spatial isolation between designs.

The structure of the paper is as follows. Section 2 reviews a number of available tools for low-level design access and analysis and summarises desired functionality of an FPGA analysis toolset. In section 3 FAT (FPGA Analysis Tool) is proposed and its architecture is described. Section 4 evaluates FAT implementation using it to analyse the Xilinx Virtex-II inter-tile routing. Finally, section 5 concludes the paper and proposes future work.

2 Background

This section reviews available tools for low-level analysis of placed and routed design netlists, bitstreams, and FPGA fabric netlists. The need for low-level extended tool support is highlighted and the main requirements of a low-level analyser toolset are summarised.

In the software domain vendors publish and popularise their hardware architecture and instruction set. In contrast, limited information provided by FPGA vendors about the internal architecture and format of the configuration bitstream can hinder the research community and 3rd party EDA software vendors from low-level design verification and design conversion between FPGA fabrics. Tools used in the FPGA design flow are typically vendor-specific, closed-source applications using proprietary file formats. This limits access to low level design information and requires peers to develop analysis tools in-house [7], [8]. Provision of open-source tools and detailed specification of proprietary file formats could benefit both system designers and design assurance researchers [9]. In applications requiring design assurance, e.g. security and design IP protection, it is vital to perform design analysis at the lowest possible level, i.e. on the placed-and-routed netlist or even configuration bitstream [3]. Also, in applications exploiting PR flow, a detailed knowledge of FPGA resources configured by dynamically loadable modules is important since the module source may be unknown (untrusted) [5].

The proposed FAT framework enables analysis of interface compatibility between dynamic modules and the rest of the FPGA design. FAT also enables verification of user-defined design constraints, e.g. the required spatial isolation between IP cores etc.

2.1 Tools for Low-Level Analysis of Design Bitstreams and FPGA Fabrics

This section reviews a number of existing tools which facilitate access to low-level design descriptions, e.g. placed and routed FPGA netlist or configuration bitstream.

The Xilinx FPGA Editor [10] is a graphical application for design visualising and configuring Xilinx FPGAs. FPGA Editor analyses a Native Circuit Description (NCD) netlist file. This file contains the design logic information mapped to components, such as Configurable Logic Blocks (CLBs) and Input-Output Blocks (IOBs). FPGA Editor provides a visual representation of the placement and routing of the design. However, FPGA Editor presents an abstract view of the FPGA fabric and does not display all of the information required to perform design assurance, e.g. IP core isolation verification analysis [4]. Nor does FPGA Editor support bitstream manipulation in PR flow. Moreover, FPGA Editor is closed-source software, which offers limited, design-oriented only, task automation through scripts.

The Xilinx JBits 3.0 SDK [11] contains class files to create Run Time Reconfigurable applications and tools using the Xilinx Virtex-II architecture. JBits is an Application Program Interface (API) to the Xilinx configuration bitstream. This API allows Java applications to dynamically read, create and modify Xilinx Virtex-II bitstreams. JBits may be used as a stand-alone tool or as a base to produce other tools. However, the current release supports Xilinx technology up to Virtex-II only. The proposed FAT framework provides similar functionality to JBits, though with support for modern Xilinx FPGA devices.

Debit [12] is an open-source project aimed at netlist recovery from FPGA proprietary bitstream formats. Debit supports Virtex II/4/5 and Spartan3 FPGAs. Debit decomposes the bitstream and extracts information about site configuration and Programmable Interconnection Points (PIPs). Debit does not process the FPGA fabric netlist and thus does not support structural analysis of the FPGA fabric architecture.

In order to address the needs of design assurance, Xilinx has developed the Isolation Verification Tool (IVT) [3]. IVT operates on placed and routed designs and performs a design analysis, including verification of design spatial isolation, in order to track all hypothetical interconnects that can be created [13]. IVT targets design assurance, but is not publicly available (provided under the Xilinx Single Chip Crypto program).

In summary, available tools either do not support automated low-level analysis of FPGA fabric resources or are not publicly available.

2.2 Functionality Requirements for Low-Level Analysis Toolset

Design assurance requires low level analysis of design files produced during the FPGA design flow. These files describe placed and routed design and the configuration bitstream. For effective design assurance, it is vital to have access to information about the internal architecture of the FPGA fabric. In a general case, FPGA fabric IP protection makes it infeasible to obtain the complete documentation on the FPGA fabric. However, the file containing the netlist of all user-configurable resources and routing can be produced using the Xilinx xdl tool.

In summary, an ideal tool low level FPGA analysis tool should:

(a) be aware of low-level architectural details (netlist) of the target FPGA device
(b) include an open and modular architecture in order to facilitate code inspection and customisation.
(c) provide read and modify access to the implemented, e.g. placed and routed, design netlist and output (partial-) bitstream
(d) provide a uniform API across device families and design input files (design and FPGA fabric netlists, bitstreams etc)
(e) provide graphical visualisation of the design and FPGA fabric resources
(f) support modern FPGA devices.

3 FPGA Analysis Tool (FAT)

This section describes the detailed architecture of the FPGA Analysis Tool. Also, the script-based definition of high-level functionality is described. The FAT system aims to address the design assurance requirements listed in section 2.2 by proposing and evaluating an open-source tool framework. The main goal of the reported tool is the support of low level analysis of the FPGA fabric and design IP cores. We address this goal by proposing a set of APIs which abstract the user design, the FPGA programming bitstream, and the FPGA fabric itself.

Depending on the data source, information obtained can be categorised into different groups:

1. The FPGA fabric netlist
2. Details of the design (IP core) implementation, logic and routing resources used, along with their configuration and placement
3. Content of FPGA configuration frames from the bitstream.

Figure 1 illustrates the FAT block diagram and its context. FAT is implemented in Python and exploits advantages of this high-level Object-Oriented (OO) scripting language.

In order to perform the required tasks, the FAT framework functionality is defined using a number of scripts, called "recipes". Recipes implement high-level algorithms

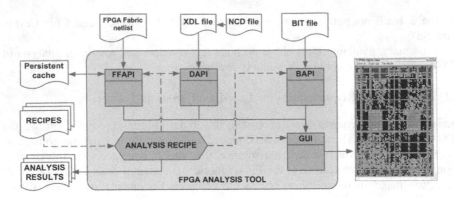

Fig. 1. The block diagram of the FPGA Analysis Tool framework

by gluing together the functionality provided by FAT modules. The use of a scripting language and a loosely-coupled architecture increase portability of the code and improve its application-oriented customisation capabilities.

3.1 FPGA Fabric API

The FPGA Fabric API (FFAPI) module provides an interface to access information about resources available within the Xilinx FPGA fabric. The data structure available via the FFAPI is depicted in Fig. 2. The relevant information is retrieved by parsing the EDIF-like FPGA fabric netlist file generated by the Xilinx xdl tool. To our knowledge, the generated xdl netlist is the only detailed description of the FPGA fabric structure provided by Xilinx in non-proprietary ASCII format. The file contains detailed information on available logic primitives, FPGA fabric routing, etc. While the netlist file is in human-readable text format, it requires automated processing and filtering to extract useful information.

The FFAPI module acts as a filter, processing an arbitrary Xilinx FPGA fabric netlist file. FFAPI extracts relevant data structures along with their context i.e. logical location within the device hierarchy and physical location within the file. The information obtained from the FPGA fabric netlist is a superset of the data available in the Xilinx FPGA Editor tool. The user experience of FPGA Editor is focused on obtaining a simplified presentation of logic resources. Thus, some information is deliberately omitted in FPGA Editor.

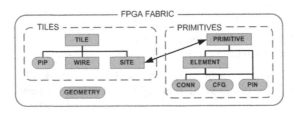

Fig. 2. Structural organisation of information available from the FPGA Fabric API (FFAPI)

FFAPI provides graphical visualisation of data representing FPGA internal re-sources. Resources are depicted in an array-like structure of tiles, see Fig. 3.a. All tiles are tagged according to their type (see Fig. 3.a) and position. User tags can also be assigned to individual tiles. This allows group selection (i.e. tiles containing user logic resources, BRAMs, clock tree etc). Moreover, when combined with the data available from the design API (described in the next section) visualisation of a user design is possible, see Fig. 3.b. The FPGA fabric view is different from that presented in the FPGA Editor and the Debit tool due to tile-centric organisation of FPGA fabric data.

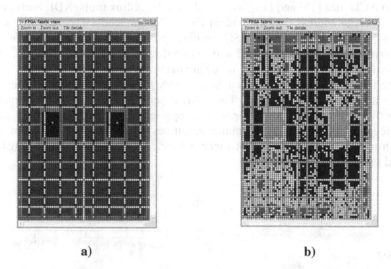

a)   b)

Fig. 3. Screenshots from the FPGA Analysis Tool (FAT); *a)* Tile view of the Xilinx Virtex-II Pro device (*dark grey* – CLB tiles); *b)* example of design logic (*black*-used, *gray*-unused) and routing(*white*) within the FPGA fabric

Methods available in the FFAPI class are organised in three functional groups based on the type of information they provide:

FPGA geometry. Methods in this group provide information about the type of FPGA package, the number of rows and columns and primitive types.

FPGA tile details. Methods in this group return information about the internal struc-ture of the tile, namely available primitive sites, routing resources and PIPs.

FPGA primitive details. Methods in this group provide information on the particular type of the site primitive, names, number and direction of the site's I/O pins, site internal routing and components, e.g. Basic Logic Elements (BELs), along with the set of valid configurations. This information is compliant with the view available in the FPGA Editor and documented by the FPGA vendor [14].

3.2 Design API

This section describes the Design API module of FAT which provides access to the user-design netlist. In the final stage of the Xilinx FPGA design flow, just before

FPGA bitstream is generated with `bitgen`, the netlist describes the design as a set of FPGA family-specific primitives and interconnections. All used primitives are annotated with information about their placement at the dedicated physical primitive site within the FPGA fabric. Also, design nets (inter-site connections) are tied to physical routing resources, namely pin-wires, wires and PIPs.

A Design API (DAPI) module has been proposed to facilitate unrestricted user access to already placed and routed designs. In order to gain access to the design netlist we use the `xdl` tool, which is part of Xilinx ISE toolsuite. Xilinx Design Language (XDL) is a fully featured physical design language that provides read and write access to NCD files [15] and [16], used by default by Xilinx tools. XDL enables users to create tools to address their individual FPGA design needs. The XDL file describes designs, using human-readable ASCII syntax and provides detailed information about e.g. physical layout of the placed and routed design, used instance names, primitive site configuration, routing details, hardware macro modules etc.

The DAPI module implements a XDL syntax parser along with a number of interfacing and conversion methods. The XDL description of the design is parsed and resource usage is reported. The parser recognises design structures such as named instances of FPGA primitives, routing resources establishing a connection network, design-module definitions (i.e. bus-macros) etc. Retrieved design structures are depicted in Fig.4.

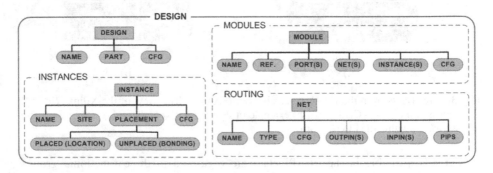

Fig. 4. Hierarchy of FPGA resources available through the Design API (DAPI) module

To ease the process of design analysis the DAPI module also provides methods for spatial grouping of occupied resources. This provides a different view on design resources used within relevant FPGA location, e.g. tile or site. This approach supports tile-by-tile analysis of the design.

3.3   Bitstream API

This section describes the Bitstream API module of FAT, which provides access to the Xilinx bitstream.

Xilinx FPGA devices are typically configured by loading the configuration data into the device configuration memory at power-up. To program configuration memory, instructions for the configuration control logic and data are included as packets in the bitstream (see Fig. 5). Configuration packets extended with a bitstream header form the complete bitstream which is delivered to the FPGA device through one of its configuration interfaces.

The structural description of the configuration bitstream for a particular device is usually provided by the FPGA vendor. However, documentation for all but obsolete devices (i.e. Virtex) does not describe the internal structure of the FPGA configuration frames [14]. Results reported in [12], [17], [18], [19] provide only partial information. The use of FAT allows discovery of the relation between the configuration of an arbitrary resource (logic, routing, IO etc) and the content of the configuration frame(s).

The Bitstream API (BAPI), depicted in Fig. 5, implements a bitstream packet processor. The packet processor reads the bitstream file and decomposes it into packets on-the-fly. Partial-bitstreams are also supported. Data packets are unpacked in order to extract the content of configuration frames and the address of their intended location within the FPGA device. The packet processor emulates behavioural functionality and part of the internal structure of the FPGA configuration control logic specified in [14].

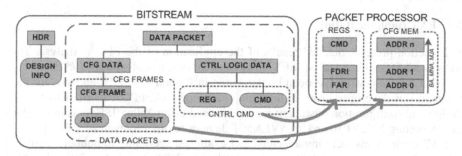

Fig. 5. Bitstream structure and information retrieved by the Bitstream API (BAPI) module

BAPI also provides methods for decoding the bitstream header and analysing the content of the frame by checking which bits are asserted and what is their location within the frame. This functionality is verified in the test scenario described in section 4.

3.4 Functionality Recipes Exploiting a Script Programming Paradigm

This section describes the script-based functionality of FAT which exploits advantages of the Python dynamic language.

In summary, the main advantages of using dynamic (scripting) languages in application development are: type-less programmability, rapid prototyping, code simplicity and ease of understanding. We propose separation of FAT functionality policies from underlying mechanisms (API modules). Functionality policies are defined as high-level analysis algorithms operating on the data sets generated by framework components (being the mechanism). Components are represented by a set of API modules, namely FFAPI, DAPI and BAPI. API modules give access to information about FPGA fabric, design, and bitstream.

The framework functionality is supported by a number of recipe scripts. Every recipe contains code for a high-level algorithm operating on data provided by underlying components or other recipes. Thus, recipes can be considered as glue for module functionality in order to provide an automated design analysis flow.

Use of recipes is depicted in Fig. 1. The FAT algorithms use FFAPI and BAPI to discover information about configuration bits for all PIPs within an arbitrary FPGA tile. As Python is an interpreted language, recipes can be dynamically generated and applied (executed) without the need for code recompilation. Also, lower-level recipes can be easily imported into advanced recipes (bottom-up algorithm composition) in order to build powerful analysis tools. This approach exploits the advantages of scripting languages and is naturally convergent with their programming paradigms.

Recipes allow the FAT user to focus on the behavioural part of the analysis algorithm rather than of on its implementation details. Use of hierarchical structures supports definition of FAT functionality at different abstraction-levels in order to maintain clarity of the algorithms, e.g. for auditing purposes. Recipes also allow applying a straightforward trial-and-error methodology for obtaining new knowledge about the FPGA fabric, the design and its bitstream.

3.5 FAT Implementation

This section presents detailed results of the application of the FPGA Analysis Tool framework for routing analysis of Xilinx FPGA fabrics, namely Virtex-II/5 devices.

The FAT framework has been implemented in Python. The GUI and visualisation frontend was developed using TkInter graphic framework. FPGA fabric netlist, XDL design and configuration bitstreams were generated using Xilinx ISE tools in standard flow targeting XC2VP30 and XC5VLX50T devices in order to evaluate FFAPI.

FAT components were implemented and evaluated according to publicly available information about Xilinx FPGA structure [10], [14], XDL design description [7], [15] and bitstream [12], [14], [18].

All API modules were implemented as separate classes with data structures based on abstract data types, e.g. sets, lists, dictionaries and tuples. The FAT framework uses a two-level caching mechanism for both permanent and temporary data storage in order speed up retrieving information from the FPGA fabric netlist (netlist size can be in range of several gigabytes). During the first run the FFAPI parser optionally produces persistent cache files containing parsed and compressed information about every tile within the FPGA fabric and location index with starting address of tile and primitive definition within the netlist. During design analysis, the required FPGA fabric information is retrieved from the persistent cache file and stored in limited-size local memory cache. The advantage of this two-level cache is that the application memory footprint is in the range of 20-60MB regardless of the netlist size, which can vary from a few MBs to tens of GBs. Moreover, the relevant FPGA fabric information is available immediately as parsing is performed only once.

4   Results of FAT Application in Analysis of Virtex-II Pro Routing

This section reports number of recipes used to verify the correct implementation of the FAT framework.

To evaluate correctness of FFAPI and BAPI modules, a *"Pip2BitMapping"* recipe was developed. The recipe (see Fig. 6) implements an algorithm determining bit patterns within FPGA configuration frames (using BAPI module) for an arbitrary configuration of the FPGA resource provided as an input. An input is the ASCII string, formatted according to the XDL syntax. The algorithm generates a list of relevant bit locations, (packet, frame and internal offset) on the output.

We have assumed, in similar way to [12], that the FPGA configuration defined by the design bitstream is a superposition of configurations of all FPGA resources and that all of these configurations are independent. Thus, identification of bits asserted for a single configuration of the particular resource (PIP, BEL etc.) reveals correct mapping.

We extended the recipe to iterate over the list of PIPs used in inter-tile routing. An exhaustive search approach was applied in an iterative loop. A single PIP is set-up during the every iteration of the algorithm. Partial results from the iteration are accumulated providing a list of possible switchbox configurations that use inter-tile routing. Accumulated results are consistent with data obtained using the JBits tool reported by Huebner et al. in [17].

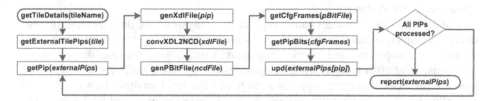

Fig. 6. Modified *"Pip2BitMapping"* recipe used in FAT framework verification test

The recipe execution time measured on the mid-class PC (1 GB RAM, Intel Pentium Dual-Core 2.16GHz) was in the order of 11 hours for all inter-tile PIPs within the CLB tile (less than 3200 algorithm iterations). Over 99% of this time was spent on conversion of XDL files back to the NCD format and partial-bitstream generation (`bitgen`). The time devoted to bitstreams parsing and XDL template generation was between 90-120s. In order to speed-up the execution time, the recipe could be modified to accommodate multiple PIPs within a single bitstream, e.g. one PIP per CLB tile.

Data obtained from the *"Pip2BitMapping"* recipe are used to detect active inter-tile routing. This type of analysis is important in the design assurance and in the PR design flow. An active inter-tile routing can possibly lead to setup of the covert communication channel e.g. violation of spatial isolation between designs [3][4].

The DAPI module was tested using a set of XDL design files, where some designs contained forced invalid syntax. In all cases the XDL parser responded correctly either by returning the recognised design structure or by raising an exception when a syntax error was detected.

The *"ShowDesign"* recipe reports and visualises areas (user-logic and routing) occupied by the design within the FPGA fabric (see Fig. 3.b). This can be used to assess logic utilisation ratio within the IP core.

The *"ResourceSelect"* recipe allows selection and grouping of FPGA resources based on arbitrary logic or regular expressions. Groups can be reported and highlighted within the GUI. Resources can be selected by their coordinates or properties. Also, user defined tags can be attached to the groups. This recipe supports, logical resource partitioning. Fig. 3.a illustrates FPGA fabric tiles grouped by type.

The device-independent syntax of the FPGA fabric netlists and XDL files allows generic support for designs targeting other Xilinx FPGA architectures (e.g. Virtex 4/5). Work is currently in progress to allow analysis of the Virtex-5 bitstreams.

5 Conclusions

The FPGA Analysis Tool is, to our knowledge, the first toolset that provides high-level and unrestricted access to the low-level description of the Xilinx FPGA fabric and the user design at the netlist- and bitstream-level. The GUI frontend extends FAT functionality by providing tile-centric visualisation of the design and FPGA resources. Use of Python programming language provides a clean syntax which is self-documenting and easy to follow. We consider this approach as a step towards full open-source FPGA design flow.

The FAT framework offers native support for analysis of the designs targeting virtually all Xilinx architectures, including Virtex 4/5. FAT is developed around the concept of component and recipe separation. Components provide the necessary mechanism and abstractions, while recipes describe policies defining its usage. The hierarchical recipe structure supports a range of high-level analysis flows and offers virtually unlimited functionality extensions. We believe the proposed FAT framework could provide increased productivity in low-level design analysis by seamlessly extending and opening the FPGA design flow. Similar tools could be developed for other FPGA fabrics, i.e. Altera, Actel etc.

The FAT framework has been tested on a V2P30 device. Minor corrections within the BAPI module are required in order to process arbitrary Xilinx bitstreams. Modifications are mainly related to package-specific geometry data and extended configuration sequence within the configuration control logic. Future work will focus on providing full support for Virtex-5 bitstreams and applying the FAT framework for bitstream analysis in FPGA IP security applications.

The long-term goal is to provide an API for bitstream-level design manipulation and recipes for automated design netlist recovery.

References

1. Lotze, J., Fahmy, S., Noguera, J., Doyle, L., Esser, R.: An FPGA-based Cognitive Radio Framework. In: IET Irish Signals and Systems Conference, NUI, Galway, pp. 138–143 (2008)
2. Bondhugula, U., Devulapalli, A., Fernando, J., Wyckoff, P., Sadayappan, P.: Parallel FPGA-based all-pairs shortest-paths in a directed graph. In: Proceedings of the 20th IEEE International Parallel and Distributed Processing Symposium (IPDPS). IEEE Computer Society, Washington (2006)

3. McLean, M., Moore, J.: FPGA-based single chip cryptographic solution. Military Embedded Systems, http://www.mil-embedded.com/pdfs/NSA.Mar07.pdf
4. Huffmire, T., Brotherton, B., Wang, G., Sherwood, T., Kastner, R., Levin, T., Nguyen, T., Irvine, C.: Moats and drawbridges: An isolation primitive for reconfigurable hardware based systems. In: IEEE Symposium on Security and Privacy, pp. 281–295. IEEE Computer Society, Los Alamitos (2007)
5. Kepa, K., Morgan, F., Kosciuszkiewicz, K., Surmacz, T.: SeReCon: a Secure Dynamic Partial Reconfiguration Controller for SoPCs. In: IEEE Computer Society Annual Symposium on VLSI, pp. 292–297. IEEE Computer Society, Los Alamitos (2008)
6. Drimer, S., Guneysu, T., Kuhn, M., Paar, C.: Protecting multiple cores in a single FPGA design,
   http://www.cl.cam.ac.uk/~sd410/papers/protect_many_cores.pdf
7. Ehliar, A., Liu, D.: Thinking Outside The Flow: Creating Customized Backend Tools For Xilinx Based Designs. In: FPGA World 2007, Sweden (2007)
8. Steiner, N., Athanas, P.: An Alternate Wire Database for Xilinx FPGAs. In: FCCM 2004: Proceedings of the 12th Annual IEEE Symposium on Field-Programmable Custom Computing Machines, pp. 336–337. IEEE Computer Society, Washington (2004)
9. Thompson, K.: Reflections on trusting trust. In: Communications of the ACM, pp. 761–763. ACM, New York (1984)
10. Xilinx ISE Foundation,
    http://www.xilinx.com/ise/logic_design_prod/foundation.htm
11. JBits 3.0 SDK, http://www.xilinx.com/labs/projects/jbits
12. Note, J., Rannaud, E.: From the bitstream to the netlist. In: Proceedings of the 16th international ACM/SIGDA symposium on FPGA, pp. 264–264. ACM, New York (2008)
13. Xilinx Single Chip Crypto Solution,
    http://www.xilinx.com/esp/aero_def/crypto.htm
14. Xilinx: Virtex-II Pro User Guide UG012 (v4.0). Xilinx (2005)
15. Xilinx: Xilinx design language, <XILINX_INST_DIR>/help/data/xdl/xdl.html in ISE 6.1
16. Raaijmakers, S., Wong, S.: Run-Time Partial Reconfiguration for Removal, Placement and Routing on the Virtex-II Pro. In: Proceedings of the 17th International Conference on Field Programmable Logic and Applications (FPL 2007). IEEE Computer Society, Amsterdam (2007)
17. Huebner, M., Braun, L., Becker, J., Claus, C., Stechele, W.: Physical Configuration On-Line Visualization of Xilinx Virtex-II FPGAs. In: IEEE Computer Society Annual Symposium on VLSI, pp. 41–46. IEEE Computer Society, Los Alamitos (2007)
18. Krasteva, Y., de la Torre, E., Riesgo, T., Joly, D.: Virtex II FPGA Bitstream Manipulation: Application to Reconfiguration Control Systems. In: Proc. of International Conference on Field Programmable Logic and Applications (FPL 2006). IEEE Computer Society, Los Alamitos (2006)
19. Steiner, N.: A Standalone Wire Database for Routing and Tracing in Xilinx Virtex, Virtex-E, and Virtex-II FPGAs. Masters thesis (2002)

An Efficient and Low-Cost Design Methodology to Improve SRAM-Based FPGA Robustness in Space and Avionics Applications

Marco Lanuzza, Paolo Zicari, Fabio Frustaci,
Stefania Perri, and Pasquale Corsonello

Department of Electronics, Computer Science and Systems
University of Calabria, Arcavacata di Rende - 87036 - Rende (CS), Italy
{lanuzza,zicari,ffrustaci,perri}@deis.unical.it,
p.corsonello@unical.it

Abstract. This paper presents an efficient approach to protect an FPGA design against Single Event Upsets (SEUs). A novel configuration scrubbing core, instantiated at the top level of the user project, is used for internal detection and correction of SEU-induced configuration errors without requiring further external radiation hardened control hardware. As demonstrated in the paper, this approach combines the benefits of fast SEU faults detection with fast restoration of the device functionality and small overhead. Moreover, the proposed technique result highly versatile and can be adopted for different FPGA device families.

Keywords: Single Event Upsets, Reconfigurable System, FPGA, Space, Avionics.

1 Introduction

SRAM-based Field Programmable Gate Arrays (SFPGAs) combine limited cost and reconfigurability with very high integration capability and performances. Such characteristics make them more attractive to be used in spacecraft electronic design with respect to their radiation-hardened anti-fuse-based counterparts [1], which are not reconfigurable, much expensive, and present considerable less performing and integration capability.

The configuration of SFPGAs is obtained by the end user through appropriate software environments which permit to move from a high-level description (behavioural or structural) of the needed functionalities, to a detailed description in which the role of each programmable resource is set. This information is called configuration *bitstream*, and when the device is switched on, it is transferred to the static configuration memory embedded into the SFPGA. Unfortunately, when used in a hostile space environment, the static memory elements storing the configuration *bitstream* (as well as the memory elements the design embeds) are particularly sensitive to Single Event Upsets (SEUs) induced by energetic particles [2-3].

SEUs affecting the configuration memory are particularly detrimental for the FPGA reliability, because they could corrupt the functionality of the implemented

J. Becker et al. (Eds.): ARC 2009, LNCS 5453, pp. 74–84, 2009.
© Springer-Verlag Berlin Heidelberg 2009

circuits. Hence, such SEUs have to be meticulously addressed in order for commercial SFPGAs to be reliably used in hostile space and avionics application environments [2].

In order to increase the robustness of commercial SFPGAs against SEUs affecting the configuration memory, the designers could exploit several Radiation-Hardening-By-Design (RHBD) methodologies [4-9].

RHDB methodologies can be divided in two main categories: redundancy-based and reconfiguration-based techniques. The former aims at masking the propagation of SEU effects to the circuit outputs [7-9], whereas the latter aims at restoring, as soon as possible, the proper values into configuration memory after SEUs occurring [4-6].

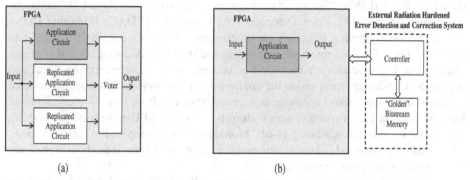

(a)   (b)

Fig. 1. Traditional RHDB methodologies; (a) *The TMR solution; (b)The external scrubbing approach*

A well-known redundancy-based technique is the Triple Modular Redundancy (TMR) with voting. It can be used to improve SEU-related reliability at user-design-level and/or at system-level. As described in Fig. 1a, the basic idea of the TMR approach consists in implementing three full copies of the same circuit and performing a bit-wise "majority vote" on the corresponding outputs [7]. The TMR mitigation strategy offers good improvements in reliability, but is often very expensive in terms of SFPGA resource utilization, power consumption, etc. [10]. Moreover the TMR technique is effective only to mask errors generated just in one of the redundant circuits, whereas it fails if multiple errors affect two or more redundant circuits [10].

In order to avoid SEU-induced errors accumulation, the configuration *scrubbing* can be exploited. *Scrubbing* is usually performed by continuously writing the valid configuration memory over the existing configuration data [4]. If no upsets have occurred, each pass of the scrubbing process will simply overwrite the same configuration data, otherwise if upsets have occurred, the corrupted configuration bits are replaced with the correct values. Alternatively, as described in Fig. 1b, configuration data can be read and compared to *"golden"* copy of the bitstream and, only when an error is detected, a configuration refresh is executed, often exploiting the partial dynamic reconfiguration feature available in several commercial SFPGAs [6]. Note that this kind of *scrubbing* is often the preferred method since reading the FPGA configuration memory is faster than writing to it.

While configuration scrubbing considerably increases the reliability of a SFPGA-based system, it requires additional external hardware resources, thus increasing the overall system complexity.

The dynamic self partial reconfiguration feature, offered by the most advanced SFPGA family chips, gives the possibility to move both the SEU check and the correction functionalities inside the same SFPGA chip without the necessity of any external radiation-hardened control hardware [11].

The development of SEU induced faults correction techniques in Self Dynamically Partially Reconfigurable SFPGAs is the main focus of this paper. The novel approach, here proposed for fast detecting and correcting SEU-induced configuration errors, exploits the internal dynamic partial readback and reconfiguration capabilities introduced in the XILINX Virtex FPGA families, extensively employed in numerous space missions [12-13]. Error Detection And Correction (EDAC) Hamming Codes [14] of the configuration bitstream are precomputed by an on purpose software, and then stored in a TMR-ed reference memory inside the SFPGA during its first configuration. The EDAC codes are then used as internal "golden" references to detect and correct SEU induced errors inside the configuration memory. In this way, no external radiation-hardened control hardware is required, thus resulting in a more efficient and less complex on board space system with respect exiting SEU mitigation methodologies based on external scrubbing [4-6]. Moreover, when compared to classical methods based on device redundancies, the novel mitigation technique leads to significant hardware cost and power savings.

The remainder of the paper is organized as follows: Section 2 describes the proposed approach for SEU mitigation in self reconfigurable SFPGAs, whereas its SFPGA-based implementation is detailed in Section 3. Finally, Section 4 summarizes the obtained results.

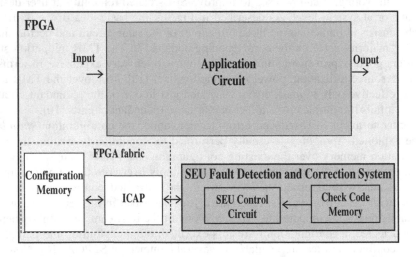

Fig. 2. The proposed SEU Fault Detection and Correction System (SFDCS)

2 Our Approach

As shown in Fig. 2, the proposed SEU Fault Detection and Correction System (SFDCS) exploits the Internal Configuration Access Port (ICAP) present in Xilinx Virtex SFPGA device families (starting from Virtex-II series) to internally detect and correct SEU-induced faults affecting the configuration data bits. The SFPGA becomes a self-repairing hardware which doesn't require any external scrubbing to restore SEU-induced configuration errors.

Pre-computed EDAC Hamming codes, stored into the Check Code Memories, are used as internal "golden" reference to detect bit errors inside the corrupted configuration frames[1].

A SEU Control Circuit, instantiated into the same SFPGA, manages the readback of the configuration data through the ICAP, detects possible SEU-induced bit errors and eventually restores the corrected configuration data into the SFPGA configuration memory.

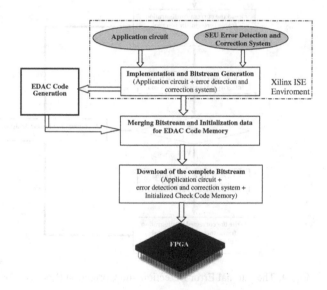

Fig. 3. The novel implementation flow

The novel design flow, shown in Fig.3, is required for radiation hardening the SFPGA. The proposed SFDCS and the application circuit are implemented at the top level of the project; the EDAC check codes of the generated bitstream are calculated by purpose-developed software. The complete bitstream to be downloaded at start-up is obtained by merging the bitstream of the application circuit and the SFDCS together with the pre-computed EDAC codes used for the initialization of the EDAC code memories.

---

[1] The configuration frame is the smallest granular portion of the configuration memory which can be accessed for both read and write operations.

Once the radiation hardened SFPGA is initially configured, the application circuit and the SFDCS can work simultaneously and independently one from each other. The latter monitors SEU-induced faults on sensitive configuration frames[2]. At each iteration, the SFDCS sets the address of the next frame to be checked, calculates the EDAC codes of the current frame and compares the result to the corresponding values stored in the Check Code memory. A discrepancy between the calculated and stored EDAC codes triggers the error correction action. The stored EDAC codes are used to correct the configuration bit errors and the restored configuration frame is then written back into the SFPGA configuration memory. As described in Fig. 4, the detection and correction operations are cyclically repeated for all the sensitive frames; after checking the last frame the process restarts with the first one, thus, the error detection and correction process works in background and never stops.

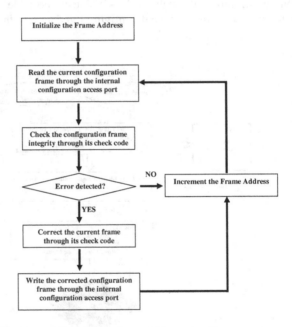

Fig. 4. The internal Error Detection and Correction Process

The proposed technique retains some limitations of the XILINX readback process [5]. During the integrity check phase, reading BRAM frames has to be avoided, as this may disrupt user data [4]. For similar reasons also the reading of configuration frames related to LUTs used as distributed RAMs or Shift Registers has to be prevented [5]. The latter limitation can be easily overcame in Virtex-4 and Virtex-5 devices by using the GLUTMASK configuration option. This option ensures that the state of LUTs being used as distributed RAMs or Shift Registers are not affected by on-line reading or writing of the SFPGA's configuration memory.

---

[2] The sensitive configuration frames correspond to configuration frames defining the application circuit and the SFDCS itself.

3   Xilinx Virtex Implementation

Only for testing and evaluations purposes, the proposed SFDCS was implemented within a XILINX Virtex-II XC2V1000 FPGA chip by using the XILINX ISE 8.1 design software.

For multiple errors per frame correction, the 3392-bit configuration frame was divided into 14 separate 256-bit Hamming data words, thus 14 SEU faults per frame can be corrected using 14 different 9-bit EDAC codes.

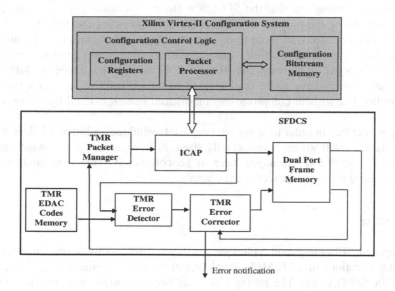

Fig. 5. The implemented SFDCS

The architecture of the implemented SFDCS is depicted in Fig. 5. Central to the proposed system is the 8-bit ICAP, which represents the interface between the built-in FPGA user logic and the embedded *Configuration Control Logic.* The latter consists of a set of *Configuration Control Registers* and a *Packet Processor* controlling the flow of packet data involved in both readback and reconfiguration operations.

In our implementation, command packets for the *Configuration Control Logic* needed to execute both the operations of reading back and writing back the configuration frames through the ICAP interface are generated by the *Packet Manager,* following the communication protocol reported in [12].

The currently analyzed sensitive configuration frame is sequentially stored into the 424x8-bit *Dual Port Frame Memory.* At the same time, the *Error Detector* checks for SEU-induced configuration faults. Each clock cycle, configuration bytes read back from the ICAP are sequentially processed to compute the current Hamming check code. When the whole 256-bit Hamming configuration data word is scanned (i.e. 32 clock cycles have elapsed), the evaluated 9-bit Hamming check code is compared to its "golden" reference and the syndrome vector is produced. The latter is a binary string used to flag error occurrences and to locate single errors inside the Hamming configuration data words [14].

If the *Error Detector* indicates an error occurred during the scan, the *Error Corrector* is activated. The latter uses the syndrome vector generated by the *Error Detector* to address the corrupted configuration byte inside the *Frame Memory*, and to correct it by flipping the fault affected configuration bit. The repaired frame inside the *Frame Memory* is then written back to the *Configuration Memory*, at the end of the current frame scanning. On the contrary, if no error is detected, the readback operation of a new frame is started without any reconfiguration operation.

It is worth pointing out that the SFDCS is the most critical portion of the entire SFPGA chip; being the only internal reference able to restore the SEU-faulted configuration memory. Thus, it needs to be opportunely radiation hardened. To this purpose, the TMR technique has been exploited with voting circuits implemented using Tri-State Buffers [8]. In Virtex-4 and Virtex-5 devices, in which Tri-State Buffers are not available, voters have to be implemented using LUTs. This increases radiation susceptibility, but without compromising the overall benefit offered by the proposed solution.

Finally, note that in order to apply the proposed technique within any Xilinx Virtex device (starting from Virtex-II series) only slight differences in the command packets generated by the *Packet Manager* have to be considered. This commands in fact strongly depend on the referenced Virtex family.

4 Results

The proposed SEU-mitigation technique has been validated by hardware emulating SEU fault injections in a MEMEC development board [16], equipped with a Xilinx XC2V1000 SFPGA chip. The testing phase has been executed on several benchmark application circuits, including five of the largest ISCAS99 benchmark circuits [17] and three CORE generated circuits optimized for the XILINX Virtex-II devices family.

The adopted hardware-assisted simulation flow starts with a conventional FPGA implementation flow executed on the application circuit hardened by the proposed SEU Detection and Correction System. As previously described, check codes are calculated by a purposely designed software routine and embedded in the configuration bitstream to initialize the *Check Code Memories*. Several bit flips, emulating SEU effects, were then randomly introduced into the configuration bitstream. Once initial configuration was performed, the correct execution of both error detection and correction phases was monitored by using the XILINX Chip Scope Logic Analyzer [18].

In Table 1, circuits implemented using the proposed approach are compared with the standalone (i.e. without any hardening) solution, in terms of FPGA resources, power and additional configuration memory requirements. All the implementations were analyzed using the XILINX Integrated Software Environment (ISE) 8.1. The proposed SEU error sclf repairing system (with triplicate resources according to the full TMR technique and voting circuits implemented using Tri-State Buffers [8]) occupies 1298 slices, which represent about the 8.8 % of the available slices in the target FPGA device; 10 to 19 BRAMs (corresponding to 19 % - 47.5% of the available 18 Kbit BRAMs) are also required depending on the number of sensitive circuit frames to be SEU hardened.

Note that the number of sensitive configuration frames to be integrity checked strongly depends on placement of both the application circuit and the SDCS. In Virtex-II devices a configuration frame is related to a whole column of CLB, thus minimizing the number of sensitive configuration frame involves the minimization of CLB columns occupied by the overall design. On the contrary, in most recent Xilinx FPGAs families, like the Virtex-4 and Virtex-5, the reconfiguration memory is divided into a number of rectangular regions, forming a grid. Each reconfiguration frame spans vertically only one of these regions, instead of the whole FPGA as in earlier families. It is therefore possible to limit the number of sensitive frames to be SEU checked also obtaining more regular design's placement.

Table 1. Characteristics of unprotected vs protected designs

	BENCHMARK	Slices	BRAMs	MULT 18x18	Dyn. Power @ 50 MHz [mW]	Sensitive Frames
	UNPROTECTED					
ISCAS99	b11	74	0	0	7.43	57
	b12	221	0	0	14.74	77
	b13	37	0	0	6.23	63
	b14	1,296	0	0	85.89	362
	b15	1,451	0	0	119.94	317
CORE GEN.	FFT	1,672	7	9	124.17	355
	CORDIC	636	0	0	30,59	190
	2-D DCT	1,152	1	0	30.26	263
	PROTECTED WITH THE PROPOSED SFDCS					
ISCAS99	b11	1,372	10	0	34.21	191
	b12	1,519	10	0	41.52	220
	b13	1,335	10	0	33.01	242
	b14	2,594	16	0	112.67	463
	b15	2,749	16	0	146.72	419
CORE GEN.	FFT	2,970	26	9	150.95	592
	CORDIC	1,934	16	0	57,37	486
	2-D DCT	2,450	14	0	57.04	327

It is worth noting that the additional logic and memory resources required by the proposed SEU mitigation approach would be also significantly reduced by using the Selective TMR methodology [8] to harden the novel SEU-mitigation system. However, when compared to the external traditional scrubbing techniques [4-6], the small increase in terms of required FPGA-resources introduced by the proposed SEU-induced errors self repairing solution is widely counterbalanced by several remarkable advantages: faster SEU faults detection and restoration of the user application without using external radiation hardened hardware. This avoids power and time consuming external data transfers. The proposed SEU Fault Detection and Correction System overcomes also the internal scrubbing method recently proposed in [11] in terms of accuracy, versatility and efficiency. In fact, our solution can detect and correct multiple errors (at most 14) inside the same configuration frame. Whereas the system presented in [11] can identify and correct just a single bit error within each configuration frame. This could be inadequate when high-energy particles induce multiple configuration bit errors [19]. Moreover, the mean time needed to detect a fault is significantly reduced since the reconfiguration process is managed by a purpose-designed circuit instead of a general purpose processor [11]; finally, differently from [11], the proposed solution can be adopted in any Virtex (starting from Virtex-II series) device family.

Table 2. Memory requirements/Reliability trade-offs for different Hamming configuration word sizes

BENCHMARK		Hamming Configuration Word Size/ Correction Capability per Configuration Frame							
		64-bit/ CC=53		128-bit/ CC=27		256-bit/ CC=14		512-bit/ CC=7	
		#check bits	#BRAMs	#check bits	#BRAMs	#check bits	#BRAMs	#check bits	#BRAMs
ISCAS99	b11	80,984	15	46,413	9	26,740	6	14,707	3
	b12	93,280	18	53,460	9	30,800	6	16,940	3
	b13	102,608	18	58,806	12	33,880	6	18,634	6
	b14	196,312	33	112,509	21	64,820	12	35,651	6
	b15	177,656	30	101,817	18	58660	12	32,263	6
CORE GEN.	FFT	251,008	42*	143,856	24	82,880	15	45,584	9
	CORDIC	206,064	36	118,098	21	68,040	12	37,422	9
	2-D DCT	138,648	24	79,461	15	45,780	9	25,179	6

* Not implementable in the used Xilinx device.

As described in Table 2, different trade-offs between FPGA memory resources utilization and SEU-related reliability can be obtained by considering different sizes for the Hamming configuration words. Note that data reported in Table 2 are related to the referenced FPGA device (i.e. a Xilinx XC2V1000 FPGA which presents a frame size of 3,392-bit). As expected, an increase of internal error correction capability CC (here expressed in terms of number of single bit errors corrigible per frame) is directly linked to an increase of the memory capability required to store the "golden" Hamming check codes.

5 Conclusions

In this paper a novel soft error mitigation technique based on internal scrubbing has been presented. The proposed SEU Fault Detection and Correction System provides considerable reliability for SFPGA-based circuits at considerable lower cost with respect external reconfiguration-based SEU mitigation techniques. The designed SEU error detection and correction system can be implemented as a VHDL/Verilog portable core easily customizable by the user. When implemented with a correction capability of 14 errors per frame and using a Virtex-II XC2V1000 device, the new system operates at a 50MHz running frequency and dissipates less than 27mW. It occupies 1298 slices independently of the implemented application circuit, whereas the number of occupied BRAMs strictly depends on the number of sensitive configuration frames.

References

1. Roosta, R.: A Comparison of Radiation-Hard and Radiation-Tolerant FPGAs for Space Applications. NASA Electronic Parts and Packaging Program (December 30, 2004), http://nepp.nasa.gov/
2. Ceschia, M., Violante, M., Reorda, M.S., Paccagnella, A., Bernardi, P., Rebaudengo, M., Bortolato, D., Bellato, M., Zambolin, P., Candelori, A.: Identification and classification of single-event upsets in the configuration memory of SRAM-based FPGAs. IEEE Transactions on Nuclear Science 50(6), 2088–2094 (2003)
3. Graham, P., Caffrey, M., Zimmerman, J., Sundararajan, P., Johnson, E., Patterson, C.: Consequences and Categories of SRAM FPGA Configuration SEUs. In: International Conference on Military and Aerospace Programmable Logic Devices MAPLD, Washington, DC, Paper C6 (2003)
4. Carmichael, C., Caffrey, M., Salazar, A.: Correcting Single-Event Upsets Through Virtex Partial Configuration. Xilinx Corp., Tech. Rep., XAPP216 (v1.0) (June 1, 2000)
5. Gokhale, M., Graham, P., Wirthlin, M., Johnson, D.E., Rollins, N.: Dynamic reconfiguration for management of radiation-induced faults in FPGAs. International journal of embedded systems 2(1-2), 28–38 (2006)
6. Gokhale, M., Graham, P., Wirthlin, M., Johnson, D.E., Rollins, N.: Dynamic Reconfiguration for Management of Radiation-Induced Faults in FPGAs. International Journal of Embedded Systems 2(1/2), 28–38 (2006)
7. Kastensmidt, F.L., Sterpone, L., Carro, L., Reorda, M.S.: On the Optimal Design of Triple Modular Redundancy Logic for SRAM-based FPGAs. In: Proceedings of Design, Automation and Test in Europe, pp. 1290–1295 (2005)
8. Samudrala, P.K., Ramos, J., Katkoori, S.: Selective triple Modular redundancy (STMR) based single-event upset (SEU) tolerant synthesis for FPGAs. IEEE Transactions on Nuclear Science 51(5), 2957–2969 (2004)
9. Carmichael, C.: Triple Modular Redundancy Design Techniques for Virtex FPGAs. In: Xilinx Application Note (XAPP) 197 (July 6, 2006)
10. Quinn, H., Morgan, K., Graham, P., Krone, J., Caffrey, M., Lundgreen, K.: Domain Crossing Errors: Limitations on Single Device Triple-Modular Redundancy Circuits in Xilinx FPGAs. IEEE Transactions on Nuclear Science 54(6), 2037–2043 (2007)
11. Heiner, J., Collins, N., Withlin, M.: Fault Tolerant ICAP Controller for High-Reliable Internal Scrubbing. In: Proceedings of IEEE Aerospace Conference, pp. 1–10 (March 2008)
12. Swift, G.M., Rezgui, S., George, J., Carmichael, C., Napier, M., Maksymowicz, J., Moore, J., Lesea, A., Koga, K., Wrobel, T.F.: Dynamic testing of Xilinx Virtex-II field programmable gate array (FPGA) input/output blocks (IOB's). IEEE Trans. Nucl. Sci. 51(6), 3469–3474 (2004)
13. Yui, C.C., Swift, G.M., Carmichael, C., Koga, R., George, J.S.: SEU Mitigation Testing of Xilinx Virtex II FPGAs. In: Radiation Effects Data Workshop, July 21-25, pp. 92–97. IEEE, Los Alamitos (2003)
14. Moon, T.K.: Error Correction Coding. John Wiley & Sons, New Jersey (2005)

15. Virtex-II Platform FPGA User Guide,
    http://www.xilinx.com/bvdocs/userguides/ug002.pdf
16. Memec-Design, "Virtex II MB",
    http://www.insight.na.memec.com/Memec/iplanet/link1
17. ISCAS99 circuit benchmarks,
    http://www.pld.ttu.ee/~maksim/benchmarks/iscas99/vhdl/
18. XILINX, Inc. Chipscope Software and ILA Cores User Manual. Xilinx User Manual,
    0401884 (v2.0) (December 2000)
19. Maiz, J., Hareland, S., Zhang, K., Armstrong, P.: Characterization of multi-bit soft error
    events in advanced srams. In: Proc. IEEE International Electron Devices Meeting, pp.
    519–522 (May 2003)

Timing Driven Placement for Fault Tolerant Circuits Implemented on SRAM-Based FPGAs

Luca Sterpone

Dipartimento di Automatica e Informatica, Politecnico di Torino
10129 Torino, Italy
luca.sterpone@polito.it

Abstract. Electronic systems for safety critical applications such as space and avionics need the maximum level of dependability for guarantee the success of their missions. Contrariwise the computation capabilities required in these fields are constantly increasing for afford the implementation of different kind of applications ranging from the signal processing to the networking. SRAM-based FPGA is the candidate device for achieve this goal thanks to their high versatility of implementing complex circuits with a very short development time. However, in critical environments, the presence of Single Event Upsets (SEUs) affecting the FPGA's functionalities, requires the adoption of specific fault tolerant techniques, like Triple Modular Redundancy (TMR), able to increase the protection capability against radiation effects, but on the other side, introducing a dramatic penalty in terms of performances. In this paper, it is proposed a new timing-driven placement algorithm for implementing soft-errors resilient circuits on SRAM-based FPGAs with a negligible degradation of performance. The algorithm is based on a placement heuristic able to remove the crossing error domains while decreasing the routing congestions and delay inserted by the TMR routing and voting scheme. Experimental analysis performed by timing analysis and SEU static analysis point out a performance improvement of 29% on the average with respect to standard TMR approach and an increased robustness against SEU affecting the FPGA's configuration memory.

Keywords: FPGA, fault tolerance, Single Event Upset, Timing-driven Placement, Triple Modular Redundancy.

1 Introduction

The interest in the use of reconfigurable computing for space and avionic based applications is increasing. Reconfigurable computations offer many advantages for these application's fields. For example, the adoption of Field Programmable Gate Array (FPGAs) enables the use of application-specific hardware platforms instead of programmable processors. The customization of the data-path directly within an FPGA allows these devices to perform several operations faster and more efficiently with respect of traditional programmable processors. In particular, SRAM-based FPGAs; unlike application-specific integrated circuits (ASICs), can be configured *on-site*,

J. Becker et al. (Eds.): ARC 2009, LNCS 5453, pp. 85–96, 2009.
© Springer-Verlag Berlin Heidelberg 2009

after the spacecraft has been launched. This flexibility allows the use of the same SRAM-based FPGA device for different instruments, missions, or spacecraft objectives. Furthermore, any error in an FPGA design can be solved by fixing the incorrect module and reconfiguring the FPGA with the new configuration bitstream. The performances and flexibility characteristics of SRAM-based FPGAs are strongly advantageous over the conventional computing methods [1].

The major drawback that limits the adoption of these devices in space and avionics environment is their sensitivity to the radiation effects. Avionics and space applications operate in harsh environments characterized by the presence of ionizing radiation such as alpha particles, atmospheric neutrons and heavy ions [2]. These radiation may induce non destructive loss of information within an integrated circuit provoking a Single Event Upset (SEU) effects. The occurrence of SEUs is an important consideration in designing fault tolerant circuits in order to tune dependability, performances and the whole cost of the system. When the dependability is considered, in space and avionics applications silicon devices need to satisfy strict dependability rules in order to guarantee the correct functionalities.

SRAM-based FPGAs are very sensitive to radiation-induced effects since SEUs may affect both the memory elements used by the design and the FPGA's configuration memory [3] [4]. In details, SEUs in FPGA affect the user design flip-flops, the FPGA configuration bitstream, and any hidden FPGA register, latch, or internal state. If an upset affects the combinational logic in the FPGA, it induces a memory cell transition in one of the LUT's cells or in the cells that control the routing. This transition, also called bit-flip, has a permanent effect, and it is correctable only at the next load of the configuration memory. Configuration upsets are especially important because they can affect either the state and the operation of the design. Since the FPGA's configuration memory totally controls the mapped circuit, any change of the configuration memory cells due to an high charged particle hitting the silicon device area, may perturb the routing resources and logic functions in a way that changes the operation of the original circuit's behavior.

Several fault tolerance methods have been proposed in order to mitigate the effects of SEUs in the SRAM-based FPGA's configuration memory. The nowadays possible solutions are two: the use of radiation-hardened FPGAs or the adoption of reconfiguration-based and redundancy-based approaches combined together. The former is able to remove permanent latch-up in the FPGA's configuration memory since radiation-hardened technology is adopted. Nevertheless the advantages it introduces, this solution is impracticable since the rad-hard devices are extremely expensive with respect to the Commercial-Off-The-Shelf (COTS) ones; besides they do not guarantee any protection against transient errors within the configuration memory. Viceversa, reconfiguration-based method combined with a redundancy-based approach is a viable solution that can be adopted on COTS FPGAs. On one side, reconfiguration-based methods can restore the proper values into the configuration bits just after a SEU happens [5], thus they can detect and remove an SEU within the configuration memory. On the other side, since stand-alone reconfiguration methods does not give complete immunity to the SEU's effects, the adoption of redundancy-based techniques avoid the SEU's effects propagation to the circuit's outputs [6] [7] [8]. The commonly adopted redundancy technique is the Triple Modular Redundancy (TMR). This technique drastically reduces the effects of SEUs within the configuration memory of

SRAM-based FPGAs. Although effective against the SEU's phenomena, this technique introduces a very high degradation in terms of operational frequency to the implemented circuit, since circuits hardened with TMR become 50 % or more slower on the average toward their original versions [9]. This reduction of the operational frequency has a severe impact on the usability of SRAM-based FPGAs in safety critical applications, because it nullifies the high performance characteristics offered by these devices.

The present work proposes a new timing-driven placement algorithm for the implementation of SEU's resilient circuits on SRAM-based FPGAs without dramatic degradation of the circuit's performances. The algorithm is based on min-cut optimization technique mixed with a set of quadratic placement rules able to implement the TMR's redundant modules and the voter architectures in a way that single-errors crossing domains induced by SEUs are mitigated and the global delay of the mapped circuit is minimized. The developed algorithm is flexible and can be easily inserted in the nowadays FPGA's tool chain.

The effectiveness of the algorithm is evaluated through experimental analyses. Two evaluations have been made. At first, the SEU's sensitiveness of the mapped circuits have been evaluated using the STAR tool [10] and reporting the total number of single-error crossing domains that affect the TMR architecture. Secondly, a timing analysis has been performed considering in details the maximum delays and the number of wiring-segments used for route each circuit. The experimental results demonstrate improvement in both cases. The running frequency of the circuits result improved of about 29 % on the average, besides the circuits placed with the developed algorithm are 5.5 more robust than standard TMR circuits.

The paper is organized as follows. Section 2 presents the related works on the techniques that can be used to mitigate the SEU's effects on FPGAs and to improve the performances of the mapped circuits. Section 3 gives the background on the TMR architecture focusing on redundancy and voting schemes and it gives the perspective on the critical timing scenario. In section 4 the developed Fault Tolerant – Timing Driven Placement (FT-TDP) is presented, while the experimental analysis are detailed in section 5. Finally, the conclusions and the future works are mentioned in section 6.

2 Related Works

In the recent years, several mitigation techniques have been proposed to avoid faults in digital circuits and to limit the overhead introduced by hardening techniques. SEU immune circuits are accomplished through a variety of mitigation techniques based on redundancy.

Time and hardware redundancy are widely used in ASIC devices [11] [12]. The full hardware redundancy obtained thanks to TMR approach is used to identify and correct logic values into a circuit, although, it presents a larger overhead in terms of area, power and especially delay, since it triplicates all the combinational and sequential logic, and the architecture introduces delay penalties for the voter propagation time and the routing congestion.

In the case of SRAM-based FPGAs, finding an efficient techniques in terms of area, performance and power is a challenge. The SEU mitigation techniques used nowadays to protect design synthesized on SRAM-based FPGAs are based on TMR combined with scrubbing that consists in periodically reloading the complete contents of the configuration memory [8]. A more complex system used to correct the information in the configuration memory exploits the readback and partial configuration procedures. Through the readback operation, the content of the FPGA's configuration memory is read and compared with the expected value, which is stored in a dedicated memory located outside the FPGA. As soon as a mismatch is found, the correct information is downloaded in the FPGA's memory. During the re-configuration only the faulty portion of the configuration memory is rewritten [13]. TMR is an attractive solution for SRAM-based FPGAs because it provides full hardware redundancy of the user's combinational and sequential logic, the routing and the I/O pad. Although effective, TMR advantages are nullified by the overhead it introduces. The TMR major concerns are the availability of the I/O pads, the circuit's frequency degradation and the area overhead.

To solve the problem of the area and of the I/O pads a solution has been proposed in [14]. However, when the circuit's frequency degradation issue is considered, few solutions have been developed. Error-Detection-And-Correction (EDAC) techniques and standard TMR with single voter [15] are interesting solutions but are expensive since they require modifications in the matrix architecture (Non-Recurrent Engineering, NRE cost). A placement and routing solution has been proposed in [16], however nevertheless the authors shown an increase of performance, the optimized circuits result more sensitive to the SEU's effects with respect to the not optimized ones, furthermore only few benchmark circuits have been analyzed, these cannot demonstrate the complete feasibility of the algorithm presented in [16].

3 Background

The traditional approach to TMR involves triplicating all registers and using voters to arbitrate between them. The basic idea of the TMR scheme is that a circuit can be hardened against SEUs by designing three copies of the same circuit and building a majority voter on the output of the replicated circuit. Implementing triple redundant circuits in other technologies, such as ASICs, is generally limited to protecting only the memory elements, because combinational logic is hard-wired and correspond to non-configurable gates. Conversely, full module redundancy is required in FPGAs, because memory elements, interconnections and combinational gates are all susceptible to SEUs. This means that three copies of the user's design have to be implemented to harden the circuit against SEUs.

The implementation of TMR circuit inside a SRAM-based FPGA depends on the type of circuit that is mapped on the FPGA device. Traditional approach to TMR involves triplicating all registers and using voters to arbitrate between them. When any of the design domains fails, the other domains continue to work properly, and thanks to the voter, the correct logic value passes to the circuit output.

An example of the TMR traditional implementation is illustrated in figure 1. This architecture presents two major drawbacks when implemented on SRAM-based FPGAs:

1- It leaves designs vulnerable to SEUs in the voting circuitry. Radiation-hardened voting circuits are available to protect against the permanent damaging of the voter induced by Single-Event Latch-Up (SEL), however CMOS devices using layout geometries below 0.25 μm are still susceptible to transient effects.

2- It does not provide any protection against the accumulation of SEUs within Flip-Flops (FFs) of state machines. After an SEU in the traditional TMR scheme the state machine is corrected through scrubbing, but the state is not reset for the synchronization.

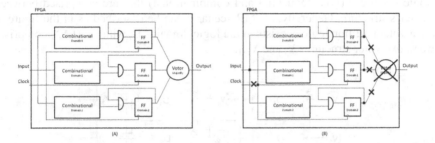

Fig. 1. The traditional TMR scheme with voter architecture (A) and an example of single fault vulnerability (B)

When implemented on SRAM-based FPGAs, TMR must follow specific rules assessing three fundamental design blocks: input and throughput logic, feedback logic and output pins. Each triplicated TMR logic domain operates independently from the other logic domains. As it is illustrated in the figure 2, all inputs, outputs, and voters are triplicated, which eliminates the presence of single points of failure in these resources. Furthermore, in order to ensure constant synchronization between the redundant state registers, majority voters with feedback paths are inserted. As a result, the feedback logic for each state machine is a function of the current state of all the three state registers. Finally, triplicated minority voters protect any possible SEUs affecting the circuit's output, that are directly connected to the device package pins as illustrated in the figure 2. If an upset occurs in throughput logic or in a state machine in a design, the voter for the affected domain detects that the output is different and disable the 3-state buffer, while the other two domains continue to operate correctly and to drive the correct output of the chip.

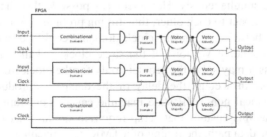

Fig. 2. The reconfigurable suggested implementation of the TMR on SRAM-based FPGAs

This scenario makes TMR circuits logically immune from upsets in the voting circuitry and against transient errors. However, recent research demonstrated that this characteristic is not sufficient to guarantee complete protection against SEU effects [9][18]. In particular, it has been demonstrated that one and only one configuration memory bit controls two or more FPGA's internal routing segments. Thus a SEU affecting the FPGA's configuration memory may provoke a domain-crossing error bypassing the TMR protection capabilities.

To decrease the possibilities to have these kinds of effects, TMR circuit on SRAM-based FPGAs may include voter partition logics. A voter partition logic is defined as the logic resources (both sequential and combinational) that are comprised between two voter's structure. Generally, a TMR scenario can be described as in the figure 3, where a voter partition logic consists in the logic domains D_i with i ∈ {1,2,3} comprises between two voter structures V_i and V_{i+1}.

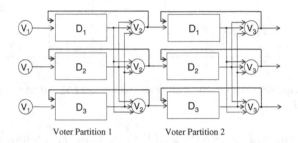

Voter Partition 1   Voter Partition 2

Fig. 3. The general TMR architecture scenario for SRAM-based FPGAs

The general TMR implementation of circuit on SRAM-based FPGAs introduces several voter levels in order to increase their protection against SEU's effects [19]. The voter scheme is particularly critical when the placement phase is executed because they congest routing interconnections coming from three domains to a single logic element. This has a severe impact on the delay of real design and the performance degradation may be between 1.5 and 2.5 times with respect of the original un-hardened circuits and depending on the overall logic density and the dependable-oriented routing introduced [9].

The timing problem in TMR designs is today only based on user's constraints to ensure cross-domain data path analysis during the place and route. The standard place and route tool chain assumes that clock signals for each redundant domain arrive at the FPGA resource simultaneously. However, it is possible that the input clocks are phase-shifted with respect to each other, thus timing problem can result. The minimization of the shift between redundant clock domains could be performed by PCB clock trances for redundant versions of the same clock and they must be of equal length. Nevertheless it may solve the problem only for the clock-tree timing propagation it does not take in account the delay of the datapath introduced by the voter scheme. While a typical non-TMR state machine can be constrained using a single period constraint, as this ensures that setup requirements are met between synchronous elements in the data path, the timing of a TMR state machine with voter partition logic cannot be fully constrained applying period constant for each path, because this will not cover the paths between all the possible cross-domains existing on the feedback logic signals.

4 FT-TDP: Fault Tolerant – Timing Driven Placement for FPGAs

The developed fault tolerant timing driven placement algorithm (FT-TDP) for implementing circuits on SRAM-based FPGAs starts by reading a description of the circuit to be placed, which consists of logic functions and the connections between them. The algorithm is compatible with the standard Xilinx design flow, depicted in figure 4.

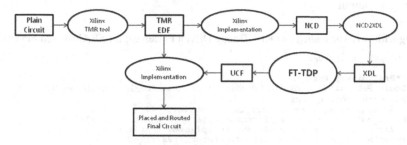

Fig. 4. The integrated Xilinx and FT-TDP flow

In detail, the integrated Xilinx and FT-TDP flow consists in generating the TMR netlist description starting from a plain circuit and using the Xilinx TMR tool [17]. The Xilinx implementation flow creates the Native Circuit Description (NCD) which contains all the physical characteristics (placement and routing information) of the mapped circuit. The FT-TDP algorithm reads the Xilinx Design Language (XDL) file created by the *ncd2xdl* tool and generates an User Constraint File (UCF) which contains the placement locations generated according to the heuristic implemented by the algorithm flow. Finally, the UCF file generated by the algorithm is used to implement the optimized TMR circuit.

4.1 The FT-TDP Algorithm

The goal of the FT-TDP placement algorithm is to find a valid placement for each configuration logic block while minimizing the total interconnection segments required and without inserting single point of failure in the circuit. The algorithm reads the XDL circuit description which includes Configurable Logic Blocks (CLBs), I/O pads, and their interconnections and generates an UCF file which binds the placement position of each CLBs within the FPGA's array.

The algorithm is based on min-cut optimization technique mixed with a quadratic placement, where the min-cut technique is applied to the general CLBs and the quadratic placement is executed for the voter's CLB.

The overall placement strategy is a three-phases approach, as is shown in Algorithm 1. After an execution of the preliminary phase which initializes the execution environment, the FT-TDP algorithm is basically working on two parts: the first aims at reducing the overall delays of connections in a global sense, while the second is a local optimization to improve the specific critical paths related to the voter resources. The circuit is loaded and stored into an undirected graph called *place_graph* where the vertices represent the logic resources such as Look-Up Tables (LUT), Multiplexers (MUXs) or Flip-Flops (FFs) and the undirected edges represent the interconnections between the logic resources. The vertices of the *place_graph* are identified by a *location* which corresponds to the physical location of the logic element into the FPGA's array, the *kind* describes the type of logic resources the vertex represents and the *domain* identifies the number of the TMR domain the logic element belongs. The relation between the locations and the *place_graph* is associated into a *placement_area* that for each logic resource it stores the related logic elements connected as input and output.

Algorithm 1. The Fault Tolerant – Timing Driven Placement for SRAM-based FPGAs

```
FT-TDP (XDL resources)
  {
    /*Preliminary Phase*/
    Logic_Set (kind, location, domain) = reading_CLB_logic(XDL resources)
    For each Logic ∈ Logic_Set
       io_net(Logic) = read_inout_logic (Logic);
    placement_area = create_placement_area (Logic_Set, io_net);
    delay_metric = create_delay_metric (placement_area);
    voter_set = create_voter_set (placement_area);
    /*Global Placement: Min-Cut, Phase 1*/
    Partitions_macro(i) = generate_bipart (placement_area);
    do until (cutting < ΔC)
       {
         cut_macro = create_minimal_cut (Partitions_macro);
         for each Logic ∈ cut_macro (i)
           {
             LF = find_local_free ();
             DR = dependability_rules (LF);
             joint (LF, DR, Macro_set);
           }
       }
    for each Macro_set ∈ Partitions_macro
       {
         find_available_macro_area (area_mac);
         logic_assignement (cut_macro, area_mac);
       }
    /*Local Placement: Quadratic, Phase 2*/
    voters_coordinates = quadratic_distance (voter_area);
    do until check_voters_coordinates (voters_coordinates))
    {
         voter_assignement (voters_coordinates, voter_area);
         estimate_voter_delay (delay_metric)
    }
    create_UCF(placement_area);
  }
```

A logic vertex is identified by a marker which distinguishes the kind of element it implements: Voter, LUT, MUX or FFs. This allows to control the distribution of the logic resources in the placement area avoiding any unreal technology mapping solution and defining the placement priority used in the quadratic placement of the voter's logic vertices. The edges modeling the interconnections have a weight metric consisting of two parameters p and cp: where p marks the position of the net within a logic critical path, and the complete critical path length is cp.

4.2 FT-TDP Global Placement

The first part of the FT-TDP algorithm consists of the global placement of all the logic resources of the circuit. In this phase, the circuit is recursively bi-partitioned, minimizing the number of cuts of the nets that connect component between the partitions. The first step of this process is executed by the function *generate_bipart* that starting from the original placement area performs the first cut. The circuit is then progressively bi-partitioned, minimizing the number of cuts of the nets that connect component between partitions, while leaving the highly-connected blocks in one partition. Each cut of a partition is executed by the function *create_minimal_cut()*. Once a cut is performed, each logic vertex of the actual cut (*cut macro*) is evaluated in terms of available space through the function *find_local_free* and in terms of dependability with the function *dependability_rules* which is based according to the rules described in [9]. The process is repeated until the number of logic element within a partition is limited to few blocks defined by the user through the parameter ΔC. The goal if this min-cut process it to make a division of partitions that cuts fewest wires. The edges of the *place_graph* are partitioned according to the weighted related to the time criticality. Therefore, by using the timing criticality as edge weight criteria, disables the partitioning algorithm with higher criticalities. This phase has the advantage that the cost function is defined by the user and is directly driven by the time cost function.

4.3 FT-TDP Local Placement

The FT-TDP local placement aims at placing the voter logic elements minimizing the delay introduced by their critical paths and feedback signals, according to the scenario described in the previous sections.

The local placement is based on a quadratic algorithm that tries to minimize the total squared length by solving linear equation of the distance between each voter input and output signals. The cost function is defined has a quadratic sum of the distance between the input sources of the voters and the related output path, considering the voter architecture as illustrated in figure 3. This process is executed in two steps.

The first step consists in calculating the expected voter's vertices position that is computed by the function *quadratic_distance* which returns the voter coordinates. The second step consists in checking if the voter coordinates are related to available logic resources and if not to compute the logic assignment of the voter's vertices by moving the vertices within the global placement partitions until an available position is find.

In details, the function *voter_assignment* executes the following steps: it adds spare nodes to the *place_graph* and expands the placement for the voter's vertices, it refines and minimizes the linear wire length. These steps are repeated until there is not a significant improvement of the estimated delay of the voter's interconnections. The advantage of the quadratic placement for the voter's element results in the ability of handle large design without affecting the global placement. The technique minimizes the wired length of the voter elements as a single optimization function where the cost of the placement is directly timing-driven.

5 Experimental Results

The developed FT-TDP algorithm has been experimentally evaluated in order to probe the efficiency and the improvements of performances with respect of standard TMR circuits implemented on SRAM-based FPGAs.

Two experimental analysis have been performed. The former aims evaluating the robustness of the circuits against SEUs effects affecting the FPGA's configuration memory. The latter consists on a detailed timing analysis measuring the maximum delay of the critical path within the implemented circuits. Both the evaluations have been performed using the benchmark circuits related to the ITC'99 benchmark. These circuits consist of 14 RTL level sequential circuits ranging from 6 to 20,000 equivalent gates and from 3 to 188 FFs. For a complete reference to the benchmark circuits adopted please refer to the document [20]. All the circuits have been synthesized using the Xilinx TMR tool and they have been implemented using different SRAM-based FPGAs of the Virtex-II family manufactured by Xilinx [21].

5.1 Analysis of the SEU Sensitiveness

The SEU sensitiveness analysis has been performed using the STAR tool [10] for analyzing the presence of single point of failure due to SEUs within the FPGA's configuration cells. All the circuits have been synthesized with the Xilinx ISE flow and then hardened with the Xilinx TMR tool and the FT-TDP algorithm. The circuit's characteristics expressed as equivalent gates are reported, together with the Critical SEUs results, in table 1.

The observed results shown that the circuits implemented with the FT-TDP algorithm present a lower number of sensitive configuration memory bit locations. In particular, the circuits hardened according to the FT-TDP algorithm are more than 5.5 times robust on the average versus the TMR circuits. Therefore, the FT-TDP algorithm is feasible in implementing fault tolerant circuits on SRAM-based FPGAs.

Table 1. Benchmark circuit's equivalent gates and Critical SEUs of the placed circuit (FT-TDP) reported by the Static Analyzer tool

TMRed Circuit	Device	Equivalent Gates	Critical SEUs	
			TMR Circuit	FT-TDP Circuit
B01	XC2V40	372	0	0
B02	XC2V40	59	0	0
B03	XC2V40	2,355	0	0
B04	XC2V40	5,235	0	0
B05	XC2V80	7,488	1	0
B06	XC2V40	525	0	0
B07	XC2V40	4,401	0	0
B08	XC2V40	1,341	2	0
B09	XC2V40	1,680	5	0
B10	XC2V40	1,719	16	3
B11	XC2V40	3,846	2	0
B12	XC2V250	10,554	29	6
B13	XC2V40	2,613	1	0
B14	XC2V1500	63,174	54	11

5.2 Analysis of the Timing Delay

The implemented circuits have been timing analyzed using Xilinx vendor's tool in order to estimate the maximum delay of the critical paths within the circuits. We compared the timing performances of circuits implemented with the standard Xilinx implementation flow, either for plain and TMR circuits, and the developed FT-TDP timing driven placement algorithm. The results obtained from the timing analysis are reported in table 2, where the maximum delay for the original and unhardened version, the standard TMR circuit and the FT-TDP ones are reported. The data indicates a delay reduction of about 29 % on the average, with respect to the standard TMR techniques, while their presents a minimal overhead of about 5% with respect to the original unhardened circuit's version. Please note that the FT-TDP circuits have not any area overhead versus original TMR circuits since the FT-TDP algorithm operates exclusively on the resource's placement without altering the synthesized circuit's netlist. This results demonstrate that the FT-TDP algorithm is efficiently implementing circuits on SRAM-based FPGAs without a drastic reduction of the circuits running frequency.

Table 2. Timing delay of the benchmark circuits

| Circuit | Critical Path Delay [ns] | | | Delay Reduction |
	Original	TMR	FT-TDP	FT-TDP / TMR [%]
B01	1.24	1.71	1.26	26.3
B02	0.85	1.35	0.91	32.6
B03	2.01	3.26	2.08	36.2
B04	2.13	2.22	1.99	10.4
B05	2.50	3.24	2.62	19.1
B06	0.96	1.98	1.04	47.5
B07	2.10	2.15	2.10	2.3
B08	1.14	1.52	1.24	18.4
B09	1.90	1.94	1.91	1.6
B10	1.71	2.11	1.83	13.3
B11	2.24	4.67	2.54	45.6
B12	2.11	4.56	2.46	46.1
B13	0.83	1.76	0.91	48.3
B14	2.18	5.03	2.20	56.3

6 Conclusions and Future Works

In this paper a new timing-driven placement algorithm for fault tolerant circuits on reconfigurable SRAM-based FPGAs has been presented. The main contribution of the present work consist in a placement heuristic able to remove the crossing error domains while reducing the routing congestions and delay inserted by the TMR routing and voting scheme. Experimental results performed shown a performance improvement of 29% on the average with respect to standard TMR approach and an increased robustness against SEU affecting the FPGA's configuration memory.

Future works are planned to evaluate the impact of the proposed placement algorithm on the circuit's power consumption.

References

[1] Sterpone, L.: Electronic System Design Techniques for Safety Critical Applications, vol. 26, p. 148. Springer, Heidelberg (2008)

[2] JEDEC standard JESD89, Measurement and Reporting of Alpha Particles and Terrestrial Cosmic Ray-Induced Soft Errors in Semiconductor Devices (August 2001)

[3] Ceschia, M., Paccagnella, A., Lee, S.-C., Wan, C., Bellato, M., Menichelli, M., Papi, A., Kaminski, A., Wyss, J.: Ion Beam Testing of Altera APEX FPGAs. In: NSREC 2002 Radiation Effects Data Workshop Record, Phoenix, AZ, USA (July 2002)

[4] Katz, R., LaBel, K., Wang, J.J., Cronquist, B., Koga, R., Penzin, S., Swift, G.: Radiation effects on current field programmable technologies. IEEE Transactions on Nuclear Science, Part 1, 44(6), 1945–1956 (1997)

[5] Xilinx Application Notes XAPP216, Correcting Single-Event Upset Through Virtex Partial Reconfiguration (2000)

[6] Habinc, S.: Gaisler Research, Functional Triple Modular Redundancy (FTMR) VHDL Design Methodology for Redundancy in Combinational and Sequential logic, http://www.gaisler.com

[7] Samudrala, P.K., Ramos, J., Katkoori, S.: Selective Triple Modular Redundancy (STMR) Based Single-Event Upset (SEU) Tolerant Synthesis for FPGAs. IEEE Transactions on Nuclear Science 51(5) (October 2004)

[8] Carmichael, C.: Triple Modular Redundancy Design Technique for Virtex FPGAs, Xilinx Application Notes XAPP197 (2001)

[9] Sterpone, L., Violante, M.: A new reliability-oriented place and route algorithm for SRAM-based FPGAs. IEEE Transactions on Computers 55(6), 732–744 (2006)

[10] Sterpone, L., Violante, M.: A new analytical approach to estimate the effects of SEUs in TMR architectures implemented through SRAM-based FPGAs. IEEE Transactions on Nuclear Science, Part 1, 52(6), 2217–2223 (2005)

[11] Anghel, L., Nicolaidis, M.: Cost Reduction and Evaluation of a Temporary Faults Detecting Technique. In: Proceedings 2000, Design Automation and Test in Europe Conference (DATE 2000), pp. 591–598. ACM Press, New York (2000)

[12] Dupont, D., Nicolaidis, M., Rohr, P.: Embedded robustness IPs for Transient-Error-Free ICs. IEEE Design and Test of Computers, 56–70 (May-June 2002)

[13] Correcting Single-Event Upsets Through Virtex Partial Reconfiguration, Xilinx Application Notes, XAPP216 (2000)

[14] Lima, F., Carro, L., Reis, R.: Designing Fault Tolerant Systems into SRAM-based FPGAs. In: ACM/IEEE Design Automation Conference, pp. 650–655 (2003)

[15] Peterson, W.W.: Error-correcting codes, 2nd edn., 560 p. MIT Press, Cambridge (1980)

[16] Sterpone, L., Battezzati, N.: A Novel Design Flow for the Performance Optimization of Fault Tolerant Circuits on SRAM-based FPGAs. In: NASA/ESA Conference on Adaptive Hardware and Systems, pp. 157–163 (2008)

[17] Xilinx User Guide, TMRTool User Guide. UG156 (v2.0) (May 30, 2005)

[18] Kastensmidt, F.L., Sterpone, L., Carro, L., Sonza Reorda, M.: On the optimal design of triple modular redundancy logic for SRAM-based FPGAs. IEEE Design, Automation and Test in Europe, 1290–1295 (2005)

[19] Sterpone, L., Violante, M., Sorensen, R.H., Merodio, D., Sturesson, F., Weigand, R., Mattsson, S.: Experimental Validation of a Tool for Predicting the Effects of Soft Errors in SRAM-based FPGAs. IEEE Transactions on Nuclear Science, Part 1, 54(6), 2576–2583 (2007)

[20] Various Authors, ITC 1999 Benchmark homepage, http://www.cerc.utexas.edu/itc99-benchmarks/bench.html

[21] Xilinx Datasheet, Virtex-II Platform FPGA: complete data sheet. rif. DS031 (2003)

A Novel Local Interconnect Architecture for Variable Grain Logic Cell

Kazuki Inoue, Motoki Amagasaki, Masahiro Iida,
and Toshinori Sueyoshi

Graduate School of
Science and Technology, Kumamoto University,
2-39-1 Kurokami Kumamoto, 860-8555, Japan

Abstract. Depending on the granularity of the basic logic cell, reconfigurable devices are classified into two types; fine-grain and coarse-grain devices. In general, each type has its own advantages; therefore, it is difficult to achieve high implementation efficiency in any applications. In this study, we propose a variable grain logic cell (VGLC) architecture. Its key feature is variable granularity which helps create a balance between these two types of device. In this paper, we propose a local interconnect structure, which is a crossbar switch circuit, for the VGLC. In order to discuss the trade-off between the number of circuit resources and flexibility, we proposed different structures and evaluated them. The results showed that a less flexible structure has almost the same effects as a more flexible structure.

1 Introduction

Reconfigurable logic devices (RLDs), which are typified by field programmable gate arrays (FPGAs), are growing importance for the implementation of digital circuits. Owing to their programmability, applications can be easily implemented.

However, in [1], the difference in area between application specific integrated circuits(ASICs) and FPGAs has been reported to be 35 times, FPGAs are 3.4 times slower, and FPGAs consume 14 times more dynamic power. Therefore, the development of high-performance RLDs is necessary. We propose a variable-grain logic cell (VGLC) architecture[2] for efficient implementation of circuits. However, the disadvantage with VGLCs is the increase in the number of routing resources. Further, routing overhead degrades the device performance. Therefore, it is important to reduce the routing resources. It is also important to reduce the number of logic cell inputs. In this paper, we propose the implementation of a local connection block (LCB), which is a programmable crossbar circuit, as shown Fig.1(b). The use of an LCB enables sharing of input signals and reduction in the number of input pins and global routing resources. However, the addition of an LCB causes area overhead. Therefore, we attempt to miniature LCB structure. The remaining part of this paper is organized as follows. Section 2

J. Becker et al. (Eds.): ARC 2009, LNCS 5453, pp. 97–109, 2009.
© Springer-Verlag Berlin Heidelberg 2009

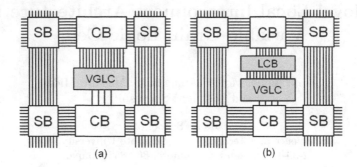

Fig. 1. Connection diagram between VGLC and global routing area (a) without LCB (b) with LCB

describes the architecture of our VGLC. Sections 3 and 4 discuss the LCB structure and its evaluation, respectively. Finally, concluding remarks and future plans are included in Section 5.

2   Variable Grain Logic Cell Architecture

As mentioned earlier, it is difficult to improve the performance of conventional RLDs, whose granularity is fixed. Thus, we propose a logic cell whose operation granularity can be changed so that it can be used in any application. The use of such a logic cell helps improve the performance efficiency. In this section, we propose a hybrid cell (HC) and VGLC (that requires four HCs) and describe their architectures and functions.

2.1   Hybrid Cell

The arithmetic computation is performed using an adder, and the random logic is expressed efficiently in a "canonical form" such as an LUT. Fig. 2(a) shows the structure of a 1-bit full adder. Fig. 2(b) shows the 2-input Reed-Muller canonical form. Both the adder and canonical form show common parts comprising EXOR and AND gates. Fig. 2(c) shows an HC comprising a full adder with four configuration memory bits. The HC can be constructed from the full adder and the 2-input canonical form according to the computation. Furthermore, in order to allow more functionality in addition to a 1-bit full adder and 2-input Reed Muller canonical form, we construct a structure known as a basic logic element (BLE), as shown in Fig. 3. A BLE consists of an HC, multiplexers, an EXOR gate, inputs (dc, dx, dy, dz, and AS), and outputs (dt and ds).

2.2   Logic Cell

Fig. 4 shows the architecture of the VGLC, which consists of four BLEs, an output selector, and a 27-bit configuration memory. It has a 21-bit input and

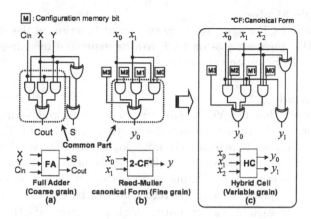

Fig. 2. Basic structure of a hybrid cell

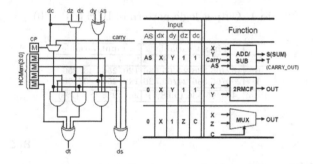

Fig. 3. Components and functions of a BLE

a 4-bit output. Carry_in, carry_out, shift_in, and shift_out signals are directly connected to neighboring VGLCs as dedicated lines. AS and CP (carry-select memory) signals are inputted together to the entire BLE in the VGLC. The following diagram explains some of the basic operations of the VGLC, they are discussed in this paper.

Arithmetic Mode

In this mode, the VGLC performs four-bit addition or subtraction operations. Here, all the BLEs are set as FAs and are connected to the carry line (controlled by the CP signal). Carry propagation between the BLEs is fast because it occurs through a dedicated carry line. In order to dynamically control the addition or subtraction process in the VGLC, the AS signal is used. The carry path between neighboring VGLCs is in the form of dedicated lines so that the width of the operation bit can be increased.

Random Logic Mode

A BLE used as a 2-CF can express any two-input function in the same manner as does a 2-LUT. Further, a 3- or 4-CF can be expressed by using two or four BLEs by using the Shannon expansion.

Misc. Logic Mode

It has been shown that the VGLC can represent 2-, 3-, and 4-input canonical forms; however, it still requires a larger area than does the LUT. In order to reduce this area overhead, we utilize the misc. logic (miscellaneous logic) function performed by the gate structure. Since a BLE can be used for a 4-input/2-output module, it can represent 3- or 4-input logic pattern with a 4-bit configuration memory. Table 1 depicts the logic pattern that can be expressed at outputs T and S. The K-input variable has 2^{2^K} output logic patterns; thus, there are 65,536 and 256 patterns in the 4-input and 3-input canonical forms, respectively. For example, since AS = 0 in the 3-input variable, T and S are capable of covering

Table 1. Output logic pattern of BLE (CP = 0)

AS	4-input variable		3-input variable	
	T	S	T	S
0	182/65,536	24/65,536	120/256	43/256
1	230/65,536	24/65,536	148/256	43/256
Total	446/65,536 (0.68%)		206/256 (80.47%)	

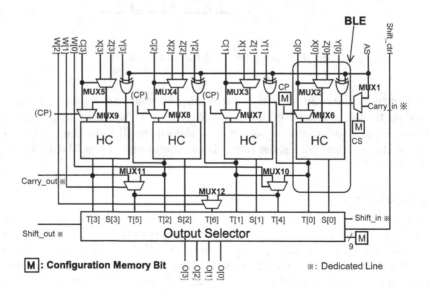

Fig. 4. VGLC Architecture

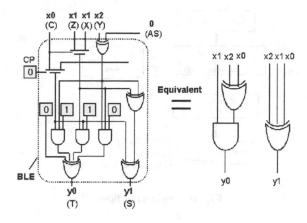

Fig. 5. Example of 3-input misc. logic function

120 and 43 logic patterns, respectively. In total, the misc. logic function can represent 80.47% of the 3-input logic patterns. Fig. 5 shows an example the usage of 3-input misc. logic.

As in the case of the random logic mode, we can construct a 4- or 5-input misc. logic function using the Shannon expression. The misc. logic function can implement 41.91% and 14.18% of the 4- and 5-input logic patterns, respectively.

2.3 Permutation Equivalence Class for Misc. Logic Mode

As shown in the previous section, the misc. logic mode can implement limited logic circuits. For this reason, boolean matching is required in a technology mapping process. The boolean matching algorithm is based on a P-representative, which is unique among the functions of a P-equivalence class[3]. The set of functions that are equivalent under permutation of variables form a P-equivalence class. In a P-equivalence class, the function that has the smallest binary number representation is the P-representative of that class.

3 Proposed Local Interconnect Architecture

In general, the number of routing resources in island-style FPGAs increases with the number of logic block inputs[4]. VGLC has a greater number of inputs than commercial FPGAs, which are based on 4-, 5-, 6-input LUTs. Therefore, we must reduce the number of VGLC inputs. For this purpose, we propose implementation of an LCB to interconnect BLEs within a VGLC. This enables sharing of input signals and a reduction in the number of input pins. Moreover, the performance is considerably improved, because signals can be propagated among BLEs within VGLC via LCB.

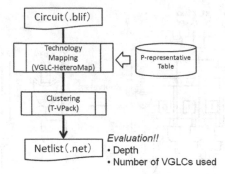

Fig. 6. Evaluation flow

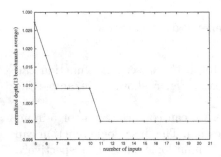

Fig. 7. Evaluation of logic depth   **Fig. 8.** Evaluation of the number of VGLCs used

3.1 Number of Logic Block Inputs

It is that important to reduce the number of LCB inputs to the maximum possible extent. However, decreasing the number of inputs beyond a certain limit can prove to be disadvantage to the system[5]. To determine the LCB structure, it is important to obtain a balance between the number of inputs and implementation-efficiency. Then, the number of inputs can be decided by pre-evaluation. Logic depth and the number of VGLCs are evaluated by implementing 13 MCNC benchmark circuits. Fig. 6 shows the evaluation flow, includes technology mapping and clustering stages. In this flow, we modify two public tools in the VGLC: HeteroMap[6] and T-VPack[7]. A modified HeteroMap is shown in [2], and the T-VPack is modified as follows. VGLC functions, for example random logic and misc. logic modes, sometimes include several BLEs by the Shannon expansion, as a multi-grain function. Therefore, we added this function to the T-VPack. Moreover, the AS signal is taken into consideration. Though each function(BLEs) requires a different AS signal value, only one AS signal value can be input into a given VGLC. Fig. 7 shows the pre-evaluation result of the normalized logic depth for the case of 21 inputs, where the obtained values are the average of the benchmark circuits. As a result, if the number of

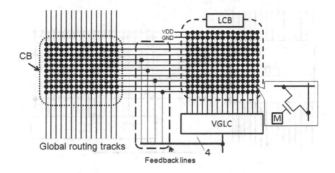

Fig. 9. The detailed structure of the LCB

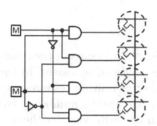

Fig. 10. Decoder circuit with two memory bits to control four switches

Table 2. Required circuit resources in LCB

	# of memory bits	# of Tr.
Without decoder	256	1804
With decoder	88	3484

inputs is more than 11, there is no overhead. If the number of inputs is 10, the logic depth increases by 1%. Fig. 8 shows the result of the normalized number of used VGLCs when there are 21 inputs. We can see that the results obtained are the same when the number of inputs is more than 10. Therefore, we set the number of inputs as 10.

3.2 Structure of Local Connection Block

Fig. 9 shows the detailed structure of the LCB, which is a full crossbar comprising nMOS switches and SRAMs[8]. Input signals to the LCB enter from global lines, feedback lines, VDD, and GND. Note that a CB(connection block) is a full crossbar structure[8]. Moreover, in order to reduce the number of required configuration memory bits, we implement a decoder circuit as shown in Fig. 10 for simultaneous control of some of the switches. It is a simple structure consisting of some AND and INVERTER gates.

Table 2 shows a comparison of the circuit resources using with and without the decoder. The number of memory bits when using a decoder is fewer than that obtained without a decoder by 75%. Meanwhile, the number of transistors with a decoder is twice that without a decoder. In this study, we consider an LCB with decoder because power consumption during the configuration stage is lesser when the number of configuration memory bits is less[9].

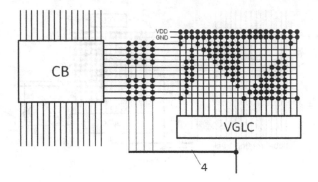

Fig. 11. LCB structure: approach (A)

3.3 Circuit Resources vs. Flexibility

As shown in Fig. 9, CB and LCB have high routability because they are made of full crossbars. However, the routing resource overhead increases. In this section, we discuss the trade-off between the number of routing resources and the flexibility of LCB. The major points of consideration are the number of switches and their positions in the LCB. In this paper, in order to consider these points, we present the following four approaches:

(A) consideration of all VGLC functions
(B) consideration of arithmetic and random logic mode
(C) consideration of (B) + a part of misc. logic functions
(D) consideration of (C) and additional functions with decoder structure

(A) Consideration of all VGLC Functions
In this approach, we present a method to reduce the number of switches without considering VGLC functionality. This method relies on the flexibility of the CB, and hence, global signals can be freely propagated to the LCB input pins. The large number of routing candidates in the routing stage bring about a considerable resource overhead. In fact, by eliminating these candidates in the LCB, the number of switches can be reduced. The CB compensates for the decrease in the flexibility of the LCB. Fig. 11 shows the detailed structure of the LCB. The switches in this LCB are reduced to half that shown in Fig. 9. However, a greater number of switches are required to connect feedback lines, because the flexibility of global and feedback signals must be equivalent.

(B) Consideration of Arithmetic and Random Logic Mode
This approach aims to reduce the number of switches by imposing the constraint of VGLC functionality. The constraint is that only arithmetic and random logic modes should be used. As shown in Fig. 3, these functions use a number of fixed pins, and therefore, high flexibility is not necessary for their implementation.

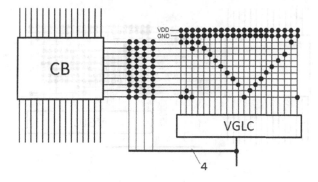

Fig. 12. LCB structure: approach (B)

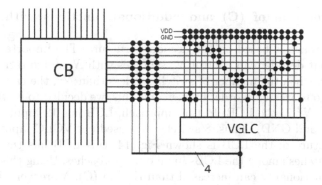

Fig. 13. LCB structure: approach (C)

On the other hand, high flexibility is required to implement the misc. logic mode because in this mode, pins are used in a random manner according to the implemented logic circuits. Thus, we aim to reduce the number of switches by ignoring the misc. logic mode. Fig. 12 shows the detailed LCB structure in this approach. As a result, each VGLC input pin has one switch for the global signals. On the other hand, the number of switches used for feedback lines are more than those used in approach (A).

(C) Consideration of (B) + a Part of Misc. Logic Functions

In a previous study[2], we found that the usage frequency of each function is different in mapping stage. Hence, in this approach, we add a part of misc. logic that is used frequently to (B). Because of this, the functionality of (C) is higher than that of (B) but lower than that of (A). The detailed structure of the LCB used in this approach is shown Fig. 13; this structure has a greater number of switches compared to that used in approach (B). The number of switches used four the feedback lines is the same as that used in approach (B).

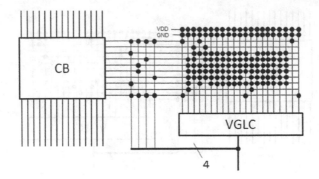

Fig. 14. LCB structure: approach (D)

(D) Consideration of (C) and additional functions with Decoder Structure

Our final approach is based on the decoder structure. The important point in this case is that decoder can control N^2 switches with N configuration memory bits. However, when the number of switches is less than N^2, the capacity of the decoder will go to waste. In order to overcome this, we decided to fix the number of switches as N^2 in the LCB. In this approach, LCB has 12 inputs (10 global inputs, VDD, and GND). Thus, 8 switches are used per VGLC inputs pin. The detailed structure of the LCB is shown Fig. 14; this LCB has the maximum number of switches among the LCBs in all our approaches. Using this structure, the VGLC functionality can increased than that in (C). Moreover, the number of switches used for feedback lines is fewer than that in other approaches.

4   Evaluation

In this section, we evaluate the circuit resources and the flexibility of the four LCB structures presented in the previous section. We also evaluate results of implementation 12 MCNC benchmark circuits.

4.1   Circuit Resources

Table 3 shows the number of circuit resources. We can see that, the number of switches, memory bits, and number of transistors in (B) are the least. However, because of this, (B) has the lowest flexibility. Further, even though the number of switches in (D) is more than that in (A), (D) has fewer transistors than (A). This is a result of the use of the decoder. Moreover, (D) has the least number of switches for feedback lines compared to other approaches.

4.2   Flexibility of LCB

In general, flexibility increases with the number of switches. However, each VGLC input pins are not equivalent unlike LUT, and each pin has different usage

Table 3. LCB circuit resources

	Crossbar part			Feedback part			Total		
	# of switches	# of memory bits	# of Tr.	# of switches	# of memory bits	# of Tr.	# of switches	# of memory bits	# of Tr.
(A)	128	60	1664	40	24	552	168	84	2216
(B)	68	43	836	50	30	690	118	73	1526
(C)	80	46	1004	50	30	690	130	76	1694
(D)	154	60	1846	22	12	246	176	72	2092

Table 4. Usable P-representative

	ratio of # of usage P-representative to that in (A) [%]		
	(B)	(C)	(D)
3-oMisc (AS = 0)	88	100	100
3-oMisc (AS = 1)	87	100	100
4-oMisc (AS = 0)	100	100	100
4-oMisc (AS = 1)	100	100	100
4-tMisc (AS = 0)	9	10	100
4-tMisc (AS = 1)	7	8	100
5-tMisc (AS = 0)	3	3	100
5-tMisc (AS = 1)	2	3	100
6-tMisc (AS = 0)	4	5	100
6-tMisc (AS = 1)	3	4	100
7-tMisc (AS = 0)	15	17	100
7-tMisc (AS = 1)	13	15	100
8-tMisc (AS = 0)	47	50	100
8-tMisc (AS = 1)	40	44	100

frequency. Hence, we must evaluate both the usage frequency of each pin and the number of switches. However, this is very difficult. Thus, in this paper, we evaluate the number of usable P-representatives as a measure of the flexibility of the LCB.

Table 4 shows the number of P-representatives that the VGLC can implement with four LCB structures. The left-hand column implies the following:

N-oMisc: N-input misc.Logic with one BLE
N-tMisc: N-input misc.Logic with two BLEs

Further, the values indicate the ratio of the number of P-representatives of the given approach to that of (A). As a result, (D) has same number of usable P-representatives as (A). Then, (B) and (C) have both high and low ratio functions (e.g. 4-oMisc, 5-tMisc). This result depends on input sharing, which requires high routability to the LCB. For example, 4-oMisc requires one BLE, which has 4 input pins, and 4 signals are propagated to each pin. In this case, input sharing is not essential. On the other hand, 5-tMisc requires two BLEs, and 5 signals are propagated to 9 input pins. In this case, these signals must be shared. Therefore, we conclude that flexibility of LCB is very important for representing several functions.

4.3   Implementation Results

In this section, in order to evaluate the effect of the number of usable P-representatives, we implement 12 MCNC benchmark circuits using the VGLC-HeteroMap. The logic depth and number of BLEs are evaluated. Fig. 15 shows

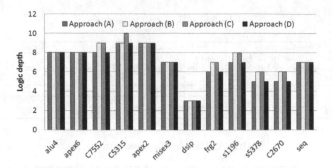

Fig. 15. Evaluation of logic depth

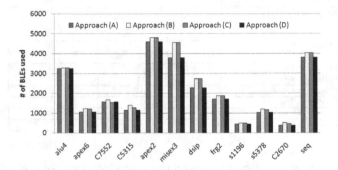

Fig. 16. Number of BLEs used for evaluation

the result of evaluation of logic depth which shows that all logic depths are almost equal. In some cases, the logic depths of (B) and (C) are greater than those of (A) and (D). Therefore, we conclude that logic depth is independent of the number of usable P-representatives.

Fig. 16 shows the result of evaluation of the number of BLEs required. The values obtained for (A) and (D) are the same. The number of BLEs required by (B) and (C) are 14% and 11% more than that used in (A), respectively. Even though (B) and (C) require very few P-representatives shown in Table 4, their implementation results are almost the same. Because some of the P-representatives are used when benchmarks are implemented, these P-representatives are included in (B) and (C). Therefore, less flexible LCB has same effect as a more flexible LCB, and the number of LCB resources can thus be reduced.

5   Conclusion and Future Plans

In this paper, we described the LCB structure composed of crossbars. In order to discuss the trade-off between its resources and flexibility, we designed four different LCB structures. Then, we implemented benchmark circuits to them. We found that area and delay overheads could be minimized by using a lesser number of P-representatives. In future, we plan to investigate the global routing architecture of VGLC. Then, we will develop clustering, placing, and routing tools for VGLC and evaluate VGLC performance.

References

1. Kuon, I., Rose, J.: Measuring the Gap Between FPGAs and ASICs. In: Proc. of the 2006 ACM/SIGDA 14th International Symposium on Field Programmable Gate Arrays, pp. 21–30 (Feburary 2006)
2. Amagasaki, M., Yamaguch, R., Koga, M., Iida, M., Sueyoshi, T.: An Embedded Reconfigurable IP Core with Variable Grain Logic Cell Architecture. International Journal of Reconfigurable Computing (2008)
3. Debnath, D., Sasao, T.: Fast Boolean Matching under Permutation by Efficient Computation of Canonical Form. IEICE Transactions on Fundamentals of Electronics, Communications and Computer Sciences 87(12) (December 2004)
4. Rose, J., El Gamal, A., Sangiovanni-Vincentelli, A.: Architecture of field-programmable gate arrays. Proceedings of the IEEE (1993)
5. Betz, V., Rose, J.: Cluster-based Logic Blocks for FPGAs: Area-efficiency vs. Inputsharing and Size. Proceedings of the IEEE (1997)
6. Cong, J., Xu, S.: Delay-Oriented Technology Mapping for Heterogeneous FPGAs with Bounded Resources. In: Proc. ACM/IEEE International Conference on Computer Aided Design, pp. 40–45 (November 1998)
7. Betz, V., Rose, J., Marquardt, A.: Architecture and CAD for Deep-Submicron FPGAs. Kluwer Academic Publishers, Dordrecht (1999)
8. Lemieux, G., Lewis, D.: Design of Interconnection Networks for Programmable Logic. Kluwer Academic Publishers, Dordrecht (2004)
9. George, V., Rabaey, J.: Low-Energy FPGA - Architecture AND Design. Kluwer Academic Publishers, Dordrecht (2001)

Dynamically Adapted Low Power ASIPs

Mateus B. Rutzig, Antonio Carlos S. Beck, and Luigi Carro

Universidade Federal do Rio Grande do Sul – Porto Alegre/Brazil
{mbrutzig,caco,carro}@inf.ufrgs.br

Abstract. New generations of embedded devices, following the trend found in personal computers, are becoming computationally powerful. A current embedded scenario presents a large amount of complex and heterogeneous functionalities, which have been forcing designers to create novel solutions to increase the performance of embedded processors while, at the same time, maintain power dissipation as low as possible. Former embedded devices could have been designed to execute a defined application set. Nowadays, in the new generation of these devices, some applications are unknown at design time. For example, in portable phones, the client is able to download new applications during the product lifetime. Hence, traditional designs can fail to deliver the required performance while executing an application behavior that has not been previously defined. On the other hand, reconfigurable architectures appear to be a possible solution to increase the processor performance, but their employment in embedded devices faces two main design constraints: power and area. In this work, we propose an ASIP reconfigurable development flow that aggregates design area optimization and a run-time technique that reduces energy consumption. The coupling of both methods builds an area optimized reconfigurable architecture to provide a high-performance and energy-efficient execution of a defined application set. Moreover, thanks to the adaptability provided by the reconfigurable ASIP approach, the execution of new application not foreseen at design time still shows high speedups rates with low energy consumption.

1 Introduction

Nowadays, the accelerated growth of the embedded devices market has already surpassed the annual manufacturing of personal computers. In 2009, it is expected that 90% of all computing devices will be embedded [1]. Designs regarding these devices tend to aggregate several functionalities in a single product, composing a heterogeneous software execution environment. This heterogeneous environment directly affects the hardware design, so that the embedded processor must be able to manipulate a wide range of software behaviors, and still support well-known embedded design constraints like area, power and energy consumption.

Furthermore, new marketing strategies have been focusing on increasing the device functionalities during the product life cycle to reach a wider market. However, the behavior of this recently installed software can be out of the range in terms of performance, not being covered by the original processor. Hence, an embedded processor must be flexible enough to speedup unknown software behaviors and, at the

J. Becker et al. (Eds.): ARC 2009, LNCS 5453, pp. 110–122, 2009.
© Springer-Verlag Berlin Heidelberg 2009

same time, guarantee the embedded system design tradeoffs. To handle this problem, current market devices employ powerful processors in their design, even if they are more expensive.

As an example, Iphone uses a system on a chip (SoC) to execute its many available functions [14]. A general-purpose ARM processor is responsible for the management of several other processing elements like 3D-graphics coprocessor, audio and video. Moreover, common desktop processors techniques running at almost 700 MHz are found in this platform: SIMD execution, ARM Jazelle technology and DSP extensions. Basically, each technology that was incorporated in this architecture attacks a specific application domain. For instance, SIMD execution aims to provide high performance on integer multimedia applications, while the ARM Jazelle technology works as a Java acceleration engine. This scenario illustrates a current embedded design strategy, which is based on several different circuits, where each one is built to perform specific operations to attack a defined application domain. This way, each circuit could be seen as an application specific instruction processor (ASIP). The main goal of the ASIP usage is the high-performance provided and small chip area overhead. However, applications added during the product lifetime cannot fit in the original ASIP designed, because of its restricted adaptability, affecting the application performance and energy consumption.

As another point of view, reconfigurable architectures appear to be an attractive solution to accelerate a wide range of applications behaviors, since they provide high adaptability, at the price of high area and power consumption [3][4][5].This work focuses on the main problems of a current embedded processor design: performance improvement, area and power constraints, time-to-market and the possibility to include new applications during the whole product lifetime. To cover all these problems we propose a reconfigurable ASIP development flow that merges the small area and power provided by an ASIP processor, together with the flexibility of reconfigurable architectures execution, decided during run-time.

The contribution of this work is a design flow targeted to a dynamic reconfigurable architecture [6]. This approach explores, at design time, the maximum ILP of a given application, building custom instructions of the main application kernels, with a customized reconfigurable data path to execute them. Using the static exploration, the designer is able to address all the embedded design constraints, ranging the amount of application code translated to custom instructions according to the power estimation provided by the proposed tool. After the chip development, it is still possible to achieve speedups even on applications that were not foreseen at design time, by turning on the dynamic detection hardware and using the very same previously designed reconfigurable data path. Hence, the dynamic detection/translation is made only for new applications, saving power. In addition, to attack dynamic and static power consumption, the Sleep Transistor technique [7] is applied to turn off idle data path functional units at run-time.

This paper is organized as follows. Section 2 shows a review of ASIPs and reconfigurable architectures. Section 3 presents the hardware of the coarse grain reconfigurable architecture used as case study. Section 4 demonstrates details about the ASIP reconfigurable development flow and presents the dynamic reconfiguration coupled to the Sleep Transistors technique. Section 5 shows the results regarding an actual case study. Finally, section 6 draws conclusions and future works.

2 Related Work

In the past, researches have focused on methodologies to allow the automatic generation of a complete instruction set architecture targeted for specific application domain. In [8] it is shown a high-level synthesis method of an ASIP-based embedded system. Basically, the method receives as input a data dependency graph of an application, an objective function, design constraints and an architecture template. With this information a micro-architecture is generated, together with an application specific instruction set and the assembly code for a given application. The main problem of this approach is the need of human intervention to describe an architecture template, which increases the design time, affecting the time to market.

More recently, several works have been proposed in order to extend the instruction set of a general-purpose processor, by building specialized units to accelerate a specific embedded application set. In [9][10] an automatic design flow is demonstrated to extend the processor instruction set focusing on the speedup of a target application. These works use a compiler to determine which parts of code must be moved to a dedicated hardware. After that, the compiler generates new instructions that replace the behavior of selected code parts. Static tools are used to identify the parts of code that will be moved to hardware, but these tools do not take into account the dynamic behavior of the application. In addition, given that the processor architecture was designed to a specified application set, the static compiler cannot guarantee the desired speedup on applications which execution was not foreseen at design time.

Reconfigurable systems have already shown to be very effective in mapping certain parts of the software to reconfigurable logic. Huge software speedups [2] as well as significant system energy reductions have been previously reported [3]. For instance, processors like Chimaera [11] have a tightly coupled reconfigurable array in the processor core, limited to combinational logic only. The array is, in fact, an additional functional unit (FU) in the processor pipeline, sharing the resources with all regular FUs. The GARP machine [4] is a MIPS compatible processor with a loosely coupled reconfigurable array. The communication is done using dedicated move instructions. However, the employment of reconfigurable architectures in embedded systems still has some problems, like the big amount of processing elements required, meaning a large area occupied and, consequently, huge power is consumed.

In [12] an architecture that merges reconfigurable hardware with an ASIP approach is demonstrated. rASIP (reconfigurable Application Specific Processor) aggregates the high performance and low power features of an ASIP design with the flexibility of reconfigurable architectures. The design flow proposes a fast methodology to create a rASIP, by the description of it on a high-level specification language. There are 2 phases on its design flow: pre-fabrication and pos-fabrication. The first one represents the traditional design of any ASIP. The second one corresponds to the product lifetime cycle, after its development. It means that new applications can be accelerated in rASIP after the chip fabrication, exploiting all the reconfigurable processing elements available. However, for the execution of applications not foreseen at design time, the designer must spend time with specialized tools to generate the new custom instructions and, again, affecting the software time to market. Besides, the pos-fabrication flow changes the original software code, breaking the backward binary compatibility.

In this work we propose a novel design flow to build a reconfigurable ASIP. We use as a case study a reconfigurable architecture that already shows good speedups on a set of applications with heterogeneous behaviors [6]. Originally, this approach exploits, at run-time, the whole application code aiming to build configurations targeted to the reconfigurable data path execution. However, the dynamic detection is not energy-efficient, since the entire application code must go through this process at run time, and only a small part of all the built configurations are accelerated in the reconfigurable data path. Hence, in this work we create a design time step to explore the application code aiming to create custom instructions regarding only the most executed application kernels. In this way, power savings are achieved after chip development by maintaining the dynamic detection hardware off when not used. For that, an ASIP hardware builder was developed to create a customized reconfigurable data path considering only the most executed applications kernels, reducing the area occupied. Moreover, to deal with the reconfigurable architecture power consumption, the Sleep Transistor technique was coupled to the ASIP design decreasing the power to feasible values for embedded systems.

Similar to [12], our design flow is divided into 2 phases: Simulation Phase and Execution Phase. As explained before, in the first phase a simulation environment was developed to exploit the execution behavior of a given application. This simulator reproduces, in a high level description language, the dynamic detection/translation hardware behavior proposed in [13]. The first phase offers to the designer easy manipulation of the ASIP characteristics, like power, area and application speedup. The Execution Phase is only activated when the consumer downloads a new application in the embedded device. When the new application is ready to execute, the dynamic detection/translation hardware is turned on to accelerate the new application code. In this phase, in contrast with other approaches, there is no human intervention, and no changes in the original code are necessary, making this process totally transparent to both the designer and the consumer.

3   Reconfigurable Architecture

The reconfigurable hardware is tightly coupled to a MIPS R3000 processor, so no external accesses (relative to the core) are necessary. The architecture is divided in three groups of simple functional units, as shown in Figure 1:

1. Formed by arithmetic and logic units (for the execution of instructions like sums, shifts and so on);
2. Composed by load/store units;
3. Responsible for executing multiplication instructions.

There are different execution times among these groups. They can vary depending on the employed technology and the way the functional units were implemented. In this case study, up to three operations that are part of the group 1 can be performed within one level, which represents one equivalent cycle of the processor. In the second and third group, a single operation needs one level to be completed (supposing that there are no cache misses). It is important to highlight that the reconfigurable data path does not support floating-point or divisions operations yet.

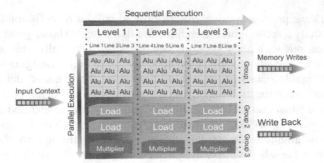

Fig. 1. Reconfigurable Architecture Hardware

Connections between these functional units are made by multiplexers, which are responsible for the routing of the operands. The input multiplexers route the sources operands from input context to the functional unit. The output multiplexer routes the target operand to the output context to make the memory writes and registers update.

4   Reconfigurable ASIP Structure

The reconfigurable ASIP design flow is divided in two phases: Simulation Phase and Execution Phase, as shown in Figure 2. The first phase is done during design time while the reconfigurable ASIP is created, based on a given application set. The second phase is enabled just when an application not foreseen at design time is detected, after the ASIP hardware was designed.

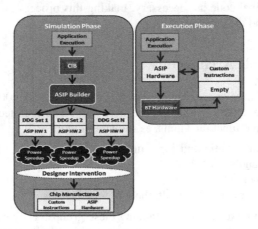

Fig. 2. The complete design flow of reconfigurable ASIP

4.1   Simulation Phase

The first phase is responsible for two tasks: design space exploration aiming to create custom instructions based on the application execution in a high level simulator; and the modeling of an optimized architecture taking into account these generated instructions. The tool explores the application execution and detects which application parts have more influence on the total execution time. After that, the tool makes a design space exploration, by combining these kernels in sets and evaluating the actual speedup and power consumption provided by the reconfigurable approach for each of them. Thus, the designer is able to choose, at an early design stage, which kernel set best fits in the design constraints and, consequently, which one should be translated to custom instructions.

The whole process is illustrated in Figure 2, and works as follows:

• The CIB (Custom Instruction Builder) explores the execution and builds the applications kernels (sequence of instructions) that have more impact on the total execution time. An example of kernel is shown in Figure 3(a). The CIB software description follows the same behavior of the binary translation (BT) hardware previously developed [13]. The BT algorithm is based on tables and bitmaps, which are used to verify the dependences between the instructions, and to provide the necessary information to fire and finalize a reconfigurable execution. Basically, for each incoming instruction, the first task is the verification of RAW (Read After Write) dependences. The current instruction source operands are compared to a bitmap of target registers of each vertical data path line (Figure 1), starting with the leftmost one. This instruction can be placed in a vertical line of reconfigurable data path, if the present line and all lines positioned on its right side do not already have instructions that contain RAW dependences with the current instruction. When a line that respects the dependences constraints is found, the algorithm seeks for one idle functional unit in a row as high as possible, depending on the group, as explained before.

• The ASIP Builder receives all kernels previously found from the CIB block and makes its Data Dependence Graph (DDG). A DDG example of the kernel illustrated in Figure 3(a) is shown in Figure 3(b). Considering the relevancy of each DDG over the entire execution time, in this stage the tool makes a design space exploration producing many DDG sets, each one composed by a different number of DDG. After that, the ASIP Builder exploits the available parallelism of each DDG set and builds a particular ASIP hardware, as shown in Figure 2, composed by the minimum number of functional units that can exploit the maximum available parallelism of the entire DDG set as possible. Finally, based on the previous data, the DDG set the tool calculates the actual ASIP hardware speedup and estimates the power consumption, by using libraries and the amount of nodes switching.

• At this moment the design exploration tool has completed its work. Now, with the speedup and power consumption estimates, the designer is able to choose which DDG Set and ASIP Hardware best fit considering design requirements and constraints. In this way, the selected DDG set is translated to custom instructions to be executed in the manufactured ASIP Hardware. The custom instructions can be stored in a non-volatile memory placed inside the processor core.

4.1.1 ASIP Hardware Building

To better explain the process, an example of an ASIP hardware built from only one DDG is shown in Figure 3(c), remembering that it was obtained from a DDG set. The ASIP Builder analyzes the dependences between the instructions in the DDG and

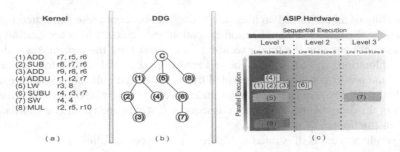

Fig. 3. ASIP simulation phase considering only one DDG

allocates functional units to exploit the maximum parallelism offered by the graph. As it can be observed in Figure 3(b), the instructions *1*, *5* and *8* can be executed at the same time, since there is no data dependence between them (Figure 3(a)). Thus, the ASIP Builder places three functional units in the first line of the ASIP hardware to support their execution, as shown in Figure 3(c). However, instructions *2* and *4* depend on instruction *1*, and cannot be placed in the first line. The ASIP Builder detects that and allocates two functional units in the second line for their execution. The same fact occurs with instruction *3* that depends on the instruction *2*. This way, the ASIP Builder places a functional unit in the third line to ensure data consistency. On the other hand, instruction *6* depends on the *load* instruction *5*, and must wait for the end of this instruction execution. Thus, the ASIP Builder places a functional unit in the fourth line, the line after of that load instruction. The firing of instruction number *7* must wait for the execution end of instruction number *6*. Thus, a functional unit is allocated in the line 7 to execute it, since that line corresponds to the next available line of this particular type of functional unit. In contrast, there are no data dependences regarding instruction number *8*, meaning that a functional unit can be placed in the first line to execute it. Figure 3(c) illustrates that the ASIP Builder only allocates the necessary functional units to explore the maximum DDG parallelism, improving energy savings and reducing silicon area.

4.2   Execution Phase

In the execution phase, when the ASIP has already been manufactured, eventually a new application could be loaded. In this phase, the dynamic reconfiguration works as an accelerator, using the same ASIP data path structure previously built. When a new application is detected, the binary translation hardware, shown in Figure 2, is turned on. It is responsible to build, at execution time, configurations to be stored into a volatile memory, labeled as *Empty* in Figure 2. Thus, the approach can achieve speedups for software which execution was unknown at design time. This means that it is able to accelerate any kind of software after the chip was manufactured. Consequently, there is no need for human intervention to make changes in the code, which sustains binary compatibility. As a result, the time to market of new application software has not been affected, unlike other approaches.

4.3 Sleep Transistor

As another contribution of this work, we coupled the CIB mechanism with Sleep transistors to create a low power reconfigurable ASIP hardware. As explained before, the main work of CIB is detecting, at design time, feasible DDG sets to be executed into the reconfigurable ASIP hardware. Therefore, we can take advantage of the CIB design time exploration to turn off unused reconfigurable blocks using Sleep Transistors.

In our study, we used a functional unit grain to switch the power off using Sleep Transistors. Figure 4 shows the schematic block diagram of one functional unit coupled to Sleep Transistors. The area overhead to build the low power architecture is of only two transistors for each functional unit. The bits that control these transistors are reused from the bits of each custom instruction (or configurations, considering dynamic detection), and hence there is almost no area overhead to control this technique.

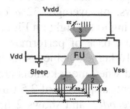

Fig. 4. Schematic of a Functional Unit using a Sleep Transistor Technique

The circuit works as follows:

• The CIB detects an instruction, at design time, and allocates it on a reconfigurable functional unit; at this moment, the sleep transistor bits in the custom instruction that represent this FU are set to the on state;

• When a custom instruction is executed into the reconfigurable architecture, all functional units with sleep transistors that have not been allocated to an instruction are kept on the off state.

When the functional units with Sleep Transistors are set to the off state, the power supply is not present in this block, and hence there is no leakage power consumption, as can be observed in Figure 4. In addition, these functional units do not dissipate dynamic power, because the switching bits in the input are not taken into account, since Vdd is not present.

5 Results

To evaluate the viability of the proposed approach, an application workload was created aiming to simulate an actual environment of a current cell phone. The applications set was extracted from MiBench, composed by: *gsm encode/decode*; *sha*; *jpeg decode*; *susan (edges,corners,smoothing)*, *stringsearch*.

First, we characterize the behavior of the chosen application workload. The *stringsearch* application is the most control flow one, showing, on average, only 5 sequential instructions executed between jumps in the code. In contrast, the *gsm_encoder* shows, in average, almost 16 sequential instructions executed between jumps, demonstrating the data flow behavior of this application, proving that this specific application subset covers a large range of different software behaviors.

The application subset was applied to the proposed ASIP design flow. As already explained, the design flow analyses all applications and generates many DDG sets and their respective ASIP hardware, allowing the design space exploration. In this way, the designer indicates which DDG set and ASIP Hardware that will be manufactured, considering the design constraints. For these experiments we generated seven DDG sets, varying the number of DDGs that composes each set, from 1 to 64, as shown in Figure 5. These DDGs are the most significant kernels extracted from the application execution.

The Figure 5 shows the speedup provided by reconfigurable ASIP Hardware in all DDG sets. The speedup is normalized by the MIPS standalone execution. Regarding the DDG set of the Figure 5, in the one next to the MIPS processor, which is composed by only one kernel, the approach has reduced by half the execution time of the *smoothing* application and shows, on average, 32% of performance improvement considering all applications. Moving to the right on Figure 5, a DDG set composed by four kernels achieves, on average, 63% of performance improvement. Considering *sha*, the DDG set composed by 16 kernels achieves its highest speedup (four times), thus no further gains are obtained when more kernels are included. Finally, the DDG set composed by 64 kernels presents a speedup of 2.5 times in most applications (*sha*, *gsm_encoder*, *smoothing*, *jpeg_decode*), and shows 2 times speedup in two applications (*gsm_decoder* and *string*).

Corners and *edges* did not follow the other applications speedup and achieved 85% of performance improvement in this case. A study of these two last applications was done to verify the difference in performance improvement when compared with other applications. It was concluded that, because of their control flow behavior, there is a large amount of kernels inside of these applications, and a total of 2048 kernels are necessary to present the ideal performance using the proposed technique. Ideal performance means the potential of the ASIP exploration when a DDG set is composed by all applications kernels. It can be noticed in the rightmost side of Figure 5 that in all applications, the DDG set composed by 64 kernels can come close to the ideal performance, showing that the design space exploration technique during design time is very effective.

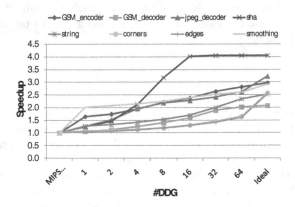

Fig. 5. Speedup provided by ASIP hardware in all DDG sets

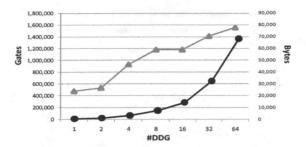

Fig. 6. Area occupied by ASIP hardware and custom instructions storage

Figure 6 illustrates the area occupied by the ASIP hardware and DDG storage for the DDG sets shown in Figure 5. The right axis scale and the dark line with the circle marker represent the area spent, in bytes, by the DDG set storage. The left axis scale and the gray line with the triangle marker illustrate the area occupied, in gates, by the reconfigurable ASIP hardware. Considering the DDG set composed by 4 kernels, to store their configuration bits one needs only 3 KB for all applications. The ASIP hardware produced by the design flow for this DDG set consumes 931.518 gates. According to [15], in 1996 the total number of transistors of the MIPS R10000 was of 2.4 million, which means approximately 600.000 gates. This fact shows the feasibility to employ such approach in nowadays CMOS technologies. Another important fact is shown in Figure 6. Due the same instruction level parallelism found in all applications, the hardware necessary to employ the ASIP hardware for 8 and 16 instructions is the same, meaning that one can achieve, on average, more 23% of performance improvements (Figure 5) with only 6.8KB of area overhead to store eight more DDGs.

The energy consumption of the application workload is shown in Figure 7. The leftmost side of this Figure illustrates the energy of the standalone MIPS processor executing all applications. The remaining items of the Figure illustrate the energy consumption of MIPS R3000 coupled to ASIP Hardware regarding different number of DDGs. As it can be observed, the energy consumption of the proposed approach is lower than the MIPS processor standalone. Three facts clarify this behavior: one avoids accesses to the instruction memory, since the custom instructions are stored in a special cache inside of the core; lower execution time thanks to the maximum parallelism exploited by the ASIP hardware; and the Sleep Transistor technique, turning off unused hardware parts. Figure 7 shows that when more DDGs are translated, more energy is saved. This fact is explained by the increasing acceleration shown in Figure 5. Considering DDG set composed by 16 DDGs the approach saves, on average, 62% for all applications increasing this value to 67% regarding 64 DDGs.

Up to this moment, all the results reproduce a design space exploration aiming to model an ASIP hardware to be manufactured. Now, after the chip has been shipped, one can simulate the second design flow phase (Execution Phase of Figure 2). By inserting two new applications not foreseen at design time one can verify the ability of the proposed ASIP to adapt to new applications that could be downloaded in the

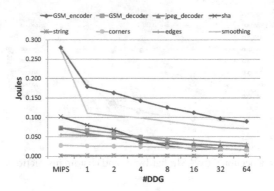

Fig. 7. Energy consumption of the proposed approach and the MIPS standalone

embedded device. The applications chosen were *mpeg_decoder* and an *mp3_decoder* from Mediabench. Both applications were executed in an already developed ASIP hardware built from the previous design exploration (Simulation Phase of Figure 2) already shown. All the results consider 32 dynamic slots for dynamic configurations (empty place in Figure 2), which means 31KB of area overhead over the previous area results shown in Figure 6. For example, to build an ASIP Hardware composed by 4 DDGs the approach spends 31 KB for dynamic slots and 6.8 KB for the custom instructions storage.

The speedup that the reconfigurable ASIP hardware shows for these new applications is illustrated in Table 1. As it can be observed, even without knowledge of the applications at design time, the proposed approach achieves speedups in these applications thanks to the adaptability of the BT hardware. Simulating the execution of the new applications over the already shipped ASIP composed by only one custom instruction, *mpeg_decoder* achieves 95% of performance improvement compared to the MIPS processor standalone execution. For *mp3_decoder,* the dynamic accelerator reaches 44% of performance improvement using the same ASIP hardware. The ideal performance, shown in the first column of Table 1, illustrates the speedup provided if a specific ASIP hardware had been built to execute these applications reflecting the speedup of the Simulation Phase of our approach. As it can be observed, the dynamic accelerator achieves almost the ideal performance in both applications, even when executing them on an ASIP hardware built to other applications.

Like in the previous energy results, the ASIP hardware also decreases the energy consumption of the new applications, even taking into account the dynamic detection hardware power. As shown in Table 2, the energy of *mpeg_decoder* decreases

Table 1. Speedup of ASIP hardware on unknown application execution

	Speedup				
	Ideal Performance	1 Custom Instruction Hardware	4 Custom Instruction Hardware	16 Custom Instruction Hardware	64 Custom Instruction Hardware
mp3_decoder	1.962	1.439	1.462	1.463	1.482
mpeg_decoder	2.462	1.953	1.977	1.977	1.977

Table 2. Energy consumption of ASIP hardware in unknown application execution

		Energy Consumption (Joules)			
	MIPS	1 Custom Instruction Hardware	4 Custom Instruction Hardware	16 Custom Instruction Hardware	64 Custom Instruction Hardware
mp3_decoder	0.0109	0.0074	0.0074	0.0074	0.0073
mpeg_decoder	1.7837	0.8545	0.8515	0.8515	0.8515

53% compared to the MIPS standalone execution, and 37% of energy consumption is obtained for the *mp3_decoder* execution. The results show that the approach provides speedups for applications unknown during design time and, at the same time, saves energy compared to the standalone MIPS execution.

6 Conclusions and Future Works

As the complexity and versatility of embedded systems continue to grow, their fabrication costs also increase. In this scenario, new acceleration techniques must be sought, aiming at providing low cost, low energy, high performance circuits also for applications that are not completely specified at design time. This paper has shown a design technique for ASIPs covering such challenges. The mixed static and dynamic mechanism takes into account a set of applications, but is able to provide acceleration and lower energy consumption also for applications not foreseen at design time.

References

1. Tsarchopoulos, P.: European Research in Embedded Systems. In: Proceeding of Embedded Computer Systems: Architectures, Modeling, and Simulation, pp. 2–4 (July 2006)
2. Venkataramani, G., Najjar, W., Kurdahi, F., Bagherzadeh, N., Bohm, W.: A compiler framework for mapping applications to a coarse-grained reconfigurable computer architecture. In: Proceedings of the 2001 international Conference on Compilers, Architecture, and Synthesis For Embedded Systems. CASES 2001, pp. 116–125. ACM, New York (2001)
3. Lysecky, R., Stitt, G., Vahid, F.: Warp Processors. In: Proceedings of the 41st Annual Conference on Design Automation. DAC 2004, pp. 659–681. ACM, New York (2004)
4. Hauser, J.R., Wawrzynek, J.: Garp: a MIPS processor with a reconfigurable coprocessor. In: Proceedings of the 5th IEEE Symposium on Fpga-Based Custom Computing Machines. FCCM, p. 12. IEEE Computer Society, Washington
5. Patel, S.J., Lumetta, S.S.: rePLay: A Hardware Framework for Dynamic Optimization. IEEE Trans. Comput. 50(6), 590–608 (2001)
6. Beck, A.C.S., Rutzig, M.B., Gaydadjiev, G., Carro, L.: Transparent Reconfigurable Acceleration for Heterogeneous Embedded Applications. In: Design, Automation and Test in Europe, 2008. DATE 2008, March 10-14, pp. 1208–1213 (2008); Yeager, K.C.: The MIPS R10000 Superscalar Microprocessor. IEEE Micro 16(2), 28–40 (1996)
7. Shi, K., Howard, D.: Challenges in sleep transistor design and implementation in low-power designs. In: Proceedings of the 43rd Annual Conference on Design Automation. DAC 2006, pp. 113–116. ACM, New York (2006)

8. Huang, I., Despain, A.M.: Generating instruction sets and microarchitectures from applications. In: Proceedings of the 1994 IEEE/ACM international Conference on Computer-Aided Design. International Conference on Computer Aided Design, pp. 391–396. IEEE Computer Society Press, Los Alamitos (1994)

9. Clark, N., Tang, W., Mahlke, S.: Automatically generating Custom instruction set extensions. In: Workshop of Application-Specific Processors (2002)

10. Clark, N., Zhong, H., Mahlke, S.: Processor Acceleration Through Automated Instruction Set Customization. In: Proceedings of the 36th Annual IEEE/ACM international Symposium on Microarchitecture. International Symposium on Microarchitecture, p. 129. IEEE Computer Society, Washington

11. Hauck, S., Fry, T.W., Hosler, M.M., Kao, J.P.: The chimaera reconfigurable functional unit. IEEE Trans. Very Large Scale Integr. Syst. 12(2), 206–217

12. Chattopadhyay, A., Ahmed, W., Karuri, K., Kammler, D., Leupers, R., Ascheid, G., Meyr, H.: Design space exploration of partially re-configurable embedded processors. In: Proceedings of the Conference on Design, Automation and Test in Europe. Design, Automation, and Test in Europe, San Jose, CA, pp. 319–324

13. Beck, A.C., Carro, L.: Dynamic reconfiguration with binary translation: breaking the ILP barrier with software compatibility. In: Proceedings of the 42nd Annual Conference on Design Automation. DAC 2005, pp. 732–737. ACM, New York (2005)

14. http://www.arm.com/products/CPUs/ARM1176.html

15. Yeager, K.C.: The Mips R10000 Superscalar Microprocessor. IEEE Micro, 28–40 (April 1996)

Fast Optical Reconfiguration of a Nine-Context DORGA

Mao Nakajima and Minoru Watanabe

Electrical and Electronic Engineering
Shizuoka University
3-5-1 Johoku, Hamamatsu, Shizuoka 432-8561, Japan
tmwatan@ipc.shizuoka.ac.jp

Abstract. Demand for fast dynamic reconfiguration has increased since dynamic reconfiguration can accelerate the performance of implementation circuits. Such dynamic reconfiguration requires two important features: fast reconfiguration and numerous contexts. However, fast reconfigurations and numerous contexts share a trade-off relation on current VLSIs. Therefore, optically reconfigurable gate arrays (ORGAs) have been developed to resolve this dilemma. ORGAs can realize a large virtual gate count that is much larger than those of current VLSI chips by exploiting the large storage capacity of a holographic memory. Also, ORGAs can realize fast reconfiguration through use of large bandwidth optical connections between a holographic memory and a programmable gate array VLSI. Among such developments, we have been developing dynamic optically reconfigurable gate arrays (DORGAs) that realize a high gate density VLSI using a photodiode memory architecture. This paper presents the first demonstration of a nine-context DORGA architecture. Furthermore, this paper presents experimental results: 1.2-8.97 μs reconfiguration times and 66-221 μs retention times.

1 Introduction

Demand for high-speed reconfigurable devices has continued to increase. If a gate array can be reconfigured rapidly, idle circuits can be removed from the gate array. Then other necessary circuits can be programmed onto the gate array, thereby increasing the overall gate array activity. However, major programmable devices, FPGAs, have been shown to be unsuitable for such dynamic reconfiguration uses because FPGAs require more than several milliseconds' reconfiguration time [1]–[3].

On the other hand, high-speed reconfigurable devices have been developed, e.g., DAP/DNA chips, DRP chips, and multi-context FPGAs [4]–[9]. They package reconfiguration memories and a microprocessor array or gate array onto a chip. The internal reconfiguration memory stores reconfiguration contexts of 4–16 banks, which can be changed from one to another during a clock cycle. Consequently, the arithmetic logic unit or gate array of such devices can be reconfigured on every clock cycle in a few nanoseconds. However, increasing the internal reconfiguration memory while maintaining the gate density is extremely difficult.

As with other rapidly reconfigurable devices, optically reconfigurable gate arrays (ORGAs) have been developed that combine a holographic memory and an optically

J. Becker et al. (Eds.): ARC 2009, LNCS 5453, pp. 123–132, 2009.
© Springer-Verlag Berlin Heidelberg 2009

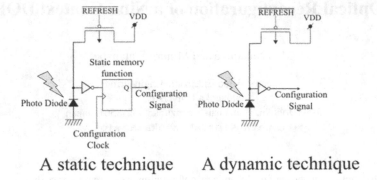

A static technique   A dynamic technique

Fig. 1. Schematic diagrams of optical reconfiguration circuits: a conventional circuit with static configuration memory and a DORGA circuit without static configuration memory

programmable gate array VLSI [10]–[12]. Contexts of the gate array are stored in a holographic memory, can be read out optically and can be programmed optically onto the gate array VLSI using photodiodes. Such ORGA architectures present the possibility of providing a virtual gate count that is much larger than those of currently available VLSIs. However, although a large virtual gate count can be realized using the large storage capacity of a holographic memory, the actual gate count— the gate count of a gate array VLSI—remains important for increasing the instantaneous performance of ORGAs. Nevertheless, the real gates of conventional ORGA-VLSIs are too few. For example, the gate counts of optically programmable gate array VLSIs [10]–[12], optically differential reconfigurable gate array VLSIs [13],[14], and latch-type ORGAs [15],[16] are, respectively, 80, 68–272, and 476–16,799 gates. The reason for their small size is that static configuration memory, as shown on the left side of Fig. 1, to store a single configuration context, occupies a large implementation area of the ORGA-VLSIs. Therefore, to realize a high-gate-count ORGA-VLSI, Dynamic Optically Reconfigurable Gate Arrays (DORGAs) were proposed: they use the junction capacitance of photodiodes as dynamic memory, as depicted on the right side of Fig. 1, thereby obviating the static configuration memory [17]. A 26,350 gate count DORGA-VLSI [18] and a 51,272 gate count DORGA-VLSI [19],[20] have been reported. In addition, to date, a DORGA architecture with four configuration contexts has been demonstrated and a 770 ns holographic configuration and $11.3\mu s$ retention time have been reported [22]. This paper presents a more advanced demonstration of a nine-context DORGA architecture. The demonstration confirmed 1.2-$8.97\mu s$ reconfiguration capability and a 66-$221\mu s$ retention capability of this architecture.

2   Hologram Generation and Simulation

2.1   Hologram Calculation

Here, a hologram for DORGAs is assumed as a thin holographic medium. A laser aperture plane, a holographic plane, and a DORGA-VLSI plane are parallelized. The laser

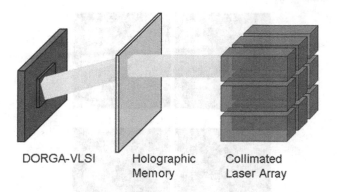

DORGA-VLSI   Holographic   Collimated
                  Memory   Laser Array

Fig. 2. Overview of a nine-context DORGA

beam is expanded. It is assumed that the aperture size is sufficiently wide for the holographic medium. Consequently, the laser beam can be considered as a plane wave. The reference wave from the laser propagates into the holographic plane. The holographic medium comprises rectangular pixels on the $x_1 - y_1$ holographic plane. The pixels are assumed as analog values. On the other hand, the input object is made up of rectangular pixels on the $x_2 - y_2$ object plane. The pixels can be modulated to be either on or off. The intensity distribution of a holographic medium is calculable using the following equation.

$$H(x_1, y_1) \propto \int_{-\infty}^{\infty} \int_{-\infty}^{\infty} O(x_2, y_2) \sin(kr) dx_2 dy_2,$$

$$r = \sqrt{Z_L^2 + (x_1 - x_2)^2 + (y_1 - y_2)^2}.$$

$$(1)$$

In that equation, $O(x_2, y_2)$ is a binary value of a reconfiguration context, k is the wave number, and Z_L represents the distance between the holographic plane and the object plane. The value $H(x_1, y_1)$ is normalized as 0–1 for minimum intensity H_{min} and maximum intensity H_{max} as the following.

$$H'(x_1, y_1) = \frac{H(x_1, y_1) - H_{min}}{H_{max} - H_{min}}.$$

$$(2)$$

Finally, the normalized image H' is used for implementing the holographic memory. Other areas on the holographic plane are opaque to the illumination.

2.2 Hologram Generation and Simulation

A nine-context holographic memory pattern was calculated using Eqs. 1 and 2, as shown in Fig. 3(g). Each parameter was selected to fit the experimental system explained in later sections. A liquid crystal spatial light modulator (LC-SLM) was used as a holographic memory. The resolution of the target LC-SLM is $8.5 \times 8.5 \ \mu m^2$. Although the

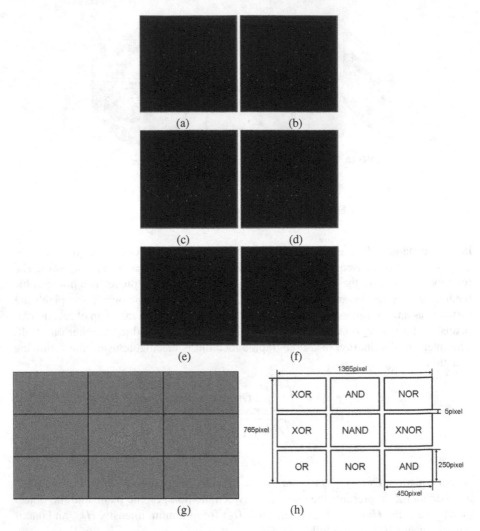

Fig. 3. Simulation results of a nine-context holographic memory pattern. Panels (a), (c), and (e) respectively depict context patterns of NAND, NOR, and AND circuits. Panel (g) shows a calculated nine-context holographic memory pattern. Panel (h) depicts a map of configuration contexts stored on the nine-context holographic memory. Panels (b), (d), and (f) respectively portray simulation results of diffraction patterns from the holographic memory of NAND, NOR, and AND circuits.

LC-SLM has 256 gradations, the intensity distribution of the holographic memory was normalized to 128 gradations to use the linearization range of the LC-SLM. Figures 3(a), 3(c), and 3(e) respectively portray context patterns of NAND, NOR, and AND circuits. Figure 3(h) shows a map of the configuration contexts stored on the nine-context holographic memory. The number of pixels of each recording area including one reconfiguration context is 450 × 250. The number of pixels of the interval between recording areas is 5. Therefore, the total number of the entire holographic memory pattern is 1365 × 765. Figures 3(b), 3(d), and 3(f) respectively portray simulation results of diffraction patterns from the holographic memories of NAND, NOR, and AND circuits. The good contrast of diffraction patterns from the holographic memory was confirmed from results of the simulations. The holographic memory pattern shown in Fig. 3(g) is used in later experiments.

3 Experimental System

Figure 4(a) presents a DORGA holographic reconfiguration system. Figures 4(b) and 4(c) show photographs of the experimental system. The DORGA holographic

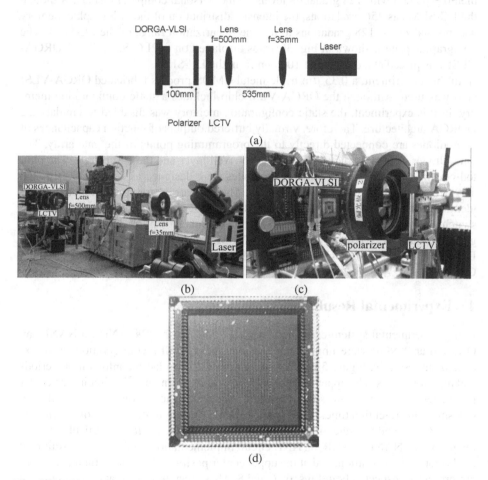

Fig. 4. Experimental system. Panel (a) shows an entire DORGA holographic reconfiguration system. Panel (b) depicts a photograph of the experimental system. Panel (c) portrays an expanded photograph of the experimental system around an emulated DORGA-VLSI. Panel (d) presents a 0.35μm CMOS process emulated DORGA-VLSI chip.

reconfiguration system was constructed using a laser—a 532 nm, 300 mW laser (torus 532; Laser Quantum)—a liquid crystal spatial light modulator (LC-SLM) as a holographic memory, and an emulated DORGA-VLSI. The beam from the laser source, the diameter of which is 1.7 mm, is expanded four times to 24.3 mm using two lenses of 35 mm focal length and 500 mm focal length. The expanded beam is incident to a holographic memory on an LC-SLM. The LC-SLM is a projection TV panel (L3D07U-81G00; Seiko Epson Corp.). It is a 90° twisted nematic device with a thin film transistor. The panel consists of 1920×1080 pixels, each having a size of $8.5 \times 8.5 \ \mu m^2$. The LC-SLM is connected to an evaluation board (L3B07-E60A; Seiko Epson Corp.). The video input of the board is connected to the external display terminal of a personal computer. Programming for the LC-SLM is executed by displaying a green holographic memory pattern with 128 gradation levels on the personal computer display. Although the LC-SLM has 256 gradations, the intensity distribution of the holographic memory was normalized to 128 gradations to use the linearization range of the LC-SLM. The holographic pattern shown in Fig. 3(g) was displayed on the LC-SLM. The DORGA-VLSI was placed at a distance of 100 mm from the LC-SLM.

In this experiment, a 0.35 μm triple-metal CMOS process fabricated ORGA-VLSI chip was used. Although the ORGA-VLSI chip includes a static configuration memory, in this experiment, the static configuration memory was disabled to emulate the DORGA architecture. Therefore, virtually buffered outputs of junction capacitances of photodiodes are connected directly to the programming points of the gate array. The photodiodes were constructed between the N-Well layer and the P-substrate. The photodiode size and distance between photodiodes were designed as $25.5 \times 25.5 \mu m$ and as $90\mu m$ to facilitate the optical alignment. The gate array structure is fundamentally identical to that of typical FPGAs. The ORGA-VLSI chip includes 4 logic blocks, 5 switching matrices, and 12 I/O bits. The total number of photodiodes used to program the gate array is 340. The DORGA-VLSI chip was controlled using a Digital Delay/Pulse Generator (DG535; Stanford Research Systems) and an FPGA (Altera Corp.).

4 Experimental Results

Using experimental system explained previously, XORs, NORs, ANDs, a NAND, an OR, and an XNOR were implemented on the system. All reconfigurations were executed successfully. Figure 5 portrays reconfiguration results: reconfiguration periods and retention times. The upper letter of each box shows the name of a circuit. The center parameter of each box shows the reconfiguration time. The bottom parameter of each box shows the retention time. It was confirmed that reconfiguration times of the circuits are 1.2-8.97μs and that retention times of the circuits are 66-221μs. In particular, timing diagrams of a NAND, a NOR, an AND circuit implementations at the center position, at the bottom center position, and at the upper center position of the holographic memory are presented respectively in Figs. 6, 7, and 8. These results show that each circuit can be reconfigured in an extremely short time. Moreover, these results clarified that the photodiode memory function can retain its state for a longer time than the reconfiguration time. Consequently, the availability of the nine-context DORGA architecture was demonstrated.

XOR	AND	NOR
7.92 μs	4.69 μs	8.97 μs
133 μs	221 μs	173.8 μs

XOR	NAND	XNOR
6.35 μs	1.2 μs	8.46 μs
133 μs	66 μs	143.8 μs

OR	NOR	AND
7.31 μs	3.46 μs	6.62 μs
131.5 μs	107.3 μs	181.8 μs

Configured circuit
Reconfiguration time
Hold time

Fig. 5. Experimental results of the reconfiguration time and retention time for each recording area on the holographic medium. The upper letter of each box shows the circuit name. The center parameter of each box shows the reconfiguration time. The bottom parameter of each box shows the retention time. It was confirmed that reconfiguration times of the circuits are 1.2-8.97μs and that retention times of the circuits are 66-221μs.

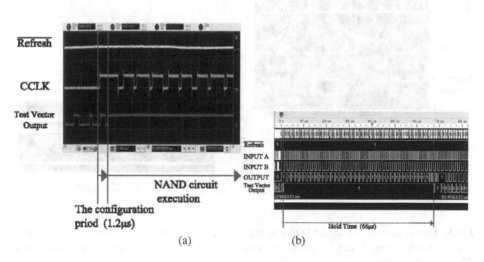

(a)   (b)

Fig. 6. Timing diagram of a NAND circuit implementation at the center position of the holographic memory. Panels (a) and (b) respectively show a 1.2μs reconfiguration time and a 66μs retention time.

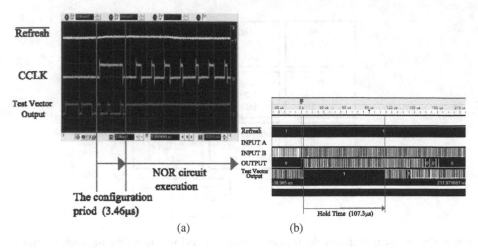

Fig. 7. Timing diagram of a NOR circuit implementation at the bottom center position of the holographic memory. Panels (a) and (b) respectively show a $3.46\mu s$ reconfiguration time and a $107.3\mu s$ retention time.

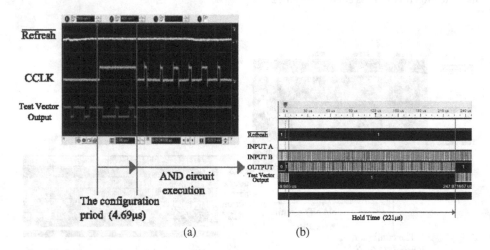

Fig. 8. Timing diagram of an AND circuit implementation at the upper center position of the holographic memory. Panels (a) and (b) respectively show a $4.69\mu s$ reconfiguration time and a $221\mu s$ retention time.

5   Conclusion

Earlier reports of the literature describe a DORGA architecture with four configuration contexts and a 770 ns holographic configuration with $11.3\mu s$ retention time. This paper has presented a more advanced demonstration of a nine-context DORGA architecture. Results show that reconfiguration times of 1.2-$8.97\mu s$ and retention times of 66-$221\mu s$ were confirmed experimentally. The reconfiguration time is sufficiently faster than those of currently available FPGAs. In addition, retention times are sufficiently long compared to the reconfiguration time. The availability of the nine-context DORGA architecture was clarified by results of this study.

Acknowledgments

This research was supported by the Ministry of Education, Science, Sports and Culture, Grant-in-Aid for Scientific Research on Innovative Areas, No. 20200027, 2008. The VLSI chip in this study was fabricated in the chip fabrication program of VLSI Design and Education Center (VDEC), the University of Tokyo in collaboration with Rohm Co. Ltd. and Toppan Printing Co. Ltd.

References

1. Altera Corporation, Altera Devices, http://www.altera.com
2. Xilinx Inc., Xilinx Product Data Sheets, http://www.xilinx.com
3. Lattice Semiconductor Corporation, LatticeECP and EC Family Data Sheet (2005), http://www.latticesemi.co.jp/products
4. http://www.ipflex.co.jp
5. Nakano, H., Shindo, T., Kazami, T., Motomura, M.: Development of dynamically reconfigurable processor LSI. NEC Tech. J (Japan) 56(4), 99–102 (2003)
6. Dehon, A.: Dynamically Programmable Gate Arrays: A Step Toward Increased Computational Density. In: Fourth Canadian Workshop on Field Programmable Devices, pp. 47–54 (1996)
7. Scalera, S.M., Vazquez, J.R.: The design and implementation of a context switching FPGA. In: IEEE symposium on FPGAs for Custom Computing Machines, pp. 78–85 (1998)
8. Trimberger, S., et al.: A Time–Multiplexed FPGA. In: FCCM, pp. 22–28 (1997)
9. Jones, D., Lewis, D.M.: A time–multiplexed FPGA architecture for logic emulation. In: Custom Integrated Circuits Conference, pp. 495–498 (1995)
10. Mumbru, J., Panotopoulos, G., Psaltis, D., An, X., Mok, F., Ay, S., Barna, S., Fossum, E.: Optically Programmable Gate Array. In: SPIE of Optics in Computing 2000, vol. 4089, pp. 763–771 (2000)
11. Mumbru, J., Zhou, G., An, X., Liu, W., Panotopoulos, G., Mok, F., Psaltis, D.: Optical memory for computing and information processing. In: SPIE on Algorithms, Devices, and Systems for Optical Information Processing III, vol. 3804, pp. 14–24 (1999)
12. Mumbru, J., Zhou, G., Ay, S., An, X., Panotopoulos, G., Mok, F., Psaltis, D.: Optically Reconfigurable Processors. In: SPIE Critical Review 1999 Euro-American Workshop on Optoelectronic Information Processing, vol. 74, pp. 265–288 (1999)
13. Watanabe, M., Kobayashi, F.: An Optically Differential Reconfigurable Gate Array using a 0.18 um CMOS process. In: IEEE International SOC Conference, pp. 281–284 (2004)
14. Watanabe, M., Shiki, T., Kobayashi, F.: 272 gate count optically differential reconfigurable gate array VLSI. In: International Conference on engineering of reconfigurable systems and algorithms (2007) (CD-ROM)
15. Watanabe, M., Kobayashi, F.: An optical reconfiguration circuit for optically reconfigurable Gate Arrays. In: 2004 IEEE International Midwest Symposium on Circuits and Systems, pp. I-529–I-532 (2004)

16. Watanabe, M., Kobayashi, F.: A 16,000-gate-count Optically Reconfigurable Gate Array in a standard 0.35um CMOS Technology. In: IEEE International Symposium on Circuits and Systems (2005)
17. Watanabe, M., Kobayashi, F.: A high-density optically reconfigurable gate array using dynamic method. In: International conference on Field-Programmable Logic and its Applications, pp. 261–269 (2004)
18. Watanabe, M., Kobayashi, F.: A dynamic optically reconfigurable gate array using dynamic method. In: International Workshop on Applied Reconfigurable Computing, pp. 50–58 (2005)
19. Watanabe, M., Kobayashi, F.: A 51,272-gate-count Dynamic Optically Reconfigurable Gate Array in a standard 0.35um CMOS Technology. In: International Conference on Solid State Devices and Materials, pp. 336–337 (2005)
20. Watanabe, M., Kobayashi, F.: A Dynamic Optically Reconfigurable Gate Array. Japanese Journal of Applied Physics 45(4B), 3510–3515 (2006)
21. Seto, D., Watanabe, M.: Reconfiguration performance analysis of a dynamic@optically reconfigurable gate array architecture. In: IEEE International Conference on Field Programmable Technology, pp. 265–268 (2007)
22. Nakajima, M., Watanabe, M.: A 770ns holographic reconfiguration of a four-contexts DORGA. In: International Conference on engineering of reconfigurable systems and algorithms, pp. 289–292 (July 2008)

Heterogeneous Architecture Exploration: Analysis vs. Parameter Sweep

Asma Kahoul, George A. Constantinides,
Alastair M. Smith, and Peter Y.K. Cheung

Department of Electrical & Electronic Engineering,
Imperial College London, Exhibition Road,
London SW7 2BT, United Kingdom
{a.kahoul,g.constantinides,a.smith,p.cheung}@imperial.ac.uk

Abstract. This paper argues the case for the use of analytical models in FPGA architecture layout exploration. We show that the problem when simplified, is amenable to formal optimization techniques such as integer linear programming. However, the simplification process may lead to inaccurate models. To test the overall methodology, we combine the resulting layouts with VPR 5.0. Our results show that the resulting architectures are better than those found using traditional parameter sweeping techniques.

Keywords: Floorplanning; Reconfigurable architectures; FPGA; integer linear programming (ILP).

1 Introduction

The advances in field programmable gate arrays (FPGAs) over the past decade have made it possible to place significantly large circuits on a single FPGA chip [1]. The need for estimation and optimization techniques has therefore become crucial to divide, conquer and explore the large design space of potential architectures. While there exists a significant amount of work on homogeneous architecture design, there is currently limited research on heterogeneous FPGA architectures consisting of a mix of coarse and fine grain components [2].

A commonly employed approach used to explore reconfigurable architecture layouts is to use tools such as Versatile Place and Route tool (VPR)[3]. This tool allows architects to have a baseline structure from which different architectures can be generated. These are in turn tested by placing and routing a set of designs using VPR's synthesis heuristic. The architecture that best suits one, or a combination of metrics such as area, delay, and power is thus selected [4]. While an exhaustive exploration of all possible layouts would lead to an optimal architecture, this would require excessive computational time. As a result, it is necessary to sample the design space, losing the scope for optimality.

This paper addresses the drawbacks of such parameter sweep techniques by using analytical modeling. Our framework targets column-based FPGA architectures consisting of different resource types such as CLBs, RAMs, and multipliers

J. Becker et al. (Eds.): ARC 2009, LNCS 5453, pp. 133–144, 2009.
© Springer-Verlag Berlin Heidelberg 2009

arranged in columns. This framework explores the design space of architecture layouts efficiently by modeling heterogeneous architecture layouts using mathematical programming in the form of Integer Linear Programming (ILP).

An ILP model has been used in our previous work to achieve optimal solutions to problems such as architecture layout generation [2]. The model allows the elimination of the dependencies on heuristic synthesis algorithms and provides more efficient ways to explore the design space. While the results have shown provably optimal bounds on the relative computational speed for various benchmarks, their efficiency is limited by the assumptions made and the accuracy of the model itself. Hence, if the architecture models are poor compared with empirical flows such as VPR, then the results will be meaningless. Moreover, if the optimization process is not scalable in execution time, this approach loses its attractiveness compared to a typical parameter sweep approach. This paper shows that the results of analytical formulations can be fed back to VPR to verify the quality of the designs. We demonstrate that the resulting architectures are an improvement over using VPR and parameter sweep for a fixed time budget.

The remainder of the paper is organized as follows: Sections 2 and 3 discuss related work and our proposed enhancements of previous mathematical formulations. In section 4 and 5 we describe our contribution in testing the efficiency of numerical methods by comparing it to a typical layout parameter sweeping technique.

The main contributions of this paper can be summarized as follows:

1. An enhanced formulation of the heterogeneous FPGA layout problem, leveraging advances in facility layout models from the operational research community.
2. The quantification of analytical modeling efficiency over a parameter sweep approach in the design of new FPGA architecture layouts.

2   Related Work

The development of advanced architectures and more efficient Computer Aided Design (CAD) mapping algorithms have improved the speed, area and power consumption over the past decade [1]. The introduction of hard specific circuits in heterogeneous FPGAs, for example, made it possible to execute their functions more efficiently. A recent study shows that coarse grain components can reduce the area gap between FPGAs and ASICs from 40X to 20X while preserving the gap of speed and static power consumption [5]. The main disadvantage of heterogeneous devices is that these coarse grain components are beneficial only when they are used and are a waste in silicon, area and routing otherwise [6]. Consequently, the exploration of the mix of these coarse grain components and different architecture layouts has become an interesting research subject [4].

The design of modern FPGA architecture layouts in particular is a challenging task. Exploring new FPGA architectures aims at finding an optimal non-overlapped layout of the FPGA chip by positioning circuit blocks while minimizing an objective function comprising selected performance metrics. There are many algorithms available in the literature for the floorplanning of Application-Specific Integrated Circuits (ASICs) [7]. Whereas these algorithms can be applied to homogeneous FPGAs consisting of only configurable logic blocks (CLBs), they must be modified significantly to be used with modern FPGAs.

In the absence of efficient floorplanning algorithms for heterogeneous architectures, methodologies based on parameter sweeping are currently used to design new FPGA architecture layouts. In comparison with such approaches, analytical tools offer the ability to explore a much wider design space within any given computational time budget. The analytical tool of [2], for instance, has been used in the past to produce optimal architectures within the accuracy of the formulation. However, the model suffers from its exponential time complexity with respect to the number of circuit blocks [2]. Enhanced formulations of the problem could result in reduced solution time and therefore be applied to larger circuits. As a result, we have taken advantage of the advances in the facility layout problem [8] in the aim of efficiently formulating the heterogeneous FPGA layout problem analytically.

Furthermore, ILP-based architecture exploration models suffer from their dependence on assumptions and simplifications which causes uncertainty about the efficiency of the results. On the other hand, empirical tools such VPR 5.0 offer much higher accuracy of the FPGA architectures models. In this paper, we propose a framework that combines the efficiency of the analytical tools with the accuracy of VPR 5.0. We present results showing the quality of architectures generated with our enhanced analytical model by feeding them back to VPR.

3 Heterogeneous Architecture Exploration Using an Enhanced ILP Formulation

The design of efficient heterogeneous architecture layouts using analytical tools and accurate models such as VPR is the primary aim of this paper. To achieve this, we initially describe our ILP model and investigate different bounding procedures to improve the solution time. A generic floorplanning model is constructed to test the efficiency of our enhanced formulation. Based on this model, further restrictions are added to describe the column-based nature of modern FPGAs. The resulting architectures are used in Section 5 to illustrate the efficiency of analytical techniques in exploring the design space of architecture layouts in comparison with a parameter sweep approach.

3.1 Generic Formulation of the Floorplanning Problem

This section describes the generic linear programming formulation of the layout floorplanning problem and provides the key notations used in this paper. We denote a set of n rectangular circuit blocks as B. The width and length of each block $i \in B$ are represented by w_i, h_i respectively. The floorplanning problem described in this paper is a fixed-die (fixed outline) problem in which the FPGA chip is modeled as a fixed rectangular shape of width W and height H. The locations of the blocks are determined by their centroid locations (x_i, y_i) in a two dimensional coordinate system aligned with the chip height, width, and its origin located at the south west corner of the chip.

Objective Function: Area minimization has been the main objective in traditional floorplanners [9]. However, due to the significant impact of interconnect on circuit delay caused by the rapidly increasing number of transistors and their switching speed, it has became necessary to design interconnect-based tools. Wire-length models are based on the fact that automatic routing tools use Manhattan geometry *i.e.* only vertical and horizontal wires to connect elements. The model initially optimizes the rectilinear distance between the centroid locations of connected blocks to obtain estimates of the total wire-length. The objective function is tuned with VPR 5.0 routing model in later sections to account for critical path. The wire-length optimization problem can be stated as follows:

$$
\boxed{
\begin{array}{l}
Minimize \\
\qquad Wire\text{-}length \\
subject\ to \\
\qquad Fit\ in\ the\ chip\ constraints \\
\qquad Non\text{-}Overlap\ constraints
\end{array}
}
$$

Fit in the Chip Constraints: To ensure that circuit blocks are contained within the die area, the origin (south west corner of the chip), the chip width, and its height are used as lower and upper bounds to the location of the blocks centroids as shown in inequalities (1).

$$
\forall i \in B \begin{cases} \frac{1}{2}w_i \leq x_i \leq W - \frac{1}{2}w_i \\[2mm] \frac{1}{2}h_i \leq y_i \leq H - \frac{1}{2}h_i \end{cases} \tag{1}
$$

Non-Overlap Constraints: In order to constrain the block placements and to prevent them from overlapping we apply a set of separation constraints. These constraints force the blocks to be separated either on the *x-axis* or the *y-axis* as shown in Fig. 1.

The non-overlapping constraints in either axes can be described using the following mathematical disjunctions:

$$
\left(x_i + \frac{1}{2}w_i \leq x_j - \frac{1}{2}w_j \right) \vee \left(y_i + \frac{1}{2}h_i \leq y_j - \frac{1}{2}h_j \right)
$$
$$
\vee \left(x_j + \frac{1}{2}w_j \leq x_i - \frac{1}{2}w_i \right) \vee \left(y_j + \frac{1}{2}h_j \leq y_i - \frac{1}{2}h_i \right)
$$

These disjunctions ensure separation by setting **at least** one of the inequalities to true. The difficulty in formulating these separation constraints in ILP, is the

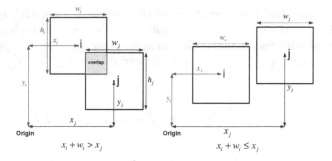

Fig. 1. Illustration of the separation constraints on the x-axis

result of introducing binary variables necessary to write the inequalities in a linear form. The most common approach to linearize a set of disjunctions is the so-called **Big-M** formulation illustrated in Equations (2).

$$Mz_{ij}^x + x_j - x_i - \frac{1}{2}w_i - \frac{1}{2}w_j \geq 0 \qquad (2a)$$

$$Mz_{ji}^x + x_i - x_j - \frac{1}{2}w_j - \frac{1}{2}w_i \geq 0 \qquad (2b)$$

$$Mz_{ij}^y + y_j - y_i - \frac{1}{2}h_i - \frac{1}{2}h_j \geq 0 \qquad (2c)$$

$$Mz_{ji}^y + y_i - y_j - \frac{1}{2}h_j - \frac{1}{2}h_i \geq 0 \qquad (2d)$$

$$z_{ij}^x + z_{ji}^x + z_{ij}^y + z_{ji}^y \leq 3 \qquad (2e)$$

$$z_{ij}^x, z_{ij}^y \in \{1, 0\}, \forall i \neq j \qquad (2f)$$

By forcing at least one of the binary variables to be zero using (2e) and (2f) we force the blocks to be separated in at least one direction. The **Big-M** formulation requires four binary variables for any pair of blocks which necessitates in total $4\binom{n}{2}$ variables. This explains the limitation of the **Big-M** formulation with regard to its exponential worst-case time complexity. Dropping the integrality constraints (LP relaxation) and solving the resulting LP problem is usually used to obtain global lower bounds on the optimal value of the problem. These are in turn used within a systematic solution technique such as the branch and bound scheme. However, this relaxation suffer tends to produce trivial bounds making the solution of the ILP problem longer to find. This motivates a tighter formulation of the floorplanning problem.

Consequently, we have taken advantage of the progress achieved in the area of disjunctive programming to obtain tighter lower bounds on the solution of the floorplanning problem which is in turn used to construct the architecture exploration framework. We aim to achieve this by adding a set of valid inequalities which capture the smallest set (convex hull) containing the feasible solutions of the disjunctions. Such a formulation should also reduce the search space for valid architectures.

Existing convex hull representations of the disjunctive constraints in [8] are constructed for variable aspect ratio problems. Since our formulation targets fixed aspect ratio blocks, we derive the corresponding convex hull representation of the disjunctions using a set of continuous variables $\forall i < j : c_{ij}^x, c_{ij}^y, \Delta_{ij}^x, \Delta_{ij}^y$ as shown in (3).

$$\frac{1}{2}(w_i + w_j)z_{ij}^x \leq c_{ij}^x \leq (W - \frac{1}{2}w_i - \frac{1}{2}w_j)z_{ij}^x, \ \forall i \neq j \tag{3}$$

$$-(W - \frac{1}{2}w_i - \frac{1}{2}w_j)(1 - z_{ij}^x - z_{ji}^x)$$

$$\leq \Delta_{ij}^x \leq (W - \frac{1}{2}w_i - \frac{1}{2}w_j)(1 - z_{ij}^x - z_{ji}^x) \tag{4}$$

$$\Delta_{ij}^x = x_j - x_i - c_{ij}^x + c_{ji}^x \tag{5}$$

$$-(H - \frac{1}{2}h_i - \frac{1}{2}h_j)(1 - z_{ij}^y - z_{ji}^y)$$

$$\leq \Delta_{ij}^y \leq (H - \frac{1}{2}h_i - \frac{1}{2}h_j)(1 - z_{ij}^y - z_{ji}^y) \tag{6}$$

$$\Delta_{ij}^y = y_j - y_i - c_{ij}^y + c_{ji}^y \tag{7}$$

$$z_{ij}^x + z_{ji}^x + z_{ij}^y + z_{ji}^y = 1 \tag{8}$$

$$z_{ij}^x, z_{ij}^y, z_{ji}^x, z_{ji}^y \in \{1, 0\} \tag{9}$$

Contrary to the **big-M** formulation, the improved model enforces separation in one direction by setting one of the binary variables z_{ij} to one, utilizing the c_{ij} variables which represent the separation distance. These equations also provide better bounds as will be demonstrated by the experimental results.

3.2   Experimental Results

In order to demonstrate the validity of this formulation, we have conducted experiments on a set of MCNC benchmarks: *apte*, *xerox*, and *hp*. For comparison purposes, we use the model of [7], which is the only formulation in the literature that provides global lower bounds on the same problem. This formulation uses a branch of mathematical programming called semi-definite programming (SDP). The big-M relaxation produced trivial bounds for this set of benchmarks and is not included in our comparison.

The commercial ILP solver CPLEX running on a 3.5GHz, 2GB pentium 4 have been used to generate the convex hull relaxation bounds shown in Table 1. The gaps in the table represent the relative gap between the optimal solution and the lower bounds and it is calculated as $\frac{Optimal - Bounds}{Optimal}$.

The results show that the convex hull reformulation has successfully been used to obtain tighter global bounds in shorter time on the optimal floorplanning problem solution. By successfully formulating the floorplanning problem more accurately, the formulation can be used to build a heterogeneous architecture model. This model along side with VPR 5.0 will be used in the following section to explore column-restricted FPGA architecture design.

Table 1. A Comparison of the lower bounds obtained using a convex hull relaxation and an SDP relaxation [7]

Benchmarks	Solution	SDP Relaxation [7]			Convex Hull relaxation		
		Bound	Gap(%)	time(sec)	Bound	Gap(%)	time(sec)
Apte	5205.4	2847.7	45.29	815	3586.03	31.11	0.29
Xerox	6538	1153.1	82.36	2721	5357.24	18.06	0.34
Hp	2101.2	773.23	63.20	7855	1384.37	34.12	0.4

3.3 Enhanced Heterogeneous FPGA Floorplanning Model Formulation

The floorplanning for column-restricted FPGAs requires the placement of circuit blocks of a particular resource type within the boundaries of the corresponding resource column. Constraints to map these nodes into their respective regions as well as setting the widths and locations of each column are added in this section. The convex hull relaxation based model discussed in the previous section is modified to include column restrictions. This will allow the exploration of different architecture floorplans of the FPGA chip. An example of the simplified FPGA architecture layout used in our formulation is shown in Fig. 2.

We introduce the following notations to model heterogenous FPGA architectures: In addition to their widths and heights, circuit blocks are constrained by their resource type denoted by $t_i \in T$ where $T = \{CLB, RAM, MULT\}$. We denote the set of resource columns available on the chip as R where each resource column $u \in R$ is a rectangular block of half-width w_u and half-height h_u which equals half the chip height, centroid locations (x_u, y_u), and resource type $t_u \in T$. The following summarizes the combined architecture and circuits floorplanning problems:

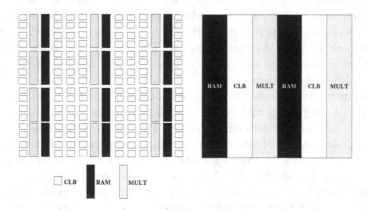

Fig. 2. A Simplified Heterogeneous Architecture Floorplan Consisting of Columns of CLBs, RAMs, and MULTs

> Minimize
> > Wire-length
> subject to
> > Circuit Block Fit in the chip constraints
> > Resource Columns Fit in the chip constraints
> > Block Placement inside Resource Columns
> > Block Non-Overlap constraints
> > Resource Columns Non-Overlap constraints

From the summary of the formulation we notice that both circuit blocks and resource columns are rectangular blocks placed within the boundaries of the FPGA chip while avoiding overlap. Consequently we use these similarities and propose a new formulation of the column-based floorplanning problem. In this formulation the non-overlap constraints are applied between circuit blocks and also resource columns. A circuit block i for instance, with resource type $t_i = CLB$, is allowed to overlap with any CLB column and is separated from the $MULTs$, $RAMs$ columns, and all other circuit blocks using the convex hull separation constraints.

Having successfully formulated the problem analytically we use this model in section 5 to generate heterogeneous architectures and compare it with a parameter sweeping approach. This latter, is described in the following section.

4 Architecture Exploration Using a Parameter Sweeping Approach

In a typical design framework, FPGA architectures are constructed using an experimental methodology. This is conducted by mapping a set of benchmarks into potential architectures and comparing the results using selected performance metrics. We have created a tool that is based on this methodology and which uses layout parameters sweeping to generate a set of architectures. A test benchmark is then placed and routed on these architectures and the architecture that provides the lowest critical path is selected. which are in turn tested with VPR 5.0. The framework takes a test benchmarks and This tool is used to vary the layout of FPGA architectures by sweeping the positions and number of the resource columns within the chip area.

The parameter sweep framework consists of three main blocks and is interfaced with VPR 5.0 for placing and routing as shown in Fig. 3. The target FPGA architectures are initially auto-sized using VPR 5.0 layout options, which find the minimal dimensions of the chip that fits a given circuit. Given this fixed chip area, the sweeping procedure targets the number r, and position p of each resource type that could be placed on the architecture. These parameters are varied using a structured approach in which the chip area is divided into subsets called repeating tiles. Each repeating tile comprises C resource columns as shown in Fig.4. All possible combinations of resources that fit in these repeating tiles are used to construct the set of potential architectures. In other words, instead

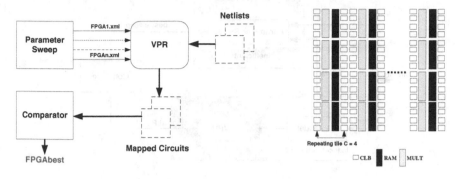

Fig. 3. Parameter-sweep approach

Fig. 4. An architecture constructed with a repeating tile of 4

of exploring all possible architecture layouts given a set of resource columns and a fixed chip area, we fully explore the layout of a smaller portion of the chip and duplicate it along the chip area. This procedure allows the exploration of architectures with significantly different layouts within a fixed time budget, resulting in a structured sampling approach of the design space.

The size of the repeating tiles is chosen based on the time frame for the architecture exploration procedure. Increasing the size of the repeating tile results in a larger number of possible permutations and therefore a larger set of explored architectures. For example, given the choice from the set of resources $\{CLB, MULT, RAM\}$ a repeating tile of size $C = 5$ results in $(3)^C$ combinations which is 243 potential architectures. The parameter sweep block output (set of combinations) are translated into VPR 5.0 architecture format, which in turn performs the placement and routing of the test circuit on the sample architectures.

The comparator block collects the results of the placement and routing of the test circuit on each architecture. The critical path is used as the comparison metric. Consequently, the architecture resulting in the lowest critical path is selected. The use of critical path as our performance metric provides information about the impact of architecture layout on circuit delays and more importantly inter-node delays. This is particulary important given the significant contribution of interconnect delays in the overall circuit delay.

This framework is used in the following section to compare the efficiency of the previously described ILP model in exploring the design space with a parameter sweep approach.

5   ILP-Based Analytical Approach vs. Parameter-Sweep Approach

5.1   Experimental Setup

The main focus of this paper is to illustrate that combining analytical models with more accurate tools such as VPR, performs better than a typical layout

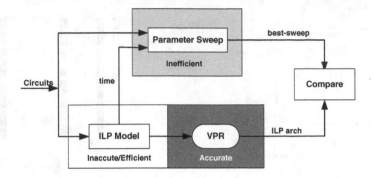

Fig. 5. Comparative experiment between ILP-based analytical model and parameter-sweep approach

parameter sweep approach. We have therefore conducted a comparative experiment on a set of test benchmarks as shown in Fig. 5. The time budget for the parameter sweep framework is tuned accordingly with the time taken by the ILP model to obtain an optimal architecture. ASIC benchmarks were selected and modified to explore a more comprehensive design space. The resource usage of the benchmark blocks was allocated based on the resource distribution obtained from the technology mapped benchmarks from [2].

This experimental approach does not only compare the efficiency of both frameworks for the same time budget, but also combines the advantages of analytical techniques and empirical models such as VPR. This is achieved by taking the results generated by the simplified ILP model and feeding it back to VPR for a more accurate architecture model as shown in Fig. 5.

The objective function of the ILP model was tuned accordingly with the routing model of VPR 5.0. This has been achieved using an experimental approach where a best fit model has been applied to the Manhattan Distance between two circuit blocks and the corresponding routing delay.

5.2   Results

The experiment described in Fig. 5 was conducted and the results are described in this section. For the ILP approach optimal solutions were obtained for smaller benchmarks and the model has been left to run for 24 hours for larger benchmarks when only upper bounds were obtained. These solutions were translated to VPR 5.0 architecture format and used for the placement and routing of the test benchmarks.

Fig. 6 shows the relative critical path gaps between the best architecture generated with the parameter sweep framework and a subset of other architectures explored with the same framework. These gaps present an important aspect of heterogencous FPGA design, which is the significant impact of architecture layout on performance. This is clearly illustrated by up to 27% increase in the critical path induced by the layout of the architecture.

On the other hand, the figure shows the gaps between architectures generated by the ILP model relative to the best parameter sweep architecture obtained

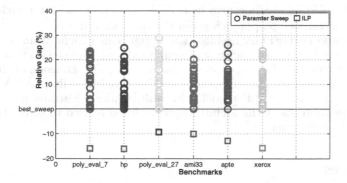

Fig. 6. Relative gap between parameter-sweeped architectures, ILP generated architecture, and the best parameter-sweeped architectures

within the same time frame. These results illustrate the significant improvement of up to 15% on the critical path using our analytical framework over architectures designed with the parameter sweep approach. This is mainly caused by limitations of the parameter sweep approach in exploring a large design space within a restricted time budget. These limitations are induced by the size of the repeating tiles which restricts the potential architecture layouts explored. On the other hand, the results show that by simplifying the problem and applying formal optimization techniques in the form of ILP, better quality architectures are generated. In fact, whereas the ILP framework does not model heterogeneous architectures accurately, it improves on the parameter sweep technique by exploring a wider range of designs.

6   Conclusion and Future Work

This paper has presented the benefits of using an analytical framework in the design of heterogeneous FPGA architecture layouts over a typical parameter sweep approach. The framework uses mathematical programming in the form of linear programming to model column-based architectures by targeting layout parameters. An enhanced formulation motivated by the advances in the facility layout problem has proved to successfully bound the design space and consequently reduce the solution time. Using this framework we have been able to simultaneously generate heterogeneous architecture layouts and reduce the critical path.

The efficiency of this framework has been tested using a comparative experiment. For this purpose, a parameter sweep tool has been developed to sample the design space of architecture layouts and test selected architectures on VPR 5.0. The experiments show an average improvement of up to 15% on the critical path induced by our analytical model in comparison with the parameter sweep approach. This shows that despite the assumptions that have been made to model the FPGA architectures in ILP, it still provides better architectures than a parameter sweep approach given the same time frame.

We conclude that FPGA architecture design can benefit from a combined framework which uses the efficiency of analytical tools and the accuracy of tools such VPR. Consequently, we propose as future work the extension of this framework to guide the search for an optimal architecture by feeding back VPR place and route results to the ILP model. This will require a learning mechanism in which information about the architectures explored is used to direct the search for optimal architectures.

References

1. Compton, K., Hauck, S.: Reconfigurable computing: a survey of systems and software. ACM Comput. Surv. 34(2), 171–210 (2002)
2. Smith, A., Constantinides, G., Cheung, P.: Removed for blind review. In: Proceedings. International Conference on Field Programmable Logic and Applications, pp. 341–346 (2005)
3. Betz, V., Rose, J.: VPR: A New Packing Placement and Routing Tool for FPGA Research. In: Workshop on Field-Programmable Logic and Applications, vol. 2(1), pp. 3–222 (1997)
4. Hutton, M.: FPGA Architecture Design Methodology. In: Proceedings. In: International Conference on Field Programmable Logic and Applications, p. 1 (August 2006)
5. Kuon, I., Rose, J.: Measuring the gap between FPGAs and ASICs. In: Proceedings. 14th International Symposium on Field Programmable Gate Arrays, pp. 21–30. ACM, New York (2006)
6. He, J., Rose, J.: Advantages of heterogeneous logic block architecture for FPGAs. In: Proceedings Custom Integrated Circuits Conference, pp. 7–4 (1993)
7. Takouda, P., Anjos, M., Vannelli, A.: Global lower bounds for the VLSI macrocell floorplanning problem using semidefinite optimization. In: Proceedings. Fifth International Workshop on System-on-Chip for Real-Time Applications, pp. 275–280 (2005)
8. Sherali, H., Fraticelli, B., Meller, R.: Enhanced Model Formulations for Optimal Facility Layout. Operations Research 51(4), 629 (2003)
9. Feng, Y., Mehta, D.: Heterogeneous Floorplanning for FPGAs. In: Proceedings IEEE International Conference on VLSI Design, pp. 257–262 (2006)

On Simplifying Placement and Routing by Extending Coarse-Grained Reconfigurable Arrays with Omega Networks

Ricardo Ferreira[1,*], Alex Damiany[1], Julio Vendramini[1], Tiago Teixeira[1], and João M. P. Cardoso[2,**]

[1] Dep. de Informática, Universidade Federal Vicosa
36570-000, Vicosa, Brazil
ricardo@ufv.br
[2] Dep. de Engenharia Informática, Faculdade de Engenharia
Universidade do Porto
Rua Dr. Roberto Frias, 4200-465 Porto, Portugal

Abstract. Most reconfigurable computing architectures suffer from computationally demanding Placement and Routing (P&R) steps which might hamper their use in contexts requiring dynamic compilation (e.g., to guarantee application portability in embedded systems). Bearing in mind the simplification of P&R steps, this paper presents and analyzes a coarse-grained reconfigurable array extended with global Omega Networks. We show that integrating one or two Omega Networks in a coarse-grained array simplifies the P&R stage with both low hardware resource overhead and low performance degradation (18% for an 8×8 array). The experimental results included permit to compare the coarse-grained array with one or two Omega Networks with a coarse-grained array based on a grid of processing elements with neighbor connections. When comparing the execution time to perform the P&R stage needed for the two arrays, we show that the array using two Omega Networks needs a far simple P&R which for the benchmarks used completed on average in about 20× less time.

1 Introduction

Reconfigurable computing architectures are becoming increasingly important in embedded and high-performance systems [1]. In many applications, coarse-grained reconfigurable arrays (CGRAs) can be valuable extensions to traditional architectures (e.g., tightly coupled to microprocessors). They are mainly based on a matrix of processing elements (PEs) seconded by routing resources, and they can be used to accelerate parts of the applications or to reduce overall energy consumption. Besides the manufacturing of a reconfigurable fabric with a CGRA architecture, CGRAs can be also used as softcores implemented by the fine-grained hardware resources of common reconfigurable fabrics (e.g., FPGAs).

* Partially supported by Bilateral Cooperation Grices/CNPq, PAEX-Capes, PNM and Pibic CNPq, Funarbe/UFV - Brazil.
** Partially supported by FCT, the Portuguese Science Foundation, under the research grant PTDC/EEA-ELC/70272/2006, and Bilateral Cooperation Grices/CNPq.

J. Becker et al. (Eds.): ARC 2009, LNCS 5453, pp. 145–156, 2009.
© Springer-Verlag Berlin Heidelberg 2009

The possibility to map computations efficiently and dynamically to CGRAs is envisaged as a feature needed for the success of those architectures in the embedded computing domain. In embedded systems, applications portability is very important and is ensured by virtual machines, just-in-time (JIT) compilers, and dynamic binary translation. However, typical CGRAs (e.g., ADRES [2], XPP [3]) need computationally demanding Placement and Routing (P&R) steps, with complexity similar to the counterpart P&R steps used in FPGAs.

In order to dynamically compile segments of an application to CGRAs, the P&R steps need to be simplified. To be successful, we believe, this simplification needs to rely in both architecture support and algorithm simplification.

One of the possibilities is to extend the CGRA with routing resources that permit to connect, with low performance degradation, every two PEs. In this case, placement can be reduced to assigning of instructions to the PEs supporting the operations involved (without location awareness), and routing is also simplified. The solutions proposed in this paper aim at simplifying the P&R steps using Omega Networks [4] - a special case of multistage interconnect networks (MINs) which uses a Perfect Shuffle connection scheme - to enrich the interconnect topologies of the CGRA. Our approach allows low overhead dynamic P&R steps.

The main contributions and main results presented in this paper are:

- A novel CGRA using Omega Networks to achieve a low-cost global network is proposed. An analysis and study of the performance degradation and hardware resources overhead are presented for the CGRA.
- A simplified P&R algorithm, with polynomial complexity, is presented for the CGRA proposed. The simplified P&R and the novel CGRA topology allowed the mapping of large dataflow graphs (with over 300 nodes) in about $70\times$ less execution time than using a grid-based CGRA.

This paper is organized as follows. Section 2 introduces the main concepts related to CGRAs and multistage interconnect networks, and the motivation behind our work. Section 3 describes our approach using CGRAs with Omega Networks and presents the P&R algorithm for these CGRAs. Section 4 presents experimental results and section 5 describes related work. Finally, section 6 draws some conclusions.

2   Background and Motivation

Coarse-grained reconfigurable arrays (CGRAs) mainly consist of a set of Processing Elements (PEs) connected with a certain interconnect topology. Each PE is associated with one or more Functional Units (FUs) which are responsible for performing a number of operations (including arithmetic, logic, special operations to deal with conditional branches, etc). CGRAs permit both spatial and temporal computations and support high degrees of parallelism.

Different interconnect topologies have been proposed [5,2,6]. For instance, grid topologies form a 2-D array of PEs with neighbor connections between them (as illustrated in Fig. 1). Inside the PE, there are hardware structures to permit the connection of each input port to an operand of the FU and each output of the FU to an output port of

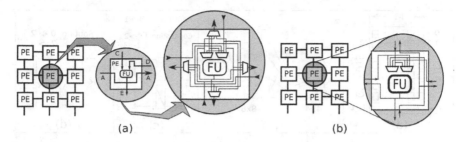

Fig. 1. A 2-D grid-based CGRA, 4 inputs and 4 outputs PE: (a) interconnect resources to connect the PE to other PEs (e.g., the neighbors in the grid) and to permit the routing of inputs directly to one or more of the outputs; (b) a simpler PE without including routing of inputs to outputs unless they pass through the FU

the PE. More complex PEs may also have interconnect resources to route inputs directly to the outputs without passing through the FU.

Previous work has shown that PEs with 8 inputs and 8 outputs, and interconnect topologies using 1-hop, achieve the best placement and routing results [2,6]. However, when a 1-hop routing PE with 8-inputs/8-outputs unidirectional is considered, the associated cost might be too high, e.g., with ten 8:1 multiplexers per PE. To reduce the PE cost they use a store-and-forward register to bypass one or two signals at each clock cycle [2]. Therefore, only one or two output multiplexers are in this case needed.

Let us suppose a 2-D grid (Fig. 1(a)) with 4/4 (unidirectional inputs/outputs) PEs. Each PE receives as inputs the signals C and D, from north and east, respectively. These inputs are connected to the FU using the multiplexers in each FU operand, and the FU result is the signal E, which is sent to the south output. This PE implements the routing for the signal A, from west to east, without passing through the FU. Four multiplexers are needed to implement all routing possibilities, as shown in Fig. 1(a). In addition, two multiplexers are needed for each FU to connect inputs from all directions.

An ideal routing topology would make possible that each PE could directly connect with zero or low-cost overhead to any other PE in the CGRA. However, such rich interconnect topologies have in practice high and usually unacceptable costs. For instance, a crossbar has a high connectivity and could be one such option, but its area cost of $O(N^2)$ prevents its use for typical CGRA sizes.

A realistic possibility, proposed and analyzed in this paper, is to diminish the number of possible interconnections by using multistage interconnection networks (MINs). They permit an intermediate solution, which has a $O(N \times log_2(N))$ area cost and offer a good cost/connectivity balance. MINs are networks with N inputs and N outputs and composed by M switch stages (see Fig. 2(a)) resulting in a total of $\frac{N}{2} \times M$ switches. Most MINs consider power of two N values with M ranging from $log_2(N)$ to $2 \times log_2(N)$ [7,8,9]. MINs have been used in many application domains such as SIMD and MIMD parallel machines, ATM switches, new reconfigurable fabrics [10], and more recently large cluster based supercomputers [11]. Although it is clear that MINs can be efficiently implemented at layout level [12], their efficiency when implemented by FPGA resources is not clear. We also analyze in this paper this efficiency.

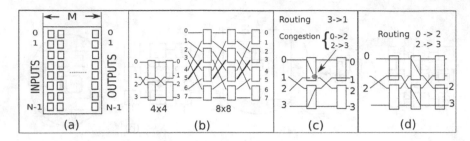

Fig. 2. A multistage interconnect network (MIN): (a) generic structure; (b) 4×4 and 8×8 Omega structure; (c) 4×4 MIN with 2 stages and a routing congestion; (d) 4×4 MIN with 3 stages without the previous routing congestion

A particular case of MINs using a Perfect Shuffle connection scheme are Omega Networks [4]. Examples of 4×4 and 8×8 Omega Networks are illustrated in Fig. 2(b). MINs are bit permutation networks, where the connections between two stages are based on bit operations. The Omega Networks use a circular rotate-left for the bit permutation. E.g., the line 5 (101) in stage i is connected to line 3 (011) at stage $i + 1$. An Omega Network with N inputs and N outputs has by definition $log_2(N)$ stages.

When the number of stages is $log_2(N)$, the MIN connectivity is restricted. These MINs are classified as blocking networks, and some input/output permutations may not be feasible. Each input/output connection has a unique path [4] and the intermediate switches can be shared by paths. Thus, it might be impossible to connect two different input/output pairs at the same time, as shown in Fig. 2(c), where the input/output pair $0 \rightarrow 2$ and $2 \rightarrow 3$ has a conflict in a 4×4 Omega Network. On the other hand, a MIN with $2 \times log_2(N)$ stages can be a rearrangeable non-blocking, and in this case it is possible to rearrange some connections to solve the routing conflicts. A Benes network [13,14] is an example of a rearrangeable non-blocking network. An intermediate solution is a network with $log_2(N) + K$ stages, where $0 \leq K \leq log_2(N)$ [9]. When $K = 0$, the MIN has a low cost and delay, but it is still a blocking network. When $K = log_2(N)$, the area cost and the latency will double, however, the connectivity will be significantly improved. A trade-off can be obtained for low values of K, as is shown in the next section. Fig. 2(d) shows how an extra level resolves the conflict illustrated in Fig. 2(c).

The work presented in this paper extends CGRAs with global MINs, in particular Omega Networks, in order to reduce the P&R complexity. To the best of our knowledge, this is the first work analyzing both the use of global Omega Networks in 2-D CGRAs in terms of area and delay overhead and in terms of the complexity of the P&R.

3 CGRA Using Omega Networks

Previous work on CGRAs proposed global buses, line and/or column buses, inter-cluster or crossbar networks [5], as routing resources to allow a complete routing on 2-D arrays. Buses have inherently low cost, but to solve congestion problems may require time-sharing of resources and scheduling. To reduce the complexity of the type

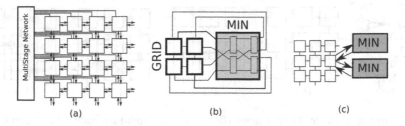

Fig. 3. (a) Grid-based CGRA with a Multistage Interconnection Network (MIN); (b) Example of PEs plus MIN interconnections; (c) Two MINs - adding routing resources to solve congestion

of interconnect resources needed to enrich the routing possibilities and the associated P&R algorithms, we propose a hybrid solution with only two types of resources for local and global interconnects, respectively.

3.1 CGRA Architecture

While most previous work has focused on PEs with routing resources [2,3,6,15], our work simplifies the PE complexity. By using MIN structures for achieving global connections between PEs, we do not need the PE complexity exhibited in Fig. 1(a) regarding routing local support. Thus, our approach permits to use PEs as the one presented in Fig. 1(b). As previously indicated, it uses only two FU multiplexers, and no bypass routing is included. The use of MINs as depicted in Fig. 3 gives to the CGRA a rich interconnect structure by also exploiting connections between PEs through the MIN. Specifically, non-local routing (i.e., routing between non-adjacent PEs) is performed through the MIN.

In addition, it is well known that the routing on a MIN requires a polynomial solution (see the routing algorithms presented in [7,9,8,14]), while the routing on a 2-D grid is NP-complete.

To decrease routing congestions, we propose to use more than one MIN (see Fig. 3(c)), each one with extra stages. The architecture proposed permits to use a polynomial P&R algorithm as the one proposed and detailed in the next section.

3.2 One Step Placement and Routing

The P&R on a 2-D array is an NP-complete problem [16]. To simplify, P&R is usually solved in a two step approach: first the placement is performed, and then a routing algorithm is applied. Previous work proposed placement based on meta-heuristics [5], such as genetic and simulated annealing algorithms. The routing step is usually based on pathfinder and similar algorithms [17,5]. Such approaches make P&R a time consuming task which hampers their use when runtime P&R is required.

This work proposes to perform P&R simultaneously by using a one step graph traversal. This approach tries to assign local routing resources in the CGRA for the edges of the graph. Naturally, after this step there might be edges without feasible routing. Those

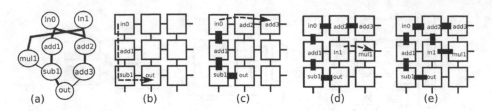

Fig. 4. Mapping: (a) input dataflow graph (DFG); (b) 1st Depth-First path; (c) 2nd Depth-First Path; (d) Last Depth-First path; (e) Final Placed and Routed Solution

unrouted remaining edges are then routed using the MIN resources. This approach has polynomial complexity.

The first stage of the P&R algorithm is based on the depth-first search, over the input DFG, previously presented in [18]. The first stage of the P&R algorithm is applied for each node n in V. A depth-first traversal starts in a node n and traverses the DFG until reaches an *end* node. Then the nodes in the path from n to the *end* node are sequentially placed on the CGRA. At the same time, neighborhood PE connections are assigned to the edges between nodes in the path. Edges without feasible routing are maintained in a set of unrouted edges to be considered by the second phase of the algorithm. The depth-first continues until all nodes and edges are visited.

Suppose the DFG and the 2-D CGRA depicted in Fig. 4(a). The algorithm starts a depth-first traversal beginning with source nodes In_0 and In_1. Let us consider the node In_0. The first path starts with In_0 and ends with *Out*. The nodes in this path are placed in the CGRA, as shown in Fig. 4(b), by using also a depth-first traversal in the CGRA. At the same time, three edges are routed: $In_0 \rightarrow Add_1$, $Add_1 \rightarrow Sub_1$, and $Sub_1 \rightarrow Out$. Then, the traversal restarts from In_0 to Add_3 (see Fig. 4(c)). The traversal continues from In_1 to Mul_1, as shown in Fig. 4(d).

As this example illustrates, all edges have been visited just once. Considering $|E|$ the number of edges in the DFG and V the set of nodes, the proposed algorithm computational complexity is $O(|E| + |V|)$. For each visited edge of the DFG, the algorithm tries to associate an interconnect resource in the CGRA. In this example, the depth-first algorithm completes with only two unrouted DFG edges (see the edges $Mul_1 \rightarrow Sub_1$ and $Add_3 \rightarrow Out$ in Fig. 4(a) and Fig. 4(e), respectively). As the proposed architecture has limited routing resources, it is not possible to complete the routing step using this simple algorithm.

The next step tries to route those remaining DFG edges using the interconnect resources given by the MIN(s) used in the CGRA. Fig. 5 shows the algorithm for the second phase of the P&R which deals with the routing on the MIN(s). Thus, after the depth-first traversal previously explained, a second routing phase is performed. This latter routing stage is responsible to route DFG edges using the routing resources provided by the MIN(s).

Consider U the set of unrouted edges. For each edge e=(source, target) in U, the routing algorithm, depicted in Fig. 5, is applied. Let us consider an $N \times N$ Omega Network with k extra stages. Let $m = log_2(N)$, and $S_{m-1} \ldots S_0$ and $T_{m-1} \ldots T_0$ be the binary code of source and target node, respectively. For ease of explanation, let us suppose

```
RoutingOmega(source, target) {
// N inputs and N outputs and M = Number of Stages = log_2(N) + K
// K = number of extra level stages and L = 2^K
// Bitmask = length log_2(N), e.g., if N=8 then Bitmask = 111

// test all possible values for extra levels
  for (inter=0; inter < L; inter++) {
    path = (source << M) OR inter << (log_2(N)) OR target
      found = true;
      for (j=0; j < log_2(N) + k; j++) { // from stage 0 to stage Log(N)+K-1
        i= path >> (log_2(N) + k + 1- j) AND bitmask;
        found = found and freeline[i][j]; // verify if all lines are free...
      }
      if (found) return true;
  }
  return found;
}
```

Fig. 5. Algorithm to perform routing in Omega Networks

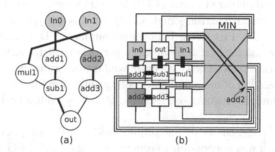

(a)   (b)

Fig. 6. (a) input DFG; (b) P&R in a 3×3 CGRA with one MIN

$k = 0$. In this case the switch line at stage 0 will be $S_{m-2} \dots S_0 T_{m-1}$, at stage 1 will be $S_{m-3} \dots S_0 T_{m-1} T_{m-2}$, until reaches the stage $log_2(N) - 1$, the last one, at the target line $T_{m-1} \dots T_0$. Let us consider again the 4×4 Omega Network shown in Fig 2(c). The routing path from the source 3 to target 1, where $S_1 S_0 = 11$ and $T_1 T_0 = 01$, will pass by the line 10 at stage 0 and line 01 at stage 1. The routing will be feasible if the lines are not busy. When $k > 0$, extra switch levels will be included. An example for a 4×4 Omega Network with one extra level (k=1) is shown in Fig. 2(d), making now possible to connect the input 2 to output 3.

The routing algorithm, shown in Fig. 5, scans the MIN network lines from the input to the output to verify if all lines are free and the routing is feasible. The algorithm is called for each unrouted connection in the previous P&R phase. Thus, the worst case computational complexity of the MIN routing stage is $O(|E| \times log_2(N))$.

Let us consider again the DFG from Fig. 4(a) and the placement shown in Fig. 6. The bold lines in DFG edges are used to mark the routed edges using local grid interconnections. There are four unrouted edges: $mul_1 \rightarrow sub_1, add_3 \rightarrow Out, In_0 \rightarrow add_2$, and $In_1 \rightarrow add_2$. The edge $mul_1 \rightarrow sub_1$ as well as the edge $add_3 \rightarrow Out$ can be routed by the MIN. Nevertheless, either the edge $In_0 \rightarrow add_2$ or the edge $In_1 \rightarrow add_2$ is routed, because the node add_2 has only one input from the MIN. Thus, only one of the two edges is routed in this example. To surpass this kind of limitations, we extend the CGRA with an additional MIN as has been previously referred. Next section includes results showing the gains in routability obtained when using two MINs and also extra levels in each MIN.

4   Experimental Results

In order to evaluate the approach presented in this paper, we have used two benchmark sets with a total of 26 data-flow graphs (DFGs). The first set is composed by DFGs representing the following benchmarks (previously used in [18]): dct, Cplx8, filterRGB, DCT line, fir64, Fir16, filterRGBpaeth, and SNN. The second set is composed by 18 DFGs from [19], a repository with DFGs carefully selected from over 1400 DFGs obtained from applications in the MediaBench benchmark suite. The DFGs used range in complexity from 18 to 359 nodes, and from 16 to 380 edges (see Table 1).

We evaluated the success of P&R when targeting 2-D Grid CGRAs, with Torus topology and 8/8 input/outputs per PE, versus CGRAs with Omega Networks and with 4/4 input/outputs per PE (referred here as simple Grid). For this study, we considered CGRAs with size from 16 to 360 PEs. Table 1 shows the number of DFG edges not routed for each CGRA option and the execution times to perform P&R for each benchmark. For the P&R to 2-D Grid-based CGRAs we employed the algorithm proposed in [18], using in this case a version of the pathfinder routing algorithm for the routing stage. For the CGRA with Omega Networks, we used the One-Step P&R algorithm presented in this paper.

Due to the low connectivity of the simple Grid and the simplicity of the greedy mapping approach, it was not possible to route all edges of each DFG. For a simple 2-D grid architecture with limited interconnect resources as shown in Fig 1(b), 33% of total DFG edges were not routed. When an Omega MIN is added to the 2-D Grid CGRA (as shown in Fig. 3(a)), the percentage of unrouted edges drops to 12%. With extra MIN stages, the percentage of unrouted DFG edges reduces to 4% and to 1.3%, when using two (K=2) and four extra stages (K=4), respectively. Using the Omega MIN with four extra levels, 15 benchmarks (out of 26) were successfully P&R as shown in Table 1.

Each congestion on a MIN has two possible causes. One happens when at least one switch is busy for all possible routing paths for an edge. In this case, extra switch levels can be added to solve the conflict. The second one happens when a node is the sink for at least two unrouted edges, and therefore it is not possible to route them because each node receives only one line from the MIN. When using additional MINs, we are diminishing such problems. The results for two MINs presented in column Two MINs in Table 1 show that all edges are routed when two MINs plus two extra levels (K=2) are added, and less than 2% of total edges are not routed when no extra level is added.

With respect to P&R execution time, using the CGRA architecture and the P&R approach proposed in this paper, we achieve speedups from about 1.9× to 70× (about 20× in average) over a fast P&R algorithm based on the algorithm previously presented in [18]. The execution times achieved and the simplicity of the P&R algorithm are a strong evidence that the novel CGRA structure proposed in this paper can be an important support for runtime compilation.

A question that may arise at the moment is related to the area and delay overhead when using Omega Networks. As we are interested in CGRAs to define a computational

Table 1. P&R results for Grid plus MIN architectures for the set of benchmarks used

			unrouted edges (proposed architecture)						CPU time (ms)				
			Grid+One MIN			Grid+Two MIN			Grid + Two MINs, K=2			Grid 4 I/O Toroidal Placement +Path Finder	P&R Speedup
									Placement Local Routing	MINs Routing	total		
	nodes	edges	grid	K=0	K=2	K=4	K=0	K=2	K=4					
dct	139	186	68	32	10	8	6	0	0	9.10	0.60	9.70	89	9.18
Cplx8	46	60	19	9	4	3	1	0	0	1.10	0.20	1.30	8	6.15
filterRGB	57	70	19	3	2	0	0	0	0	1.80	0.20	2.00	10	5.00
DCT	92	124	41	15	4	2	1	0	0	5.50	0.50	6.00	65	10.83
fir64	193	255	92	32	10	6	11	0	0	3.70	1.00	4.70	189	40.21
Fir16	49	63	30	6	0	0	2	0	0	0.90	0.20	1.10	41	37.27
filterRGBpaeth	84	106	31	8	5	0	1	0	0	2.00	0.60	2.60	30	11.54
snn	253	299	77	31	8	1	6	0	0	9.30	1.10	10.40	324	31.15
fir1	44	43	20	7	1	0	1	0	0	1.40	0.30	1.70	7	4.12
arf	28	30	10	2	0	0	0	0	0	0.70	0.50	1.20	21	17.50
jpeg_idct_ifast	170	210	74	30	15	6	7	0	0	3.10	0.90	4.00	116	29.00
smooth_color_z	197	196	64	24	7	4	2	0	0	8.90	2.50	11.40	166	14.56
collapse_pyr	72	89	28	11	5	0	0	0	0	1.10	0.90	2.00	51	25.50
horner_bezier_surf	18	16	3	0	0	0	0	0	0	0.20	0.10	0.30	3	10.00
jpeg_fdct_islow	175	210	71	32	8	0	6	0	0	3.90	1.00	4.90	145	29.59
matmul	117	124	33	15	5	0	4	0	0	1.70	0.40	2.10	49	23.33
fir2	40	39	15	4	2	0	1	0	0	0.80	0.10	0.90	6	6.67
motion_vectors	32	29	11	3	0	0	0	0	0	1.60	0.10	1.70	4	2.35
cosine1	66	76	29	7	2	2	0	0	0	2.10	0.40	2.50	61	24.40
idctcol	186	236	84	31	15	6	4	0	0	3.00	3.20	6.20	222	35.81
interpolate_aux	108	104	41	12	3	0	1	0	0	1.40	0.50	1.90	54	28.42
feedback_points	54	51	17	4	1	0	0	0	0	0.80	0.20	1.00	10	10.00
ewf	42	55	18	3	1	0	0	0	0	0.40	0.40	0.80	7	8.75
write_bmp_header	111	93	23	5	1	1	0	0	0	2.10	0.60	2.70	41	15.19
h2v2_smooth	54	55	19	7	2	0	1	0	0	1.00	4.80	5.80	11	1.90
invert_matrix_gen	359	380	106	36	8	1	5	0	0	9.50	2.70	12.20	857	70.25
Average	107	123	40.1	14.2	4.6	1.5	2.3	0.0	0.0	2.97	0.92	3.89	99.50	19.56
Total	2786	3199	1043	369	119	40	60	0	0				**Maximum**	70.25
% unrouted edges			32.6	11.5	3.7	1.3	1.9	0.0	0.0				**Minimum**	1.90

layer implemented in fine-grained reconfigurable fabrics, we show here implementations of CGRAs in a Xilinx Virtex-5 FPGA (xc5vlx50-3ff324). We consider in these experiments PEs with 32-bit FUs implementing arithmetic operations (addition, multiplication, subtraction, negation, comparisons), shifts, and bitwise operations (and, or, xor, not). We also consider that all outputs of the PEs are registered.

Fig. 7 presents the number of FPGA resources (#LUTs) and maximum delays obtained for different sizes of Omega Networks dealing with 32-bit input/outputs. The area cost in LUTs is a function of $N \times log_2(N)$. The delay increases by about 0.5 ns for each additional input/output of the network. Note that even an Omega Network with 128 input/outputs only uses about 11% of the total LUTs available in the FPGA considered.

We show in Table 2 the number of #LUTs used and the maximum clock frequencies achieved for simple 2-D Grid-based CGRAs and for CGRAs with Omega Networks proposed in this paper. The Grid with simple routing resources (i.e., with PEs with a small number of neighbor connections) has a very low cost, but suffers from congestions and may need long P&R execution times. The Grid plus one MIN has an area cost below the Grid with 4/4 inputs/outputs PEs with routing resources. With respect to maximum clock frequencies, they decrease for the CGRA with MIN when the MIN is

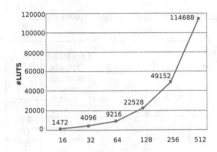 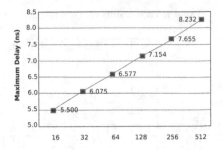

Fig. 7. Results for 32-bit Omega Networks considering different number of input/outputs: (a) area in terms of #LUTs; (b) maximum delay

Table 2. FPGA resources used and maximum frequencies for a number of CGRAs (percentages of used resources are given; for the 8×8 arrays the DSP48 resources were not used)

32-bit FUs, PEs w/ 5 inputs and 5 outputs	Size	# LUTs		#DSP48Es		#FF		Max Freq (MHz)
2D Grid-Based CGRA +	2x2	4495	2.2%	12	6.3%	256	0.1%	104.58
routing resources	4x4	19289	9.3%	48	25.0%	1536	0.7%	106.79
	8x8	130750	63.1%		0.0%	7239	3.5%	10.4.13
2D Grid-Based CGRA +	2x2	3854	1.9%	12	6.3%	128	0.1%	103.61
1-MIN, K=0	4x4	15812	7.6%	48	25.0%	512	0.2%	93.89
	8x8	119008	57.4%		0.0%	2048	1.0%	85.45
2D Grid-Based CGRA +	2x2	3912	1.9%	12	6.3%	256	0.1%	110.48
1-MIN, K=0	4x4	16130	7.8%	48	25.0%	1024	0.5%	109.25
w/ 1 clock cycle for MIN	8x8	116602	56.2%		0.0%	4543	2.2%	103.26
2D Grid-Based CGRA +	2x2	4090	2.0%	24	12.5%	384	0.2%	109.86
2-MINs, K=0	4x4	17347	8.4%	96	50.0%	1536	0.7%	107.88
w/ 1 clock cycle for MINs	8x8	132561	63.9%		0.0%	6144	3.0%	100.60

not registered (MIN delay adds to the maximum delay of the PE). In this case, the clock frequency decreases about 12% and 18% for the 4×4 and 8×8 CGRA with 1-MIN, respectively, when compared to the ones obtained for the original CGRA (these frequencies correspond also to the performance decrease as the latencies of the applications in the CGRA do not change). When using MINs with registered outputs, we achieve maximum clock frequencies similar to the baseline 2-D Grid-based CGRA without MINs. In this case, we are including interconnect resources that route in a clock cycle and thus the latencies may change, especially with P&R algorithms not aware of the critical path of the DFGs (i.e., without assigning local interconnects to edges of the critical path). In the improbably worst case assumption, this may increase twice the latencies of the applications in the CGRA.

As can be seen, CGRAs with Omega Networks are promising solutions, especially in systems where one needs to avoid long P&R runtimes, e.g., in systems needing runtime P&R.

5   Related Work

Most P&R algorithms are based on simulated annealing (SA) and pathfinder approaches [5]. Long P&R execution times have been shown for a number of CGRAs. E.g., a modulo scheduling algorithm based on SA is used in [17]. The execution time is around 100 seconds for DFGs with about 200 nodes. Recently, a CGRA based on a 2-D stripe model has been presented in [20]. However, even for the greedy P&R, the reported execution times are around few seconds.

Our previous work also addressed a polynomial placement [18] for 2-D grid-based CGRAs. However, to be successful, it needed that the target architecture used rich local interconnection resources and 1-hop interconnections.

Recently, some authors focused on runtime P&R in the context of just-in-time compilation. The most notorious work is the one related to the Warp processors [21]. They simplify P&R by using a greedy placement algorithm and by reducing the interconnect resources of their fine-grained reconfigurable logic array. P&R execution times reported are in the order of seconds when considering examples with similar complexity as the ones presented in this paper.

Recognizing that we need both new P&R algorithms and CGRA specific hardware support to achieve fast P&R (envisioning runtime operation), we propose the use of global Multistage Interconnect Networks (MINs) in 2-D Grid-based CGRAs. Our approach is different from the previous ones in a number of aspects. The support given by MINs allows a P&R algorithm with polynomial complexity, flexible, and achieving execution times in the order of milliseconds, even for large DFGs (around 300 nodes).

6 Conclusions

This paper proposes the use of global multistage interconnection networks in coarse-grained reconfigurable array architectures based on 2-D grids. The main idea is to extend local routing resources with global multistage interconnection networks. These multistage interconnection networks easier the routing by giving a richer interconnect topology which permits to connect directly processing elements independently of their position in the grid. By doing so, a simple and efficient placement and routing algorithm can be used as is demonstrated in this paper.

The results presented in this paper are very promising. The new architecture leads to a very fast placement and routing (on average in $20\times$ less time than when using a similar architecture, but without global interconnection networks) with acceptable area overhead and low performance degradation (less than 18% for an 8×8 array). Our approach can be especially useful for reconfigurable computing systems needing runtime placement and routing, e.g., to accomplish efficient just-in-time compilation.

Our ongoing work intends to study the impact on performance of a critical path aware placement and routing algorithm.

References

1. Hauck, S., DeHon, A.: Reconfigurable Computing: The Theory and Practice of FPGA-Based Computation. Morgan Kaufmann, San Francisco (2007)
2. Mei, B., Lambrechts, A., Verkest, D., Mignolet, J.Y., Lauwereins, R.: Architecture exploration for a reconfigurable architecture template. IEEE Des. Test 22(2), 90–101 (2005)
3. Volker Baumgarten, E.: PACT XPP - A Self-Reconfigurable Data Processing Architecture. The Journal of Supercomputing (TJS) 26(2), 167–184 (2003)

4. Lawrie, D.H.: Access and alignment of data in an array processor. IEEE Trans. Comput. 24(12) (1975)
5. Hartenstein, R.: A decade of reconfigurable computing: a visionary retrospective. In: DATE 2001: Proceedings of the conference on Design, automation and test in Europe, pp. 642–649. IEEE Press, Piscataway (2001)
6. Bansal, N., Gupta, S., Dutt, N., Nicolau, A., Gupta, R.: Network topology exploration of mesh-based coarse-grain reconfigurable architectures. In: DATE 2004: Proceedings of the conference on Design, automation and test in Europe, p. 10474. IEEE Computer Society, Washington (2004)
7. Yeh, Y.M., yun Feng, T.: On a class of rearrangeable networks. IEEE Trans. Comput. 41(11), 1361–1379 (1992)
8. Andresen, S.: The looping algorithm extended to base 2t rearrangeable switching networks. IEEE Trans. Commun. 25(10), 1057–1063 (1977)
9. Hu, Q., Shen, X., Liang, W.: Optimally routing lc permutations on k-extra-stage cube-type networks. IEEE Trans. Comput. 45(1), 97–103 (1996)
10. Zied, M., Hayder, M., Emna, A., Habib, M.: Efficient tree topology for fpga interconnect network. In: GLSVLSI 2008: Proceedings of the 18th ACM Great Lakes symposium on VLSI, pp. 321–326. ACM, New York (2008)
11. Kim, J., Dally, W.J., Abts, D.: Flattened butterfly: a cost-efficient topology for high-radix networks. SIGARCH Comput. Archit. News 35(2), 126–137 (2007)
12. DeHon, A., Huang, R., Wawrzynek, J.: Hardware-assisted fast routing. In: FCCM 2002: Proceedings of the 10th Annual IEEE Symposium on Field-Programmable Custom Computing Machines, p. 205. IEEE Computer Society, Washington (2002)
13. Benes, V.E.: Mathematical Theory of Connecting Networks and Telephone Traffic. Academic Press, New York (1965)
14. Lee, K.Y.: A new benes network control algorithm. IEEE Trans. Comput. 36(6), 768–772 (1987)
15. Goldstein, S.C., Schmit, H., Moe, M., Budiu, M., Cadambi, S., Taylor, R.R., Laufer, R.: Piperench: a co/processor for streaming multimedia acceleration. In: ISCA 1999: Proceedings of the 26th annual international symposium on Computer architecture, pp. 28–39. IEEE Computer Society, Washington (1999)
16. Tessier, R.G.: Fast Place and Route Approaches for FPGAs. Phd thesis, MIT, Massachusetts Institute of Technology (1999)
17. Mei, B., Vernalde, S., Verkest, D., Man, H.D., Lauwereins, R.: Exploiting loop-level parallelism on coarse-grained reconfigurable architectures using modulo scheduling. In: DATE 2003: Proceedings of the conference on Design, Automation and Test in Europe, p. 10296. IEEE Computer Society, Washington (2003)
18. Ferreira, R., Garcia, A., Teixeira, T., Cardoso, J.M.P.: A polynomial placement algorithm for data driven coarse-grained reconfigurable architectures. In: ISVLSI, pp. 61–66. IEEE Computer Society, Los Alamitos (2007)
19. ExPRESS Benchmarks: Electrical & Computer Engineering Department at the UCSB, USA (last access on November 3rd 2008), http://express.ece.ucsb.edu/benchmark/
20. Mehta, G., Stander, J., Baz, M., Hunsaker, B., Jones, A.K.: Interconnect customization for a coarse-grained reconfigurable fabric. In: Parallel and Distributed Processing Symposium, International, pp. 1–8. IEEE Computer Society, Los Alamitos (2007)
21. Lysecky, R., Vahid, F., Tan, S.X.D.: Dynamic fpga routing for just-in-time fpga compilation. In: DAC 2004: Proceedings of the 41st annual conference on Design automation, pp. 954–959. ACM, New York (2004)

A New Datapath Merging Method for Reconfigurable System

Mahmood Fazlali, Mohammad K. Fallah, Mahdy Zolghadr, and Ali Zakerolhosseini

Department of Computer Enginiering, Faculty of Elecrical& Computer Enginiering,
Shahid Beheshti University,G.C, Evin 1983963113
Tehran, Iran
Fazlali@cc.sbu.ac.ir, {mk_fallah,mzolghadr}@std.sbu.ac.ir,
a-zaker@ sbu.ac.ir

Abstract. Reconfigurable systems have been proved to achieve significant performance speed-up by mapping the most time-consuming loops to a reconfigurable units. Datapath merging (DPM) synthesis has identified the similarities
among the Data Flow Graphs (DFGs) corresponding to the loops, and produces
a single reconfigurable datapath that can be dynamically reconfigured to execute each DFG. This paper presents a new datapath merging method that produces a reconfigurable datapath with minimal area usage. At first it merges
DFGs together one by one to create the reconfigurable datapath. Then it merges
the functional units and interconnection units inside the reconfigurable datapath
to reduce resource area usage. To do this, a new graph-based technique to
merge the resources in the reconfigurable datapath is presented. We evaluate
the proposed method using programs from the Media-bench benchmarks and
experimental results show a decrease from 5% to 15% in reconfigurable data
path resource area in comparison to previous algorithms.

Keywords: Reconfigurable Computing, High Level Synthesis, Datapath Merging, Maximum Weighted Clique Algorithm.

1 Introduction

Reconfigurable hardware has been shown to provide an efficient compromise between the flexibility of software and the performance of hardware especially in embedded systems [1]. Due to power consumption resulting from area usage, these
systems need a synthesizer to use their reconfigurable resources efficiently. Traditional High-Level Synthesis (HLS) shares the resources where a datapath is synthesized from a DFG to optimize a certain goal such as the resource area usage. The
synthesis process comprises the major tasks of scheduling, resource allocation, resource binding and interconnection binding [2] [3]. Datapath merging is a synthesis
method which has been presented for sharing a datapath among a number of DFGs
and reducing the resource area usage in partially reconfigurable systems. That way, it
merges vertices and edges of a number of DFGs to create a reconfigurable datapath.
In traditional HLS, the resulting datapath corresponds to only one input DFG while by
using DPM as a HLS synthesizer, the synthesized resulting datapath is able to

J. Becker et al. (Eds.): ARC 2009, LNCS 5453, pp. 157–168, 2009.
© Springer-Verlag Berlin Heidelberg 2009

perform the computation of several DFGs [4] so, traditional HLS allocation enables intra-DFG resource sharing, while DPM provides inter-DFG resource sharing and it is compatible to the partially reconfigurable systems.

Finding a merging of the vertices from the DFGs to minimize the area usage cost can turn into the maximum weight bipartite matching which has a polynomial complexity time [5]. On the other hand, merging the edges from the DFGs to minimize the interconnection cost is an NP-complete problem, because merging edges depends on merging their adjacent vertices [6]. That is, two edges from two DFGs can only be merged if their source vertices are merged as well as their destination vertices. If vertices are merged without considering the interconnection cost or using only estimates, we may have a reconfigurable datapath that its interconnection cost is not minimized and consequently, the total area cost is not optimal. To solve this problem, we need a merging method that reduces the total area cost by considering the functional unit area usage and interconnection area usage.

In previous works, [6] defines an algorithm for partitioning a DFG consisting of datapath operators into reconfigurable clusters. [7] presents a technique to perform global resource sharing for automatic synthesis of Control Data Flow Graphs (CDFGs). [8] presents an efficient heuristic which transforms a set of custom instructions into a single hardware datapath on which they can execute. [9] addresses the design of multi-mode architectures for digital signal processing applications and present a dedicated design flow and its associated high-level synthesis tool, named GAUT. Given a unified description of a set of time-wise mutually exclusive tasks and their associated throughput constraints, a single RTL hardware architecture optimized in area is generated.

[10] presents the initial idea of DPM. It merges DFGs in a sequence. The edges from DFGs are merged and the vertices would have been merged if their edges had been merged together. [11] achieves a better resource area usage resulted by merging DFGs all at once. It uses integer programming algorithm for merging the edges that is so time-consuming and can be used only for a few number of DFGs. [4] completes the idea of [10] for minimizing the resource area usage and achieves the novel and the fastest solution for DPM but it heuristically chooses the sequence of DFGs from a biggest DFG to the smallest one for merging. In this paper, we represent a new merging technique that merges the functional units and interconnection units in the reconfigurable datapath to the more reduction of the resource area usage, after merging DFGs together one by one. Therefore it can optimize the resource area usage for each sequence of merging.

Next section explains the reduction of the resource area usage by datapath merging. Section 3 explains the proposed DPM technique while its method is presented in section 4. Section 5 evaluates the proposed method by comparing its experimental results to the previous algorithm. Ultimately, section 6 concludes the paper.

2   Merging DFGs to Reduce Resource Area Usage

In datapath merging, DFGs are merged together to make the reconfigurable datapath that can execute each DFG and has the minimal resource area usage. Let a DFG as a directed graph $G=(V,E)$, where $V=\{v_1,v_2,...v_n\}$ is the set of vertices *and* $E=\{e_{1=}$ $(u_1,v_1,p_1),...e_{n=}(u_n,v_n,p_n)\}$ is the set of edges. A vertex $v \in V$ represents a function that can be performed with a functional unit while each v has a set of input ports p. An edge $e_=(u,v,p) \in E$ indicates a data transfer from vertex u to the input port p of vertex v. The resulting reconfigurable datapath RDP is the merge of all DFGs. Therefore, a reconfigurable datapath, $RDP=(V',E')$, corresponding to DFGs $G_{i, i=1...n}$ is a directed graph, where: a vertex $v' \in V'$ represents a merging of vertices v from various V_i. An edge $e'=(u',v',p') \in E'$ represents a merging of edges, $e_i=(u_i,v_i,p_i)$, each one from a different E_i, in such a way that all u_i have been mapped onto u' and all v_i have been mapped onto v' and corresponding input ports p_i have been matched together and mapped to p'.

Fig.1 illustrates an example of datapath merging where DFGs G_1 and G_2 from this figure are merged and the reconfigurable datapaths (resulting datapaths) RDP_1, RDP_2, RDP_3, are produced. Considering these DFGs, if the function of a vertex from G_1 and the function of a vertex from G_2 can be performed with a functional unit, they will become a potential for merging. For example, the vertex a_1 from G_1 and the vertex b_1 from G_2 can be executed by a functional unit. Thus, these vertices are merged together and the vertex (a_1 / b_1) is made for them in the reconfigurable

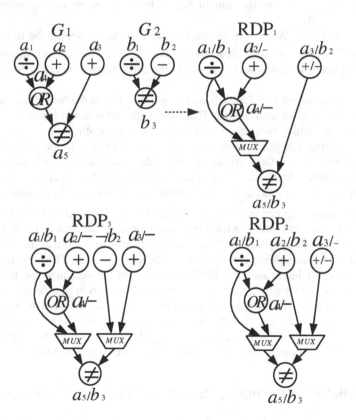

Fig. 1. Making the reconfigurable datapaths (RDP_1, RDP_2 and RDP_3) that have various resource area usage ($A_{RDP1} < A_{RDP2} < A_{RDP3}$) for the input DFGs G_1 and G_2 [4]

datapaths in this figure. If a vertex can not be merged onto other vertices, it will be used in the reconfigurable datapath itself. After merging two vertices, a multiplexer is employed in the input ports of their corresponding vertex in the reconfigurable datapath to select the input operand. This is illustrated in the input ports of vertex (a_5 / b_3) in the reconfigurable datapaths in this figure.

Among these DFGs, if couple vertices of an edge from G_1 are merged onto couple vertices of an edge from G_2, these edges will be merged together. As it is apparent, in Fig.1, because of merging the couple vertices a_3 and a_5 from G_1 onto the another couple vertices b_2 and b_3 in G_2, these edges (a_3, a_5) and (b_2, b_3) are merged together and the edge $(a_3/ b_2 , a_5/ b_3)$ is made instead, in the reconfigurable datapath RDP_1 so, it does not use any multiplexer in the input ports of the vertex (a_5 / b_3) in this reconfigurable datapath to select the input operands. The reconfigurable datapath should have the minimum resource area usage.

Definition 1. The resource area usage of the reconfigurable datapath RDP is:

$$A = A_f + A_i$$

Where $A_f = \sum_{\forall v \in V} A_v$ is the functional units' area usage in the reconfigurable datapath and $A_i = \sum A \, mux_i$ is the interconnection area usage in the reconfigurable datapath [4]. A_v is the resource area usage allocated to v, and since our interconnection is based on multiplexers, $Amux_i$ represents the area usage equivalent to each multiplexer.

As a result, reconfigurable datapath area usage depends on the functional unit area usage and the multiplexer area usages. That is, the optimal solution for reducing the area usage is the one which produces the reconfigurable datapath with the minimum area usage, considering functional units and interconnections area usage. In fig.1 DFG G_1 and G_2 are merged and three reconfigurable datapaths, (RDP_1, RDP_2 and RDP_3), are made for them. Area cost of these reconfigurable datapaths is different ($A_{RDP_1} \prec A_{RDP_2} \prec A_{RDP_3}$). The area cost depends on which vertices or edges from DFGs are merged together. In this way, we should merge the edges and vertices that make the reconfigurable datapath with the minimum area usage. Although merging DFGs altogether (using integer programming) has the best results to minimize the resource area usage, it is a time-consuming process and can be used for a few DFGs with small sizes [11]. On the other hand, merging DFGs, one by one, to minimize the resource area usage is a crude minimization and can not optimize the reconfigurable datapath area. A better approach to the more reduction in reconfigurable data path area usage is, once the DFGs are merged in a one by one fashion, the vertices and edges in the obtained reconfigurable datapath are merged together. This way the reconfigurable datapath area usage is minimized. What comes later is our specific technique to perform this idea.

3   Technique for Reconstructing Reconfigurable Datapath

Our ultimate purpose is to merge the resources in the reconfigurable datapath to minimize the resource area usage. The merging technique should solve the resource selection, resource binding and minimizing the resource area usage by simultaneously merging functional units and interconnection units to reconstruct the reconfigurable datapath. For reconstructing reconfigurable datapath, we have presented a new graph-based technique which is explained as follows.

3.1 Making the Compatibility Graph

Consider the DFGs are merged and the reconfigurable datapath is obtained. For merging the resources of the reconfigurable datapath, at first all merging possibilities among the vertices or among the edges of the input reconfigurable datapath *RDP* should be taken into consideration. The compatibility graph shows the merging possibility among all vertices from *RDP* to share the same vertex in the next reconfigurable datapath or, all merging possibility among all edges from *RDP* to share the same edge in the next reconfigurable datapath. Below, compatibility graph G_{cc} for the input reconfigurable datapath *RDP* is defined formally.

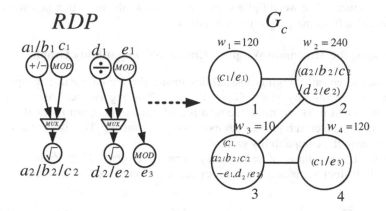

Fig. 2. Making compatibility graph G_{cc} for the input reconfigurable datapath *RDP*

Definition 2. A compatibility graph corresponding to input reconfigurable datapath, RDP, is an undirected weighted graph $G_{cc}=(V_c,E_c)$ where:

• Each vertex $v_c \in V_c$ with weight w corresponds to:

— Vertex-merging that is a possible merging of the vertices $v_i, v_j \ldots v_k \in RDP$ to create a vertex $v_{i..k}$ in the next reconfigurable datapath where it does not cause merging of the same vertex from a G_x onto a different vertices from a G_y or vice-versa.

— Edge-merging that is a possible merging of edges $e_i=(u_i, v_i, p_i)$, $e_j=(u_j, v_j, p_j) \ldots e_k=(u_k, v_k, p_k) \in RDP$ to create an edge $e_{i..k}$, in the next reconfigurable datapath where it does not cause merging the same vertex from a G_x onto a different vertices from a G_y or vice-versa.

• Each edge $e_c=(u_c, v_c) \in G_{cc}$ illustrates that using the vertices u_c and v_c together in data path merging, do not cause to merge the same vertex from a G_x onto different vertices from a G_y or vice-versa.

- Each vertex weight w represents the reduction in resource area usage resulting from merging the vertices or merging the edges.

After merging five DFGs $G_1=(a_1,a_2,(a_1,a_2))$, $G_2=(b_1,b_2,(b_1,b_2))$, $G_3=(c_1,c_1(c_1,c_2))$, $G_4=(d_1,d_2,(d_1,d_2))$, $G_5=(e_1,e_2,e_3,(e_1,e_2),(e_1,e_3))$ one bye one, the reconfigurable datapath RDP is made for them that is illustrated in fig.2. Afterwards, we should make the compatibility graph for the RDP. Fig 2 illustrates the compatibility graph for the input reconfigurable datapath RDP. In this figure, vertex (c_1/e_1) is made in compatibility graph G_{cc} for merging possibility between vertices $c_1,e_1 \in RDP$. Similarly, $(c_1/e_3) \in G_{cc}$ is made for merging possibility between vertices $c_1,e_3 \in RDP$. Vertices $(a_2/b_2/c_2)$ and $(d_2/e_2) \in RDP$ can be merged together so, the vertex $(a_2/b_2/c_2/d_2/e_2) \in G_{cc}$ is made for them to show these merging possibilities. A pair of vertices c_1 and $e_1 \in RDP$ and an other pair of vertices $a_2/b_2/c_2$ and $d_2/e_2 \in RDP$, are merged together, thus their edges $(c_1,a_2/b_2/c_2)$ and $(e_1,d_2/e_2)$ can also be merged. This way, a node $(c_1,a_2/b_2/c_2/- e_1,d_2/e_2)$ is made in G_{cc} for this edge-merging. All vertices of G_{cc} are compatible except (c_1/e_1) and (c_1/e_3) which merge a vertex c_1 from a DFG onto two vertices e_1 and e_3 from another DFG so all vertices of G_{cc} are connected except these two vertices. The weight of a vertex in G_{cc} shows the reduction in resource area usage resulting from merging vertices or edges.

3.2   Finding the Maximum Weighted Clique in Compatibility Graph

In previous stage, all merging possibilities inside the reconfigurable datapath were found as a compatibility graph $G_{cc}=(V_c, E_c)$. Choosing compatible vertices with maximum weight in G_{cc} to make the next reconfigurable datapath is equal to finding completely connected sub graph with more weight from G_{cc}. This is the classic graph called clique in the compatibility graph G_{cc}.

A clique C_c is a subset of vertices in compatibility graph $C_c \subset V_c$, in such a way that for all distinct vertices $u,v \in C_c$, they are adjacent $u,v \in E_c$ (are compatible). A

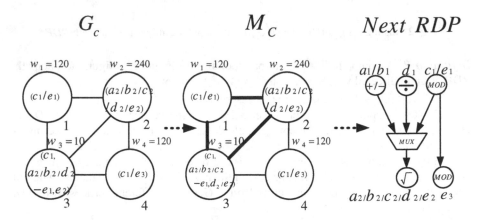

Fig. 3. Finding the maximum weighted clique in compatibility graph to make the next reconfigurable datapath

clique is called maximum clique if there are no larger cliques than it is in the compatibility graph G_{cc}.

Maximum weighted clique MC_c, is a maximum clique in compatibility graph G_{cc} that total weight of its vertices is more than any other clique C_c in the compatibility graph.

Choosing compatible vertices with larger weight in G_{cc} to make the next reconfigurable datapath is equal to finding completely connected sub graph with larger weight from compatibility graph G_{cc}. Therefore, our problem is actually the maximum weighted clique problem. As illustrated in fig.3, by using this clique, the next reconfigurable datapath will be made.

4 The Proposed Datapath Merging Method

Since merging great number of DFGs (or large DFGs) all at once, is so time- consuming, we do merge DFGs in a step by step fashion [4]. Our method merges DFGs in a one-by-one fashion. In the first stage of our method, the inputs DFGs are added to the reconfigurable datapath while the resource area usage is minimized. For merging DFGs onto reconfigurable datapath, we use the technique in [4]. After merging all DFGs to make the reconfigurable datapath, in the second stage we should minimize the resource area usage by reconstructing the reconfigurable datapath. This way, a graph-based technique that was presented in previous section is employed to perform our merging method. Below, the pseudo code of our method is shown in fig.4.

The algorithm considers the first input DFGs as a reconfigurable datapath in the first stage of merging. Then the compatibility graph, G_c, between the reconfigurable is made in the first stage of the algorithm. In the second stage, the compatibility graph finds the intra-reconfigurable datapath similarity using function *MakeCompatibilityGraph2*. By finding the maximum weighted clique for the compatibility graph and

```
program DPM ( output: reconfigurable datapath RDP=(V,E) such that
A(RDP) is minimum input: n DFGs G_i=(V_i,E_i, i=1..n))
   {assuming G_i is sorted};

begin  /*Merging DFGs to create the reconfigurable datapath*/

RDP<-G_1;
   for i<-2 to n do /*Iteratively merge RDP with input G_i*/
      G_c<-MakeCompatibilityGraph1(RDP,G_i);
      MC_c<-FindMaximumWeightedClique(G_c);
      RDP<-ReconstructReconfigurableDatapath1(MC_c, RDP,G_i);

   endfor

        /*Reconstructing the reconfigurable datapath */
   G_cc<-MakeCompatibilityGraph2(RDP);
   MC_c<-FindMaximumWeightedClique(G_cc);
   RDP<-ReconstructReconfigurableDatapath2(MC_c, RDP);

End DPM.
```

Fig. 4. Pseudo code of the proposed datapath merging method

```
function MakeCompatibilityGraph2 ( output: Compatibility Graph
Gcc=(V_c,E_c) input: reconfigurable datapats RDP =(V,E))

{Assuming |V| , |E| the number of vertices and the number of
edges in the reconfigurable datapath respectively. Assuming |N|
and |A| number of vertices and edges in G_cc respectively }

/* Creating vertices in G_cc for merging All vertex couples or all
edge couples in RDP*/
Begin
1   K=2;
2   For i<-1 to |V|
3     For j<-i+1 to |V| do
4         If ((v_i Ĉ v_j) then
5             n^k <- v_i + v_j;
6             N = N ∪ n^k;

7         EndIf;
8   For i<-1 to |E|
9     For j<-i+1 to |E| do
10        If ((e_i Ĉ e_j) then
11            n^k <- e_i + e_j;
12            N = N ∪ n^k;

14        EndIf;

/* create vertices in G_cc for merging all vertices and all edges
in RDP*/
15   While(IsMergingVertex)do
16     k++
17     IsMergingVertex = False
18     For i<-1 to |N|
19       For j<-1 to |V| do
20         If ((n_i Ĉ v_j) then IsMergingVertex = True;
21             n^k <-n_i + v_j;
22             N = N ∪ n^k;

23         EndIf;
24     For i<-1 to |A|
26       For j<-1 to |E| do
26         If ((a_i Ĉ e_j) then IsMergingVertex = True;
27             n^k <-a_i + e_j;
28             N = N ∪ n^k;

29         EndIf;
30   EndWhile

/* create edges in G_cc */
31   For i<-1 to |N|)
32     For j<-i+1 to |N|) do
33         If (n_i Ĉ m_j)then
34             makeEdge a=(n_i,m_j)in G_cc;
End MakeCompatibilityGraph2;

A Ĉ B: /* A is compatible to B*/
n^k :/* a vertex in G_cc for merging k vertices or k edges in RDP
```

Fig. 5. *MakeCompatibilityGraph2* function for making the compatibility graph G_{cc} for the input reconfigurable datapath

reconstructing the reconfigurable datapath using graph, the desired reconfigurable datapath is made.

To make the compatibility graph, G_{cc}, for the second stage of the algorithm, we implement our function according to definition.2. Fig.5 shows the *MakeCompatibilityGraph2* function that makes G_{cc} for the input reconfigurable datapath. In the first stages of the proposed function, all vertices in *RDP* are compared together to find each merging possibility between the vertex couples in the *RDP*. A vertex n^2 is made in G_{cc} for the merging possibility between the vertex couples. This way, each merging possibility between an edge couples in the *RDP* is found and their corresponding vertex is made in G_{cc}. In the second stage, in a While Loop, each vertex in G_{cc} is compared to all vertices in *RDP* to find the possibility of merging k vertices, and to do so, vertex n^k is made in G_{cc}. Similarly, each edge in G_{cc} is compared to all edges in *RDP* to make the vertex n^k in G_{cc} for merging k edges from *RDP*. k shows the number of vertices or edges merged to make the vertex n^k in G_{cc}.

In the final stage, after making the vertices of G_{cc}, each vertex couples from G_{cc} is compared together to find their compatibility between. Now, if they do not cause the merge in two vertices from a DFG, they are compatible and an edge is made between them in G_{cc}. Using the proposed algorithm in fig.5, the compatibility graph for the input *RDP* is made that shows all merging possibilities among the vertices and among the edges in *RDP*.

The maximum weighted clique problem is known to be an NP-complete problem [12]. For finding the maximum weighted clique from a graph, [13] has presented a Branch&Bound algorithm and has optimized its execution time. It chooses efficient order for selecting vertices and predicts bounds for quick backtracking. The method in [13] for searching the search space of the problem and its optimizations are suitable for solving our problem. By adding conditions of our problem to algorithm in [13] and modifying it, the proposed Branch&Bound function (*FindMaximumWeightedClique*) to find the desired maximum weighted clique is achieved. This function finds the maximum weighted clique $M_C = (V_{mc}, E_{mc})$ for graph $G_{cc} = (V_c, E_c)$. At the end of running this function, the maximum weighted clique M_C is obtained. The function which we implemented for making the maximum weighted clique is used for two stages of the algorithm.

After finding M_C of the compatibility graph, the merging possibility represented by the vertices of M_C is used to reconstruct the reconfigurable datapath. Each vertex from this clique gives a merging possibility between an edge (a vertex) from *RDP* and an edge (a vertex) from the DFG, in the first stage of merging or among the resources of *RDP* in the second stage of merging. These edges (vertices) are merged together. This solution reconstructs *RDP* to minimize the resource area usage.

5 Experimental Results

Many experiments exist to support the fact that there are some Inner-loop sections in Media-bench benchmark which have the largest share of execution time [14]. The entity of these inner loops makes them suitable for mapping on reconfigurable unit. Initially these benchmarks should be converted to intermediate representation. At first, each program was compiled using the GCC compiler, and was profiled so as to determine which inner loops contributed the most to the program execution time [15]. For each such loop, a DFG was generated from the loop body RTL code (GCC inter-mediated representation). Using RTL instead of machine instructions permitted us to extract the loop code after most machine-independent code optimizations, but before register allocation and machine-dependent optimizations. After attaining DFGs for each benchmark, up to 8 Inner-Loops have been considered and the DFGs were itera-tively merged from a larger DFG to the smaller DFG.

For evaluating our method, we compared the resource area usage of the obtained reconfigurable datapath by the proposed algorithm to the reconfigurable datapath in [4]. HLS was performed on the DFGs corresponding to the inner loops for each benchmark beforehand, using an in-house tool. Chaining was exploited during sched-uling and no intra-DFG resource sharing was exploited. After applying our DPM algorithms and the algorithms in [4] to the DFGs, the reduction in resource area usage of the reconfigurable datapath indicates the efficiency of the proposed method.

Fig.6 illustrates the percentage of decrease in area usage for reconfigurable datapath of various DFGs from GSM-Coder benchmark after applying the proposed algorithm in comparison to algorithm in [4]. As illustrated in this figure, the results of merging two DFGs are the same for two algorithms but, by augmenting the number of DFGs, the difference between reconfigurable datapath area usages for these algo-rithms increases.

We repeat this experiment for some benchmarks from Media-bench to make their reconfigurable datapaths. Fig.7 shows the percentage of decreases in the reconfigur-able datapath area usage for these benchmarks after applying the proposed algorithm in comparison to algorithm in [4]. There is a noticeable decrease in reconfigurable datapath area usage mostly for benchmarks that have more number of DFGs.

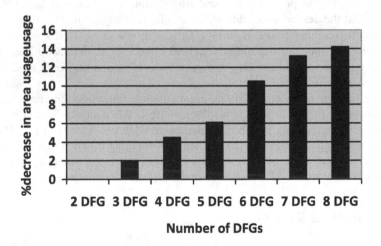

Fig. 6. Percentage of decrease in area usage for reconfigurable datapath of various DFGs from GSM-Coder benchmark after applying the proposed algorithm in comparison to the algorithm in [4]

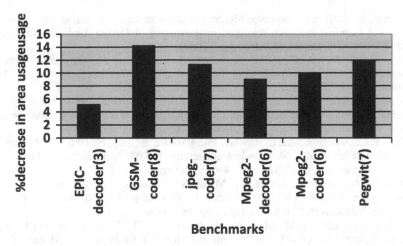

Fig. 7. Percentage of decrease in resource area usage for reconfigurable datapath of Media-bench benchmarks after applying the proposed algorithm in comparison to the algorithm in [4]

6 Conclusion

This paper presented a new data path merging method for minimizing the resource area usage of reconfigurable datapath in reconfigurable system. Our method merges the DFGs one by one to make the reconfigurable datapath. Then it reconstructs the datapath by merging its functional units and interconnection units all at once. By such a method, we presented a new graph-based technique for reconstructing the reconfigurable datapath. It allocates and binds functional units and multiplexers at the same time besides minimizing the resource area usage of the resulting datapath that is an *NP*-complete problem. The maximum weighted clique algorithm is modified to solve this problem. We added our method to high computational For-Loop sections of Mediabench benchmarks. The experimental results show the improvement from %5 to %15 for reducing the resource area usage after using this method in comparison to previous algorithms. This method is more efficient than previous DPM methods especially whenever the number of DFGs for merging increases.

References

1. Compton, K., Hauck, S.: Automatic Design of Area-Efficient Configurable ASIC Cores. IEEE Transaction on Computers (TC) 56(5), 1–11 (2007)
2. Gajski, D., Dutt, N., Wu, A., Lin, S.: High-Level Synthesis-Introduction to Chip and System Design. Kluwer, Boston (1992)
3. De Micheli, G.: Synthesis and Optimization of Digital Circuits. McGraw-Hill, New York (1994)
4. Moreano, N., Borin, Ed., Souza, Cd., Araujo, G.: Efficient Datapath Merging for Partially Reconfigurable architectures. IEEE Transaction on Computer Aided Design 24(7), 969–980 (2005)
5. Papadimitriou, C., Steiglitz, K.: Combinatorial Optimization-Algorithms and Complexity. Dover, New York (1998)

6. Mathur, A., Sanjive, S.: Improved Merging of Datapath Operators Using Information Content and Required Precision Analysis. In: Proceding of Design Automation Conference (DAC), Rhode Island, pp. 462–467 (April 2001)
7. Memik, S.O., Memik, G., Jafari, R., Kursun, E.: Global resource sharing for synthesis of control data flow graphs on FPGAs. In: Proceedings of the 40th Conference on Design Automation (DAC), Anaheim, CA, USA, pp. 2–6 (June 2003)
8. Brisk, P., Kaplan, A., Sarrafzadeh, M.: Area-efficient instruction set synthesis for reconfigurable system-on-chip designs. In: Proceedings of the 41st Annual Conference on Design Automation (DAC), San Diego, CA, USA, pp. 395–400 (June 2004)
9. Chavet, C., Andriamisaina, C., Coussy, Ph., Casseau, E., Juin, E., Urard, P., Martin, E.: A design flow dedicated to Multimode Architectures for DSP Applications. In: Proceeding of (ICCAD), San Jose, CA, USA, pp. 604–611 (November 2007)
10. Moreano, N., Araujo, G., Huang, Zh., Majlik, S.H.: Datapath Merging and Interconnection Sharing for Reconfigurable Architectures. In: Proceding of International Symposium on Systems Synthesis (ISSS), Kyoto, Japan, pp. 38–43 (January 2002)
11. de Souza, C., Lima, A.M., Moreano, N., Araujo, G.: The Datapath Merging Problem in Reconfigurable Systems: Lower Bounds and Heuristic Evaluation. ACM Journal of Experimental Algorithmics (JEA) 10(2), 1–19 (2006)
12. Garey, M., Johnson, D.S.: Computers and Intractability-A Guide to the Theory of NP-Completeness. Freeman, San Francisco (1979)
13. Ostergard, P.R.J.: A New Algorithm for the Maximum-Weight Clique Problem. Nordic Journal of Computing (NJC) 8(4), 424–436 (2002)
14. Lee, C., Potkonjak, M., Mangione, W.S.: Media-bench: a tool for evaluating and synthesizing multimedia and communication systems. In: Proceedings of The thirtieth Annual IEEE/ACM International Symposium on Microarchitecture (MICRO-03), California, USA, pp. 330–335 (December 1997)
15. GNU Compiler Collection Internals, http://gcc.gnu.org/onlinedocs

Optimizing the Control Hierarchy of an ECC Coprocessor Design on an FPGA Based SoC Platform

Xu Guo and Patrick Schaumont

Virginia Tech, Blacksburg VA 24061, USA
{xuguo,schaum}@vt.edu

Abstract. Most hardware/software codesigns of Elliptic Curve Cryptography only have one central control unit, typically a 32 bit or 8 bit processor core. With the ability of integrating several soft processor cores into one FPGA fabric, we can have a hierarchy of controllers in one SoC design. Compared to the previous codesigns trying to optimize the communication overhead between the central control unit and coprocessor over bus by using different bus protocols (e.g. OPB, PLB and FSL) or advanced techniques (e.g. DMA), our approach prevents overhead in bus transactions by introducing a local 8 bit microcontroller, PicoBlaze, in the coprocessor. As a result, the performance of the ECC coprocessor can be almost independent of the selection of bus protocols. To further accelerate the Uni-PicoBlaze based ECC SoC design, a Dual-PicoBlaze based architecture is proposed, which can achieve the maximum instruction rate of 1 instruction/cycle to the ECC datapath. Using design space exploration of a large number of system configurations of different architectures discussed in this paper, our proposed Dual-PicoBlaze based design also shows best trade-off between area and speed.

1   Introduction

FPGAs are ideal for System-on-Chip (SoC) or Hardware/Software (HW/SW) codesign. Embedded processor soft-cores enable integration of various peripherals or coprocessors. Computationally intensive kernels are well suited for hardware acceleration. In this work we investigate the acceleration of the point operations from Elliptic Curve Cryptography (ECC). This task remains a challenge because of the implementation complexity of ECC, which requires optimizations at multiple abstraction levels. We will demonstrate that there is a strong interaction between the target architecture and the most suitable HW/SW partitioning.

Many HW/SW codesigns have been proposed to evaluate trade-offs between cost, performance and security in ECC system designs. Most of the target platforms fall into two categories: 8 bit platforms (e.g. AVR or 8051) [1,2,3,4,5,6] and 32 bit microprocessors and bus systems (e.g. MicroBlaze with PLB bus) [7,8,9]. Although the design goals in these two platforms may differ due to different applications (e.g. low power sensor nodes *vs.* high performance security

J. Becker et al. (Eds.): ARC 2009, LNCS 5453, pp. 169–180, 2009.
© Springer-Verlag Berlin Heidelberg 2009

systems), both of them have to deal with the same problem of how to minimize the communication overhead resulting from using a single, central controller.

The work discussed in this paper differs from previous research by realizing the fact that both of the 8 bit microcontrollers and 32 bit microprocessors can co-exist in modern FPGAs and the combination of them in one SoC design may result in a better trade-off between area and speed. In this work, we propose an SoC architecture for ECC Point Multiplication that uses a central 32 bit microprocessor, an 8 bit local control processor, and a dedicated field arithmetic datapath. The contribution of our work is two-fold. First, we use HW/SW cosimulation to do system profiling of the bus bottleneck, and we explore multiple control hierarchies in a typical FPGA based SoC system. We show that, using proper partitioning of control and data, the ECC system execution time can be made almost independent of the selection of bus protocols between the central controller and the coprocessor. Second, we optimize the local control unit by converting a Uni-Picoblaze sequencer architecture into a Dual-Picoblaze architecture which runs interleaved instruction sequences. This novel Dual-PicoBlaze based architecture achieves the instruction transfer rate of 1 instruction/cycle, while a Uni-Picoblaze architecture only provides half that speed, 1 instruction per 2 cycles. Moreover, the FPGA implementation results show that our proposed ECC SoC architecture with the Dual-PicoBlaze based coprocessor has a better trade-off between area and speed.

The remainder of this paper is organized as follows. Section 2 gives a brief description of current available processor cores in FPGAs and their different usages. Our complete ECC SoC system design will be presented in Section 3 and detailed discussion on our proposed Uni-PicoBlaze and Dual-PicoBlaze based coprocessor designs is given. Section 4 explains the system-level design flow used in the paper, and performance results are analyzed and compared between cosimulation and FPGA implementation. Section 5 concludes the paper.

2   Embedded Processor Cores in FPGAs

Modern FPGAs are considered as configurable systems on chip (CSoC) [21]. A primary component for such CSoC systems is the processor core. A wide range of bit widths from 8 to 32 bit are used in SoC designs. Small bit widths have the advantage of a small memory footprint for simple applications, but also imply a limited complexity. Wide instructions allow for much more complex applications, but will also require a large amount of memory even for small applications [10].

Various synthesizable processor cores are available for FPGAs. On one hand we have some popular embedded processors like AVR8[11] and Leon2 [12]. These cores are not tailored to the specific resources available in FPGAs. On the other hand there are specialized processor cores for FPGAs, such as Altera NIOS II, Xilinx MicroBlaze and PicoBlaze, and Lattice Mico8. They can be classified into two categories: 8 bit cores like the Xilinx PicoBlaze or the Lattice Mico8 and 32 bit cores like the NIOS II and the Microblaze. The use of 32 bit cores targets at high performance applications and sometimes requires external memory. Compared with the 32 bit cores, the 8 bit cores have very simple IO interfaces and are very limited in computation power. The on-chip program memory is always very small, typically less than 1K instruction store with simplified instruction set. Hence, they consume very few hardware resources on FPGAs, which makes them sometimes be an ideal alternative for complicated FSMs.

As indicated above, either type of core has its own advantages, which may be complementary to each other in one SoC design. However, most current research only considers them as separate control units and rarely combines them in a single system-level design.

3   ECC SoC Design

Curve-based cryptography, especially ECC, has become very popular in the past several years [22]. These cryptographic primitives are used for exchanging keys over an insecure channel and for digital signatures. Furthermore, these algorithms show good properties for software and hardware implementation because of the relatively short operand length compared to other public-key scheme, like RSA. However, ECC is still considered as a computational intensive application due to the complexity of scalar or point multiplications. As shown in Fig. 1, a scalar multiplication, $k \cdot P$, with k is an integer and P is a point on an elliptic curve, needs to be realized through a sequence of point additions and doublings. These group operations can be further decomposed in several types of finite field arithmetic with ultra-long operand word length (e.g. 163 bit or above).

There are many design options for ECC designs, and different approaches differ in the selection of coordinate system, field and type of curve[13]. Since in our design the main focus lies on the architectural optimization of the ECC SoC system, we start with a baseline design using Montgomery Scalar Multiplication on $GF(2^{163})$ based on L-D projective coordinates [14]. For hardware implementations of the lowest level field arithmetic, the GF multiplication is implemented both as bit-serial [15] and digit-serial multipliers [16] with different digit sizes; the GF addition is simply logic XORs; the GF square is implemented by dedicated hardware with square and reduction circuits [13]; the GF inversion consists of a sequence of GF multiplications and squares based on Fermat's Theorem [17].

Since the core component of our ECC coprocessor is the field multiplier, here we define a design space based on the use of different field multipliers to discuss the design trade-offs between area and speed. A basic bit-serial multiplication in $GF(2^m)$ can be realized through an classic 'shift-and-XOR' based MSB-first bit-serial multiplier with interleaved reduction modulo the irreducible polynomial [15]. It can finish one $GF(2^{163})$ multiplication in 163 clock cycles. A digit-serial multiplier [16] on the other hand can process multiple bits of the operands in parallel with a processing time proportional to $\lceil m/D \rceil$ cycles, with digit size D $\leq$ m - k, where m is 163 and k is 7 for the B-163 curve. It is obvious that within a certain range of D, when increasing the D, the area will increase accordingly, but the processing time will be the same. For example, for all D$\in$[55,81], the

Table 1. System profiling from GEZEL cosimulation

# Access 163 bit local reg.	Baseline Design bus transactions		Uni-PicoBlaze bus transactions		Dual-PicoBlaze bus transactions	
	# Ins.	# Data	# Ins.	# Data	# Ins.	# Data
2,788	26,791	1,294	481	489	468	476

multiplication time is 3 clock cycles. In this case we only select D size of 55 for our implementations.

The HW/SW partitioning adopted in this design is trying to offload the field arithmetic operations from the microprocessor and execute them in a dedicated coprocessor [2,7]. For our baseline design, all other operations, such as point addition/doubling, are implemented in software running on microprocessor. However, this partitioning may result in a HW/SW communication bottleneck since the lower-level field multiplication function will always be called by upper-level point operations, including a large amount of instruction and data transfers.

From the above analysis on the HW/SW partitioning, we already know where the system bottleneck will be, so before starting the system-level design we should first quantitatively measure the bus transactions in the baseline design, and estimate the optimization room left for us. Table 1 shows the system profiling from GEZEL cosimulation [18,19], and more details can be found in section 4.1. Since our system bus interface uses the memory-mapped registers, the way we collect the number of instruction and data transfers over the bus is to measure how many write and read on these registers for instruction or data transfers.

3.1   Baseline ECC SoC Design with Coprocessor Local Storage

In a straightforward design (see Fig.1 (a)), the ECC system will implement the point operations on the main processor. This requires storing all parameters and intermediate results in Processor Local Memory, so that the main processor can access and manipulate them. From Table 1, it is observed that for a 163 bit scalar multiplication, there are 2,788 times read/write on eight 163 bit coprocessor local registers, so if all parameters and intermediate results are stored in main memory, this may result in 16,728 times 32 bit data transfers over the bus. This represents a significant amount of time (around 60% of the total execution time of a point multiplication, assuming the typical PLB bus HW-SW latency of 9 clock cycles). Hence, a simple optimization can be achieved by adding local storage to the coprocessor, like scheme (b) in Fig. 1, so that the amount of data transfers over the processor-to-coprocessor bus can be minimized.

3.2   Uni-PicoBlaze Based ECC SoC Design

The above design mitigates the overall bus communication overhead by optimizing the data transfer side; however, instruction transfers still dominate the

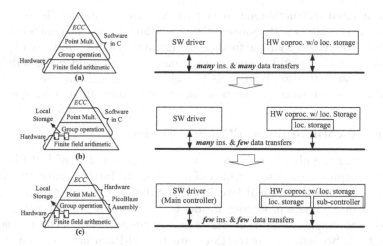

Fig. 1. System architecture modeling of different schemes

entire scalar multiplication time. From the cosimulation profiling (see Table.1), we can see for a 163 bit scalar multiplication, there are 26,791 times instruction transfers though the data transfers have been reduced to 1,294 (mostly composed of reading status registers) with a typical PLB bus. One area for further optimization is that of coprocessor control. Indeed, for each operation performed by the coprocessor, the processor needs to perform a command transfer over the PLB bus. These command transfers are still needed, even after local registers are added to the coprocessor. In order to reduce the amount of command transfers, we must change the way to control the coprocessor.

The PicoBlaze microcontroller is a compact and cost-effective embedded 8 bit RISC microcontroller core optimized for Xilinx FPGAs. It has predictable performance, always 2 clock cycles per instruction, and 1K instructions of programmable on-chip program store, automatically loaded during FPGA configuration. It only costs 63 slices and 1 block RAM on Virtex-5 XC5VLX50 FPGA.

By introducing PicoBlaze as a sub-control hierarchy to be in charge of sending out the point addition and doubling instructions, the main controller, MicroBlaze, only needs to start a scalar multiplication once, after which the detailed sequencing will be completed by the PicoBlaze (like Scheme (c) in Fig. 1). The PicoBlaze has the additional advantage of having a fixed instruction rate (2 clock cycles per operation). This means that the local instruction decoder in the coprocessor can be simplified: no additional synchronization is needed between the PicoBlaze and the local instruction decoder FSM. From the cosimulation system profiling (see Table. 1), we can see that for the Uni-PicoBlaze design the instruction and data transfers have been greatly reduced to 481 and 489, respectively. Here, we want to further point out that the lower-bound on the amount of instruction and data transfers is around 18 and 6, respectively. Most of the current measured instruction and data transfers are devoted to the continuous read on status registers with associated instructions during the coprocessor execution time. Therefore, a simple further optimization can be conducted by using 'interrupt' control, and this improvement may not only reduce the number of bus transactions but also save the ECC task's occupation time on MicroBlaze and PLB bus, which then may be used for other peripherals in a large system.

3.3   Dual-PicoBlaze Based ECC SoC Design

After analyzing the above design we find two characteristics of Uni-PicoBlaze based ECC coprocessor design, which can help us to further refine the design. First, the sub-control unit, PicoBlaze, in current design is acting as an instruction generator. It has no data processing inside, which means it is feasible to split the Picoblaze program into several subsets as long as the sequence of the instructions is guaranteed. Second, the instruction rate of Uni-PicoBlaze is fixed 2 clock cycles per operation, which means that there is still one cycle per operation wasted. So, from the above two observations we propose the idea of optimizing the local control unit by converting an Uni-Picoblaze sequencer architecture into a Dual-Picoblaze architecture which runs interleaved instruction sequences. Hence, this novel Dual-PicoBlaze based architecture can achieve the maximum instruction transfer rate of 1 instruction/cycle. To illustrate the conversion from Uni-PicoBlaze to the Dual-PicoBlaze, a simple example of PicoBlaze assembly codes executing one field multiplication followed by an addition is shown in Fig.2. Compared with the Uni-PicoBlaze design our proposed Dual-PicoBlaze design can save additional 18% of total clock cycles in average, at the expense of very small hardware overhead (81 slices in average from FPGA implementation results on XC5VLX50). Detailed comparison between cosimulation and FPGA implementation results are presented in section 4.3.

As we know there are some traditional ways which can achieve the maximum instruction rate of 1 instruction/cycle, such as implementing the point operations in FSM or using microcoded controller with pre-set micro codes [7].

Compared with the first approach using FSMs, our Dual-PicoBlaze architecture is more flexible and efficient. In general, the field operations can already be very fast (a digit-serial multiplier with D size of 82 can finish one 163 bit field multiplication in 2 clock cycles) and big performance gain of the whole underlying ECC system can only be obtained if new point operation algorithms are proposed. In this case, by fixing the lowest level field operations in hardware, updating an ECC system is just replacing the software assembly codes in PicoBlaze with the new point operation algorithms without the need to rewrite the HDLs. In addition, this method can also enable the integration of the latest countermeasures against side-channel attack into the algorithm for scalar multiplication. Moreover, many people regard the 8 bit microcontroller, like PicoBlaze, as a replacement for large and complicated FSMs since they are always hard to write and debug.

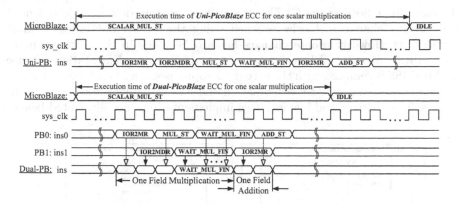

Fig. 2. An example of interleaving instructions

Compared with the second approach using microcoded controller, the Dual-PicoBlaze architecture is much easier to be programmed since instead of designing sometimes complex dedicated controller with FSMs to dispatch instructions, we can simply use several PicoBlaze instructions to achieve efficient communication and synchronization with the hardware decoder without additional logic.

4   Design Flow and Implementation

4.1   System-Level Design and Co-simulation Using GEZEL

In order to narrow the gap between performance and flexibility, to reduce the time required to complete a design and to reduce the risk of errors that might result from translating a high-level prototype (e.g. C model) into HDLs, we use GEZEL to perform system-level design [18,19,20]. GEZEL is especially suitable for the exploration of domain-specific coprocessor and multiprocessor micro architectures as it can provide cycle-true hardware/software co-simulation with various embedded core instruction set simulators. This shortens the design time for both HW and SW. After finishing cosimulation the GEZEL file can be automatically translated into synthesizable VHDL files.

As shown in Fig. 3, the cosimulation is based ARM and PicoBlaze with PLB IPIF and all of them are instantiated as 'ipblock' in GEZEL. The implementation of the whole ECC coprocessor in GEZEL is based on Finite State Machine with Datapah (FSMD) model. The ARM communicates with the coprocessor through three 32 bit memory-mapped registers. An instruction decoder with a FSM and PicoBlazes are added on the top of the hardware field multiplier to dispatch instructions. Then, it will be attached to an interface module, 'user_ logic', to be connected with ARM through PLB IPIF. The last step is to develop software drivers in C. It should be pointed out that the GEZEL cosimulation can not only verify the correctness of the coprocessor and generate the corresponding VHDLs of the function unit, but also generate the bus interface module in VHDL.

Therefore, by following the GEZEL design flow, system designers do not need to make any change in hardware when doing the FPGA SoC integration of coprocessors. However, minor changes have to be made in the software driver when shifting from GEZEL cosimulation to the FPGA implementation because the ARM ISS is replaced with the actual microprocessor, a MicroBlaze core. The comparison between GEZEL cosimulation and FPGA implementation, in terms of the software driver and bus interface implementations, are illustrated below.

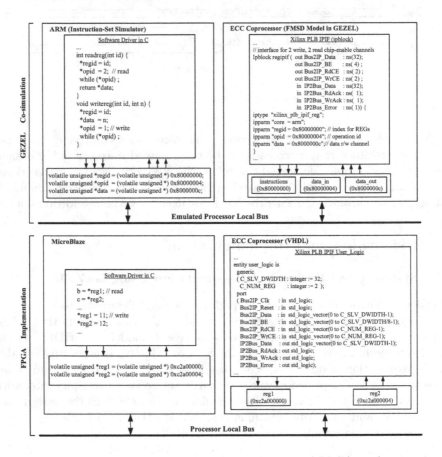

Fig. 3. Comparison between the GEZEL cosimulation and FPGA implementation

4.2   FPGA Implementation

After GEZEL cosimulation we can translate the GEZEL description of the ECC datapath and control wrappers into synthesizable VHDLs, which can be added as coprocessors in the Xilinx Platform Studio (XPS) 9.2.02i. The system shown in Fig. 4 is built on Xilinx Virtex-5 XC5VLX50 ML501 development board. A hardware timer is added for measuring cycle counts for each design configuration.

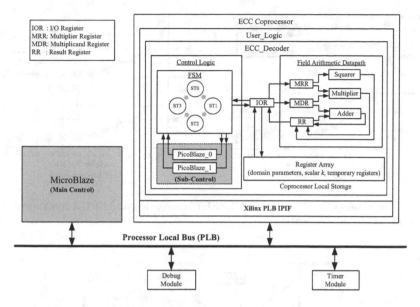

Fig. 4. FPGA implementation block diagram of ECC SoC system

4.3 Discussion of Experimental Results

From the deterministic and cycle-accurate GEZEL cosimulation, we can obtain both of the standalone hardware design profiles and the system profiles (e.g. cycle and toggle counts) [20]. This is very helpful for system designers to evaluate performance at a very early design stage and accelerate their design space exploration. To verify the correctness of our cosimulation, the FPGA implementation performance results measured by hardware timer are also added for comparison.

As indicated in Fig. 5, for the baseline design without PicoBlaze, the two systems are limited by the throughput of the PLB bus. For example, for the FPGA implementation with the PLB bus latency of 9 clock cycles, if a field multiplication in hardware can finish in 9 clock cycles (e.g. 8 clock cycles for digit-serial multiplier of D size of 24), the speedup of standalone field multiplication brought by D-sizes beyond 24 become invisible. Similarly, due to overhead introduced in the ARM ISS model, the bus latency is much higher, around 44 clock cycles, which results in no overall system speedup observed after D size of 2. Whereas, for the other PicoBlaze based designs, since the bus transactions are no longer the bottleneck, we can observe comparable results between the FPGA implementation and GEZEL cosimulation. Since the control hierarchy optimization by introducing PicoBlaze also features small hardware overhead, from Fig. 6 we can see our proposed Dual-PicoBlaze based design can achieve the best trade-off design with D size of 28.

In order to make a fair comparison with other published results, we also synthesize our design based on Virtex-2 Pro XC2VP30 FPGA. As shown in Table 2, our Dual-PicoBlaze based ECC (with maximum frequency around 200MHz on

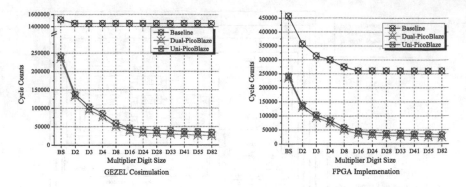

Fig. 5. Comparison of cycle counts of GEZEL cosimulation and FPGA implementation for one full scalar multiplication

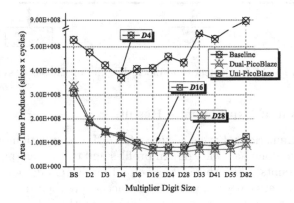

Fig. 6. Comparison of time-area products for each configuration of coprocessors

XC2VP30) shows a better trade-off between cost and performance: compare our fastest design with ref. 2, it gains 13.4% speedup; compare our best trade-off design with ref.1 and ref.2, its area-time product is 50.3% and 53.4% smaller. Although the current version of Dual-PicoBlaze design does not support arbitrary field size as [7], it still offers an ideal alternative since in most cases the arbitrary field size is not required. We want to also point out that the optimizations of ECC SoC design can be done in several levels (e.g. architecture, algorithm, and circuit) and the results shown here might not be the optimal ones even in terms of the area-time product since the performance optimization focus in this paper only lies on the architectural-level. However, we believe our proposed ECC SoC architecture can be easily adapted to other system requirements, such as the integration of high-level (e.g. algorithmic level) countermeasures against simple power analysis (SPA) and differential power analysis (DPA) attacks [23].

Table 2. Comparison of ECC coprocessor implementations on FPGAs

	Field	Platform	Slices	Cycle Counts	Field Size	Comments
Dual-PB w/ D28	$GF(2^{163})$	V2Pro	5,158	29,897	Fixed	Best trade-off
Dual-PB w/ D82	$GF(2^{163})$	V2Pro	8,944	24,689	Fixed	Fastest
ref.1 in [7]	$GF(2^{163})$	V2Pro	4,749	48,800	Arbitrary	1xMALU163
ref.2 in [7]	$GF(2^{163})$	V2Pro	8,450	28,000	Arbitrary	2xMALU163

5 Conclusions

This paper introduced an ECC coprocessor design using PicoBlaze as sub-control hierarchy. Starting from the system profiling of a baseline ECC design using cosimulation, we tried to not repeat the conventional optimization techniques on bus communication, but instead explore new system architectures with multiple control hierarchies. This results in the Uni-PicoBlaze based ECC coprocessor design. Since with this architecture, the impact of the bus latency is almost negligible, we then focus on improving the computational performance of the design to achieve the maximum instruction rate. This leads to a novel Dual-PicoBlaze based ECC architecture is proposed, which can achieve a better trade-off between area and speed with proper choosing the digit size of field multiplier. With flexibility, ease of integration of multiple PicoBlazes into current FPGA systems and predictable performance, this Dual-PicoBlaze based architecture can not only be extended to other curve-based cryptography systems, but also to some other computational intensive applications.

Acknowledgments. This project was supported in part by the National Science Foundation through grant 0644070. The authors would like to thank the Xilinx University Program for their hardware support.

References

1. Gura, N., et al.: An End-to-End Systems Approach to Elliptic Curve Cryptography. In: Kaliski Jr., B.S., Koç, Ç.K., Paar, C. (eds.) CHES 2002. LNCS, vol. 2523, pp. 349–365. Springer, Heidelberg (2003)
2. Koschuch, M., et al.: Hardware/Software Co-design of Elliptic Curve Cryptography on an 8051 Microcontroller. In: Goubin, L., Matsui, M. (eds.) CHES 2006. LNCS, vol. 4249, pp. 430–444. Springer, Heidelberg (2006)
3. Gura, N., et al.: Comparing elliptic curve cryptography and RSA on 8-bit CPUs. In: Joye, M., Quisquater, J.-J. (eds.) CHES 2004. LNCS, vol. 3156, pp. 119–132. Springer, Heidelberg (2004)
4. Aigner, H., Bock, H., Hütter, M., Wolkerstorfer, J.: A low-cost ECC coprocessor for smartcards. In: Joye, M., Quisquater, J.-J. (eds.) CHES 2004. LNCS, vol. 3156, pp. 107–118. Springer, Heidelberg (2004)

5. Batina, L., et al.: Hardware/software co-design for hyperelliptic curve cryptography (HECC) on the 8051 μP. In: Rao, J.R., Sunar, B. (eds.) CHES 2005. LNCS, vol. 3659, pp. 106–118. Springer, Heidelberg (2005)
6. Hodjat, A., Hwang, D., Batina, L., Verbauwhede, I.: A hyperelliptic curve crypto coprocessor for an 8051 microcontroller. In: SIPS 2005, pp. 93–98. IEEE, Los Alamitos (2005)
7. Sakiyama, K., Batina, L., Preneel, B., Verbauwhede, I.: Superscalar Coprocessor for High-Speed Curve-Based Cryptography. In: Goubin, L., Matsui, M. (eds.) CHES 2006. LNCS, vol. 4249, pp. 415–429. Springer, Heidelberg (2006)
8. Cheung, R.C.C., Luk, W., Cheung, P.Y.K.: Reconfigurable Elliptic Curve Cryptosystems on a Chip. In: DATE 2005, vol. 1, pp. 24–29. IEEE, Los Alamitos (2005)
9. Klimm, A., Sander, O., Becker, J., Subileau, S.: A Hardware/Software Codesign of a Co-processor for Real-Time Hyperelliptic Curve Cryptography on a Spartan3 FPGA. In: Brinkschulte, U., Ungerer, T., Hochberger, C., Spallek, R.G. (eds.) ARCS 2008. LNCS, vol. 4934, pp. 188–201. Springer, Heidelberg (2008)
10. Hemple, G., Hochberger, C.: A resource optimized Processor Core for FPGA based SoCs. In: DSD 2007, pp. 51–58. IEEE, Los Alamitos (2007)
11. AVR Core at opencores.org (2008),
    http://www.opencores.com/projects/avr_core/
12. Gaisler Research: LEON2 Processor User's Manual (2005)
13. Hankerson, D., Menezes, A.J., Vanston, S.A.: Guide to Elliptic Curve Cryptography. Springer, Heidelberg (2004)
14. López, J., Dahab, R.: Fast multiplication on elliptic curves over $GF(2^m)$. In: Koç, Ç.K., Paar, C. (eds.) CHES 1999. LNCS, vol. 1717, pp. 316–327. Springer, Heidelberg (1999)
15. Großschädl, J.: A low-power bit-serial multiplier for finite fields $GF(2^m)$. In: ISCAS 2001, vol. IV, pp. 37–40. IEEE, Los Alamitos (2001)
16. Kumar, S., Wollinger, T., Paar, C.: Optimum Digit Serial $GF(2^m)$ Multipliers for Curve-Based Cryptography. IEEE Transactions on Computers 55(10), 1306–1311 (2006)
17. Rodríguez-Henríquez, F., Saqib, N.A., Díaz-Pérez, A., Koç, Ç.K.: Cryptographic Algorithms on Reconfigurable Hardware. Springer, Heidelberg (2006)
18. Schaumont, P., Ching, D., Verbauwhede, I.: An Interactive Codesign Environment for Domain-specific Coprocessors. ACM Transactions on Design Automation of Electronic Systems 11(1), 70–87 (2006)
19. Schaumont, P., Verbauwhede, I.: A Component-based Design Environment for Electronic System-level Design. IEEE Design and Test of Computers Magazine, special issue on Electronic System-Level Design 23(5), 338–347 (2006)
20. Guo, X., Chen, Z., Schaumont, P.: Energy and Performance Evaluation of an FPGA-Based SoC Platform with AES and PRESENT Coprocessors. In: Bereković, M., Dimopoulos, N., Wong, S. (eds.) SAMOS 2008. LNCS, vol. 5114, pp. 106–115. Springer, Heidelberg (2008)
21. Becker, J.: Configurable systems-on-chip (CSoC). In: SBCCI 2002, pp. 379–384. IEEE, Los Alamitos (2002)
22. Koblitz, A. H., Koblitz, N., Menezes, A.: Elliptic Curve Cryptography: The Serpentine Course of a Paradigm Shift (2008), http://eprint.iacr.org/2008/390
23. Coron, J.-S.: Resistance against Differential Power Analysis for Elliptic Curve Cryptosystems. In: Koç, Ç.K., Paar, C. (eds.) CHES 1999. LNCS, vol. 1717, pp. 292–302. Springer, Heidelberg (1999)

Fully Pipelined Hardware Implementation of 128-Bit SEED Block Cipher Algorithm

Jaeyoung Yi[1], Karam Park[1], Joonseok Park[2], and Won W. Ro[1]

[1] School of Electrical and Electronic Engineering
Yonsei University, Seoul, Korea
jaeyoung@yonsei.ac.kr
[2] College of Information Technology
Inha University, Seoul, Korea

Abstract. As the need for information security increases in our everyday life, the job of encoding/decoding for secure information delivery becomes a critical issue in data network systems. High-speed data encoding for cryptography is required especially when sending a large amount of important data with high-speed transmission. In order to accomplish the procedure more efficiently, previous research focused on implementing existing algorithms using hardware accelerators. In this paper, we discuss and propose the FPGA implementation of the SEED block cipher algorithm, which is a Korean national industrial association standard for secured systems. Our implementation, which is written in Verilog HDL, is synthesized and tested on a Virtex-V XC5LX110T FPGA device. Our results show that the proposed fully pipelined design achieves high throughput and can support as high as 6.4 Gbps network speed. Compared to a full software implementation on the Intel Core 2 Duo 2.53 GHz processor, our implementation provides 34 times higher performance in terms of encoding/decoding throughput.

Keywords: Field Programmable Gate Arrays (FPGA), Block Cipher Algorithm, Cryptography, SEED.

1 Introduction

Cryptography has long been a major application domain of the diplomatic and military area. Moreover, the importance of cryptography is continuously growing in our current world of informational society, highly used in electronic commerce, electronic signature and digital authorization. Cryptosystems must ensure that private information does not leak out to unauthorized users. Therefore, various encryption algorithms such as DES (Data Encryption Standard) [1], AES (Advanced Encryption Standard) [2], and FEAL (Fast Data Encryption Algorithm)[3] have been developed to fulfill this function. With high network transmission rate, the process of encryption/decryption is one of the major bottlenecks in contemporary secure systems. As a result, high-speed encoding is required especially when sending a large amount of important information with high-speed transmission or on Virtual Private Networks (VPN). In order to accomplish secure and high-speed information transmission, previous researches have focused on implementing existing algorithms using various hardware structures.

J. Becker et al. (Eds.): ARC 2009, LNCS 5453, pp. 181–192, 2009.
© Springer-Verlag Berlin Heidelberg 2009

To embed this security functionality to an application, the secured system uses hardware implementations of encryption (or decryption) protocols. The performance requirements of the cryptosystem include high computational ability, high data throughput, and adaptability to the protocol changes. To address these requirements, an FPGA-based platform is an attractive match for the cryptosystem implementation. Since many cryptographic algorithms are consisted of a large amount of homogenous computations, using an FPGA can exploit a high level of parallelism and achieve increased computational performance which will ensure high data throughput. More-over, the re-configurability of FPGA can provide customized hardware for changed encryption protocols with lesser design efforts.

Our contribution in this paper is that we have implemented a fully pipelined block cipher algorithm in an FPGA with maximum parallelism. The design is fully functional in the most recent FPGA device and we achieved a 6.4 Gbps throughput. The results exceed the performance achieved by most recent general performance processors.

The rest of this paper is organized as follows. In Section 2, we will discuss the background of this research, which include an overall description of the SEED block algorithm. In Section 3, we present some related works. We explain the details of our design implementation in Section 4. Experimental results are shown in Section 5, and we conclude in Section 6.

2 Overview of the SEED Algorithm

The SEED block cipher algorithm has been developed by KISA (Korea Information Security Agency) in 1998, by the government's concern on the importance of cipher systems. (The name "SEED" only means an English word "*seed*" implying this tech-nique can be a source of later block cipher algorithms). It has become a national stan-dard since year 2000, and has been adapted to most of the security systems in [4]. Especially, the SEED algorithm is designed for strong resistance against differential cryptanalysis and linear cryptanalysis.

2.1 Structure of the SEED Algorithm

The SEED block cipher algorithm processes a block size of 128-bit plain text using a 128-bit cipher key, producing a 128-bit cipher-text. The SEED algorithm is a private key algorithm, meaning that it uses the same key for encryption and decryption. It has a *Feistel* structure with 16 rounds, in order to make it secure. A *Feistel* structure receives two t-bit blocks $L0$, $R0$ and repeats r rounds($r \geq 1$) of encryption [5]. A *Feis-tel* structure is generally used in more than three rounds, in an even number of rounds.

The general overview of the SEED algorithm is depicted in Fig. 1. The initial in-put data stream is 128 bit wide. Internally, the 128-bit input text stream is divided into two 64-bit blocks (named $L0$ and $R0$, in the diagram). The whole procedure of SEED is composed of 16 rounds. After the data goes through 16 rounds, they will result in two 64-bit blocks forming the 128-bit cipher-text.

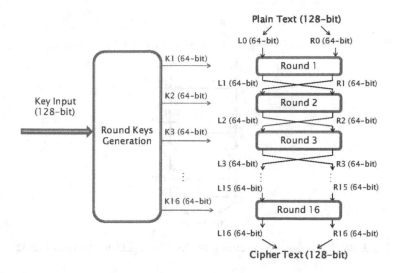

Fig. 1. SEED algorithm structure

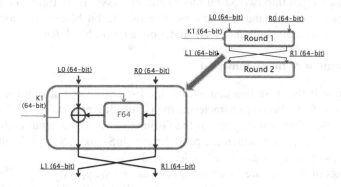

Fig. 2. Each round of SEED

The specific details of each round are shown in Fig. 2. Focusing on Round 1 first, there are two inputs to the round: *L0* and *R0*. *L0* includes the left 64 bits of the original input stream and *R0* matches to the remaining right 64 bits. The output of the first round is *L1* and *R1*. The first output *R1* is the result of *L0* exclusive-or *F(R0)* – the *F* operation will be presented in the following section. On the other side, *R0* just flows to *L1;* in other words, Round 1 bypasses *R0* to *L1* which becomes one of the inputs to Round 2. The SEED design consists of the round-key generator, F-function, G-function, and S-boxes.

2.2 Descriptions of the F-Function

The F-function of SEED has a Feistel structure as you can see in Fig. 3. It provides resistance against differential cryptanalysis, linear analysis, and other known attacks.

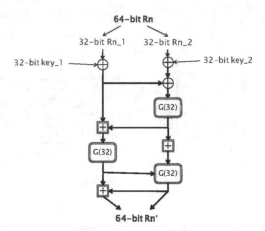

Fig. 3. Block diagram of F-function   ⊕ : XOR,   a ⊞ b = (a+b) mod 2^32

The F-function receives a 64-bit block Rn and a 64-bit round key as inputs. It divides the 64-bit block input into two 32-bit blocks and processes them through a mixture of *xors,* additions (mod 32) and G-functions. The two 32-bit blocks that come out are concatenated to form the output of the F-function, a 64-bit block Rn'.

2.3 Descriptions of the G-Function

The G-function is the main function used in the F-function and also in the round key generation. The formulas that characterize the G-function are laid out in Table 1, and Fig. 4 shows the structural diagram of the G-function. A 32-bit input is divided into four 8-bit blocks ($x_0 \sim x_3$), which are passed through S-boxes, S_1 and S_2; the detailed operation of the S-boxes is described in Section 2.5.

The outputs of S-boxes are four 8-bit blocks named y_0, y_1, y_2, and y_3. Those blocks are distributed over m_0, m_1, m_2, and m_3 as described in the diagram and a bitwise AND operation is performed. Finally, the four 8-bit outputs of four AND operations are exclusive-ORed to produce z_0, z_1, z_2, and z_3. Those four 8-bit blocks that come out are combined to make the 32-bit output of the G-function.

Table 1. Formulas for G-function   ⊕ stands for the exclusive-OR, & is the bitwise AND

$$y_0 = S_1(x_0), \; y_1 = S_2(x_1), \; y_2 = S_1(x_2), \; y_3 = S_2(x_3),$$
$$z_0 = (y_0 \& m_0) \oplus (y_1 \& m_1) \oplus (y_2 \& m_2) \oplus (y_3 \& m_3),$$
$$z_1 = (y_0 \& m_1) \oplus (y_1 \& m_2) \oplus (y_2 \& m_3) \oplus (y_3 \& m_0),$$
$$z_2 = (y_0 \& m_2) \oplus (y_1 \& m_3) \oplus (y_2 \& m_0) \oplus (y_3 \& m_1),$$
$$z_3 = (y_0 \& m_3) \oplus (y_1 \& m_0) \oplus (y_2 \& m_1) \oplus (y_3 \& m_2),$$
$$(m_0 = 0xfc, m_1 = 0xf3, m_2 = 0xcf, m_3 = 0x3f)$$

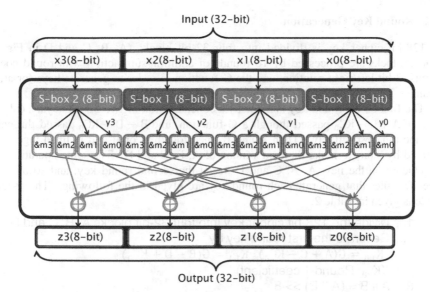

Fig. 4. Structural Diagram of G-Function

$\oplus$ stands for the exclusive-OR, & is the bitwise AND

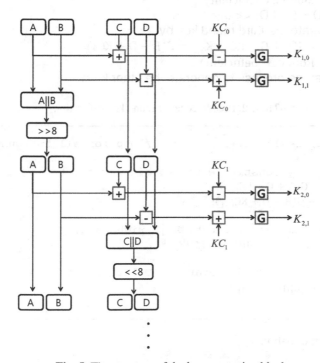

Fig. 5. The structure of the key generation block

2.4 Round Key Generation

A 128-bit cipher key is divided into four 32-bit blocks (A, B, C and D in Fig. 5). Those blocks are processed by 16 rounds of addition/subtraction with round coefficients, 8-bit left/right rotation, and the G-function in order to generate keys for all 16 rounds. The structure of the key generation block is shown in Fig. 5.

The first 64-bit round key is made by a concatenation of two 32-bit keys, a calculation of $A + C - KC_0$ passed though a G-function, and $B - D + KC_0$ passed through a G-function, respectively. Then A and B lined together, or B and D lined together is rotated by 8 bits to make the next version of A, B, C and D. The same operations are conducted on the new A, B, C and D to get the second round key, and so on. The specific rules that generate each round key are given in the following. The pseudo-code is given in Table 2.

1. Divide the 128-bit cipher key into four 32-bit blocks A, B, C and D
2. Generate the first round key by
   $K_{1,0} = G(A + C - KC_0)$, $K_{1,1} = G(B - D + KC_0)$
   (KC_0: Round 1 coefficient)
3. A ǁ B = (A ǁ B) >> 8
4. Generate the second round key by
   $K_{2,0} = G(A + C - KC_1)$, $K_{2,1} = G(B - D + KC_1)$ (
   KC_1: Round 2 coefficient)
5. C ǁ D = (C ǁ D) << 8
6. Generate the third round key by
   $K_{3,0} = G(A + C - KC_2)$, $K_{3,1} = G(B - D + KC_2)$
   (KC_2: Round 3 coefficient)
7. Repeat the process to generate the other keys.

Table 2. Pseudo-code for round key generation

```
for (i=1; i<=16, i++)          //loop for all 16 rounds
{
    //K_{i,0},K_{i,1} constitute the 64-bit key for the i^th round
    K_{i,0} ← G(A + C − KC_{i−1});
    K_{i,1} ← G(B − D + KC_{i−1});

    //if odd round, rotate A||B right 8 bits
    if(i%2==1) (A||B) ← (A||B)^{≫8}

    //if even round, rotate C||D left 8 bits
    else (C||D) ← (C||D)^{≪8}
}
```

2.5 Operation of S-box

The two S-boxes S_1 and S_2 are represented by two lookup tables [4]. The S-boxes are derived from nonlinear functions and each S-box has the address from 0 to 255. The S-boxes are defined as following.

$$S_i: Z_{2^8} \rightarrow Z_{2^8}, S_i(x) = A^i \bullet x^{n_i} \oplus b_i$$

where $n_1 = 247$, $n_2 = 251$, $b_1 = 169$, $b_2 = 56$ and

$$A^1 = \begin{pmatrix} 1 & 0 & 0 & 0 & 1 & 0 & 1 & 0 \\ 1 & 1 & 1 & 1 & 1 & 1 & 1 & 0 \\ 1 & 0 & 0 & 0 & 0 & 1 & 0 & 1 \\ 0 & 1 & 0 & 0 & 0 & 0 & 1 & 0 \\ 0 & 1 & 0 & 0 & 0 & 1 & 0 & 1 \\ 0 & 0 & 1 & 0 & 0 & 0 & 0 & 1 \\ 1 & 0 & 0 & 0 & 1 & 0 & 0 & 0 \\ 0 & 0 & 0 & 1 & 0 & 1 & 0 & 0 \end{pmatrix} \quad A^2 = \begin{pmatrix} 0 & 1 & 0 & 0 & 0 & 1 & 0 & 1 \\ 1 & 0 & 0 & 0 & 0 & 1 & 0 & 1 \\ 1 & 1 & 1 & 1 & 1 & 1 & 1 & 0 \\ 0 & 0 & 1 & 0 & 0 & 0 & 0 & 1 \\ 1 & 0 & 0 & 0 & 1 & 0 & 1 & 0 \\ 1 & 0 & 0 & 0 & 1 & 0 & 0 & 0 \\ 0 & 1 & 0 & 0 & 0 & 0 & 1 & 0 \\ 0 & 0 & 0 & 1 & 0 & 1 & 0 & 0 \end{pmatrix}$$

For any x in Z_{2^8}, x can be expressed as a binary vector form of $x = (x_7, ..., x_0)$. That is, $x = x_7 2^7 + x_6 2^6 + \cdots + x_1 2 + x_0$. To represent x^{n_i} in Z_{2^n}, we use the primitive polynomial $p(x) = x^8 + x^6 + x^5 + x + 1$. Using this affine transformation allows us to avoid cases where a fixed input value yields a fixed output value.

In our implementation, we pre-calculate all of the possible output values for input 0 to 255, and construct a lookup table for each box. As a result, the processing time of the S-box is insignificant; each output value can just be accessed directly from the input address.

3 Related Works

Many researchers have implemented efficient versions of block cipher algorithms in FPGAs included in New European Schemes for Signatures, Integrity, and Encryption (NESSIE) [6] and Cryptography Research and Evaluation Committee (CRYPTREC) in Japan [7]. In most cases, the large amount of parallelism of FPGA enables Giga scale of data processing in cryptosystems.

Denning *et al.* implemented a fully pipelined *Camellia* algorithm in FPGAs [8]. They implemented 3 variation versions for a key generation/schedule schemes. They achieved up to a 17.4 Gbps throughput. Zambreno *et al.* implemented the AES algorithm in Xilinx FPGAs. Their work focuses on design space explorations for area, data throughput and latency. They compared various designs with different round unrolling factors, and pipeline depth. They use Mbps/slice metric to find the most efficient design point of explored design spaces [9]. Rouvroy *et al.* implemented MISTY1 on FPGAs. They compared their implementations with other block cipher algorithms, such as AES RIJNDAEL, SERPENT and KHZAD [10]. Beuchat implemented RC6 block cipher in FPGAs. They implemented 4 different hardware designs for transformation functions to compare FPGA resource utilization and execution delays [11].

Seo *et al.* implemented SEED algorithm in FPGAs [12]. Their implementation is composed of modules of the key generator, the F-function, the G-function, the two S-boxes and the round process. While the SEED algorithm requires a large amount of hardware resources; they focused to minimize resource utilization for small FPGA devices. Each functional module is implemented only once and is used sequentially in order to minimize the area, which results in a small throughput. Our approach rather focuses on performance than resource utilization and enables fully pipelined operations of each round.

4   General Descriptions of the SEED Implementation

Nowadays, FPGAs become very efficient and suitable devices for fast hardware implementation. When an appropriate hardware algorithm is mapped on an FPGA, it can improve the throughput greatly compared to a software version of the application. Our SEED implementation pipelines the 16 rounds and implements all required modules as many times as needed. We have chosen to exploit the maximum possible speed while compromising the area-efficiency on the chip. The block diagram is shown in Fig. 6. The key generation block receives a 128-bit encryption key and outputs 16 round keys. As it is a combinational circuit each round key is not generated at the exact same time; yet it outputs its values stably after a certain delay time.

In the pipelined SEED architecture, a plain-text block is divided into two 64-bit blocks and goes through 16 rounds of encryption, input in each round together with the round keys generated from the key generation block. The outputs of the rounds form the inputs to the next round on consecutive clock cycles. After 16 iterations, the two 64-bit blocks that have passed through the *Feistel* structure are concatenated to form the 128-bit cipher-text. The main components in the fully pipelined architecture are the F-function and the key generator. Each F-function uses three carry look-ahead adders and three G-functions.

One round is implemented as a module and the top module generates and uses a total of 16 rounds. Registers are stationed at the beginning and end of each round to keep the encrypted values stable when sending them on to the next round. Thus, it takes an initial delay of 32 clock cycles until the first encrypted block is generated as the output of the 16th round. New plain text blocks can be received in each clock cycle, and after an initial delay, the corresponding cipher-text blocks will come out on consecutive clock cycles, one cipher-text block per clock cycle. This leads to a major throughput increase compared to the iterative architecture, which processes all 16 rounds per plain-text block before letting the next plain-text block progress.

The key generator is also implemented in hardware in order to change the key dynamically. The key generator receives as input a 128-bit encryption key. It is consisted of shifters, carry look-ahead adders, and two G-functions, which are each implemented in hardware for all 16 rounds of keys that are supposed to be generated. This way we implemented the key generator as a combinational circuit and after the round keys are generated, the values of the output round keys do not change before the encryption key is modified. It has no need for the clock, and the delay time that occurs here does not affect the minimal clock cycle time of the encryption part of the circuit. After a certain delay time, all of the round key values are stabilized.

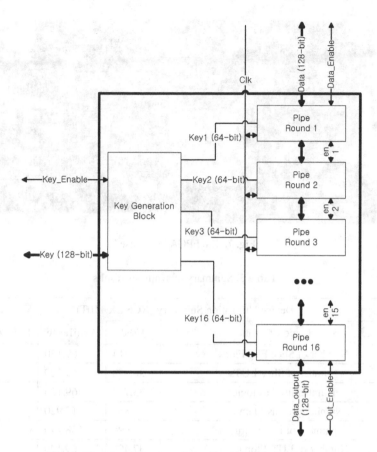

Fig. 6. The block diagram of pipelined SEED algorithm

5 Experimental Results

We have implemented the fully pipelined SEED block cipher algorithms using Verilog HDL. To demonstrate the correctness of the proposed design, we have tested it on an FPGA chip; the actual implementation has been synthesized targeting for Xilinx® Virtex-V XC5LX110T using Xilinx® ISE®. Indeed, our target board is consisted of Virtex-V XC5LX110T, PCI-Express Interface, 196MB DDR2 RAM, 16MB Flash, PC4/USB JTAG port and a 100MHz LVTTL OSC. A snapshot of the board is given in Fig. 7.

Table 3 summarizes synthesis results. As seen in the compilation report, the design occupies 53% chip area. After we have downloaded the design on the board, we have performed a full experiment on the device; the target Virtex-V XC5LX110T device runs at an external clock speed of 100MHz. As the maximum delay time calculated from the timing simulation results is 17.9ns, the highest possible speed achievable while getting the correct results is approximately 55.8MHz. Here, we use a 50MHz clock speed for the verification of the design. We have conducted on-chip

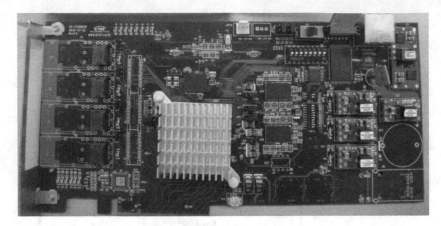

Fig. 7. The FPGA board used

Table 3. Summary of synthesis results

Device Utilization Summary (XC5 LX 110T)			
Slice Logic Utilization	Used	Available	Utilization
Number of Slice Flip Flops	5,314	69,120	7%
Number of Slice LUTs	36,678	69,120	53%
Number used as logic	33,752	69,120	48%
Number used as Memory	2,882	17,920	16%
Number of route-thrus	996	138,240	1%
Number of LUT-Flop pairs	37,408	69,120	54%
Number of bonded IOBs	644	800	80%
Total equivalent gate count for design	737,328		
Additional JTAG gate count for IOBs	3,220		

simulation with diverse test vectors and every variation of 128-bit plain text and 128-bit key input data sets. The 128-bit data and key were incremented separately in the test bench to test every possible combination. The results are analyzed with Xilinx® ChipScope Pro® 10.1 by comparing input plain-text and once encoded and then decoded plain-text. The chip operates successfully with the given clock frequency of 50MHz and hence we achieve a throughput of 6.4 Gbps (since the bit-width for each round is 128) on both SEED encoding and decoding process.

To compare these performance results to the desktop computing environment, we have tested a full software SEED implementation on three different commercial processors. The experimental results of executing the SEED algorithm on current systems are shown in Table 4. We have measured the total execution time to encode plaint-text to cipher-text with 128 bits x 10^8 data size. The average execution times on the three different systems over ten trials were measured as 92 sec, 88 sec, and 68.6 sec.

Table 4. Experimental results on general purpose processors

CPU name	Clock speed	L1 cache	L2 cache	OS	throughput
Intel Core Duo	1.83GHz	64KB	2MB shared	MacOS	139Mbps
AMD Phenom 9550	2.2GHz	128KB	L2 : 512KB L3: 2M shared	Linux	145Mbps
Intel Core 2 Duo E7200	2.53GHz	32KB	3MB shared	Windows XP	188Mbps

The corresponding throughputs are 139Mbps, 145Mbps and 188Mbps, respectively. In the near future, it is predicted that the transmission rate of high-speed network will become as fast as 1Gbps. The encryption rate of the software implemented SEED algorithm that current available desktop systems can provide is too slow and will be a bottleneck. Accordingly, other methods than software implementation are required to fulfill the needs of fast encryption speed. Using an FPGA is one of those alternatives. Comparing the software implementation to our performance achievement, our proposed FPGA implementation provides about 34 to 46 times faster encoding/decoding speed.

6 Conclusion

In this paper, we have shown a hardware implementation of the SEED block cipher algorithm and have mapped it to an FPGA chip. The proposed designed is fully pipelined and provides 6.4Gbps performance. In addition, it has been shown that it efficiently fits in the Virtex-V XC5LX110T board. The achieved throughput, 6.4 Gbps, is a sufficient performance rate to prevent the SEED block cipher from being a bottleneck in high-performance network systems. Toward the era of 1 Gbps network environment, the encoding and decoding speed of network security algorithms is very crucial. As SEED is a widely used algorithm in Korea, where high-speed network transmission rates are typical, this pipelined hardware accelerator would be of great use.

As future work, we will perform more variations on our basic pipeline approach considering the performance and area requirement. We will also investigate the internal structure optimization such as the table look up inside S-Box implementation or the adders inside the F-function.

References

1. Federal Information Processing Standards Publication 46-3: Data Encryption Standard (1999)
2. Federal Information Processing Standards Publication 197: Advanced Encryption Standard (2001)
3. Miyaguchi, S.: The FEAL Cipher Family. In: Menezes, A., Vanstone, S.A. (eds.) CRYPTO 1990. LNCS, vol. 537, pp. 627–637. Springer, Heidelberg (1991)
4. Korea Information Security Agency: A Design and Analysis of 128-bit Symmetric Block Cipher (SEED) (1999)

5. Beuchat, J.L.: FPGA Implementations of the RC6 Block Cipher. In: Proc. of the 13th Int'l Conference on Field-Programmable Logic and its Applications, Portugal (2003)
6. NESSIE: NESSIE Project Announces Final Selection of Crypto Algorithms, IST-199-12324 (2003)
7. Information-Technology Promotion Agency, Japan, CRYPTREC Report (2002)
8. Denning, D., Irvine, J., Delvin, M.: A KeyAgile 4Gbit/sec Camellia Implementation. In: Becker, J., Platzner, M., Vernalde, S. (eds.) FPL 2004. LNCS, vol. 3203, pp. 546–554. Springer, Heidelberg (2004)
9. Zambreno, J., Nguyen, D., Choudhary, A.: Exploring Area/Delay Tradeoffs in an AES FPGA Implementation. In: Proc of Int'l Conference on Field-Programmable Logic and its Applications, Belguim (2004)
10. Rouvroy, G., Standaert, F.X.: Efficient FPGA Implementation of Block Cipher MISTY1. In: Proc of IEEE International Parallel & Distributed Processing Symposium, France (2003)
11. Schneier, B.: Applied Cryptography. Wiley, Chichester (1996)
12. Seo, Y.H., Kim, I.H., Kim, D.W.: Hardware Implementation of 128-bit Symmetric Cipher SEED. In: Proc. of the Second IEEE Asia Pacific Conference on AP-SIC 2000, pp. 183–186 (2000)

Improving Throughput of AES-GCM with Pipelined Karatsuba Multipliers on FPGAs

Gang Zhou[1], Harald Michalik[1], and László Hinsenkamp[2]

[1] Institute of Computer and Communication Network Engineering,
Technical University of Braunschweig, Germany
{zhou,michalik}@ida.ing.tu-bs.de
[2] Digital Signalprocessing and Information Technology, Otto-Lilienthal-Strasse 1,
D-28199, Bremen, Germany
hinsenk@dsi-it.de

Abstract. Two main components in AES-GCM (Advanced Encryption Standard with Galois Counter Mode) are an AES engine and a finite field multiplier over $GF(2^{128})$ in the universal hashing function (GHASH). Because of the inherent computation feedback, the system performance is usually determined by the finite field multiplier based on the known FPGA implementations to date. In this paper, we present the throughput optimization of AES-GCM with a 4-stage pipelined finite field multiplier based on Karatsuba-Ofman algorithm on FPGAs. The critical delay of the pipelined multiplier then matches that of the AES implementation with either the BlockRAM *SubBytes*, pipelined composite field *SubBytes* or LUT-based *SubBytes*. The AES-GCM throughput reaches more than 30Gbps on a single Xilinx Virtex Chip. The experimental results show that we achieve the most efficient AES-GCM implementations on FPGAs to date.

Keywords: AES-GCM, pipelined Karatsuba multiplier, finite field arithmetic, FPGAs.

1   Introduction

The GCM (Galois Counter Mode) [1], [2] was finalized as a new mode of operation of AES (Advanced Encryption Standard) [3] by National Institute of Standards and Technology (NIST) in 2007. GCM was designed to meet the need for an authenticated encryption mode that can efficiently achieve speeds of 10Gigabps and higher in hardware. Many working groups recommended the use of GCM, such as IPsec Encapsulating Security Payload in RFC4106[4] and RFC 4543[5], Media Access Control Security in IEEE 802.1AE[6], Security Storage in IEEE P1619.1[7] and ANSI Fibre Channel Security Protocols[8] and so on.

Two main components in GCM are an AES engine and a Finite Field Multiplier (FFM) over $GF(2^{128})$ in the universal hashing function (GHASH). The AES implementation has been extensively discussed, e.g., in [9], [10], [11], [12] and [13]. The BlockRAM based *Subbytes* or inner-round pipelined composite field *Subbytes* can easily run at frequency higher than 200Mhz on modern FPGAs (Field Programmable Gate Arrays). However, the GHASH calculation with FFM has inherent feedback operations. Therefore the GCM system performance is usually determined by the FFM as shown in the two published AES-GCM FPGA implementations in [14] and [15]. Both works did

J. Becker et al. (Eds.): ARC 2009, LNCS 5453, pp. 193–203, 2009.
© Springer-Verlag Berlin Heidelberg 2009

not exploit the inner-round pipelining techniques because it will not improve the GCM system performance due to the critical delay of the modular multiplier. In this paper, we show that by our method of implementing the GHASH multiplier, the inner-round pipelining can be applied in the AES engine.

In ASICs (Application-Specific Integrated Circuits), Satoh et. al in [16] showed that the GHASH function can be achieved by a 2-stage pipelined multiplier when the input data is interleaved to even and odd sequences, or by a 4-stage pipelined multiplier when the input data is interleaved to four sequences. The pipelined multiplier in [17] is built by using four concatenated digital-serial (128 by 32) multipliers. Therefore the complexity is quadratic. In this paper, we show that the sub-quadratic FFM based on Karatsuba-Ofman Algorithm (KOA), which reduces the area consumption, can be also pipelined and achieves the same functionality. Furthermore, Satoh et. al evaluated only the performance with composite field *Subbytes* based on 0.13um CMOS technology. We will show the performance for BlockRAM based *Subbytes* and LUT-based *Subbytes* on reconfigurable devices. In security sensitive applications reconfigurable FPGA devices are commonly preferred because of the inherent capability to protect the firmware against tampering by safe outside storage of the firmware and fast erase capabilities of SRAM based FPGAs.

This paper is organized as follows. In next section we review the GCM algorithm for completeness. Then, in section 3 the pipelined FFM based on Karatsuba-Ofman algorithm is presented and compared with the pipelined quadratic multiplier. In section 4 the high throughput GCM architecture is shown and the experimental results are presented in section 5. Section 6 concludes this work.

2   GCM Algorithm

$$
\begin{cases}
H = E(K, 0^{128}) \\
Y_0 = \begin{cases} IV \parallel 0^{31} \parallel 1 & if\ len(IV) = 96 \\ GHASH(H,, IV) & otherwise \end{cases} \\
Y_i = incr(Y_{i-1})\ for\ i = 1 \cdots, n \\
C_i = P_i \oplus E(K, Y_i)\ for\ i = 1 \cdots, n-1 \\
C_n^* = P_n^* \oplus MSB_u(E(K, Y_n)) \\
T = MSB_t(GHASH(H, A, C) \oplus E(K, Y_0))
\end{cases}
\tag{1}
$$

The GCM encryption [1], [2] accepts four inputs: a secret key K, an initialization vector IV, a plaintext P and an additional authenticated data A. It produces a cipher text C and an authentication tag T. P and A are segmented into 128-bit blocks $(P_1, P_2, \cdots, P_n^*)$ and $(A_1, A_2, \cdots, A_n^*)$. The last bit blocks P_n^* and A_n^* may be incomplete blocks and are assumed to have only u-bit and v-bit, where $1 \leq u, v \leq 128$. The GCM authenticated encryption operation is defined in (1): where $A \parallel B$ denotes the concatenation of two strings A and B; $E(K, X)$ denotes the block cipher encryption of the value X with the key K; $incr()$ generates successive counter values for AES; $MSB_t(S)$ returns the bit strings containing only the most significant t bits of S.

The universal GHASH function is defined over a sequence of finite/Galois field operations over $GF(2^{128})$ with the irreducible polynomial $F(x)_{128} = x^{128}+x^7+x^2+x+1$. It accepts A, C and H as inputs where C and H are variables defined in (1) and generates a 128-bit hash value GHASH=X_{m+n+1}.

$$X_i = \begin{cases} 0 & for\ i = 0 \\ (X_{i-1} \oplus A_i) \cdot H & for\ i = 1 \cdots m \\ (X_{i-1} \oplus C_{i-m}) \cdot H & for\ i = m+1 \cdots m+n \\ (X_{m+n} \oplus (len(A) \parallel len(C))) \cdot H & for\ i = m+n+1 \end{cases} \tag{2}$$

where $len(A)$ and $len(C)$ return the bit string length of A and C in 64-bit, respectively.

As recommended in [16], (2) can be rewritten as (3), where I_i denotes the sequence of A, C and $(len(A) \parallel len(C))$.

$$X_i = Q_1 \oplus Q_2 \oplus Q_3 \oplus Q_4, where \tag{3}$$
$$Q_1 = (((I_1 H^4 \oplus I_5)H^4 \oplus I_9)H^4 \oplus \cdots)H^4 \tag{4}$$
$$Q_2 = (((I_2 H^4 \oplus I_6)H^4 \oplus I_{10})H^4 \oplus \cdots)H^3 \tag{5}$$
$$Q_3 = (((I_3 H^4 \oplus I_7)H^4 \oplus I_{11})H^4 \oplus \cdots)H^2 \tag{6}$$
$$Q_4 = (((I_4 H^4 \oplus I_8)H^4 \oplus I_{12})H^4 \oplus \cdots)H \tag{7}$$

3   Pipelined FFM Based on KOA

3.1   Quadratic FFM over $GF(2^m)$

Assume the two operands are $A(x) = \sum_{i=0}^{m} a_i x^i$ and $B(x) = \sum_{i=0}^{m} b_i x^i$. The objective is to calculate $C(x) = A(x)B(x)\ mod\ F(x)$ efficiently. The modular multiplication can be divided into two steps as the architecture described in Fig. 1: a classic polynomial multiplication and then a modular reduction.

The first stage generates a polynomial with $2m-1$ terms

$$D(x) = \sum_{i=0}^{2m-2} d_i x^i,\ where\ d_k = \sum_{i+j=k} a_i b_j,\ 0 \le i, j \le m-1 \tag{8}$$

$$[x^m, \cdots, x^{2m-2}]^T = [Q][1, \cdots, x^{m-1}]^T \tag{9}$$

The computations in the 1st stage need m^2 AND gates and $(m-1)^2$ XOR gates as shown in Fig. 1. The critical delay occurs at the d_{m-1}, which is $T_A + log_2 m T_X$. T_A and T_X is the delay of a single AND and XOR gate, respectively. In the second stage, the most significant $m-1$ terms of $D(x)$ are iteratively reduced to polynomials with degree less than m by using the irreducible polynomial $F(x)$ as shown in (9). Because $F(x)_{128}$ is a pentanomial, the second stage requires only a small number of XOR gates compared with the first stage. More precisely, the count of XOR gates for each c_k can be calculated by (10), where $H(Q(k))$ is the Hamming weight of the k-th column of

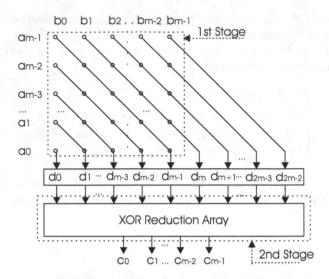

Fig. 1. Bit parallel modular multiplier

matrix $[Q]$. The required number of XOR gates for $F(x)_{128}$ is bounded by 527 and the critical delay is $2T_X$.

$$gates(c_k) = H(Q(k)), k = 0..m - 1 \qquad (10)$$

3.2   Polynomial Multiplication with KOA

The KOA can reduce the complexity of the classic school multiplication. Suppose $A = A_l A_h$ and $B = B_l B_h$, where A_l, A_h, B_l, B_h are $\frac{m}{2}$-bit terms. The 1-step iteration of KOA can be described as:

$$\begin{cases} D_0 = A_l B_l \\ D_{01} = (A_h + A_l)(B_h + B_l) \\ D_1 = A_h B_h \\ D = D_0 + x^{\frac{m}{2}}(D_0 + D_{01} + D_1) + x^m D_1 \end{cases}$$

As indicated in Fig. 2, the splitting stage requires $2u$ XOR gates to calculate $A_h + A_l$ and $B_h + B_l$, where $u = \frac{m}{2}$ holds. The alignment stage aligns the outputs of three concurrently executed sub-multipliers. The straightforward calculation requires $6(u - 1) + 2$ XOR gates. More precisely, aligning each d_k requires 3 XOR gates if $u \leq k \leq 2u - 2$ or $2u \leq k \leq 3u - 2$. Two XOR gates are required for d_{2u-1}. In total, the complexity of 1-step KOA can be generalized as (11), where the number of AND gates, XOR gates for a given bit-depth m is denoted by $\mathcal{A}(m)$, $\mathcal{X}(m)$. Their corresponding delay is denoted by $\mathcal{T}_A(m)$, $\mathcal{T}_X(m)$, respectively. Recursively applying KOA on the

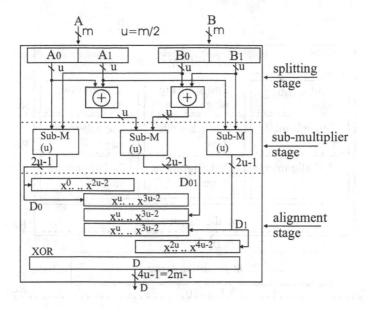

Fig. 2. Polynomial Multiplication with 1-step KOA

sub-multiplier can reduce the complexity to sub-quadratic as shown in (12), where r denotes the iteration step and $m = 2^r n$ holds.

$$\begin{cases} \mathcal{A}_{kom}(m) = 3\mathcal{A}_{kom}(u) \\ \mathcal{X}_{kom}(m) = 3\mathcal{X}_{kom}(u) + 8u - 4 \\ \mathcal{T}_{A kom}(m) = \mathcal{T}_{A kom}(u) \\ \mathcal{T}_{X kom}(m) = \mathcal{T}_{X kom}(u) + 3 \end{cases} \qquad (11)$$

$$\begin{cases} \#XOR = (\frac{m}{n})^{log_2 3}(n^2 + 6n - 1) - 8m + 2 \\ \#AND = (\frac{m}{n})^{log_2 3} n^2 \\ Delay \leq T_A + T_X(log_2 n + 4 log_2 r) \end{cases} \qquad (12)$$

3.3 Pipelined FFMs Based on KOA

As shown in (3), each $Q_j, 1 \leq j \leq 4$ is dependent on I_i, where $mod(i, 4) = (j - 1)$ holds. Which means each Q_j can be calculated independently. Only 1 final XOR is required to get $Q_1 \oplus Q_2 \oplus Q_3 \oplus Q_4$. There exist 4 clock intervals between the calculation of Q_j and its next value. Therefore, we propose a 4-stage pipelined FFM based on KOA for the GHASH calculation. An example is illustrated in Fig. 3 for the pipelined FFM with 2-step KOA. For the FFM with r-step KOA, the registers are inserted after the rth splitting stages, the sub-multiplier stages, the 1st alignment stage and the XOR reduction array.

Based on the complexity analysis of 1-step KOA, we can summarize the number of gates, the number of registers and the critical delay for the pipelined FFMs with

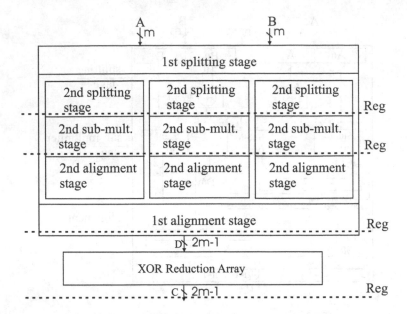

Fig. 3. 4-stage pipelined FFM with 2-step KOA

Table 1. Complexity of Pipelined FFMs for $F(x)_{128}$

FFM	Analysis						Synthesis					
							Virtex4			Virtex5		
	AND	XOR	Total	FF	Delay	AT	LUT	D	AT	LUT	D	AT
	#	#	#	#		T_X	#	ns	10^3	#	ns	10^3
$KOA_{r=1}$	12288	12942	25230	1148	T_A+6T_X	176k	8736	4.186	36.5	5379	3.425	18.4
$KOA_{r=2}$	9216	10440	19656	1526	T_A+5T_X	117k	7096	3.632	25.8	4574	3.392	15.5
$KOA_{r=3}$	6912	8982	15894	2084	$6T_X$	**95k**	6189	3.632	**22.5**	4214	3.347	**14.1**
$KOA_{r=4}$	5184	8496	13680	2894	$8T_X$	109k	5932	5.241	31.1	4364	3.759	16.4
$KOA_{r=5}$	3888	8982	12870	4028	$10T_X$	128k	6409	6.603	42.3	5097	4.643	23.7
$KOA_{r=6}$	2916	10440	13356	5486	$12T_X$	160k	7727	7.702	59.5	6941	5.487	38.1
4xDSM[16]	16384	16248	32632	1280	T_A+7T_X	261k	11194	5.338	59.7	7496	4.3	32.2

different iteration steps of KOA in Table 1. The last row is based on the pipelined architecture proposed in [16], in which 4 Digital-Serial Multipliers (DSM) are concatenated together. Therefore the multiplier has the quadratic complexity and it consumes much more gates compared with KOA-based FFMs. For the KOA-based FFMs, the total number of gates first decreases, then increases along the increasing iteration step r. The number of registers (FF) increases monotonically along r. The minimal number of gates occurs at $r=5$. The critical delay is determined by the longest propagation path among all stages, in which $T_A = T_X$ is assumed. For example, the longest path occurs at the sub-multipliers when $r=1$ or 2, while the longest path is determined by the alignment stages when $r > 2$. In total, the best Area-Time (AT) product occurs at $r=3$.

Table 1 also lists the synthesis results of different FFMs [1]. The smallest area occurs at different r with the gate-oriented analysis since the main primitives in FPGAs are Look-Up-Tables, e.g., LUT4 in Virtex4 [18] and LUT6 in Virtex5 [19]. On Virtex4 FPGAs, the smallest area occurs at $r=4$ while on Virtex5 it occurs at $r=3$. The variation on the critical delay is consistent with the gate-oriented analysis. For example, the delay is 5.241ns when $r=4$, which ich 30% larger than the delay of FFM with $r=3$ on Virtex4. In total, the best AT products based on analysis, synthesis on Virtex4 and Virtex5 are consistent with each other, Which is $r=3$. Finally, we choose the FFMs of $r=3$ for our GCM designs.

3.4 GHASH Calculation with the 4-Stage Pipelined FFM

Fig. 4 shows the hardware architecture for the GHASH calculation with the 4-stage pipelined FFM. Once the operands I_i is loaded into the multiplier, the product will be ready after 4 clocks on port c, which is then feeded back and XORed with the next input I_{i+4}. However, according to (5), (6) and (7), the multiplications with H, H^2 and H^3 are also required. They are achieved by the multiplexer between H and H^4. The operations $\otimes H^2$ and $\otimes H^3$ are accomplished by invoking the multiplier twice and three times, respectively.

An example of data flow control for the GHASH control is shown in Table 2, where $I_1 \cdots I_8$ is the input sequence and "-" denotes "don't care". At the beginning H^4 is passed to port b. After the input of I_6, H is passed to port b. The multiplier is invoked at the 6th, 10th and 14th clock to perform $(I_2 H^4 \oplus I_6) H^3$. The calculation is done in the same manner for $(I_3 H^4 \oplus I_7) H^2$. The partial GHASH values Q_1, Q_2, Q_3 and Q_4 are ready at the 9th 15th 18th and 12th clock, respectively. An additional clock is required to generate the final GHASH.

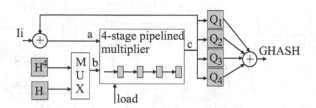

Fig. 4. GHASH calculation with the 4-stage pipelined FFM

4   High Throughput GCM Architecture

Fig. 5 shows the high throughput architecture for GCM encryption. The IV length is fixed to 96 bits for efficient implementations as recommended in the standard. The shadowed boxes denote registers and the symbols conform with the GCM algorithm. The register $Mask$ is used to indicate the valid bits of the last data block. Both inputs and outputs are registered to minimize the IO influences and the register OP and

---

[1] Synthesis tool used is Synplicity Pro 9.01 with default settings.

Table 2. Example of data flow control for GHASH calculation

clk	load	I_i	a	b	c	Comment
1	1	I_1	I_1	H^4	0	
2	1	I_2	I_2	H^4	0	
3	1	I_3	I_3	H^4	0	
4	1	I_4	I_4	H^4	0	
5	1	I_5	$I_1 H^4 \oplus I_5$	H^4	$I_1 H^4$	
6	1	I_6	$I_2 H^4 \oplus I_6$	H	$I_2 H^4$	
7	1	I_7	$I_3 H^4 \oplus I_7$	H	$I_3 H^4$	
8	1	I_8	$I_4 H^4 \oplus I_8$	H	$I_4 H^4$	
9	0	−	−	−	$(I_1 H^4 \oplus I_5)H^4$	$c = Q_1$
10	1	0	$(I_2 H^4 \oplus I_6)H$	H	$(I_2 H^4 \oplus I_6)H$	
11	1	0	$(I_3 H^4 \oplus I_7)H$	H	$(I_3 H^4 \oplus I_7)H$	
12	0	−	−	−	$(I_4 H^4 \oplus I_8)H$	$c = Q_4$
13	0	−	−	−	−	
14	1	0	$(I_2 H^4 \oplus I_6)H^2$	H	$(I_2 H^4 \oplus I_6)H^2$	
15	0	−	−	−	$(I_3 H^4 \oplus I_7)H^2$	$c = Q_2$
16	0	−	−	−	−	
17	0	−	−	−	−	
18	0	−	−	−	$(I_2 H^4 \oplus I_6)H^3$	$c = Q_3$
19	0	−	−	−	−	GHASH

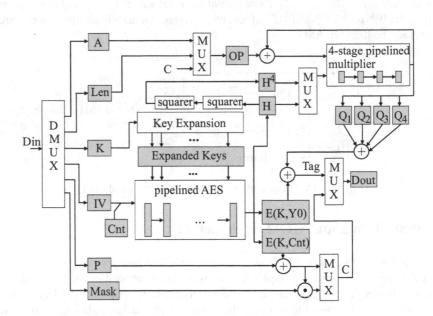

Fig. 5. GCM encryption hardware architecture

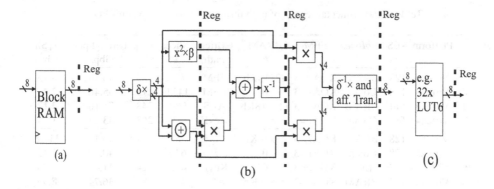

Fig. 6. *SubBytes* implementation with BlockRAMs (a), with composite field approach (b), with LUTs (c)

$E(K, Cnt)$ are inserted to reduce the critical delay. The expanded keys are stored in registers so that the expansion of next keys (KeyE) could be executed in parallel to the encryption with the current key.

The pipelined AES engine generates one H, one $E(K, Y0)$ and then continuous $E(K, Cnt)$. The *SubBytes* transformation can be implemented either by BlockRAMs, composite field approach or direct LUT approach as shown in Fig. 6. The LUT approach is especially interesting on Virtex5 devices. On Virtex5, with its the 6-input LUT technology only 32 LUTs are needed for the *SubBytes* transformation [13]. The number of LUTs required on Virtex4 is 128 because of the 4-input LUT technology. In order to balance the critical delay of the pipelined FFM, a register are inserted each after the block memory (Fig. 6(a)) and the LUTs (Fig. 6(c)). Three levels of registers are added into the composite field based *SubBytes* (Fig. 6(b)). Therefore the pipelined AES latencies for BlockRAM-based *SubBytes*, composite field *SubBytes* and LUT-based *SubBytes* are $NR \times 3$, $NR \times 4$ and $NR \times 2$, respectively. NR is 10 for 128-bit AES, 12 for 192-bit AES and 14 for 256-bit AES as specified in the standard.

5   Experimental Results

We implemented the pipelined FFMs and different types of *SubBytes* in VHDL code and targeted on both Virtex4 (V4LX60ff668-11, 26624Slices and 160*18KbBlockRAMs available) and Virtex5 (V5LX85ff668-2, 12960Slices and 96*36KbBlockRAMs available) devices. The Synplicity Pro 9.0.1 was used to perform the synthesis and Xilinx ISE10.1 was adopted to run the Place And Route (PAR). All tools were kept with default settings. The critical delay of PAR is derived from the design by gradually adjusting the timing constraints with resolution 0.1ns. The GCM cores with both 128-bit AES and full-AES were evaluated. The experimental results are illustrated in Table 3.

On Virtex4 platforms, the GCM core with full-AES support reaches the throughput of 31Gbps with the area consumption of 9800 slices and 118*18KbBlockRAMs. The GCM core with composite field *SubBytes* consumes twice more slices, however no BlockRAM is required. The implementation is technology independent and can

Table 3. Experimental results of high throughput AES-GCM on FPGAs

	Platform	AES Type	*SubBytes*	FFM	BRAM #	Critical Path	Slices #	Freq. Mhz	Throughput Gbps	Thr./Slice Mbps
	Virtex4	128	BRAM	KOAr=3	82x18Kb	FFM	7712	285	36.48	4.73
T	Virtex4	128	Comp.	KOAr=3	0	FFM	14349	277	35.46	2.47
H	Virtex4	full	BRAM	KOAr=3	118x18Kb	AES	9800	243	31.10	**3.17**
I	Virtex4	full	Comp.	KOAr=3	0	KeyE	19301	263	33.66	1.74
S	Virtex5	128	BRAM	KOAr=3	41x36Kb	KeyE	3533	314	40.19	11.38
	Virtex5	128	Comp.	KOAr=3	0	*SubBytes*	6492	314	40.19	6.19
W	Virtex5	128	LUT	KOAr=3	0	KeyE	4628	324	41.47	8.96
O	Virtex5	full	BRAM	KOAr=3	59x36Kb	AES	4115	287	36.74	**8.93**
R	Virtex5	full	Comp	KOAr=3	0	*SubBytes*	8077	305	39.04	4.83
K	Virtex5	full	LUT	KOAr=3	0	KeyE	5961	296	37.89	6.36
[15]	Virtex4	128	Comp.	quadratic	0	-	16378	161	20.61	1.27
[15]	Virtex4	128	Comp.	KOAr=4	0	-	13523	119	15.23	1.13
[14]	Virtex4	full	BRAM	quadratic	114	-	13200	110	14.08	1.07
[14]	Virtex4	full	Comp.	quadratic	0	-	21600	90	11.52	0.53
[14]	Virtex4	full	LUT	quadratic	0	-	27800	120	15.36	0.55

be transformed to other FPGA devices without much extra efforts. On Virtex5, the most efficient implementation reaches the throughput 36.74Gbps with 4115 slices and 59*36KbBlockRAMs. The Throughput per Slice (Thr./Slice) is 8.93Mbps in this case. Although the composite field *SubBytes* achieves the highest throughput (39.04Gbps), the LUT-based GCM core becomes more efficient than the composite field *SubBytes* (6.36/4.83) thanks to the LUT6 technology. The timing analysis shows that the critical path is not always the FFM any more. Compared with previous FPGA implementations of 128-bit AES-GCM in [15], the operating frequency of our design is doubled due to the pipelined FFMs. Therefore our implementation boosts both the throughput and the Thr./slice twice higher. Compared with the full AES-GCM in [14], the efficiency of our systems is three time better (3.17/1.07 and 1.74/0.53).

The most efficient ASIC implementations reported in the literature were designed by Satoh et. al. in [16]. The throughput on 0.13um CMOS technology reaches 54Gbps with 272K gates and 38Gbps with 262K gates. Considering the huge NRE (Non-Recurring Engineering) cost, the relatively long verification period and the adaptation inflexibility of the ASIC development, our reconfigurable AES-GCM cores are competitive alternatives against the ASIC implementations, being also attractive for security sensitive applications.

6 Conclusion

In this paper, we presented the throughput improvement of AES-GCM with pipelined Karatsuab-Ofman based finite field multipliers. With our proposed 4-stage sub-quadratic finite field multipliers, the GHASH function is not the bottleneck any more in GCM hardware systems, no matter which one of the three AES implementations is selected

(BlockRAM based *SubBytes*, composite field *SubBytes* or LUT-based *SubBytes*). The presented AES-GCM cores reach the throughput of 31Gbps and 39Gbps on Virtex4 and Virtex5, respectively. The experimental results show that a single modern FPGA chip can provide the throughput of more than 30Gbps for the authenticated AES-GCM, which exhibits the advantage of field programmable devices in high performance computing systems.

References

1. McGrew, D.A., Viega, J.: The Galois/Counter Mode of Operation (GCM). Updated submission to NIST, Modes of Operation Process (May 2005)
2. NIST, Recommendation for Block Cipher Modes of Operation: Galois/Counter Mode (GCM) and GMAC. NIST Special Publication 800-38D (November 2007)
3. NIST, Advanced Encryption Standard (AES). FIPS Publication 197 (November 26, 2001)
4. Viega, J., McGrew, D.: The Use of Galois/Counter Mode (GCM) in IPsec Encapsulating Security Payload. RFC 4106 (2005)
5. McGrew, D., Viega, J.: The Use of Galois Message Authentication Code (GMAC) in IPsec ESP and AH. RFC 4543 (2006)
6. IEEE, 802.1AE - Media Access Control (MAC) Security (2006)
7. IEEE, P1619.1, Standard for Authenticated Encryption with Length Expansion for Storage Devices (2006)
8. INCITS, Fibre Channel Security Protocols, REC 1.74 (2006)
9. Jaervinen, K.U., Tommiska, M.T., Skyttae, J.O.: A Fully Pipelined Memoryless 17.8Gbps AES-128 Encrypto. FPGA (2003)
10. Standaert, F.-X., Rouvroy, G., Quisquater, J.-J., Legat, J.-D.: Efficient Implementation of Rijndael Encryption in Reconfigurable Hardware: Improvements and Design Tradeoffs. In: Walter, C.D., Koç, Ç.K., Paar, C. (eds.) CHES 2003. LNCS, vol. 2779, pp. 334–350. Springer, Heidelberg (2003)
11. Zhang, X., Parhi, K.K.: High-Speed VLSI Architectures for the AES Algorithm. IEEE Transaction on VLSI 12(9), 957–967 (2004)
12. Good, T., Benaissa, M.: AES on FPGA: from the fastest to the smallest. In: Rao, J.R., Sunar, B. (eds.) CHES 2005. LNCS, vol. 3659, pp. 427–440. Springer, Heidelberg (2005)
13. Bulens, P., Standaert, F.-X., Quisquater, J.-J., Pellegrin, P., Rouvroy, G.: Implementation of the AES-128 on Virtex-5 FPGAs. In: Vaudenay, S. (ed.) AFRICACRYPT 2008. LNCS, vol. 5023, pp. 16–26. Springer, Heidelberg (2008)
14. Lemsitzer, S., Wolkerstorfer, J., Felber, N., Braendli, M.: Multi-gigabit GCM-AES Architecture Optimized for FPGAs. In: Paillier, P., Verbauwhede, I. (eds.) CHES 2007. LNCS, vol. 4727, pp. 227–238. Springer, Heidelberg (2007)
15. Zhou, G., Michalik, H., Hinsenkamp, L.: Efficient and High-Throughput Implementations of AES-GCM on FPGAs. In: Proceedings of International Conference on Field Programmable Technology, ICFPT 2007, pp. 185–192 (December 2007)
16. Satoh, A., Sugawara, T., Aoki, T.: High-speed Pipelined Hardware architecture for Galois Counter Mode. In: Garay, J.A., Lenstra, A.K., Mambo, M., Peralta, R. (eds.) ISC 2007. LNCS, vol. 4779, pp. 118–129. Springer, Heidelberg (2007)
17. Satoh, A.: High-speed hardware architectures for authenticated encryption mode GCM. In: Proceedings IEEE International Symposium on Circuits and Systems (ISCAS) (May 2006)
18. Xilinx, Virtex-4 User Guide, V2.3 (August 2007), http://www.xilinx.com
19. Xilinx, Virtex-5 User Guide, V3.3 (Feburary 2008), http://www.xilinx.com

Compiling Techniques for Coarse Grained Runtime Reconfigurable Architectures

Mythri Alle[1], Keshavan Varadarajan[1], Alexander Fell[1], S.K. Nandy[1],
and Ranjani Narayan[2]

[1] CAD Lab, Bangalore, Indian Institute Of Science
{mythri,keshavan,alefel,nandy}@cadl.iisc.ernet.in
[2] Morphing Machines Pvt. Ltd, Bangalore
ranjani.narayan@morphingmachines.com

Abstract. In this paper we develop compilation techniques for the realization of applications described in a High Level Language (HLL) onto a Runtime Reconfigurable Architecture. The compiler determines Hyper Operations (HyperOps) that are subgraphs of a data flow graph (of an application) and comprise elementary operations that have strong producer-consumer relationship. These HyperOps are hosted on computation structures that are provisioned on demand at runtime. We also report compiler optimizations that collectively reduce the overheads of data-driven computations in runtime reconfigurable architectures. On an average, HyperOps offer a 44% reduction in total execution time and a 18% reduction in management overheads as compared to using basic blocks as coarse grained operations. We show that HyperOps formed using our compiler are suitable to support data flow software pipelining.

1   Introduction

Reconfigurability in hardware is its ability to recast itself in order to emulate an operation[1]. General Purpose Processors (GPP) support reconfiguration across different opcodes, while Field Programmable Gate Array (FPGA) allows reconfiguration of the logic blocks and their interconnect so as to execute logic circuits that correspond to fine granular operations (as described in RTL). A runtime reconfigurable hardware provides the ability to emulate different operations at runtime. While GPPs allow very fast reconfigurations, they are inefficient in terms of performance and power. On the other hand, FPGAs are very slow to reconfigure due to the large reconfiguration data. In the architectures reported in [15], [10], [16] overheads of reconfiguration is reduced due to the use of coarse grained computations supported on computation structures. Computation structures are not Logic Blocks but elements of higher granularity like Function Units (FU) and/or Arithmetic Logic Units (ALU). As mentioned in [10], Compute Elements (CEs) are connected by a NoC. In order to exploit parallelism between

---

[1] We are of the opinion that reconfigurability and programmability are the same, except that these terminologies are used in different domains.

J. Becker et al. (Eds.): ARC 2009, LNCS 5453, pp. 204–215, 2009.
© Springer-Verlag Berlin Heidelberg 2009

elementary operations of a coarse grained computation, these elementary operations are distributed over several CEs that define a computation structure [1]. The computation structures for coarse grained computations are identified at compile time in terms of compute metadata (identifying the computations to be performed) and transport metadata (identifying the communications of results of computations). The compute and transport metadata together define the configuration of the computation structure. The computation structures are provisioned at run time.

Architectures described in [15], [10], [16] adopt a distributed data driven execution paradigm to mimic the hardware behaviour. The use of High level Language (HLL) hastens development time. Transforming HLL descriptions to GPP configurations (i.e. executables) have long been mastered. However the same is not true for the aforementioned architectures. We, in this paper present a generic compilation framework for architectures based on dataflow execution paradigm. We also assume a dynamic dataflow paradigm which schedules various operations in a data driven manner. In section 2.4 we describe extentions to the compilation framework to support architectures without dynamic dataflow support.

The rest of the paper is organized as follows. In section 2, we describe a method to transform applications described in HLL to Data flow graphs (DFGs) and techniques to optimize the same. Creation of coarse grained operations and generation of tags, (which are needed to identify data belonging to different iterations of loops) is also described in the same section. We present a technique to pipeline the coarse grained operations to further reduce management overheads. We establish the effectiveness of our compiler framework in section 3. We discuss the related work in section 4 and conclude in section 5.

2 Compilation Trajectory

In our compilation process, a HLL description of the application is first reduced to Static Single Assignment (SSA) form by the LLVM [3] infrastructure. It is then transformed into an application DFG. The nodes in the DFG represent the operations that are to be performed and the edges of the DFG represent the transports. ϕ operations are translated into DFG by adding additional nodes to transfer the data only when required. The control flow present in the imperative language is transformed into data flow using predicates. The control constructs of the C language are converted into conditional and unconditional branches by LLVM infrastructure. Since we handle both of these constructs, we can support all control structures that are expressed using C language. The number of predicates required depends on the complexity of control path. The edges in the DFG which transport these predicates are termed as *Predicate edges*. Higher the number of predicate edges higher is the transport overhead (i.e. the communication between two operations) and higher is the configuration data. To minimize transport overhead we perform Reduced Order Binary Decision Diagram (ROBDD) based optimizations (section 2.1). In the next step, subgraphs of DFG are identified to form HyperOps which are coarse grained operations.

Definition 1. *A **HyperOp** is defined as a directed acyclic graph $H(V', E')$. H is a vertex induced subgraph of DFG $G(V, E)$, where V, V' are the vertex sets of DFG G and HyperOp H respectively and E, E' are the edge sets of DFG G and HyperOp H respectively such that $V \subseteq V'$. For every edge $(v_i, v_j) \in G$ such that $v_i, v_j \in V' \exists$ an edge in E'*

*   Given two HyperOps $H_i(V_i, E_i)$ and $H_j(V_j, E_j) \forall i, j$ where $i \neq j$, $V_i' \bigcap V_j' = \{\}$ where V_i' is the vertex set of H_i and V_j' is the vertex set of H_j. A HyperOp must also satisfy the Convexity condition.*

Convexity condition: HyperOp interconnection graph should be a directed acyclic graph. The HyperOp interconnection graph captures producer consumer relationship between the set of HyperOps. More formally, HyperOp interconnection graph $I(H'', E'')$ where H'' is the set of HyperOps. For every edge (v_i, v_j) in the DFG such that $v_i \in Hi$ and $v_j \in Hj$, $i \neq j$, there exists an edge between H_i and H_j.

From the definition of the HyperOp it can be seen that a Hyper Block [11], Super Block also satisfies this definition. Hyper Block typically aggregates basic blocks (BBs) from the most frequently executed path based on the profile information. HyperOps on the other hand do not distinguish between more frequently and less frequently executed operations. Code duplication is another optimization that is performed to obtain larger code blocks. These optimizations are not suitable in our context as the primary goal is to find coarse grained operations across the entire application making profile information irrelevant for our framework. Code duplication leads to larger configuration size leading to less efficient implementation. HyperOps are atomically scheduled on dynamically composed computation structures.

    The Compiler needs to be aware of the structure and interconnection of CEs in order to optimally generate the compute and transport metadata. Refer to [1] for details of this step. Further, as shown in section 2.4 the compiler combines one or more HyperOps to form HyperOp Pipelines thus reducing management overheads. This technique is very useful for streaming applications where high throughput must be supported.

2.1   Optimizations Using ROBDD Technique

To minimize overhead due to predicate edges, we need to eliminate all control dependencies from redundant intermediate BBs which do not play a role in determining the execution of the BB under consideration. For example in figure 1 (a), BB H will be executed whenever BB B is executed. Execution of BB H does not depend on whether BB D or BB E is executed. Hence control edges DH and EH are redundant. The problem of identifying redundant control edges is modeled as the problem of obtaining a Reduced Ordered Binary Decision Diagram (ROBDD) from a given Binary Decision Diagram (BDD). ROBDD is formed by eliminating all the paths and variables, which do not play a role in determining the value of the function represented by the BDD [14].

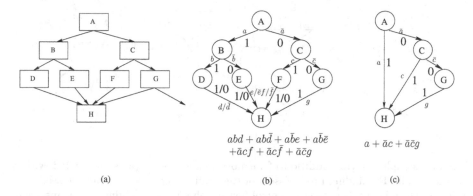

$$abd + ab\bar{d} + a\bar{b}e + a\bar{b}\bar{e}$$
$$+\bar{a}cf + \bar{a}c\bar{f} + \bar{a}\bar{c}g$$

$$a + \bar{a}c + \bar{a}\bar{c}g$$

(a)   (b)   (c)

Fig. 1. Example showing ROBDD optimization. (a) shows control flow graph rooted at A which is immediate dominator of H (b) shows the corresponding BDD and also the logic expression for execution of BB H. We use a to represent a true path from A and $\bar{a}$ to represent a false path from A. and (c) shows the ROBDD.

Predicate Minimization: Control flow graph is transformed into a BDD, treating each BB as a logic variable and the "true" edge as an edge corresponding to 1 and a "false" edge as an edge corresponding to 0. A unconditional branch is treated as having two edges one on "true" and another on "false". These edges are not added in the dataflow graph, but are just used for the computation of minimal set of predicates. In a BDD, each edge needs to be annotated with a value of 0 or 1. An Unconditional branch is equivalent to having both edges (1 and 0) pointing to the same node. For this transformation, the subgraph of the CFG rooted at the immediate dominator of the BB whose predicate is being minimized is considered. Since by definition [4], all paths to any node in the CFG has the immediate dominator as one of the predecessors. To compute the minimal set of predicates we obtain a ROBDD corresponding to this BDD. Standard techniques are applied to obtain ROBDD [14]. An example of this technique is shown in figure 1. Figure 1(a) shows a CFG rooted at BB A, which is the immediate dominator of BB H. Figure 1(b) shows the BDD corresponding to this control flow graph. It can be seen that BBs B, D, E, F do not play any role in determining the execution of H. Hence they are eliminated. Figure 1(c) shows the ROBDD corresponding to BB H. The ROBDD optimization when applied to all BBs can potentially reduce the number of predicates required, leading to a reduction in transports.

Minimization of Memory Dependencies: The order of the memory operations can be maintained at the time of issue as determined by the compiler or when they are being serviced. Swanson et al. [16] take the latter approach. In this approach additional hardware is required to detect the dependencies at the execution time, which increases power and area of the target hardware. We maintain the order at the time of issue by adding a dependency between the memory operations. Memory dependencies within a BB are identified and

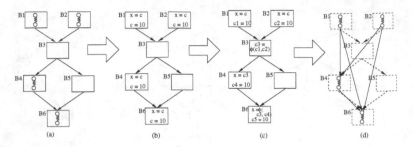

Fig. 2. Example showing addition of memory dependencies (a) shows a BB with a memory chain. For finding predecessors of the chain is replaced by read followed by a write as shown in (b). (c) shows a control flow graph after performing SSA translation. BB B3 has a ϕ node, but does not have a memory operation. Instead of adding a dummy operation ϕ nodes are iteratively replaced. (d) shows links added from all predecessors after iterative replacement.

dependency links are added. These memory chains should be linked with memory chains of all preceding BBs. To achieve this, each memory chain is replaced by a read followed by a write to a variable. All memory operations in an alias set perform a read and write from the same variable. This is done so that no unnecessary dependencies are added from memory operations which do not alias. The problem of finding the preceding operations translates to that of finding all reachable definitions for that variable. This is achieved through the process of SSA translation. An example is shown in figure 2. While our technique uses dominance frontiers to analyze memory dependencies, Beck et al. [2] use a post dominator approach. Both techniques are equivalent, but the use of dominance frontiers allow us to reuse the SSA based techniques. To add memory dependencies across functions, function call is predicated appropriately using the alias information obtained by the inter procedural analysis. Further, to reduce the number of memory dependency edges that are added we use ROBDD based techniques described earlier in this section. In applications where there is a long `if else` ladder or `switch` statement, ROBDD optimization is highly effective. As shown in the section 3 for applications like Deblocking Filter of H.264 video decoding application this technique is highly effective.

2.2   Construction of a HyperOp

When a HyperOp is formed by grouping together BBs, it is easier to check for convexity. The CFG of the application provides the necessary information to perform these checks. In most of the cases the operations within a BB have strong producer consumer relationship. Hence it is beneficial to group all these operations into one HyperOp. BBs are considered in a topologically sorted order for inclusion into a HyperOp. A new HyperOp is created when the current HyperOp cannot include any more BBs either due to resource constraints or due to correctness constraints. To ensure correctness, it is sufficient to check if immediate dominator [4] of BB is already included in a HyperOp. A BB may have to be partitioned before including into a HyperOp in case HyperOp exceeds limits imposed by the particular implementation of the architecture.

2.3 Tag Generation

Traditionally Dataflow Machines use "tags" to distinguish data tokens from multiple instances of same operation [18], [13], [9]. In these approaches, tags are associative with every data instance (token = data + tag) and this increases the overhead of data transfer (since additional bits needs to transferred). To minimize this overhead we generate tags only for the inputs and outputs of a HyperOp. Since a HyperOp is a Directed Acyclic Graph (DAG), intra HyperOp data tokens do not need a tag.

Compiler provides hints to the hardware for generation of tags for dynamic instances of tokens at run time. These hints include identifying the loop nesting relation of the producer and consumer and specifying the iteration dependence distance. The DFG is appropriately modified by adding additional nodes to ensure that a loop receives its data only from its immediate parent. Our observations indicate that in most cases this structure (of a loop receiving data only from its parent) naturally exists. In less than 1% of all cases we need to add additional nodes. With these additional nodes there can be only three relationships between a producer and a consumer for scalar variables. (i) Producer and consumer belong to the same loop, (ii) consumer is the parent of producer and (iii) producer is the parent of consumer. These three scenarios are encoded using two bits. The other information required is the iteration dependence distance. It can be clearly seen that any scalar data produced is consumed in the same loop instance or in the next loop instance. Hence the iteration dependence distance can be "0" or "1". This is encoded using one additional bit. These three bits are sufficient to generate the tag at the execution time. Using these three bits and the producer tag, hardware generates the consumer tag. Vector data (for ex: array data) are not delivered directly to the consumer, but are handled using loads and stores. Hence tags are not required for such data. However this scheme can be extended to array dependencies with statically known dependence distance. More number of bits are required to encode this dependence distance. When the number of bits available is not sufficient to encode the dependence distance, or when the dependence distance is not known at compile time (for ex: non-affine array accesses) loads and stores are introduced. In our current implementation, we add loads and stores for all vector data.

2.4 Pipelined HyperOps

Management overheads include wait time for all input operands of a HyperOp to arrive, time to launch HyperOps for execution and time to transport results. This overhead can be reduced, if the HyperOp is launched once and is retained for execution on the computation structure for complete lifetime of all dynamic instances of the HyperOp. Similarly, when HyperOps serve as sources to other HyperOps which are executed multiple times, management overheads (both due to launching and transport of results) can be reduced if the source and destination HyperOps are launched once and retained for the complete life time of all dynamic instances. In other words, we can create a *Pipeline of HyperOps*. We assume in-order delivery of results and existence of appropriate flow control mechanism in hardware ([7]) for this pipeline to function correctly. The execution model in such a scenario is identical to a pipelined static data flow machine [5]. Further in our case, the need for intra-HyperOp acknowledgments is obviated, since the HyperOps are DAGs.

Also, to have an efficient pipeline, it is important to use data flow software pipelining techniques [6] to balance the delays. Balancing of delays in the cited literature is done at the level of individual operations. In our solution, since we pipeline at the level of HyperOps, delay balancing is also done at the level of HyperOps. The NoC doubles up as delay balancing buffers. Generation of appropriate mapping of HyperOps to computation structures at compile time achieves the effect of delay balancing.

3   Results

The effectiveness of the compiler framework is established for different media related kernels/applications. In the following, we present the results of the evaluation. To evaluate the compiler, we have built a simulator, which mimics the behaviour of architecture described in [10]. In our simulator, we can configure different delays to depict overheads incurred due to launching of HyperOps, overheads incurred as input operand wait time and overheads due to inter HyperOp transports.

We carry out experiments in two scenarios; one in which a single BB is treated as a HyperOp (referred to as SBB HyperOp) and the other in which multiple BBs are aggregated to form HyperOps using algorithm proposed in this paper (referred to as MBB HyperOp). Intuitively, the management overheads in MBB HyperOps is expected to be lower than that in SBB HyperOps due to higher number of Intra HyperOp transports. The efficiency of generation of DFG is measured in terms of the additional nodes and edges introduced to transform the application into a DFG. To quantify improvement in performance, we measure execution time using the simulator. We also measure the buffer size required to store HyperOps waiting for inputs. The buffer size indicates the hardware complexity.

3.1   Effectiveness of ROBDD Optimization for DFG Generation

Table 1 shows the percentage of nodes added during conversion of control flow to data flow. Less control intensive applications (IDCT and Deblocking Filter) result in least amount of additional nodes. More control intensive applications (Edge detection algorithm, Sobel) show a greater amount of additional nodes.

Table 1. Percentage of Additional nodes added due to conversion from CFG to DFG and Reduction in Predicate Edges using ROBDD technique

Application	No. of Compute Nodes	No. of Additional Nodes	% of Additional Nodes	Number of Predicates		% of reduction due to ROBDD optimization
				before ROBDD optimization	after ROBDD optimization	
FIR	32	14	43.7	13	13	0
FFT	80	27	33.7	23	23	0
Edge De-tection	386	114	29.6	36	34	5.5
IDCT	1138	180	15.8	195	150	23.0
Deblocking Filter	1248	182	14.6	465	290	37.6

Table 1 also summarizes the reduction in predicates using ROBDD technique. For FIR, FFT and Edge detection we observe very small reduction as the control flow is very simple and the number of predicates required are low. We see maximum reduction of predicates in Deblocking filter (37% reduction) due to the complex control structure of this application. On an average, we observe 13.22% reduction in predicates.

3.2   Efficiency of HyperOp Formation

Gain in terms of reduced management overheads in MBB HyperOps could potentially get offset by increased wait time for input operands. To quantify this effect, we compare the execution time of SBB and MBB HyperOps. In both the cases (SBB and MBB) we measure Raw Execution time and Total Execution time. Raw execution time refers to the execution time ignoring the management overheads. Total execution time is the execution time including these overheads. To measure these overheads we assign single clock cycle delay for consumption of input operand, a single cycle delay for transportation of results to destinations and eight clock cycle delay to launch a HyperOp onto the execution structure. From the figure 3, we observe that for the case of MBB an average reduction of 26% in the raw execution time and 44% reduction in total execution time when compared to SBB.

To quantify management overheads, we measure the amount of inter HyperOp transports with respect to the total amount of transports (inter and intra HyperOp transports put together), waiting time of HyperOps for its inputs and the buffer size needed to store HyperOps waiting for inputs. Inter HyperOp transports contributes towards overheads incurred for matching operands. As expected, we observe in table 2 that the inter HyperOp transports in SBB is much higher than that in MBB. This is due to higher consolidation of operations in MBB HyperOps. The potential reduction in parallelism due to grouping together operations into a HyperOp can be quantified by the time HyperOp spends

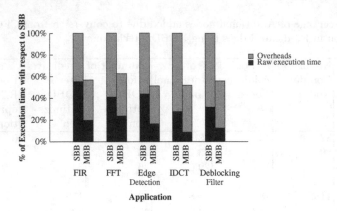

Fig. 3. Execution time comparison of SBB and MBB

Table 2. Efficiency of HyperOp Formation

Application	% of transports that are inter HyperOp		Average Wait time for Input Operands		Maximum number of Buffers Required		Average number of Buffers Required	
	SBB	MBB	SBB	MBB	SBB	MBB	SBB	MBB
FIR	25.14	7.3	20.7	26.3	4	2	1.8	1.2
FFT	11.2	6.8	86.4	66.3	4	4	2.6	2.7
Edge De-tection	18.4	7.4	61.8	57.8	9	6	5.4	3.2
IDCT	27.2	10.1	262.7	462.2	71	36	50.0	29.0
Deblocking Filter	27.1	19	249.3	344	251	55	143.1	28.4

in waiting for all its input operands. This time is measured as the elapsed time between the arrival of first operand and the last operand. These results are presented in table 2. The average waiting time of a HyperOp depends on the number of inputs and program characteristics. In case of FIR and Edge Detection, the number of BBs that can be included in a HyperOp is very small and hence the impact is very less in MBB. In IDCT we observe a very high impact and the waiting time increases as a large number of BBs are included in the HyperOp. In FFT and Edge Detection, unlike other applications we observe reduction in waiting time. This is because some of the high latency inter BB transports are converted into intra HyperOp transports.

Table 2 summarizes the maximum buffer size needed to store HyperOps waiting for input operands. More the buffer size, more is the complexity of hardware, which primarily matches the operands. We observe an average reduction of 42.6% in the maximum buffer requirement in MBB. Table 2 also shows average buffer requirement in both cases.

3.3 Efficiency Due to Tag Generation

In our scheme, we generate tags for HyperOps with the intention of reducing
tag matching overhead. Reduction in inter HyperOp transports proportionately
reduces tag matching overheads since tags are required only for inter HyperOp
transports. For MBB, our results show there is a 90.1% reduction in this overhead
when compared to generating tags for every operation. For SBB, we observe an
average reduction of 78%.

3.4 HyperOp Pipeline

To study the impact of HyperOp pipeline we simulate an ideal case of executing
the entire application as HyperOp pipeline. Figure 4 summarizes these results.
We observe an average of 26% improvement in performance ignoring launch overheads and an average of 44% improvement in performance ignoring both launch
and inter HyperOp transport overheads. It can be observed from the figure 4
that the launch delays for Deblocking filter are much higher than the average.
This is due to the larger size of HyperOps. Also, the reduction in execution time
points to the existence of high amount of parallelism. In the case of IDCT, close
to 50% of the time is spent in inter HyperOp transport delays. This is due to
smaller size of HyperOps, lesser parallelism exploited and large number of inputs
to each HyperOp. From the above it can be concluded that the benefits of HyperOp pipeline is significant in streaming applications since all inter HyperOp
delays are overlapped with HyperOp execution, and HyperOp launch delay is
eliminated since HyperOps are launched only for pipeline setup.

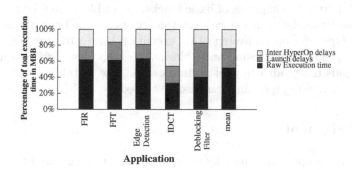

Fig. 4. Time spent in various stages during execution in MBB

4   Related Work

Transforming an application written in control oriented imperative languages
into data flow graphs is well researched topic. Like most of the techniques ([2]
, [16]) we also use predicates to construct DFG. Loop Invariant data is identified as special data and the hardware is expected to store it and deliver it to
the consumer HyperOps. In [16] and [9] these tokens are recirculated multiple

times with appropriate tags. To handle memory dependencies, we add static dependencies unlike [13] which uses hardware support.

The HyperOp pipeline is similar to data flow software pipeline [6]. However, our framework is at a coarser granularity. Further, the delay balancing is ensured by the appropriate placement of HyperOps in our framework. Gao et. al. [6] use delay balancing algorithms to introduce additional operations to perform the same.

Few synthesis methodologies use existing languages like C as input. Most of these tools proposed in [12], [17], and [8] translate a part of C application to hardware. It is not possible to translate entire application efficiently because of scheduling and resource allocation considerations. The important distinction between the proposed technique and other high level synthesis techniques is that the run time reconfigurable architecture is exposed to the compiler as a dynamic dataflow engine. Currently, we support only architectures that support dataflow execution paradigm. In future, we would like to extend our work to make it more generic.

5   Conclusion

In this paper we presented a framework to compile applications described in High level language onto runtime reconfigurable architectures. The architecture considered is data flow oriented in which hardware resources can be provisioned on demand at runtime. The demand for hardware resources are in terms of computation structures to support execution of coarse grained operations determined by the compiler. The notion of HyperOp as a coarse grained operation was introduced. HyperOp is a superset of basic blocks, Super blocks and Hyper blocks. Through quantitative evaluation we show that coarse grained operations formed using HyperOps offer on an average 44% execution time advantage over coarse grained operations formed using basic blocks. We also incur 18% less management overheads using our compilation framework. The suitability of HyperOps for data flow software pipelining was also discussed.

Acknowledgments

The research is supported in part by research grants from the Ministry of Communication and Information Technology, Govt. of India.

References

1. Alle, M., Varadarajan, K., Joseph, N., Reddy, C.R., Fell, A., Nandy, S.K., Narayan, R.: Synthesis of Application Accelerators on Runtime Reconfigurable Hardware. In: ASAP 2008: Proceedings of the 19th IEEE International Conference on Application specific Systems, Architectures and Processors (2008)
2. Beck, M., Johnson, R., Pingali, K.: From Control Flow to Data Flow. Journal of Parallel and Distributed Computing 12(2), 118–129 (1991)

3. Lattner, C., Adve, V.: LLVM: A Compilation Framework for Lifelong Program Analysis & Transformation. In: CGO 2004: Proceedings of the international symposium on Code generation and optimization, Washington, DC, USA (2004)
4. Cytron, R., Ferrante, J., Rosen, B.K., Wegman, M.N., Zadeck, F.K.: Efficiently Computing Static Single Assignment Form and the Control Dependence Graph. ACM Transactions on Programming Languages and Systems 13(4), 451–490 (1991)
5. Dennis, J.B., Gao, G.R.: An efficient pipelined dataflow processor architecture. In: Supercomputing 1988: Proceedings of the 1988 ACM/IEEE conference on Supercomputing, Los Alamitos, CA, USA (1988)
6. Gao, G.R.: Algorithmic aspects of balancing techniques for pipelined data flow code generation. J. Parallel Distrib. Comput. 6(1), 39–61 (1989)
7. Goossens, K., Dielissen, J., Radulescu, A.: Æthereal Network on Chip: Concepts, Architectures and Implementations. IEEE Design & Test of Computers 22(5), 414–421 (2005)
8. Gupta, S., Dutt, N., Gupta, R., Nicolau, A.: Spark: A high-level synthesis framework for applying parallelizing compiler transformations. In: Proceedings of 16th International Conference on VLSI Design, pp. 461–466 (2003)
9. Inagami, Y., Foley, J.F.: The specification of a new Manchester Dataflow Machine. In: ICS 1989: Proceedings of the 3rd International Conference on Supercomputing, New York, NY, USA (1989)
10. Joseph, N., Ramesh Reddy, C., Varadarajan, K., Alle, M., Fell, A., Nandy, S.K., Narayan, R.: RECONNECT: A NoC for polymorphic ASICs using a Low Overhead Single Cycle Router. In: ASAP 2008: Proceedings of the 19th IEEE International Conference on Application specific Systems, Architectures and Processors (2008)
11. Mahlke, S.A., Lin, D.C., Chen, W.Y., Hank, R.E., Bringmann, R.A.: Effective Compiler Support for Predicated Execution Using the Hyperblock. In: MICRO 25: Proceedings of the 25th Annual International Symposium on Microarchitecture, Portland, Oregon, December 1–4 (1992)
12. Mentor Graphics. Catapult C synthesis, http://www.mentor.com/products/esl/high_level_synthesis/catapult_synthesis/
13. Petersen, A., Putnam, A., Mercaldi, M., Schwerin, A., Eggers, S.J., Swanson, S., Oskin, M.: Reducing control overhead in dataflow architectures. In: Altman, E., Skadron, K., Zorn, B.G. (eds.) 15th PACT 2006: Proceedings of the 15th International Conference on Parallel Architecture and Compilation Techniques, Seattle, Washington, USA, pp. 182–191. ACM, New York (2006)
14. Akers, S.B.: Binary Decision Diagrams. IEEE Transactions on Computers C-27(6), 509–516 (1978)
15. Satrawala, A.N., Varadarajan, K., Alle, M., Nandy, S.K., Narayan, R.: REDEFINE: Architecture of a SOC Fabric for Runtime Composition of Computation Structures. In: FPL 2007: Proceedings of the International Conference on Field Programmable Logic and Applications (August 2007)
16. Swanson, S., Schwerin, A., Mercaldi, M., Petersen, A., Putnam, A., Michelson, K., Oskin, M., Eggers, S.J.: The WaveScalar architecture. ACM Transactions on Computer Systems 25(2), 1–54 (2007)
17. Vassiliadis, S., Wong, S., Cotofana, S.: The molen rho-mu-coded processor. In: Brebner, G., Woods, R. (eds.) FPL 2001. LNCS, vol. 2147, pp. 275–285. Springer, Heidelberg (2001)
18. Kathail Vinod, A., Pingali, K.: A Dataflow Architecure with tagged Tokens. Technical Report MIT/LCS/TM-174, Massachusetts Institute of Technology, Laboratory for Computer Science (September 1980)

Online Task Scheduling for the FPGA-Based Partially Reconfigurable Systems

Yi Lu, Thomas Marconi, Koen Bertels, and Georgi Gaydadjiev

Computer Engineering
Delft University of Technology, The Netherlands
{yilu,thomas,k.l.m.bertels,georgi}@ce.et.tudelft.nl

Abstract. Given the FPGA-based partially reconfigurable systems, hardware tasks can be configured into (or removed from) the FPGA fabric without interfering with other tasks running on the same device. In such systems, the efficiency of task scheduling algorithms directly impacts the overall system performance. By using previously proposed 2D scheduling model, existing algorithms could not provide an efficient way to find all suitable allocations. In addition, most of them ignored the single reconfiguration port constraint and inter-task dependencies. Further more, to our best knowledge there is no previous work investigating in the impact on the scheduling result by reusing already placed tasks. In this paper, we focus on online task scheduling and propose task scheduling solution that takes the ignored constraints into account. In addition, a novel "reuse and partial reuse" approach is proposed. The simulation results show that our proposed solution achieves shorter application completion time up to 43.9% and faster single task response time up to 63.8% compared to the previously proposed $stuffing$ algorithm.

1 Introduction

The reconfigurability of the FPGA has received much more attentions from various fields in the last decade. Usually, the FPGA is treated as a slave component in a reconfigurable system, when required, the complete FPGA is configured to offload the main processor. In this way, the FPGA can be easily managed as a solid part. With the development of the partially reconfigurable FPGAs, only the necessary part of the FPGA can be partially reconfigured when needed. By doing this, such partially reconfigurable systems can provide real multi-task function. The partial reconfiguration technology brings higher FPGA resource usage and faster partial reconfiguration time, but also introduce a need of an efficient scheduler to manage the hardware tasks.

Offline and online solutions can be used to solve this problem. In an offline solution, the scheduling decision is optimized when the application is compiled. In an online solution, the information of each task (e.g. execution time, configuration time) is unknown until it arrives. The online solution provides more adaptivity to various applications and avoids the application profile step, which is time-consuming. The online scheduler should, at runtime, assign a required time period to the arrival task. During

J. Becker et al. (Eds.): ARC 2009, LNCS 5453, pp. 216–230, 2009.
© Springer-Verlag Berlin Heidelberg 2009

this time period the task can be loaded and execute on the FPGA. The efficiency of the online scheduler will directly impact the overall performance of the whole system. In this paper, we focus on this online task scheduling and propose our solution.

In our solution, the basic configuration unit of the target FPGA is a column with the complete height of the FPGA. This configuration is supported by the popular Xilinx Virtex FPGA. Each task used in our system occupies a set of continuous columns. In this way, the size of a task can be only represented by its width. Then the task scheduling can be processed by using the 2D scheduling model (referred as **2D model** in this paper) described in [10]. As shown in Figure 1(b), in this model, the horizontal axis stands for the width of the FPGA and the vertical axis represents time. Each task can be treated as a rectangle in which the height represents the time (e.g. execution time and configuration time of the task) and the width keeps its original meaning. The scheduling problem now is similar to the strip packing as presented in [10]. Based on the 2D model, in this paper, we propose our solution to the online task scheduling problem. The main contributions of our solution are:

– to provide a modified algorithm which is suitable for searching the complete set of free allocations(stored as maximum free rectangles) on the 2D model;
– to present an example scheduling heuristic implied on the found allocations;
– to demonstrate a "reuse and partial reuse" approach;

In section 2, related work and our observation are presented. Thereafter, we detail our proposal in section 3. In section 4, we present the simulation results and evaluate its performance while comparing against previously proposed $stuffing$ algorithm [10]. Finally, we conclude this paper and discuss future works in section 5.

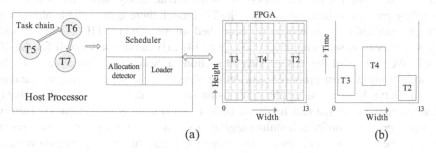

(a)   (b)

Fig. 1. The system architecture and scheduling model

2   Related Work

Online task scheduling is one of the key components of reconfigurable hardware operating systems [12]. In [10], Steiger et al. described the picture of the online scheduling for real-time tasks running on partially reconfigurable systems. They introduced a convenient 2D model which can convert the online scheduling problem to the strip packing. In addition, two online scheduling algorithms (1D Horizon and Stuffing) were proposed and evaluated in their work. However, their algorithms can not find all suitable scheduling positions for arrival tasks. In some cases, the arrival task is assigned to a later start time although there are other allocations allowing it to start earlier. Their algorithms also ignored the hardware constraint brought by the single reconfiguration port on the single-context FPGA (e.g. Xilinx FPGA), which will bring serious resource conflict when implementing the algorithms on real hardware. Zhou et al. [15] proposed a"window-based stuffing" online scheduling algorithm which is based on the 2D model from [10]. In this algorithm, for each arrival task, a time interval (the start time and the end time are decided according to the parameters of the arrival task) is defined on the 2D model. The occupied areas of scheduled tasks in the time window are passed to a placement algorithm (e.g. algorithms from [14][3][2]) to find available allocations for the arrival tasks. If found, the task is scheduled. This algorithm also ignored the hardware constraint as happened in [12]. Although the algorithm focused on a higher task acceptance ratio, it did not show obvious reduction of the completion time of the overall application, which reflects the overall performance of the partially reconfigurable systems. In [4], Danne et al. proposed a scheduling algorithm for periodic real-time tasks. In this algorithm, the FPGA area is partitioned into one dimensional slots and each task has several variants with different size and execution time. All possible combinations of available tasks are measured by the utilization metrics which is defined in the algorithm. Then the combination of tasks with minimum resource usage will be loaded into the proper slot. In [7], Jeong et al. described an ILP algorithm. Although their ILP approach considers prefetch and the hardware constraint of a single configuration port, the real hardware usage is not taken into account when implementing scheduling. In some cases, although the ILP shows successful task scheduling result, the assigned areas on the FPGA are not continuous, which actually leads a fail result.

By investigating the related works, we noticed that, firstly, when the online task scheduling problem is handled by using the 2D model, there is no suitable algorithms searching available allocations as we described above (e.g.[12] [10]). The previous proposed allocation searching algorithms (e.g.[14] [5]) can not serve well for the 2D model. (We will detail the reasons later in section 3). Secondly, in order to make the 2D model simple, most proposed scheduling algorithms ignored the reconfiguration port constraint. In this case, applications using such scheduling results will probably fail when running on the real hardware (detail explanation is in section 3). Thirdly, previously proposed online scheduling algorithms have not investigated the task reuse. However, the task reuse is the most direct way to decrease the reconfiguration overhead and is practical for many applications (details in section 3.5). Fourthly, task dependency is not well supported by the proposed algorithms, most algorithms used a large number of random independent tasks as their testbench.

Given these consideration, our proposed online task scheduling solution provides an allocation searching algorithm running on the 2D model and take the constraint of the configuration port into account as well as the task dependency. In addition, the "reuse and partial reuse" is explored. The goals of our solution are: 1) to provide a frame work solution to solve online task scheduling problems; 2) to generate a shorter completion time of the overall application running on the FPGA-based partial reconfigurable systems; 3) to ensure a faster response time for each task in an application.

3   Our Proposal

In this section we first present the unsuitability of the previously proposed algorithms aiming to find free allocations when they work on the 2D model. Then, the modified flow scanning (FS) algorithm [9] which is suitable for the 2D model is detailed. Next, the approach to overcome the configuration port constraint is detailed. Thereafter, a "best fit" scheduling heuristic is described. Last the "reuse and partial reuse" approach is presented.

In our solution, the base part is the algorithm which can find the complete set of free allocations. The "best fit" scheduling heuristic is an example of using the found free allocations, other heuristics can also be implied(e.g. we use the found free allocations in a different way when implementing the "reuse and partial reuse", which is detailed in section 3.5). In our solution, the allocation searching algorithm and "reuse and partial reuse" are highlighted.

3.1   Allocation Searching Algorithms

The previously proposed algorithms(e.g. [14] [5]) aiming to find the complete set of available free allocation are mostly based on the 2D matrix model. As shown in Figure 2(a), the target is modeled as a 2D matrix, all cells are encoded with meaningful information(e.g. the negative value is assigned to the occupied area, and the positive value is to the free area). By processing the information of all cells, the complete set of free allocations can be found. These algorithms work well for the target models which have exact height and width (e.g. FPGA and multi-processor mesh). However, when implementing such algorithms on the 2D model, things become much more complicated. As shown in Figure 2(b), if a task arrives at t_s and is expected to complete by t_e, in order to find all available allocations between this interval by using the algorithms based on the matrix model, information in almost all the cells has to be updated as shown in Figure 2(c). In addition, the t_s and t_e will probably be different for every task, which means the size of the matrix has to be changed and all the information encoded in the cells has to be recalculated and updated every time a task arrives.

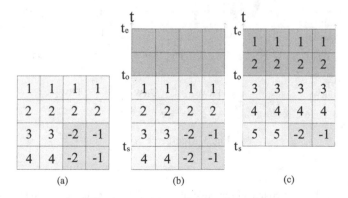

Fig. 2. Algorithms with matrix model

3.2 Modified Flow Scanning Algorithm

In [9], we previously proposed the flow scanning (**FS**) algorithm which finds the complete set of maximum free rectangles on the FPGA at runtime. To achieve this, the FS algorithm only need the positions of placed tasks and the width and height of the FPGA. In this work, the original FS algorithm was modified to be easily implied to the 2D model. The modified FS (mFS) algorithm is use to find all suitable allocations in the 2D model for arrival tasks. In this section, we will describe how the mFS algorithm works on the 2D model.

We start the description with an example to explain how the mFS works on the 2D model as shown in the Figure 3. Assume that a new task arrives at time t_s and is expected to complete by time t_e. An maximum free rectangle between t_s and t_e is needed to allocate this task. In the beginning, an initial FRW_1 is created at the task arrival time t_s (the FRW in the mFS is defined as a rectangle which has no top line and can only be expanded upwards). The bottom of this FRW_1 is t_s and it covers the complete width of the model, as shown in Figure 3(a). The scanning flow which is from t_s to t_e in the t direction, will reach the in-edge[1] of a previously placed task 1 (PT_1) at time t_{in} in the t direction (shorthand **At time = t_{in}:**), the initial FRW_1 is overlapped with this edge in X direction, so it becomes a maximum free rectangle (0, 10, t_s, t_{in}) (in this paper, we define such maximum free rectangle as **scheduling rectangle (sRectangle)**). Thereafter, two new FRWs are created for the non-overlapping area, as shown in Figure 3(b), the FRW_2 and FRW_3. **At time = t_{out}:** the out-edge of task PT_1 is met at this level, so the out-edge process is performed, which creates a new FRW: FRW_4 shown in Figure 3(c). **At time = t_e:** when reaching the top edge (t_e), which is defined as an in-edge, all existing FRWs are transferred to maximum free rectangles with top at $t = t_e$. During the scanning process described above, totally four sRectangles were found: (0, 10, t_s, t_{in}), (0, 3, t_s, t_e), (6, 10, t_s, t_e) and (0, 10, t_{out}, t_e).

In the mFS, there are two basic processes as shown in above example, the in-edge process and out-edge process. The in-edge process happens when the scanning flow

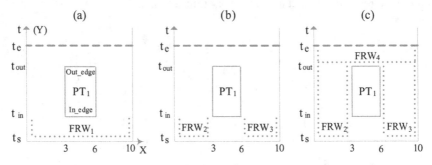

Fig. 3. Modified F S

---

[1] In the mFS, the bottom edge and top edge of a placed task are named in-edge and out-edge respectively.

reaches an in-edge and the out-edge process is called when leaving an out-edge. In the in-edge process, if a FRW is overlapped with an in-edge in the X direction, a sRectangle is created by adding to the FRW a top line at the height of the in-edge. New FRW(s) will also be created if the FRW is not fully overlapped with the in-edge. In the out-edge process, only one new FRW is created with the bottom at the same height as the out-edge. Every time when a task arrives, a searching interval is set, which is the time period between the t_s and t_e. By implying the mFS to the 2D model, we do not need to rebuild the meaningful matrix every time. The available allocations are found only by running mFS to scan the searching interval.

3.3 Reconfiguration Port Scheduling

The reconfiguration port is a hardware interface located on the FGPA to implement the run-time partial reconfiguration. On current FPGAs (e.g. Xilinx FPGAs), only one reconfiguration port is supported, which means that the configuration of tasks is a sequential process. As shown in Figure 4 (a), three tasks PT_1, PT_2 and PT_3 arrive at t_s and are to be scheduled on the same FPGA. If the availability of the reconfiguration port on the FPGA is not taken into account, the three tasks are scheduled as shown in Figure 4 (b), which can be treated as a simple strip packing problem. However, if we check the availability of the reconfiguration port shown in Figure 4 (c), it is obvious that the configuration of the PT_3 can not start at time t_s, because the reconfiguration port is occupied by the PT_1. So the scheduling result shown in Figure 4 (b) is not feasible in reality. A reasonable scheduling result is shown in the Figure 4 (d). Figure 4 (e) reflects the availability of the reconfiguration port after scheduling the three tasks.

In our algorithm, a reconfiguration port checking process is added to avoid the confliction of the reconfiguration port scheduling. After the mFS finds the complete set of sRectangles, the reconfiguration port checking process can be run to check the confliction between the reconfiguration port availability and the sRectangles. If there is any conflict, the temporal values of the related sRectangles will be reset. As shown in Figure 5 (b), the checking process finds that the start time (t_s) of original R_2 is overlapped with the configuration time of PT_1 and PT_2. Consequently, the start time of R_2 is reset to the value shown in the figure.

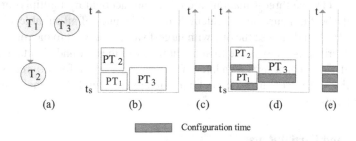

Configuration time

Fig. 4. Sequential reconfiguration port

3.4   Best Fit Scheduling Heuristic

In our solution, the scheduling heuristics can be various. We are not aiming to provide a specific scheduling heuristic for all applications. Because by using our mFS algorithm, all available allocations on the 2D model can be easily found, we can implement various heuristics to use these found allocations for different applications.

In this paper, we will give an example scheduling heuristic, the best fit. The best fit heuristic is to schedule the arrival task into an available sRectangle which results in less fragmentation and better time performance in the 2D model. Based on our observation, we created equation (1). For all available allocations, we calculate their BF value by using equation (1), then the best fit one is chosen according to the values. In equation (1), A_{task} stands for the arrival time of a task; S_{task} represents the starting time for the task running on the FPGA; T_{width} and R_{width} are the width of the task and the chosen sRectangle respectively; the $E_{overlap}$ stands for the length of overlapped edges between placed tasks and the new task when placed in a chosen rectangle and the E_{task} is the perimeter of the arrival task.

$$BF = \frac{A_{task}}{S_{task}} \times \frac{T_{width}}{R_{width}} \times \frac{E_{overlap}}{E_{task}} \qquad \dots\dots(1)$$

Equation (1) consists of three components which reflects the time issue and the de-fragmentation requirements by using the 2D model, as shown in the Figure 5. PT_x(x = 1,2...) stands for the placed task; PT_a is the arrival task; R_x(x = 1,2...)is the suitable sRectangle to locate the arrival task. In Figure 5 (a) (b), when a new task PT_a arrives at t_s and is expected to complete by t_e, R_1 and R_2 are both suitable for the PT_a. However, allocating PT_a in these suitable sRectangles will give different response time and completion time. In our approach, we allocate the PT_a into R_2 in order to achieve shorter response time as well as the earlier completion time. Corresponding to the equation (1), for various suitable allocations, we choose the one with biggest $\frac{A_{task}}{S_{task}}$ value. In Figure 5 (c) (d), it can be observed that when the arrival task is placed in the suitable sRectangle with shorter width (R_1), less fragmentation will be created. This reflects the requirement of larger $\frac{T_{width}}{R_{width}}$ value. In Figure 5 (e) (f), we observed that when placed the arrival task with more overlapped edges with placed tasks, less fragmentation will be created. Corresponding to the equation (1), the chosen sRectangle should have largest value of $\frac{E_{overlap}}{E_{task}}$.

In equation (1), the three situations are taken into account by multiplying them to-gether. For the best fit heuristic, we calculate the BF values of all suitable sRectangles for the arrival task and choose the one with largest value. We want to mention again that the best fit heuristic is an example to show how to use these found sRectangles, it can achieve good performance as shown later in section 4, however, for different situations, we believe that different heuristics can be applied to the found sRectangles in order to achieve better results.

3.5   Reuse and Partial Reuse

For the FPGA-based partially reconfigurable systems, the reconfiguration overhead de-creases the overall performance of systems, some researches were done to reduce or

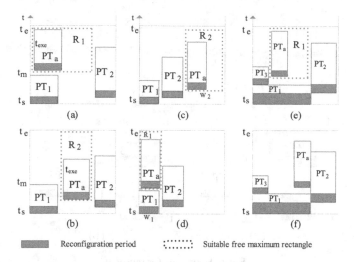

Reconfiguration period   ┊┄┄┄┄┊ Suitable free maximum rectangle

Fig. 5. Heuristics for defragmentation

hide this overhead(e.g. [1] [6]). Most previous work focus on hiding the reconfiguration time to the users, however, the reconfiguration port is still occupied by these tasks. In most current FPGAs, only one reconfiguration port is supported, which means that the reconfiguration is a sequential process. This reflects that the overall configuration time of all hardware modules in an application is a fixed value. When the number of the hardware modules is increased and the size of modules becomes bigger (usually because the logic of modules become complicated), this overall configuration time will become much longer (sometime even comparable to the execution time of applications). This is one of the critical reasons to limit the use of partially reconfigurable systems in real applications. So, the most efficient way to avoid the reconfiguration overhead is to support reuse of the tasks which have been already placed on the FPGA as much as possible. During our investigation to many applications, we noticed that different hardware function modules in the same application usually work on the same objects, which makes the logic of each module can be reused by others (e.g. the pixel operation functions in H.264 applications). In addition, many hardware modules contain common functions (e.g. multiply, memory address generator). Given these reasons, the reuse of placed tasks is efficient and practical. In this paper, we propose our task reuse and partial reuse (RPR) approach. The "reuse" means to use the logic of placed task T_p to implement the arrival task T_a, which save the configuration time of the arrival task. The partial reuse happens in two situations: 1) the logic of placed task T_p can not implement the complete function of the arrival task T_a but a part; 2) T_p can implement the function of T_a, but T_p will be removed before it can complete the execution for T_a. When the partial reuse is applied, the logic of T_p is used for T_a, meanwhile, the T_a itself is also configured on the FPGA. Once the T_a is ready, the partially processed data will be transferred from T_p to T_a, then T_a can complete the computation. In this way, the partial reuse hide the configuration time of T_a to the user.

For the online scheduling, the information about arrival task is unknown until it arrives, which implies that when implementing the RPR technology, the reusable task

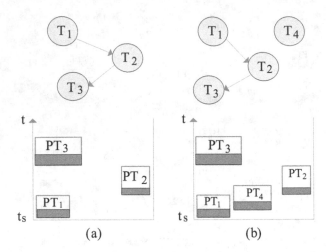

Fig. 6. Heuristics for reuse

should exist on the FPGA as long as possible. Given this, we apply another heuristic to allocate the arrival tasks as shown in the Figure 6. For the data independent task or the first task in a task graph, it is placed at the bottom left corner of the sRectangle with fastest response time, e.g. the PT_4 and PT_1 shown in Figure 6 (b). For the tasks having data dependence, each task is placed as far as possible (in the horizontal direction) from its ancestor task, e.g. PT_1, PT_2 and PT_3 shown in Figure 6 (a).

An example of the RPR process is shown in the Figure 7. Assume that the task PT_1 to PT_4 have already been scheduled and the task PT_1 meets the requirements of being reused by the task PT_a arriving at t_s. In the 2D model, if the height of sRectangle above the PT_1 is no less than the value of execution time when reusing PT_1 for PT_a, the PT_1 can be directly reused for execution of PT_a after PT_1 completes, as shown in Figure 7 (a). On the contrary, if the height is less than the value, the partial reuse approach can be implied. The difference of implementing scheduling solution with and without partial reuse approach is shown in Figure 7 (b) and (c). In Figure 7 (b), PT_a is placed as usual, Instead, the Figure 7 (c) shows that the result of implementing partial reuse approach. Comparing the task ending time t_e, the partial reuse approach gives a better performance. When implementing the partial reuse, an extra period is added into the task execution time. This price is paid for the necessary data (e.g. state information of the hardware module) extracting and transferring from the reused task to the new configured task(e.g. PT_{a1} to PT_{a2} in Figure 7 (c)). The mechanism of this process is presented in [8]. When a running task is to be reallocated into other position, only the bitstreams containing state information will be read back from reconfiguration port(ICAP). The state information of the running task will be extracted and combined into the initial bitstream for the target position. According to the experimental results shown in [8], the total state information exacting and combining time is about 18% of the task configuration time. In our simulation, we added the same amount extra time as the task state setting period to the task when implying the partial reuse approach. The communication structure in our solution is the homogeneous busmacro system which

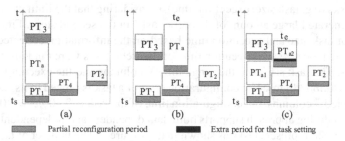

Fig. 7. Reuse and partial reuse

was presented in [8]. By using this type of busmacro system, tasks placed on the FPGA have the same bus interface and share the buses. The connecting interface of tasks to the buses is same as the interface of custom unit in the "Molen" architecture [11].

The overall algorithm is shown as follow:

Algorithm:

Input: arrival task, searching starting time, searching ending time

  if Reuse_function_checking is true **then**

    assign the arrival task to the reusable module;

  else if Partial_reuse_checking is true **then**

    assign a part of calculation of the arrival task to the reusable module;

    searching all free allocations for the rest of the arrival task;

    implying scheduling heuristic to choose an allocation;

  else

    searching all free allocations;

    checking conflict of the reconfiguration port;

    implying scheduling heuristic;

  end if

4 Experimental Evaluation

The target FPGA is Xilinx Virtex II XC2V4000 FPGA which contains 80(row) x 72(column) CLBs. The total configuration time of the complete FPGA is 39.15ms (SelectMAP port at 50MHz). On the FPGA, there are total 2156 frames, which is the minimum configuration unit. All the CLBs in one column use 22 frames. The reconfiguration time of one column is calculated by using the equation shown in [1]: T_{column} =(frames per column) x ((total configuration time) / (total frames)) = 22 x (39.15 / 2156) = 0.40ms. The partial reconfiguration time of each task will be calculated based on these data.

The tasks we used in the experiment were created via two steps. In the first step, VHDL codes of real hardware tasks (e.g. $fmult$ and $update$ [2] for G721 encoder, DCT and AES) were generated by DWARV [3] [13]. Then they were synthesized by Xilinx ISE and implemented on the "Molen" [11]. In this step, we collected information of the real

---

[2] The $fmult$ performs table look-up and the $update$ is control dominated processing of multiple scalar variables.

[3] The DWARV is a toolset performing automatic C-to-VHDL generation [13].

hardware tasks (e.g. task size, execution time). Considering that the limit number of real tasks, we generated large amount of theoretic tasks in the second steps. Firstly, we set the ranges of task size and execution time based on the information collected from the real tasks. Then the size and execution time of theoretic tasks were randomly chosen in these ranges. The task size is in the range [5..20] columns and the execution time is in the range [1.00..50.00] ms. The configuration time of a task is related to its size, e.g. for a task occupied 5 columns, the configuration time of the task is 0.40 x 5 = 2.00 ms. Our proposed scheduling approach supports both data dependent and independent tasks. We used task graph to represent tasks as shown in the Figure 7. The number of tasks in each task graph was randomly chosen in the range [1..5].

Usually, the partially reconfigurable systems can be categorized into two types. The hardware operation only and the hardware-software (Hw/Sw) cooperation. In the first type, all tasks in an application can only run on the hardware target (e.g. FPGAs). For the second type which supports Hw/Sw cooperation, each task in the application can either run on the hardware target or the general purpose processor (GPP). In the experiment, we considered both types. In the simulation of Hw/Sw cooperation type, two extra parameters of tasks were given: the software execution time of a task (T_{set}) and the dummy time (T_{dummy}) of a task. The T_{set} is the task execution time when it runs on the GPP and the T_{dummy} represents the time that a task can wait for the scheduling on the FPGA. If the scheduling can not be made within the T_{dummy}, the task will run on the GPP. For the tasks generated via DWARV, the two parameters are collected from the real hardware implementation. For the randomly created tasks, the T_{set} is randomly set as 3 to 5 times of the execution time of the task, and the T_{dummy} is randomly set as 0.5 to 2.5 times of the execution of the task.

In the experiment, the performance of our proposed approaches (BF and RPR) and the $stuffing$ [10] were evaluated. The original $stuffing$ algorithm did not support data dependent tasks and reconfiguration port check, in order to fairly compare our approaches to the $stuffing$ algorithm, we modified the $stuffing$ algorithm to support these features. All algorithms were programmed using C, and executed under Linux 2.6 with Intel(R) Pentium(R) 4 CPU 3.00GHz. All algorithms were evaluated in term of application completion time and single task response time.

4.1   Application Completion Time

The application completion time (ACT) is defined as the completion time of the application. In each simulation run, firstly an application was generated by randomly creating the task graph and tasks (each application consists of 50 task graphs). Then the $Stuffing$, BF and RPR were implied to the application respectively and the ACT were measured. Totally, 1000 simulation runs were implemented and the results shown in the table 1 were evaluated by using the following equation:

$$\frac{A}{B} = \frac{AET_B - AET_A}{AET_B} \times 100\% \qquad ......(2)$$

The 'A' and 'B' stands for scheduling algorithms. The AET_A and AET_B represent the AET values of the same application when implying 'A' and 'B' algorithms respectively.

The $\frac{A}{B}$ stands for the comparison of A to B and its value is calculated by the right side of equation (2). The positive value means that the AET_A is shorter than AET_B, which reflects that algorithm 'A' outperforms algorithm 'B' (similarly, 'B' is better than 'A' for a negative value). If comparing serval algorithms to 'B', the best algorithm will show the closest value to "100%".

As shown in the table 1, the "$Average$" column gives the average value of the 1000 simulation runs, and the "$Best$" and "$Worst$" columns show the largest and smallest values respectively. It can be observed in the third row that averagely the BF outperforms the $stuffing$ by 11. 3% in term of ACT, and the worst and best cases among the 1000 simulation runs are 3. 9% and 20.4% respectively. The BF outperforming $stuffing$ can be explained with 2 reasons: 1) the mFS algorithm used in BF can find all suitable sRectangles for arrival tasks, which can not be granted by $stuffing$; 2) by using equation (1), less fragmentation, shorter response time and shorter completion time can be achieved for the allocation of each task. When implementing our RPR technology, averagely around 20% tasks are reused or partially reused in an application. As shown in the second and fourth rows of the table 1, the RPR achieved better performance compared to BF and $stuffing$. This is because when reusing a placed task T_p for an arrival task T_a, the reconfiguration time of T_a is removed. In addition, the reconfiguration port can be used to load other tasks during the period when the T_a should be loaded (the T_a should be loaded when RPR is not implied). Further more, although extra communication time is required when implying partial reuse, it helps to achieves shorter completion time and response time as described earlier in the section 3.5.

Table 1. Comparison of ACT

	Average	Best	Worst
RPR / BF	28. 9%	39.1%	11. 6%
BF / stuffing	11. 3%	20.4%	3. 9%
RPR / stuffing	34.7%	43. 9%	20.8%

4.2 Single Task Response Time

The single task response time (STRT) is defined as the time interval represented by: $T_{response}$ - $T_{arrival}$. The $T_{arrival}$ stands for the arrival time of a task, and the $T_{response}$ is the starting time of the task configuration or the starting time of the execution when reusing a placed task. The STRT is an very important character to measure the system performance especially for the real-time systems. The results shown in the table 2 are in the same format as the table 1. The results are calculated by using equation (3) which holds the similar explanation as the equation (2).

$$\frac{A}{B} = \frac{STRT_B - STRT_A}{STRT_B} \times 100\% \qquad \text{......(3)}$$

The BF achieves a better performance at least around 2.4% and averagely 11.7% less STRT compared to the $stuffing$. When implementing the RPR technology, the

Table 2. Comparison of STRT

	Average	Best	Worst
RPR / BF	41.6%	61.6%	12. 5%
BF / stuffing	11.7%	23.4%	2.4%
RPR / stuffing	49. 9%	63.8%	28. 5%

reductions of STRT are averagely around 28. 9% and 34.7% compared to the BF and $stuffing$ respectively. The explanation for the BF and RPR having better STRT results can also be referred to the reasons described for the comparison of ACT results.

In our simulation, the execution time for scheduling a task is in a range from 0.09ms to 0.13ms, averagely 0.11ms. Compared to the reconfiguration time of tasks used in our simulation (which is from 2.0ms to 8.0ms), the time used for a single task scheduling is acceptable.

4.3   Hw / Sw System Scenario

In the previous two subsections, we assumed that all tasks can only run on the hardware and we presented the comparison of ACT and $STRT$ among the BF, RPR and $stuffing$. In this subsection, the system is assumed to run in the Hw/ Sw mode. In our approach, when a task arrives, the mFS algorithm finds all suitable sRectangles for the task in the required searching interval, which is defined as: $T_{arrive} + T_{dummy} + T_{configuration} + T_{execution}$. The T_{arrive} stands for the arrival time of the task, the $T_{configuration}$ is the configuration time of the task and the $T_{execution}$ is the hardware execution time of the task. By using the mFS algorithm, all suitable sRectangles in the required time interval are aware, the schedule of a task to the FPGA or the GPP can be processed immediately when the task arrives. In previously proposed algorithms, because of unknowing all suitable sRectangles, if an arrival task can not be scheduled to the FPGA immediately, it has to wait until the end of the dummy time. During that period, if any suitable allocation found, it will be scheduled to the FPGA, otherwise, it will be assigned to the GPP after the dummy time.

In the simulation, we used a linked list to represent the availability of the GPP. Each node in the linked list shows a continuous free period of the processor. If an arrival task is assigned to the GPP, the task is scheduled in the nearest node(s). An example of scheduling a task to the GPP is shown in the Figure 8. When task T_x and T_y arrive at t_s, the mFS can not find a suitable allocation for the T_x during the time interval $[T_s$ $T_d]$, so the T_x is decided to run on the GPP. The resource availability of the FPGA and the GPP are shown in Figure 8 (b)(c) respectively. According to Figure 8 (c), the T_x is scheduled on the GPP into two time interval t_{xs1} and t_{xs2}. The T_y which is data-dependent with the T_x can only run after the t_{xe} (the completion time of the T_x). The comparison of ACT results of 1000 simulations for the Hw/ Sw cooperation is shown in the table 3. The BF shows worse performances compared to the $stuffing$. By tracing the scheduling process, we found an interesting phenomenon. Under the

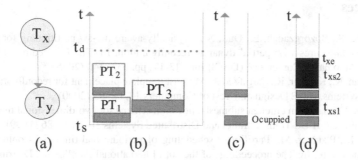

Fig. 8. Task software execution

Table 3. comparison of ACT for Hw/Sw mode

	Average	Best	Worst
RPR/BF	20.74%	39.9%	0.3%
BF/stuffing	-4.5%	15.5%	-28.5%
RPR/stuffing	21.2%	54.2%	-6.7%

HW/ SW mode, although in the beginning, the BF scheduled more tasks to the FPGA compared to $stuffing$, the free time periods of the reconfiguration port become much smaller fragmentation, which results in unusable for the later tasks. On the contrary, although the $stuffing$ created more fragmentation on the 2D model, it kept the relative longer free time periods of reconfiguration port, which helped to achieve a good overall performance. Then we simulated the RPR, as expected, by decreasing the impaction from availability of reconfiguration port, the PRP achieved averagely 21.2% reduction of ACT compared to the $stuffing$.

5 Conclusion and Future Work

In this paper, we proposed an online task scheduling solution for the FPGA-based partially reconfigurable systems. Building upon our allocation search approach, various scheduling heuristics could be applied to different situations. In addition out "reuse and partial reuse" approach showed the potential to shorter the ACT and STRT. Our experimental validation has shown that our solution has up to 43.9% shorter ACT and 63.8% faster STRT compared to the $stuffing$ algorithm. In the future, our work will focus on: (i) implementing the "reuse and partial reuse" method on our "Molen" prototype board; (ii) considering the heterogenous resource distribution on the FPGA.

Acknowledgment. This work is sponsored by the hArtes project (IST-035143) supported by the Sixth Framework Programme of the European Community under the thematic area "Embedded Systems".

References

1. Banerjee, S., Bozorgzadeh, E., Dutt, N.: Physically-aware hw-sw partitioning for reconfigurable architectures with partial dynamic reconfiguration. In: The Proceeding of the 42nd Design Automaion Conference (DAC), June 13-17, pp. 335–340 (2005)
2. Bazargan, K., Kastner, R., Sarrafzadeh, M.: Fast template placement for reconfigurable computing systems. IEEE Design and Test of Computers 17, 68–83 (2000)
3. Chiu, G., Chen, S.: An efficient submesh allocation scheme for two-dimensional meshes with little overhead. IEEE Trans. Parallel and Distributed Systems 10, 471–486 (1999)
4. Danne, K., Platzner, M.: Partitioned scheduling of periodic real-time tasks onto reconfigurable hardware. In: The proceedings of the 20th International Parallel and Distributed Processing Symposium (IPDPS), April 25-29 (2006)
5. Handa, M., Vemuri, R.: An efficient algorithm for finding empty space for online fpga placemen. In: Proceedings of the 41st annual conference on desing automation, San Diego, pp. 960–965 (June 2004)
6. Hauck, S.: Configuration prefetch for single context reconfigurable coprocessors. In: Proceedings of the sixth International Symposium on Field Programmable Gate Arrays (FPGA 1998), pp. 65–74 (1998)
7. Jeong, B., Yoo, S., Lee, S., Choi, K.: Hardware-software cosynthesis for run-time incrementally reconfigurable fpgas. In: The Proceeding of the Asia and South Pacific Design Automation Conference (ASP-DAC), pp. 169–174 (2000)
8. Kalte, H., Porrmann, M.: Context saving and restoring for multitasking in reconfigurable systems. In: Proceedings of the International Conference on Field Programmable Logic and Applications (FPL), pp. 223–228 (2005)
9. Lu, Y., Marconi, T., Gaydadjiev, G., Bertels, K.: An efficient algorithm for free resource management on the fpga. In: Proceedings of Design, Automation and Test in Europe (DATE 2008), Munich, Germany (March 2008)
10. Steiger, C., Walder, H., Platzner, M.: Operating systems for reconfigurable embedded platforms: Onlline scheduling of real-time tasks. IEEE Transactions on Computers 53 (November 2004)
11. Vassiliadis, S., Wong, S., Gaydadjiev, G., Bertels, K., Kuzmanov, G., Panainte, E.M.: The molen polymorphic processor. IEEE Transactions on Computers archive 53 (November 2004)
12. Walder, H., Platzner, M.: Reconfigurable hardware operating systems: From concepts to realizations. In: Proc. Int'l Conf. Eng. of Reconfigurable Systems and Algorithms (ERSA), pp. 284–287 (2003)
13. Yankova, Y., Kuzmanov, G., Bertels, K., Gaydadjiev, G., Lu, Y., Vassiliadis, S.: Dwarv: Delft workbech automated reconfigurable vhdl generator. In: International Conference on Field Programmable Logic and Applications (FPL), August 27-29, pp. 697–701 (2007)
14. Yoo, S., Youn, H., Shirazi, B.: An efficient task allocation scheme for 2d mesh architectures. IEEE Trans. Parallel and Distributed Systems 8, 934–942 (1997)
15. Zhou, X., Wang, Y., Huang, X., Peng, C.: On-line scheduling of real-time tasks for reconfigurable computing system. In: IEEE International Conference on Field Programmable Technology (FPT), Thailand, pp. 57–64 (December 2006)

Word-Length Optimization and Error Analysis of a Multivariate Gaussian Random Number Generator

Chalermpol Saiprasert, Christos-Savvas Bouganis,
and George A. Constantinides

Department of Electrical & Electronic Engineering, Imperial College London
Exhibition Road, London SW7 2BT, United Kingdom
{cs405,christos-savvas.bouganis,g.constantinides}@imperial.ac.uk

Abstract. Monte Carlo simulation is one of the most widely used techniques for computationally intensive simulations in mathematical analysis and modeling. A multivariate Gaussian random number generator is one of the main building blocks of such a system. Field Programmable Gate Arrays (FPGAs) are gaining increased popularity as an alternative means to the traditional general purpose processors targeting the acceleration of the computationally expensive random number generator block. This paper presents a novel approach for mapping a multivariate Gaussian random number generator onto an FPGA by automatically optimizing the computational path with respect to the resource usage. The proposed approach is based on the Eigenvalue decomposition algorithm which decomposes the design into computational paths with different precision requirements. Moreover, an error analysis on the impact of the error due to truncation is performed in order to provide upper bounds of the error inserted into the system. The proposed methodology optimises the usage of the available FPGA resources leading to area efficient designs without any significant penalty on the overall performance. Experimental results reveal that the hardware resource usage on an FPGA is reduced by a factor of two in comparison to current methods.

Keywords: Multivariate Gaussian Distribution; Word-length optimization; FPGA.

1 Introduction

Many stochastic processes in scientific experiments and mathematical analysis are modeled using Stochastic Differential Equations (SDE). In order to determine the solution to these stochastic processes, time consuming and computationally expensive simulations are employed. Financial mathematics is one of many fields that heavily relies on the simulation of SDE in which many financial instruments can be modeled. Examples can be found in value-at-risk [1] and credit-risk calculation [2]. The Monte Carlo method is one of the most widely used techniques to carry out these simulations [3]. At the heart of Monte Carlo simulation lies

J. Becker et al. (Eds.): ARC 2009, LNCS 5453, pp. 231–242, 2009.
© Springer-Verlag Berlin Heidelberg 2009

a sequence of randomly generated numbers which is one of the essential pre-requisites for almost all Monte Carlo simulations. These random numbers are produced from a variety of distributions, and one of the most commonly in use is the multivariate Gaussian distribution.

In recent years there is an increasingly high demand for computationally in-tensive calculations in finance due to the ever increasing assets and portfolios size. Traditionally, the random number generator and the financial application it-self have been implemented on general purpose processors. Recently, alternative methods based on Graphics Processing Unit (GPU) and Field Programmable Gate Array (FPGA) have gained a great deal of attention due to their higher throughput performance and lower power consumption. In this work we tar-get an FPGA device due to its capability to provide fine-grain parallelism and reconfigurability. Existing works in literature concerning hardware acceleration of financial applications include the calculation of Monte Carlo based credit derivative pricing [4] and interest rates simulation [5]. In order to maximize the performance of the system, many researches have focused on the mimization of the hardware resources occupied by the random number generator. In the case of FPGA based Multivariate Gaussian random number generator, two pieces of work have been published so far [6], [7]. The approach in [6] is capable of produc-ing samples at a high throughput but it lacks the flexibility to meet any given resource constraints. This has been addressed by the technique in [7] which of-fers the flexibility to accommodate a range of resource constraints when certain conditions are met.

The presented work differs from the previous published works as follows:

- It proposes a novel methodology that minimizes the resource usage of a multivariate Gaussian random number generator based on the Eigenvalue decomposition algorithm which decomposes the design into computational paths with different precision requirements. As a result, the number of hard-ware resource usage is reduced by up to a factor of two in comparison with existing techniques.
- An error analysis on the impact of the error due to truncation in the dat-apath is performed providing upper bounds of the error inserted into the system. To the best of the authors knowledge, this error analysis has not been previously addressed in the literature in the case of multivariate Gaus-sian random number generator.

2   Background

A multivariate Gaussian random distribution is defined by two parameters, its mean denoted by $\mathbf{m}$ and its covariance matrix $\mathbf{\Sigma}$. Many techniques have been deployed to generate random samples from this distribution and some of the most widely used are the Cholesky Factorization technique and the Eigenvalue decomposition technique.

Under the Cholesky Factorization technique, $\mathbf{\Sigma}$ is decomposed using Cholesky decomposition into a product of a lower triangular matrix $\mathbf{A}$ and its transpose [3].

Then, the required samples are generated through a linear combination of univariate Gaussian samples $\mathbf{z}$ that follow a standard Gaussian distribution $N(0, 1)$. Due to the lower triangular property of matrix $\mathbf{A}$, the number of computations are reduced by half in comparison to full matrix-vector multiplication. Hence, this method is widely used in software based applications as well as in some hardware approaches as in [6].

An alternative method is to decompose $\boldsymbol{\Sigma}$ by Eigenvalue decomposition [8] and using the Singular Value Decomposition algorithm (SVD). Since an $N \times N$ covariance matrix $\boldsymbol{\Sigma}$ is symmetric and semi-positive definite, all of its eigenvalues λ are non-negative and its eigenvectors $\mathbf{u}$ are orthogonal. SVD expresses a matrix as a linear combination of three separable matrices [9]. Hence using SVD, $\boldsymbol{\Sigma}$ can be expressed as $\boldsymbol{\Sigma} = \mathbf{U} \boldsymbol{\Lambda} \mathbf{U}^T$ where $\mathbf{U}$ is an orthogonal matrix ($\mathbf{U}\mathbf{U}^T = \mathbf{I}$) containing columns $\mathbf{u}_1, ..., \mathbf{u}_N$ while $\boldsymbol{\Lambda}$ is a diagonal matrix with diagonal elements being $\lambda_1, ..., \lambda_N$. By letting $\mathbf{A} = \mathbf{U} \boldsymbol{\Lambda}^{1/2}$, multivariate Gaussian random samples that follow $N(\mathbf{m}, \boldsymbol{\Sigma})$ can be generated as in (1), where $\mathbf{z} \sim N(0, \mathbf{I})$.

$$\begin{aligned}
\mathbf{x} = \mathbf{A}\mathbf{z} + \mathbf{m} &= \mathbf{U}\boldsymbol{\Lambda}^{1/2}\mathbf{z} + \mathbf{m} \\
&= (\sqrt{\lambda_1}\mathbf{u}_1 z_1 + \sqrt{\lambda_2}\mathbf{u}_2 z_2 + ... + \sqrt{\lambda_N}\mathbf{u}_N z_N) + \mathbf{m} \\
&= \sum_{i=1}^{N}(\sqrt{\lambda_i}\mathbf{u}_i z_i) + \mathbf{m}.
\end{aligned} \tag{1}$$

As it will be demonstrated later on in this paper, this decomposition enables us to exploit different precision requirements of each decomposition level leading to an optimized hardware design. To the best of authors knowledge, this technique has not previously been applied to the hardware implementation of a multivariate Gaussian random number generator.

3 Related Work

The first FPGA based multivariate Gaussian random number generator has been published by Thomas and Luk [6]. Their approach is based on factorizing a covariance matrix using Cholesky decomposition in order to take advantage of the lower triangular property of the resulting matrix. The design has the capability to serially generate a vector of multivariate Gaussian numbers every N clock cycles where N denotes the dimensionality of the distribution, and hence the size of the generated random vectors. In addition, the multiply-add operation in the algorithm is mapped onto DSP48 blocks on an FPGA, requiring N blocks for an N-dimensional Gaussian distribution. One apparent shortcoming of their approach is the restriction in resource usage where the dimension of the distribution under consideration dictates the number of required DSP48 blocks on an FPGA.

An alternative approach has been proposed to solve the problem encountered in [6] where an algorithm based on the use of Singular Value Decomposition algorithm was introduced to approximate the lower triangular matrix $\mathbf{A}$, the result of applying Cholesky decomposition on the covariance matrix $\boldsymbol{\Sigma}$, by trading off "accuracy" for an improved resource usage [7]. In [7], "accuracy" is defined as the mean square error in the approximation of covariance matrix Σ by the SVD algorithm. With reference to resource usage, the approach in [7] requires $2K$ DSP48 blocks to produce a vector of size N, where K denotes the number of decomposition levels required by using SVD to approximate the lower triangular matrix $\mathbf{A}$ within a certain accuracy. The resource usage can be reduced in comparison to [6] if K is less than $N/2$ while achieving the same throughput performance. As well as an improved resource usage, this approach offers the flexibility to produce a hardware system that meets any given resource constraint, that is the dimensionality of the Gaussian distribution no longer dictates the number of required DSP48 blocks, by trading off the "accuracy" in the approximation of Σ.

4   Proposed Methodology

The objective of the proposed system is to generate random samples from a multivariate Gaussian distribution using a hardware architecture implemented on an FPGA. Similar to the existing approaches, the elements of each random vector are serially generated resulting to a throughput of one vector per N clock cycles for an N dimensional Gaussian distribution. The main feature of the proposed methodology is that it exploits different precision requirements of different parts of the system in order to achieve a design that has the least error in the approximation of the input covariance matrix Σ and at the same time the least area requirements. The essential properties of the proposed algorithm are:

– It is based on the Eigenvalue decomposition where the computation path is decomposed into paths with different precision requirements in order to minimize the resource usage with minimal impact to the quality of the random samples.
– It produces ordered decompositions according to the impact on the error of the approximation of the covariance matrix. Hence, decompositions with less impact on the approximation error can be discarded resulting in the flexibility to exploit designs with specified resource constraint.

The full exploration of all possible precision requirements for each computational path is time consuming and computationally expensive. Hence, the proposed approach exploits a subset of the possible designs by introducing a library containing pre-defined hardware blocks with different user-specified precisions for the implementation of each computational path. Therefore, there is a trade-off between the complexity of the search and the optimum solution.

4.1   Overview of Algorithm and Architecture

Consider a covariance matrix Σ, the algorithm applies the Eigenvalue decomposition algorithm to express $\Sigma = \mathbf{U}\Lambda\mathbf{U}^T$. According to (1), the random samples can be generated as in (2)

$$\mathbf{x} = \sum_{i=1}^{N} \sqrt{\lambda_i} \mathbf{u}_i z_i \tag{2}$$

Since the multivariate Gaussian samples are generated from a sum of the products of $\mathbf{u}$ and z, different levels of computation i of (2) are broken down into decompositions which are mapped onto computational blocks (CB) designed for an FPGA. The proposed algorithm maps computational paths over this set of CBs targeting to reduce the resource usage and the approximation error of the covariance matrix. The objective of the exploration is to determine the best combination of CBs in order to construct a design which has the least approximation error as well as the least resource usage. The architecture is mapped to only logic elements on an FPGA so that the precision of the datapath can be varied as opposed to [6] and [7] where the precision of the architecture is fixed to 18bits as DSP48 blocks were utilized. Moreover, it has been shown that it is not a necessity to dedicate as much as 18 bits, which is the word-length supported by a DSP48. Quantizing the coefficients of the vectors to lower bit widths could be sufficient depending on the structure of the matrix under consideration [7]. The addition of mapping to DSP48 blocks can easily be included to the library whenever this is required.

The overall architecture of a multivariate Gaussian random number generator can be constructed from any combination of CBs. An instance is shown in Figure 2 where five blocks are selected out of a set of three types of CBs with different precisions namely p_1, p_2 and p_3. In the figure, $\mathbf{u}$ denotes the vector coefficient which is stored in on chip RAM blocks while z denotes the univariate Gaussian random numbers. The above precisions refer to the word-length of the coefficients. The word-length of z is fixed to a user-specified precision. In order for an improved throughput performance to be achieved, the operation is pipelined so that all of the computational blocks operate in parallel. As far as the number representation is concerned, fixed point precision is used throughout the entire design. Fixed point arithmetic produces designs which consume fewer resources and operate at a higher frequency in comparison to floating point arithmetic. The Eigenvalue decomposition algorithm also provides an order in the range of the coefficients. This has been exploited by the proposed algorithm in order for the resulting architecture to perform computations between intermediate results of similar dynamic range. A significant advantage for this is that the error due to truncation is minimized.

4.2 Proposed Algorithm

Figure 1 shows an overview of the algorithm. The inputs to the proposed algorithm are a correlation matrix $\mathbf{\Sigma}$, the allowed resource usage (in LUTs) a set of types of CBs that are available along with resource usage information for each CB and the word-length of its datapath, and finally the target mean square error (MSE) between the original input matrix and the approximated one. Moreover, the proposed algorithm is fully parameterized such that it is able to support any number of pre-defined hardware blocks. The algorithm is divided into three

Algorithm: Decompose a correlation matrix Σ given a target *MSE* and select the appropriate pre-defined hardware blocks to be mapped onto FPGA

```
MSE_min = 1
WHILE MSE_min > MSE_target
    STAGE 1: SVD and Coefficients Quantization
    FOR i = 1:Number of Σ matrices
        Calculate the first decomposition level of Σ using [u, λ, u^T] = SVD(Σ)
        FOR j = 1:Number of hardware blocks
            Quantize √λu : ū ← √λu with p_j bits precision
            Σ̄ = Σ̄ + (ūū^T)
        END LOOP
    END LOOP
    STAGE 2: Calculate MSE
    FOR a = 1:Number of all possible designs
        For each design calculate  MSE
    END LOOP
    Sort designs in the order of ascending MSE
    STAGE 3: Remove bad designs
    FOR b = 1:Number of all possible designs
        IF resource_{b-1} >= resource_b THEN
            Remove design b
        END IF
        Store remaining designs in a pool
    END LOOP
    IF Number of design in the pool > pool_size
        Keep design_1 up to design_pool_size
    END IF
    Calculate the remaining of Σ matrices which will become new Σ
    matrices for next iteration
    Σ = Σ - Σ̄
    MSE_min = min(MSE_all designs)
END LOOP
RETURN Valid Designs
```

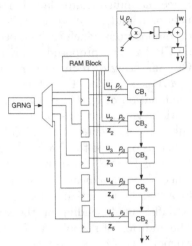

Fig. 1. Outline of the proposed algorithm   **Fig. 2.** Hardware architecture

stages. In the first stage, the correlation matrix Σ is decomposed into a vector **u** and a scalar λ. Then the vectors are converted into fixed point representation using one of the pre-defined available word-lengths. The effect of decomposing Σ and mapping it into different precision hardware blocks generates many possible designs. Note that the number of designs increases exponentially as the number of decomposition level increases. At a certain decomposition level K the number of possible designs is expressed as $\sum_{i=1}^{K} B^i$, where B denotes the number of hardware blocks.

The second stage of the algorithm calculates the MSE for all of the possible designs using

$$MSE_K = \frac{1}{N^2} \sum_{i=1}^{N} \sum_{j=1}^{N} \left(\Sigma_{i,j}^K - \overline{\Sigma}_{i,j}^K \right)^2, \tag{3}$$

where $\overline{\Sigma}$ represents the approximated correlation matrix, N corresponds to the dimensionality of the distribution, K refers to the number of decomposition levels, while i and j are the row and column indices of the matrix respectively.

The third stage of the algorithm discards any inferior designs. An inferior design is a design which, in comparison to another design, uses more hardware resources but produces worse MSE. Thus, the proposed algorithm is optimizing for the $MSE - Area$ design space. In order to further tune the required search time, a parameter called "pool size" is introduced. A pool size indicates the maximum number of designs to be kept from one iteration to the next during the execution of the algorithm. These steps are repeated until the design with the minimum MSE meets the target value specified by the user.

4.3   Overall System

In order to visualize the full functionality of the proposed approach, the overall structure of this methodology is illustrated in Figure 3 in which there are two main processes. The first process is the proposed algorithm which decomposes any given correlation matrix for a specified MSE into distinct vectors. The hardware library contains relevant information regarding the pre-defined hardware blocks including the word-length and the corresponding resource usage of each block. Finally, the second process generates VHDL files based on the information acquired from the first process together with the specification from the hardware library. The entire process is fully automated and parameterizable to accommodate any type of resources and any precision requirements.

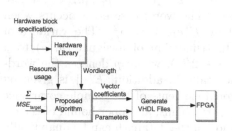   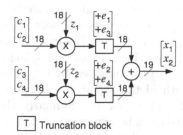

Fig. 3. Overall structure   **Fig. 4.** Analysis of truncation error

5   Error Analysis

The quantization of the coefficients and the truncation in the datapath of the proposed approach introduce two sources of errors in the system. The first source of error originates from the quantization of the coefficients of the correlation matrix. Assuming that no truncation takes place, the sole impact of this is that the sample correlation matrix of the generated samples will deviate from the original one. This error can be analytically calculated and the metric that is used to quantify this is the mean square error (MSE) in (3).

The second source of error is initiated by the truncation effect in the datapath where the multiplication and addition occur. Figure 4 illustrates a circuit diagram to generate a 2-dimensional vector $\mathbf{x}$. The numbers on the datapaths denote the word-length employed. c_1 and c_2 are the coefficients that correspond to the first decomposition level while c_3 and c_4 are the coefficients of the second decomposition level. Thus, the system implements the following expression:

$$\begin{bmatrix} x_1 \\ x_2 \end{bmatrix} = \begin{bmatrix} c_1 \\ c_2 \end{bmatrix} z_1 + \begin{bmatrix} c_3 \\ c_4 \end{bmatrix} z_2 \tag{4}$$

where $z_1, z_2 \sim N(0,1)$. The truncation of the datapath introduces an error e to the system resulting in the final value of $\mathbf{x}$ expressed as in (5).

$$\begin{aligned} x_1 &= (c_1 z_1 + e_1) + (c_3 z_2 + e_2) \\ x_2 &= (c_2 z_1 + e_3) + (c_4 z_2 + e_4). \end{aligned} \tag{5}$$

The covariance between x_1 and x_2 which is given by the expectation $E\{x_1x_2\}$ is shown in (6).

$$
\begin{aligned}
E\{x_1x_2\} &= E\{(c_1z_1 + e_1 + c_3z_2 + e_2).(c_2z_1 + e_3 + c_4z_2 + e_4)\} \\
&= c_1c_2 + c_3c_4 + E\{e_1e_3\} + E\{e_1\}E\{e_4\} + E\{e_2\}E\{e_3\} + E\{e_2e_4\} \\
&= E\{x_1x_2\}_{original} + E\{e_1e_3\} + E\{e_1\}E\{e_4\} + E\{e_2\}E\{e_3\} + E\{e_2e_4\}
\end{aligned}
\tag{6}
$$

where $E\{x_1x_2\}_{original}$ denotes the original targeted covariance between x_1 and x_2. It should be noted that $E\{e_1e_3\}$ and $E\{e_2e_4\}$ are non-zero since e_1 is correlated to e_3 and e_2 is correlated to e_4. Focusing on e_1 and e_3, the covariance between e_1 and e_3 can be expressed as $E\{e_1e_3\} = \rho_{e_1e_3}\sigma_{e_1}\sigma_{e_3}$, where $\rho_{e_1e_3}$ is the correlation between e_1 and e_3. The worst case error occurs when $\rho_{e_1e_3}$ is 1. Hence, $E\{e_1e_3\}$ is bounded by $E\{e_1e_3\} \leq \sigma_{e_1}^2$. The variance of the error inserted to the system due to truncation of a signal (p_1, d) to a signal (p_2, d) is given by $\sigma_e^2 = \frac{1}{12}2^{2d}(2^{2p_2} - 2^{2p_1})$, where p denotes the word-length of the signal and d refers to the scale. In addition, $E\{e\}$ is given by $-2^{d-1}(2^{-p_2} - 2^{-p_1})$. Similarly, the diagonal elements of the sample covariance matrix can be expressed as $E\{x_1^2\} = \sigma_{e_1}^2 + \sigma_{e_2}^2$. Thus, an upper bound of the error inserted to the system due to truncation of the datapath can be analytically calculated.

6   Results

The architecture has been implemented on a Stratix III EP3SE50F484C2 FPGA from Altera and Quartus II was utilized as a hardware synthesis tools. With regards to the word-length of the univariate samples z, a fixed 18 bits precision is allocated throughout the entire design. z is an 18 bit signed number with 3 bits dedicated for the integer part and 14 bits dedicated for the decimal part. Hence, approximately 99.7% of the dynamic range of a standard normal distribution can be represented.

6.1   Library Construction

The set of computational blocks that is used in the proposed framework is chosen in order to cover the range between 4 to 18 bits precision in an almost uniform way. Four CBs with 4, 9, 15 and 18 bits precision have been pre-defined in the hardware library for the construction of the multivariate Gaussian random number generator. The synthesis stage from Quartus II reports a resource usage of 115, 206, 300, and 332 LUTs for a CB with 4, 9, 15, and 18 precision bits respectively. These results are used by the proposed algorithm in order to optimize the architecture. In order to make a direct comparison between the the proposed approach and [6] and [7], DSP48 functionality has been mapped to logic on an FPGA and the reported resource usage are used accordingly.

6.2   Eigenvalue Analysis

This section investigates the impact of the matrix structure on the proposed algorithm and the other two existing approaches [6],[7]. Four 5x5 correlation matrices with different eigenvalue profiles are randomly created, namely **A,B,C** and **D**. The three approaches under consideration are applied to the four generated matrices and the MSE calculated using (3) is plotted against the corresponding resource usage. It should be noted that this MSE does not take into account the truncation and the quantization effects. The MSE of approach [6] is used as a target MSE for the other two algorithms.

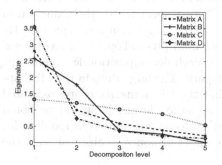   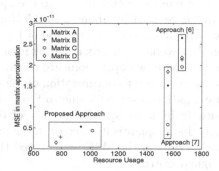

Fig. 5. Eigenvalue profiles of **A,B,C** and **D**   **Fig. 6.** MSE of **A,B,C** and **D** without truncation and quantization effects

Figure 5 illustrates a plot of the eigenvalues of the four matrices against the decomposition level. From the graph, four distinct lines can be observed indicating the difference in matrix structure where the eigenvalues of **A**, **B** and **D** drop rapidly in the first few levels of decomposition in comparison to **C** where the line is more flat. The MSE obtained from applying the proposed approach and approaches [6] and [7] is presented in Figure 6. The graph clearly demonstrates that the proposed approach provides the best designs for all four matrices in comparison to the other two approaches since a lower MSE is obtained using fewer resources. This is due to the use of hardware blocks with different precisions in order to map matrices with different precision requirements.

6.3   Evaluation of the Proposed Approach

The objective of this experiment is to assess the performance of the proposed algorithm in comparison to the approaches in [6] and [7]. In this experiment the three methods under consideration are applied to a 10x10 randomly generated correlation matrix **C**. The pool size of the proposed approach is set to 30 designs. The value of MSE in the approximation of **C** is plotted for all three approaches. In [6] and [7], the architecture is mapped onto DSP blocks as opposed to the proposed method where only logic elements are utilized. Note that the only error under consideration in this experiment is due to the quantization of the coefficients. Therefore, the MSE plotted on the graph indicates the lower bound of the approximation.

It can be observed from Figure 7 that the generated architectures from the proposed algorithm are the best designs in comparison with those from the other two approaches since the proposed algorithm obtains the same error using fewer resources. In particular, 10 DSP blocks which is equivalent to approximately 3,120 LUTs are required for approach [6] to achieve the same error as the proposed algorithm where only 1,250 LUTs are required. Hence, the resource usage is reduced by approximately a factor of 2.5. There is also an improvement in the resource usage in comparison to the approach in [7] where the resource requirement is reduced by about 2 to 2.5 times. With respect to [7], the reduction in resource usage is due to the use of Eigenvalue decomposition technique directly on the covariance matrix resulting in only one multiply-add operation as opposed to [7] where two operations are required for each decomposition level, and due to the word-length optimization of the datapath. The large drop in the MSE approximation observed is due to the fact that the whole matrix is approximated entirely by using specific number of decomposition levels. It should be noted that due to quantization error, the number of decomposition levels required for such a drop in the MSE may exceed the number of non-zero eigenvalues of the original matrix.

In order to assess the quality of the random numbers produced by the proposed algorithm a large number of multivariate Gaussian samples are generated. They enable us to evaluate the sample correlation matrix which is then compared with the original correlation matrix in order to calculate the empirical MSE of the approximation. Thus, the error inserted due to truncation in the datapath as well as the quantization of the coefficients are taken into account as the correlation matrix is calculated from the empirical samples produced by the FPGA.

After applying the proposed algorithm to the matrix of interest and collecting all of the samples produced, the results are illustrated in Figure 8 where the empirical MSE of the proposed algorithm and the approach in [6] are plotted

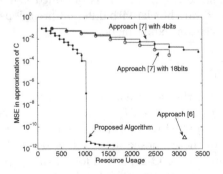

Fig. 7. Lower bound MSE

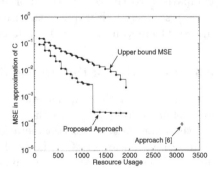

Fig. 8. Empirical MSE

against the corresponding resource usage in which 100,000 vectors are generated. Note that the reported resource usage is obtained after synthesizing and performing place and route on all of the generated designs on the target device. The graph also illustrates the upper bound of the empirical MSE calculated using (6) from the error analysis model. As anticipated, the values of empirical MSE obtained in this experiment are much higher than the lower bound due to the error inserted from the truncation in the datapath. Figure 8 illustrates that the empirical MSE of the proposed approach converges to approximately 2.5×10^{-4}. This is slightly higher than the error obtained from [6] which is the reference design but much fewer resources are consumed by the designs produced by the proposed approach. In addition, it should be noted that the proposed approach offers more flexibility than [6] allowing the selection of designs for any given resource constraint.

6.4 Timing Analysis

Since the proposed approach targets applications where the architecture of multivariate Gaussian random number generator has to be mapped to various systems, the execution and synthesis and place and route time are of high importance. Figure 9 illustrates the execution time of the proposed algorithm for a range of matrices with different sizes. In addition, the pool size is varied between 30 to 120 for each matrix. The results show that the execution time increases linearly with the size of the matrix as well as the pool size. Figure 10 shows the required time for synthesizing and performing place and route for the generated designs with varying number of CB instantiations. It is apparent that as the number of CB instantiations increases the synthesis time also increases. The total time for a 50x50 matrix using 23 CBs is under 11 minutes where in the case of small matrix sizes the total time is much less where the entire process takes up to 3 minutes. It should also be noted that the average operating frequency of the designs is 411.32MHz bringing the actual throughput of the proposed design to the same level as in [6] and higher than [7].

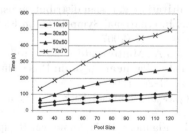 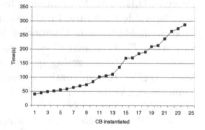

Fig. 9. Execution time of the algorithm   **Fig. 10.** Synthesis and Place and Route time

7 Conclusion

This paper has presented a novel approach to construct hardware architectures to generate random samples from a multivariate Gaussian distribution. The proposed approach is based on the Eigenvalue decomposition technique where the computation path is decomposed into paths with different precision requirements in order to minimize the resource usage with minimal impact to the quality of the random samples. In addition, an analysis of the error due to the truncation operation along the datapath has been presented and an upper bound of this error is determined. Experimental results have demonstrated that by dedicating appropriate precisions to different computational paths, both the resource usage and the mean square error of the approximation of the targeted correlation matrix can be minimized. Future work includes the investigation of the relationship between the eigenvalue profile of the input correlation matrix and the type of the computational blocks that are required, targeting to optimize the performance and to reduce the run-time of the algorithm.

References

1. Glasserman, P., Heidelberger, P., Shahabuddin, P.: Variance reduction techniques for value-at-risk with heavy-tailed risk factors. In: Proceedings of the 32nd conference on Winter simulation, pp. 604–609 (2000)
2. Glasserman, P., Li, J.: Importance sampling for portfolio credit risk. Management Science 51, 1643–1656 (2003)
3. Glasserman, P.: Monte Carlo Methods in Financial Engineering. Springer, Heidelberg (2004)
4. Kaganov, A., Chow, P., Lakhany, A.: Fpga acceleration of monte-carlo based credit derivative pricing. In: Proceedings IEEE International Conference on Field Programmable Logic and Applications, pp. 329–334 (2008)
5. Thomas, D.B., Bower, J.A., Luk, W.: Automatic generation and optimization of reconfigurable financial monte-carlo simulations. In: Proceedings IEEE International Conference on Application-Specific Systems Architectures and Processors, pp. 168–173 (2007)
6. Thomas, D.B., Luk, W.: Sampling from the multivariate gaussian distribution using reconfigurable hardware. In: Proceedings IEEE International Symposium on Field-Programmable Custom Computing Machines, pp. 3–12 (2007)
7. Saiprasert, C., Bouganis, C.-S., Constantinides, G.A.: Multivariate gaussian random number generator targeting specific resource utilization in an fpga. In: Proceedings IEEE Applied Reconfigurable Computing, pp. 233–244 (2008)
8. Chan, N.H., Wong, H.Y.: Simulation Techniques in Financial Risk Management. Wiley, Chichester (2006)
9. Press, W.H., Teukolsky, S.A., Vetterling, W.T., Flannery, B.P.: Numerical Recipes in C. Cambridge University Press, Cambridge (1992)

FPGA-Based Anomalous Trajectory Detection Using SOFM

Kofi Appiah[1], Andrew Hunter[1], Tino Kluge[2], Philip Aiken[3],
and Patrick Dickinson[1]

[1] Dept. of Computing & Informatics, University of Lincoln, UK
[2] Statistical Laboratory, University of Cambridge, UK
[3] SecuraCorp, Kirkland, USA

Abstract. A system for automatically classifying the trajectory of a
moving object in a scene as usual or suspicious is presented. The system uses an unsupervised neural network (Self Organising Feature Map)
fully implemented on a reconfigurable hardware architecture (Field Programmable Gate Array) to cluster trajectories acquired over a period,
in order to detect novel ones. First order motion information, including
first order moving average smoothing, is generated from the 2D image
coordinates (trajectories). The classification is dynamic and achieved in
real-time. The dynamic classifier is achieved using a SOFM and a prob-
abilistic model. Experimental results show less than 15% classification
error, showing the robustness of our approach over others in literature
and the speed-up over the use of conventional microprocessor as compared to the use of an off-the-shelf FPGA prototyping board.

1 Introduction

An intelligent video surveillance system should be able to keep track of objects in
a camera view *(identity tracking)*, determine where the objects are in the camera
view *(location tracking)* and what the people, vehicles or objects are doing in the
scene *(activity tracking)*[1]. Increasing safety and security concerns have resulted
in the development of complex video surveillance and traffic monitoring systems
in both research and industrial communities [2]. An intelligent surveillance system should have the capability to process video streams and characterize the
actions taking place, to distinguish between normal and abnormal actions, and
to draw the attention of a human operator when an action poses a threat.

CCTV systems have a human operator monitoring a number of cameras at
the same time. Typically, the concentration level of the operator reduces after
15 minutes monitoring a non-active camera scene. Increasing demands for use of
surveillance cameras in crime prevention calls for the development of automated
techniques capable of detecting actions that poses a threat in a camera scene
and subsequently signal an alert to the human operator for verification. Such
automation will augment rather than replace the human operator.

Evolution of computer vision algorithms as well as Ambient intelligence (AmI)
[20], oriented towards ubiquitous computing and smart environments that react

J. Becker et al. (Eds.): ARC 2009, LNCS 5453, pp. 243–254, 2009.
© Springer-Verlag Berlin Heidelberg 2009

in an adaptive and active way to the presence and actions of objects implemented on embedded systems, has become an interesting area of research over the past decade. Such systems allow the implementation of early vision processes similar to the first neural layer in the retina, for pre-filtering conspicuous information [21]. Field Programmable Gate Arrays (FPGAs) are a technology which has been available to researchers for the past two decades. However, recent increases in programmable fabric density has made this an appealing platform for accelerating computer vision and digital image processing algorithms[19].

The potential uses of FPGAs in areas like medical image processing, computational fluid dynamics, target recognition, embedded vision systems, gesture recognition and automotive infotainment have been demonstrated in [19,20,21,22,23].

We use a reconfigurable architecture, FPGA, in conjunction with an image sensor to process trajectory information of moving objects and only send alerts to a central monitoring station. The system architecture is based upon the commercially available *Algorithm Based Object Recognition and Tracking (ABO-RAT)* system designed for wireless IP cameras for highly sophisticated security surveillance systems[24]. Whereas ABORAT uses an Intel Bulverde (PXA270) in this paper an FPGA is used for the pre-filtering and classification of trajectories as either normal or abnormal.

2   Related Work

Abnormal activity detection has been divided into two categories: parametric and non-parametric by Zhou et. al[13]. The parametric approach models normal and abnormal activities using visual features like position, speed and appearance, while the non-parametric learns the normal and abnormal patterns from the statistical properties of the observed data. In this paper we further divide the non-parametric into two sub-groups; the on-line and the batch approach. The batch approach trains and detects normal and abnormal activities using complete trajectories. The on-line approach may or may not train the system using complete trajectories, yet it is able to detect normal/abnormal activities using incomplete trajectories; hence the ability to detect abnormalities as they happen.

Generally, the trajectory data of tracked objects are recorded as a set of (x, y) locations of the tracked object's centre of mass from frame to frame. In [10], they used flow vectors $f = \{x, y, \delta x, \delta y\}$ rather than sequence of positions to describe an object's movement. Thus if an object i appears in n frames it can be represented by a set Q_i of n flow vectors all lying within a unit hypercube in 4D phase space: $Q_i = \{f_1, f_2, \ldots, f_{n-1}, f_n\}$. Owens et. al in [8], used a hierarchical neural network as a novelty detector. Normal trajectories are used during training, and experiment conducted shows a high detection rate. Humphreys et. al [7] has extensively use cost functions based on SOFM to detect, track and classify object trajectories. The paper also demonstrates improved performance, by breaking down the SOFM into three parts.

Grimson et. al [15] used the (x, y) location, speed/direction (dx, dy) and size to develop a codebook using an on-line Vector Quantization(VQ). A co-occurrence statistic is accumulated over the codebook and a hierarchical classification performed to identify normal and abnormal activities. In [14] a Dynamic Oriented Graph (DOG) is used to structure common patterns of objects activities. The entrance, path and departure nodes are used to construct the graph. The spatial motion information, size and colour of the objects are used to classify their activity. During testing, known or normal object patterns should match an existing node, else the activity is rejected and classified as unusual or abnormal.

Jiang et. al [5] uses an information-based trajectory dissimilarity measure making use of Bayesian information criterion (BIC) to determine the number of clusters in the agglomerative hierarchical clustering algorithm. Each trajectory or feature sequence is modelled by a hidden Markov model (HMM) and the number of clusters in the BIC decreases as similar trajectories are merged. In [13] an unsupervised spectral clustering, represented by the mean and variance of their data points is used for clustering trajectories. An unusual approach is taken by Dickinson et. al [6], who use HMMs to differentiate between normal and unusual behaviour in domestic scenes. The hidden states correspond to learned inactive states, such as sitting on a particular chair, and transitions correspond to movement between them. Trajectories are therefore represented as movements between familiar static events. The learned model of normal behaviour is used in conjunction with a threshold model to classify test sequences.

A multi-sample-based similarity measure using a dynamic hierarchical clustering method has been present in [2]. Trajectory data acquired over a period of time are represented by a 5-state HMM with Gaussian emission probability and used as the training data. HMMs are learnt from clusters with large number of samples and are used for detecting abnormal trajectories. Han et. al[25] used an unsupervised fuzzy self-organising map trained with normal activities. Trajectory features $(x, y, \sqrt{\delta x^2 + \delta y^2}, \tan^{-1}(\delta y/\delta x))$ are translated into a fixed length vector of size $4N$. An object with trajectory length less than N, is padded with it last centre position (x, y), zero speed and zero direction. The $4N$ vector is used to train the FSOM, which is then used for the abnormal activity detection in real-time/on-line mode.

A Spatial Occupancy Map (SpOM) built from object trajectories has been used in [4] for detection of unusual trajectories in a camera scene. Object trajectories are modelled as motion time series in [12] to train a coefficient feature space, which is subsequently used for trajectory classification. Principal Component Analysis (PCA) trained with sub trajectories, used in conjunction with HMM has been presented in [3] for classifying motion trajectories. In [11] trajectories are collected and processed on-line as a list of vectors representing the spatial position of the object. Rather than the Euclidean distance, a new distance measure has been introduced to check if a trajectory fits a given cluster.

Owens et. al in [9] used a self-organising feature map to learn and characterize normal trajectories. The 4D flow vector $(x, y, \delta x, \delta y)$ used in [15] has been extended into 8D $(x, y, s(x), s(y), s(\delta x), s(\delta y), s(\delta^2 x), s(\delta^2 y))$ to include a second order motion information. The on-line system presented in [9] is capable of detecting abnormalities in both instantaneous and whole trajectory motion. In [16] a feature vector γ_t which encapsulates the local curvature of the trajectory as well as the local velocity magnitude is used to represent the tracked object's position. The feature vectors are modelled with a HMM and the similarity between trajectories expressed with a quantization-based HMM. Piciarelli et. al in [17] used a support vector machine (SVM) for the classification and clustering of 2D trajectory data. Mixtures of Gaussians (MoGs) have been used in [18] to group 4D motion histogram data into coherent trajectories and used to identify events after training.

In this paper we present an on-line base event detection system using trajectory data and implemented on Field Programmable Gate Array (FPGA) for real-time purposes. The system is able to detect abnormal trajectory data point-by-point using SOFM in conjunction with a Gaussian distribution. The paper is structured as follows. Section 3 introduces our approach with the theoretical background to the parameter selection for SOFM neural network. This is followed by details of our FPGA implementation in section 4. Experimental details are given in section 5 and we conclude with some future pointers to this work in section 6.

3   Our Approach

To efficiently implement a trajectory discriminator in hardware using Self Organising Feature Map (SOFM) and Gaussian distribution, we have conducted two basic analyses. First, we analyse the minimal dimension that can be used to represent the point-to-point trajectory data (x_t, y_t) without losing any behavioural information. Intuitively, the minimum dimension is 2D, yet in [16] the (x_t, y_t) coordinate information has been reduced to a single value γ_t encoding the local curvature and velocity information. The penalty for the model is the high dimensional vector used in the HMM. Secondly, we analyse the most efficient way to represent the trajectory data in the SOFM. By reducing the dimension of the trajectory data we are able to implement the SOFM on FPGA using the internal/embedded Block RAM.

3.1   Curse of Dimensionality

In general, the more data put into the state vector the better one would expect to be able to distinguish between usual and unusual behaviour. Obvious variables are the (x_t, y_t) coordinates, their time derivatives representing speed as well as their second time derivatives representing acceleration, which would leave us with a 6D vector $(x, y, \delta x, \delta y, \delta^2 x, \delta^2 y)$. Other papers [16,18,11,9] have used even higher dimensions. However, as the dimensionality of the input increase the number of nodes required in the SOFM grows very rapidly. The number of nodes required to populate the input state space to a given density increase exponentially with the dimension, and although the data may lie on a lower-dimensional manifold, this does mean that performance can drop if too many

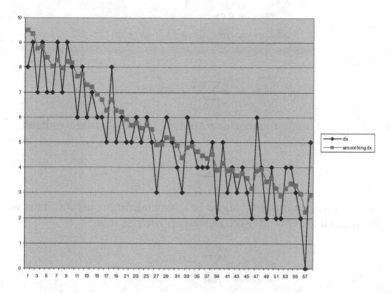

Fig. 1. A graph showing the effect of smoothing the speed component (δx)

input features are used. Therefore, dimensionality reduction should be performed whenever the setup allows, e.g. if the speed of an object is generally independent of its position then the state variables (x, y) and $(\delta x, \delta y)$ can be represented in different networks. However, this is not the case in general, for example if the scene contains a highly obstructed footpath and a clear road, then object speed will be higher on the road than the footpath. In conclusion, we will use a 4D vector with the objects position (centroid) (x, y) and speed $(\delta x, \delta y)$ to model nodes in the SOFM.

3.2   Importance of Smoothing the Speed Data

The trajectory coordinates obtained represent the centroid of the object tracked over the input image frames. However, due to camera jitter and slight movement, the centroid includes some noise. Let the observed trajectory be given by $\{(x_1, y_1), \ldots, (x_n, y_n)\}$ then we say $x_i = x_i^* + \epsilon_i$ where x_i^* are the true x coordinates and ϵ_i independent identically distributed random variables representing the error. The same applies to the y coordinates.

We also assume the spatial error ϵ_i is small compared to the size of the moving object. When calculating changes in position between two frames, however, relative errors can be very large because $\delta x_i = x_i - x_{i-1} = \delta x_i^* + \epsilon_i - \epsilon_{i-1}$ and $\delta x_i^* = x_i^* - x_{i-1}^*$ is likely to be small, and the standard deviation of the error is $\sqrt{2}$ times that of the spatial error. Figure 1 shows a plot of δx for a sample trajectory with 58 points and the corresponding smoothed versions $s\delta x$. We use an exponential moving average as it is faster and simpler to implement on FPGA:

$$s\delta x_1 = \delta x_1,$$
$$s\delta x_{i+1} = \alpha\delta x_{i+1} + (1-\alpha)s\delta x_i,$$

or equivalently

$$s\delta x_k = \alpha\sum_{i=0}^{k-1}(1-\alpha)^i\delta x_{k-i}. \qquad (1)$$

Note, [16] uses a similar smoothing applied to the coordinates itself:

$$sx_k = c^{-1}\sum_{i=0}^{k-1}e^{-\left(\frac{i}{h}\right)^2}x_{k-i}, \qquad (2)$$

where h is chosen appropriately and c is a normalising constant. This is similar to the exponential moving average as we can rewrite it as

$$s\delta x_k = \alpha\sum_{i=0}^{k-1}e^{\ln(1-\alpha)i}\delta x_{k-i}. \qquad (3)$$

Small values of α indicate a long history of coordinates is taken into account whereas values of α close to 1 are used to prioritise the current coordinates. There is a trade off between reducing errors and taking averages over too long a period (say more than one second) which would give us outdated information. The error in the moving average due to the noise term can be described as follows. Assuming an infinite series for simplicity we have

$$\mathrm{Var}[s\delta x_k] = \mathrm{Var}\left[\alpha\sum_{i=0}^{\infty}(1-\alpha)^i\epsilon_{k-i}\right],$$
$$= \alpha^2\sum_{i=0}^{\infty}(1-\alpha)^{2i}\mathrm{Var}[\epsilon_{k-i}],$$
$$= \frac{\alpha^2}{1-(1-\alpha)^2}\mathrm{Var}[\epsilon],$$

and hence the standard deviation of the error of the moving average is $\sqrt{\frac{\alpha}{2-\alpha}}$ times that of the error in δx. For values $\alpha = 1/4$ down to $\alpha = 1/10$ we get a reasonable reduction of noise to the order of about 0.38 and 0.23, respectively, and assuming we have 25 frames per second the contribution of frames older than a second to the moving average is negligible.

3.3   Trajectory Modelling with SOFM

Similar to [9], our systems monitors trajectories as they are generated as opposed to other systems [2,13] which need the entire trajectory to make a decision. Hence the trajectory encoding used here converts both full and sub trajectories into a fixed length feature vector $F = (x, y, s\delta x, s\delta y)$, where $s\delta x$ and $s\delta y$ are the moving averages for the change in x and y respectively. As the feature vector generated for each individual point is of fixed length, a SOFM-based has been used for classification.

The self-organising feature map (SOFM) is a neural network model based on Kohonen's discovery that important topological information can be obtained through an unsupervised learning process[26]. It has an input layer, with one weight each for all elements in the feature vector F. It has two phases: the training and the test phases. During the training phase, data is presented to the network and the winning node (typically the Euclidean distance measure) is updated to reflect the input data. Similarly, during the test phase an Euclidean distance measure is used to identify the winning node *(winner)* and a decision made on how close the input is to the network node.

We have designed our SOFM with 100 network nodes, each with four weights representing the 4-input feature vector $(x, y, \delta x, \delta y)$. During the training, we maintain four extra parameters for each node in the network: the total number of training samples that get associated with each node T_i, the maximum distance between the node and all associated inputs, M_i, the mean μ_i and variance σ_i^2 of the distances. A Gaussian distribution of all distances associated with every node is also maintained.

The training data is made up of both normal and abnormal trajectories, yet our implementation is able to distinguish between normal and abnormal trajectories after training. Trajectory data (x, y) is collected over a period of time from a stationary camera and converted into a 4D feature vector F for training the SOFM. During training, the 100 network nodes are randomly initialized, then for every input vector (feature vector), the Manhattan distance between the input vector and every network node is computed to estimate the winner. For a winner w_t and input vector x, all the weights i of the winning node are updated as follows $w_{i,t+1} = w_{i,t} + \beta(x - w_{i,t})$ to reflect the input data. If the Manhattan distance $m_{w,x}$ between w_t and x is the maximum for node w_t, $M_w = m_{w,x}$. Similarly, the total distance for the winner T_w is increased by $m_{w,x}$.

The training of the SOFM is repeated for a number of epochs with the same input data. The Gaussian distribution for each node is generated for a random iteration $t \leq (epoch - 1)$ during training. The network is ready for use after the training phase. During the test phase, point-to-point trajectory data (x, y) is converted into a 4D vector and used as input to the SOFM. Again, the winning node is identified as the node with the minimum Manhattan distance to the input vector. In the test phase the network isn't subjected to any further modification, but rather is used to make a decision on the input vector or trajectory.

An input trajectory data for tracked objects is identified as abnormal if any of the following conditions is true:

1. If the Manhattan distance $m_{w,x}$ between the input vector x and the winner w is greater than the maximum allowable distance for the winner M_w.
2. If T_w (the total number of input vectors associated with the winner during training) is less than a gobal threshold Th set as $0.01\% * total\ train\ points$.
3. If the Manhattan distance $m_{w,x}$ is outside 2.5 standard deviation of the Gaussian distribution for the winner.

The penalty for option 1 is the highest, followed by options 2 and 3 respectively. An input node whose Manhattan distance is greater than M_w is abnormal on the assumption that such a point is new to the SOFM. Since the system is trained with both normal and abnormal trajectories, it is possible for a node in the network to represent only abnormal trajectory points. Since unusual trajectories are rare, an assumption that no more than $Th = 0.01\%$ of the entire trajectory points are abnormal is made. Hence, any network node with less than the global threshold value Th of points, is labelled as an abnormal network node n_{ab}. Thus any input vector whose winner is n_ab is also considered abnormal.

It is also possible to associate an abnormal point to a normal network node n_{nor} during training. If this happens, we expect the Manhattan distance between the abnormal point x_{ab} and the network node n to be much greater than all other points associated with n_{nor}. The Gaussian distribution maintained for n_{nor} is then used to identify such abnormal trajectory points. Figure 2 shows two images with normal and abnormal trajectory points.

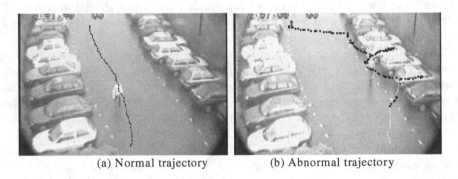

(a) Normal trajectory   (b) Abnormal trajectory

Fig. 2. Images showing (a) normal and (b) abnormal trajectories. In (b), abnormal points are labelled black.

4   Hardware Implementation

The training and testing of the trajectory classifier has been implemented on an FPGA architecture, making use of the embedded RAM to store the network node values. Figure 3 is a high-level block diagram of the FPGA classifier. The bold lines show the part of the system activated when in the test phase. During the training phase, the trajectory data is read from the external RAM and converted into 4D feature vector for the training the SOFM. In the test phase, point-to-point trajectory data is sent to the FPGA via the RS232/USB port on the development board. The entire design has been accomplished on RC340 development board packaged with Xilinx Virtex-4 FPGA chip (XC4VLX160) with approximately 152,064 logic cells with embedded Block RAM totalling 5,184 Kbits.

The design is made up of four hardware blocks: the initialization, feature extraction, winner identification and update (for the training phase). The initialization block is used to initialize all weights for all the network nodes in the

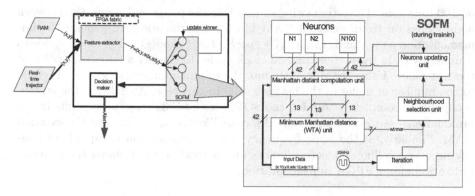

Fig. 3. A block diagram of the FPGA based trajectory classifier

Table 1. Implementation results for the SOFM classifier, using Virtex-4 *XC4VLX160*, package *FF1148* and speed grade *-10*

Resource			Total Used	
Name	Total	Used	Per.(%)	
Flip Flops	135,168	3,826	2	
4 input LUTs	135,168	25,821	19	
bonded IOBs	768	156	20	
Occupied Slices	67,584	15744	23	
Block RAM	5,184kb	9,800b	-	

10 × 10 SOFM neural network. It takes exactly 100 cycles to initialize all the 100 nodes. Note that this is done once before training the SOFM. The feature extraction block converts the trajectory data (x, y) into 4D feature vector. It takes exactly two clock cycles in the test phase and an extra two cycles in the training phase to read the trajectory data from external ZBT RAM. The first cycle is used to convert the data into $(x, y, \delta x, \delta y)$. The second cycle is used to compute the moving averages of the first derivatives $(s\delta x, s\delta y)$.

The winner identification block is use to identify the winning node (winner). The feature vector from the feature extraction block is sent to all the 100 SOFM nodes in parallel. It takes exactly four clock cycles to compute the Manhattan distance from the input feature vector to all the nodes. Note, the feature vector is 4D, hence the four clock cycles. This can further be reduced to a single clock cycle depending on the memory structure used. The node with the minimum Manhattan distance is computed in approximately seven cycles from the 100 distances. Again, the number of cycles here is dependent on the number of network nodes.

The update block takes exactly two cycles to update the winning node and its neighbouring nodes. This is only done in the training phase. After training on 100 iterations the system switches into test the phase and writes the network node values on to an external RAM block for verification. In general the implementation as it stands takes $(17 * epoch * total\ inputs) + 100$ clock cycles to completely train the system, and 13 clock cycles to classify a trajectory point in the test phase. Using the rule of thumb, the minimum acceptable *epoch* is equal to the number of nodes in the network, 100 in this case. At 25MHz, the system is capable of completely training the SOFM with 65535 trajectory points in approximately $5sec$, excluding external factors like the access time to the external RAM. Similarly, at the same frequency the implementation is capable of classifying over a million trajectory points in a second. Table 1 shows the resource utilization of our FPGA implementation.

5   Experimental Results

Three different datasets have been used in testing the implementation on a PC with a general purpose processor clocked at 2.8GHz and on an FPGA with Xilinx Virtex-4 clocked at 25MHz. All the images have been obtained using a stationary camera. The input image is sent to an object tracker and the trajectory fed to this system. Two of the image sequences have been acquired on a normal day while the last of the three has been collected on a rainy day. They have all been collected over a period of 3 hours. The datasets are made of 34713 and 21867 trajectory points for the normal day and 12636 trajectory points for the rainy day. Table 2 is a summary of the test conducted on the FPGA and PC with the same input data and epoch.

Table 2. Timing results for train the SOFM on FPGA and PC

Day	Points	PC(min.)	FPGA(min.)	epoch
Normal	34713	45	7.2	346
Normal	21867	27	4.5	218
Rainy	12636	10	2	126

A test has also been conducted on the number of trajectory points correctly classified with the implementation. For 520 trajectory points collected on a normal day, 421 were correctly classified as normal, 76 correctly classified as abnormal and 23 were incorrectly classified as normal, representing approximately 4.4% error. A similar test conducted on the same scene, on a rainy day with a total of 151 trajectory points gave 97 correctly classified as normal, 32 correctly classified as abnormal, 19 incorrectly classified as normal with 3 classified incorrectly as abnormal. This represents a total of 14.5% error. Even though the error level is high on a rainy day its fairly acceptable on a normal day. The implementation on FPGA with approximately 5 fold speed improvement is a significant advantage over our PC-based implementations.

6 Conclusion

A system for classifying trajectories in real-time have been presented in this paper. The architecture is fully implemented on an FPGA making it possible to break the training time bottlenecks. This is not the first implementation of SOFM on FPGA, but the use of SOFM on FPGA as a trajectory classifier makes our implementation novel. Again, the on-line classifier based on point-to-point makes this architecture more usable for today's embedded security surveillance systems. A possible extension is to incorporate an object tracker on the FPGA architecture.

References

1. Hampapur, A., Brown, L., Connell, J., Ekin, A., Haas, N., Lu, M., Merkl, H., Pankanti, S.: Smart video surveillance: exploring the concept of multiscale spatiotemporal tracking. IEEE Signal Processing Magazine 22(2), 38–51 (2005)
2. Jiang, F., Wu, Y., Katsaggelos, K.A.: Abnormal Event Detection From Surveillance Video By Dynamic Hierarchical Clustering. In: Proc. IEEE Int'l Conf. on Image Processing (ICIP 2007), San Antonio, TX (September 2007)
3. Bashir, F., Khokhar, A., Schonfeld, D.: Object Trajectory-Based Motion Modeling and Classification using Hidden Markov Models. IEEE Transactions on Image Processing 16(7), 1912–1919 (2007)
4. Jung, C., Jacques, J., Soldera, J., Musse, S.: Detection of Unusual Motion Using Computer Vision. In: Jung, C., Jacques, J., Soldera, J., Musse, S. (eds.) XIX Brazilian Symposium on Computer Graphics and Image Processing (SIBGRAPI 2006), pp. 349–356 (2006)
5. Jiang, F., Wu, Y., Katsaggelos, A.K.: Abnormal event detection based on trajectory clustering by 2-depth greedy search. In: IEEE International Conference on Speech and Signal Processing, 2008. ICASSP (2008)
6. Dickinson, P., Hunter, A.: Using Inactivity to Detect Unusual Behaviour. In: Proc. of IEEE Workshop on Motion and Video Computing, Colorado (January 2008)
7. Humphreys, J., Hunter, A.: Multiple object tracking using a neural cost function. In: Image and Vision Computing (June 2008)
8. Owens, J., Hunter, A., Fletcher, E.: Novelty Detection in Video Surveillance Using Hierarchical Neural Networks. In: Dorronsoro, J.R. (ed.) ICANN 2002. LNCS, vol. 2415, p. 1249. Springer, Heidelberg (2002)
9. Owens, J., Hunter, A.: Application of the Self-Organizing Map to Trajectory Classification. In: IEEE Computer Society Proceedings of the Third IEEE international Workshop on Visual Surveillance (Vs 2000), July 1 (2000)
10. Johnson, N., Hogg, D.: Learning the distribution of object trajectories for event recognition. In: Proceedings of the 6th British Conference on Machine Vision, UK, vol. 2, pp. 583–592 (1995)
11. Piciarelli, C., Foresti, G.L., Snidara, L.: Trajectory clustering and its applications for video surveillance. In: IEEE Conference on AVSS (2005)
12. Naftel, A., Anwar, F.B.: Visual Recognition of Manual Tasks Using Object Motion Trajectories. In: Proceedings of the IEEE international Conference on AVSS (2006)
13. Yue Zhou, Y., Yan, S., Huang, T.S.: Detecting Anomaly in Videos from Trajectory Similarity Analysis. In: IEEE International Conference on Multimedia and Expo (2007)

14. Duque, D., dos Santos, H.D., Cortez, P.: Prediction of abnormal behaviors for intelligent video surveillance systems. In: Proceedings of IEEE Symposium on computational intelligence and data mining, USA (2007)
15. Stauffer, C., Grimson, W.E.: Learning Patterns of Activity Using Real-Time Tracking. IEEE Trans. Pattern Anal. Mach. Intell. 22(8), 747–757 (2000)
16. Hervieu, A., Bouthemy, P., Le Cadre, J.-P.: A statistical video content recognition method using invariant features on object trajectories. IEEE Trans. on CSVT (Special Issue on "Event Analysis in Videos") (2008)
17. Piciarelli, C., Micheloni, C., Foresti, G.L.: Trajectory-based anomalous event detection. IEEE Transactions on Circuits and Systems for Video Technology (2008)
18. Jung, C.R., Hennemann, L., Musse, S.R.: Event Detection Using Trajectory Clustering and 4D Histograms. In: Special issue on Event Analysis in Videos in IEEE Transactions on Circuits and Systems for Video Technology (2008)
19. Appiah, K., Hunter, A.: A single-chip FPGA implementation of real-time adaptive background model. In: IEEE International Conference on Field-Programmable Technology, pp. 95–102 (December 2005)
20. Meng, H., Freeman, M., Pears, N., Bailey, C.: Real-time human action recognition on an embedded, reconfigurable video processing architecture. Special Issue of Journal on Real-Time Image Processing 3(3), 163–176 (2008)
21. Chalimbaud, P., Berry, F.: Embedded Active Vision System Based on an FPGA Architecture. EURASIP Journal on Embedded Systems (2007)
22. Yamaoka, K., Morimoto, T., Adachi, H., Koide, T., Mattausch, H.J.: Image segmentation and pattern matching based FPGA/ASIC implementation architecture of real-time object tracking. In: Proceedings of the 2006 Conference on Asia South Pacific Design Automation, Yokohama, Japan, January 24-27 (2006)
23. Tomasi, M., Díaz, J., Ros, E.: Real Time Architectures for Moving-Objects Tracking. In: Diniz, P.C., Marques, E., Bertels, K., Fernandes, M.M., Cardoso, J.M.P. (eds.) ARCS 2007. LNCS, vol. 4419, pp. 365–372. Springer, Heidelberg (2007)
24. ABORAT Project: Eastern Kentucky University -College of Justice and Safety (2006), www.jsc.eku.edu/projAborat.asp
25. Han, C., Lin, C., Ho, G., Fan, K.: Abnormal Event Detection Using Trajectory Features. In: International Computer Symposium, Taiwan (December 2006)
26. Kumar, S.: Neural Networks a classroom approach. McGraw-Hill, New York (2004)

SORU: A Reconfigurable Vector Unit for Adaptable Embedded Systems

José M. Moya, Javier Rodríguez, Julio Martín,
Juan Carlos Vallejo, Pedro Malagón, Álvaro Araujo,
Juan-Mariano de Goyeneche, Agustín Rubio, Elena Romero,
Daniel Villanueva, Octavio Nieto-Taladriz, and Carlos A. López Barrio

Universidad Politécnica de Madrid, Dpto. Ingeniería Electrónica,
ETSI de Telecomunicación, Ciudad Universitaria s/n, 28040 Madrid, Spain

Abstract. In this article we describe SORU, a reconfigurable instruction set processor architecture (RISP) specially designed for run-time self-adaptation in environments with tight resource and power restrictions. It allows to accelerate computationally intensive multimedia processing on portable/embedded devices while maintaining a low energy consumption.

The experimental results show a mean speedup of 4 with half the energy consumption. The main datapath can be left in a hibernate state during more than 75% of the execution time in our experiments, what leads also to a significant reduction of energy consumption in the I-cache and the main datapath, including the register file.

Keywords: Reconfigurable hardware, Adaptable architectures, Application-transparent adaptation, Ubiquitous computing.

1 Introduction

As Ambient Intelligence (AmI) is becoming a reality, embedded systems designers have to face new challenges related to the continuously changing environment (processing demand, processing power, time constraints, energy constraints, network topology, etc.). Much effort has been focused on the management of these issues at the operating system level, but there is little or no consideration of the run-time adaptability of hardware resources.

We envision a global heterogeneous network, mainly composed of low-end processing elements, that is capable to migrate computation between the nodes to adapt to power failures, or just to dynamically re-optimize the overall network performance when new hardware is added to the network. These computing nodes should also be able to adapt themselves to the changing external requirements.

In this article we present SORU (Stream Oriented Reconfigurable Unit), a reconfigurable instruction set processor architecture (RISP) specially designed for run-time self-adaptation. There are many existing RISP designs, but to the best of our knowledge none of them is suitable for the described scenario because the configuration generation is usually a very computing-intensive task. It is important to note that we require online synthesis of loops. We need to dynamically

J. Becker et al. (Eds.): ARC 2009, LNCS 5453, pp. 255–260, 2009.
© Springer-Verlag Berlin Heidelberg 2009

create new configuration contexts, not just changing between a limited set of previously generated configuration contexts.

2 Previous Work

The SORU architecture is based on a general-purpose RISC processor with a reconfigurable functional unit inside the processor datapath. In this sense it is similar to the Nano Processor [1], PRISC [2], DISC [3], Chimaera [4], or OneChip98 [5].

However, our reconfigurable functional unit (RFU) is pipelined, with multiple per-stage configuration contexts, and coarse reconfigurable blocks, what resembles the PipeRench coprocessor [6].

Unlike most previous RISP designs, the RFU is a vector unit using in-memory vectors, with an internal register file that can be used to minimize and homogenize memory accesses. It includes a simple control unit that allows the execution of complete loops without any intervention from the main datapath. RSVP [7] is a previously designed reconfigurable vector coprocessor aimed at providing a simple yet efficient programming interface. SORU is designed to be simpler to use for dynamic optimization and much smaller, as the main goal was not to boost performance, but to better adapt the available resources for the functionality they should provide, even for low-end processors.

3 SORU Structure

The SORU RFU has been originally designed as an extension to the execution stage of a classical MIPS-like RISC processor, although it should be easy to adapt to any general-purpose RISC processor.

A vector load/store unit, integrated into the execution unit of the main processor, decouples operand fetch of SORU operations from the normal processor operation. It allows to feed the SORU RFU with up to four independent in-memory vectors, and store the results in data memory with no further intervention from the main datapath. This feature lets the processor execute any non memory-dependent data processing at the same time the SORU unit is executing a complex vector operation.

The SORU functional unit is a 32 bit dynamically reconfigurable datapath. Its internal structure is shown in figure 1. It is designed as a three stage pipeline structure.

SORU Decode stage. The first stage gets the operation information and the operands involved in its execution. It has a simple control unit and a general purpose register file, that stores new data from the main processor and partial results from the running SORU operations. It contributes significantly to reduce the register pressure in the main register file and the coupling between SORU operations and normal operations.

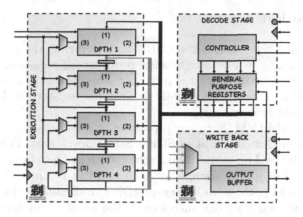

Fig. 1. SORU datapath

SORU Execution stage. This stage is divided into four cascade-connected basic reconfigurable units (BRU). Each BRU gets three 32 bit data operators: 1) the result from the previous BRU, 2) a new data item from the SORU register file, and 3) the last result computed by itself.

The result of a BRU operation is stored in the pipeline register, so it can be used by the next BRU at the next clock cycle. In our current prototype, each BRU has some multiplexers, three 3-LUTs per bit, and a shifter. The control inputs of these elements and the LUT memories form the BRU context, which is replicated to enable the BRU to perform different operations at every clock cycle.

SORU Write back stage. This stage writes the intermediate results into the SORU internal register file. It is also the output data interface from the SORU RFU to the main processor. A FIFO buffer stores ordered data from the SORU execution stage.

4   ISA Extensions

We have defined new operations for:

- Configuring a BRU context (SCONF).
- Programming the vector load units to iteratively load a new element into a SORU register every n clock cycles (LDV).
- Programming the vector store unit to extract the output data from the SORU unit when it is ready (STV).
- Scalar data movement between the main register file and the SORU register file (overloaded as MOVE in assembler code).
- Executing SORU SIMD operations (EXECV).
- Stop the main datapath to save energy when possible (WAIT).

Memory-mapped registers configure the vector load/store units, allowing the programmer to specify the vector lengths and shapes in a similar way to RSVP[7].

5 Compilation

One of the main advantages of the SORU architecture is the ease of compilation, which is a major requirement to allow run-time self-adaptation. The simple pipeline-oriented structure allows a very easy mapping of data processing kernels into SORU basic operations, while the internal register file decouples data fetching from data processing.

We have ported LLVM [8] to our prototype processor, adding a new vectorization pass to implement loops as SORU SIMD operations. This compilation framework can be used for static off-line compilation and also for dynamic on-line optimization and re-optimization, when used as a just-in-time (JIT) compiler.

To vectorize a loop, the data flow graph (DFG) is decomposed into subgraphs where every node has only one successor. If the result of an operation is used by more than one successor, it is stored in a temporary SORU register. Finally, all the independent subgraphs are scheduled following an ALAP policy (as late as possible). As the different subgraphs are scheduled independently, chances are that the data dependencies between them are not met. These are fixed by adding a prologue and a epilogue. The result is a kind of software pipelining transformation, but very fast and easy to implement.

6 Results

We have implemented a SystemC RTL simulator of the proposed architecture in order to evaluate not only the performance and energy consumption of the hardware architecture, but also the quality of the compilation process.

To evaluate the performance, we have supposed that the BRUs reconfiguration will be driven by a DMA controller during unused memory cycles, and therefore it will not degrade the overall performance.

Taking into account that the main datapath is quite simple and we focus on multimedia applications, to evaluate the energy consumption we have considered the memories to be dominant, as in DSP systems. Also, the energy consumption of external buses have been modeled, in a similar way to [9]. For the simulation results, we have set $Vdd = 3.3V$, $C = 10pF$, and $E_{access} = 4.95nJ$ for a $0.8\mu m$ technology, as justified in [10].

We have simulated the performance and the energy consumption of the proposed architecture with a collection of classical DSP algorithms. The benchmark programs have been created from direct translation to ANSI C of the algorithms in the Texas Instruments C64x Core Benchmarks[1]. Table 1 summarizes the results. Absolute times are given in clock cycles, and energy in μJ.

These benchmarks saw a speedup ranging from 2 to 4.5, while reducing the energy consumption up to 80%. Also, the main datapath is mostly idle during the execution of the SORU SIMD operations. This idle time can be used to

---

[1] Available from http://focus.ti.com/dsp/docs/dspplatformscontentaut.tsp?sectionId=2&familyId=477&tabId=496

Table 1. Benchmark tests and simulation results for the maximum number of elements

Test	Cycles base	Cycles SORU	Speed-Up	Energy base	Energy SORU	Energy Reduction
Vec · Vec	2280	1153	1.98	17.11	7.60	55.58%
Vec · Mat	149233	34172	4.37	1052.81	836.39	20.56%
Mat · Vec	588272	133239	4.42	4197.88	834.73	80.12%
Mat · Mat	18598258	4259838	4.36	$128.79 \cdot 10^3$	$22.83 \cdot 10^3$	82.27%
Max. val.	2278	848	2.68	15.70	5.74	63.44%
Vec + Vec	2782	1382	2.01	21.22	9.21	56.60%
Sum	1511	848	1.78	11.31	5.75	49.16%
Vec. copy	2277	1068	2.13	17.04	7.31	57.11%

schedule other independent operations (leading to a better global speedup), or alternatively the main datapath can be left in a hibernate state until the SORU unit finishes (leading to a better energy reduction).

For small vector sizes the configuration overload cause the SIMD solution to have more memory accesses than the scalar alternative. For the vector dot product example, the execution of the SORU implementation is faster with vector lengths larger than 40 elements, and it may be up to 42% faster, with a 52% reduction in energy consumption.

Also, the scalar implementation requires more register accesses (up to 70% more) to keep values from previous iterations, and for the induction variables.

7   Conclusions

We have designed a dynamically reconfigurable computing architecture specially easy to target from the point of view of the compiler. This is an important feature to take into account when the application requires dynamic reconfiguration of the available resources. In particular, it is well suited for intelligent ambients (AmI), with changing resources, changing requirements, tight restrictions on power consumption, etc.

The experimental results on a DSP benchmark show a mean speedup of 4 with a simultaneous reduction in energy consumption up to 80%. As opposed to typical FPGA devices, where interconnect power consumption is dominant, SORU units force a predefined pipelined data flow, reducing significantly the length of interconnections and the load capacitance. The loss in flexibility is highly compensated by the ease of mapping complete loops into a single SORU instruction, enabling the use of dynamic optimization techniques.

Acknowledgments. This work was funded partly by the Spanish Ministry of Industry, Tourism and Trade, under the CENIT Project Segur@, and partly by DGUI de la Comunidad Autónoma de Madrid and Universidad Politécnica de Madrid under Grant CCG07-UPM/TIC-1742.

References

1. Wirthlin, M.J., Hutchings, B.L., Gilson, K.L.: The nano processor: A low resource reconfigurable processor. In: Buell, D.A., Pocek, K.L. (eds.) IEEE Workshop on FPGAs for Custom Computing Machines, pp. 23–30. IEEE Computer Society Press, Los Alamitos (1994)
2. Razdan, R., Smith, M.D.: A high-performance microarchitecture with hardware-programmable functional units. In: Proceedings of the 27th Annual International Symposium on Microarchitecture, pp. 172–80 (1994)
3. Wirthlin, M., Hutchings, B.: A dynamic instruction set computer. In: Athanas, P., Pocek, K.L. (eds.) IEEE Symposium on FPGAs for Custom Computing Machines, pp. 99–107. IEEE Computer Society Press, Los Alamitos (1995)
4. Hauck, S., Fry, T.W., Hosler, M.M., Kao, J.P.: The chimaera reconfigurable functional unit. IEEE Trans. Very Large Scale Integr. Syst. 12(2), 206–217 (2004)
5. Jacob, J.A., Chow, P.: Memory interfacing and instruction specification for reconfigurable processors. In: FPGA 1999: Proceedings of the 1999 ACM/SIGDA seventh international symposium on Field programmable gate arrays, pp. 145–154. ACM Press, New York (1999)
6. Goldstein, S.C., Schmit, H., Moe, M., Budiu, M., Cadambi, S., Taylor, R.R., Laufer, R.: PipeRench: a co/processor for streaming multimedia acceleration. In: ISCA 1999: Proceedings of the 26th annual international symposium on Computer architecture, pp. 28–39. IEEE Computer Society, Washington (1999)
7. Ciricescu, S., Essick, R., Lucas, B., May, P., Moat, K., Norris, J., Schuette, M., Saidi, A.: The reconfigurable streaming vector processor (rsvptm). In: MICRO 36: Proceedings of the 36th annual IEEE/ACM International Symposium on Microarchitecture, p. 141. IEEE Computer Society, Washington (2003)
8. Lattner, C., Adve, V.: LLVM: A Compilation Framework for Lifelong Program Analysis & Transformation. In: Proceedings of the 2004 International Symposium on Code Generation and Optimization (CGO 2004), Palo Alto, California (March 2004)
9. Ning, K., Kaeli, D.: Power aware external bus arbitration for system-on-a-chip embedded systems. In: Conte, T., Navarro, N., Hwu, W.-m.W., Valero, M., Ungerer, T. (eds.) HiPEAC 2005. LNCS, vol. 3793, pp. 87–101. Springer, Heidelberg (2005)
10. Kim, H.S., Narayanan, V., Kandemir, M., Irwin, M.J.: Multiple access caches: Energy implications. In: WVLSI 2000: Proceedings of the IEEE Computer Society Annual Workshop on VLSI (WVLSI 2000). IEEE Computer Society, Washington (2000)

A Parallel Branching Program Machine for Emulation of Sequential Circuits

Hiroki Nakahara[1], Tsutomu Sasao[1], Munehiro Matsuura[1], and Yoshifumi Kawamura[2]

[1] Kyushu Institute of Technology, Japan
[2] Renesas Technology Corp., Japan

Abstract. The parallel branching program machine (PBM128) consists of 128 branching program machines (BMs) and a programmable interconnection. To represent logic functions on BMs, we use quaternary decision diagrams. To evaluate functions, we use 3-address quaternary branch instructions. We emulated many benchmark circuits on PBM128, and compared its memory size and computation time with the Intel's Core2Duo microprocessor. PBM128 requires approximately quarter of the memory for the Core2Duo, and is 21.4-96.1 times faster than the Core2Duo.

1 Introduction

A **Branching Program Machine (BM)** is a special-purpose processor that evaluates binary decision diagrams (BDDs)[3,2,14]. The BM uses only two kind of instructions: Branch and output instructions. Thus, the architecture for the BM is much simpler than that for a general-purpose microprocessor (MPU). Since the BM uses the dedicated instructions to evaluate BDDs, it is faster than the MPU. In fact, for control applications, the BM is much faster than the MPU [2]. The applications of BMs include sequencers [3,14], logic simulators [11,1], and networks (e.g., packet classification).

In this paper, we show the parallel branching machine (PBM128) that consists of 128 BMs and a programmable interconnection. To reduce computation time and memory size, we use special instructions that evaluate consecutive two nodes at a time.

2 Branching Program Machine to Emulate Sequential Circuits

We show the branching program machine (BM) that emulates the sequential circuit shown in Fig. 1. First, the combinational circuit is represented by a decision diagram. Next, it is translated into the codes of the BM. Finally, the BM executes those codes. To emulate the sequential circuit, the BM uses registers that store state variables. We assume that the BM uses 32-bit instructions, which match the data structure of embedded systems and the embedded memory of FPGAs.

2.1 MTQDD

In this paper, we use standard terminologies for reduced ordered binary decision diagrams (BDDs)[4], and reduced ordered multi-valued decision diagrams (MDDs)[9].

J. Becker et al. (Eds.): ARC 2009, LNCS 5453, pp. 261–267, 2009.
© Springer-Verlag Berlin Heidelberg 2009

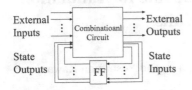

External Inputs ⋮ Combinatioanl Circuit ⋮ External Outputs

State Outputs ⋮ FF ⋮ State Inputs

Fig. 1. Model for a Sequential Circuit

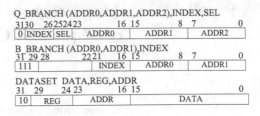

Q_BRANCH (ADDR0,ADDR1,ADDR2),INDEX,SEL

31 30		26 25 24 23		16 15		8 7		0
0	INDEX	SEL	ADDR0		ADDR1		ADDR2	

B_BRANCH (ADDR0,ADDR1),INDEX

31	29 28		22 21	16 15		8 7		0
111			INDEX	ADDR0		ADDR1		

DATASET DATA,REG,ADDR

31	29		24 23		16 15			0
10	REG		ADDR		DATA			

Fig. 2. Mnemonics and Internal Representations

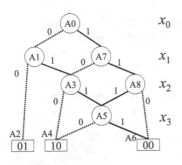

Fig. 3. Example of MTBDD

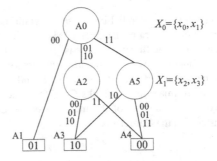

Fig. 4. MTQDD derived from MTBDD in Fig. 3

An **MTBDD (Multi-Terminal Binary Decision Diagram)** [8] can evaluate many outputs at a time. Evaluation of an MTBDD requires n table look-ups. The **APL (average path length)** of a BDD denotes the average number of nodes to traverse for the BDD. Evaluation time for a BDD is proportional to the APL [5]. To further speed up the evaluation, an **MTMDD(k) (Multi-terminal Multi-valued Decision Diagram)** is used. In the MTMDD(k), k variables are grouped to form a 2^k-valued **super variable**. Note that a BDD is equivalent to an MDD(1). For many benchmark functions, in logic evaluation, with regard to the area-time complexity, MDD(2)s are more suitable than BDDs. Since MDD(2) has 4 branches, it is denoted by a **QDD (Quaternary Decision Diagram)**. In this paper, we use an **MTQDD (Multi-terminal Multi-valued QDD)**.

Example 2.1 *Fig. 3 shows an example of MTBDD. Fig. 4 shows the MTQDD that is derived from the MTBDD in Fig. 3.* *(End of Example)*

2.2 Instructions to Evaluate MTQDDs

Three types of instructions are used to evaluate an MTQDD. A **2-address binary branch instruction** (B_BRANCH) and a **3-address quaternary branch instruction** (Q_BRANCH) evaluate a non-terminal node, while a **dataset instruction** (DATASET) evaluates a terminal node. Mnemonics and their internal representations for *B_BRANCH*, *Q_BRANCH* and *DATASET* are shown in Fig. 2.

B_BRANCH performs a binary branch: If the value of the variable specified by IN-DEX is equal to 0, then GOTO ADDR0, else GOTO ADDR1. **DATASET** performs an output operation and a jump operation. First, *DATASET* writes DATA (16 bits) to a register specified by REG. Then, GOTO ADDR. **Q_BRANCH** jumps to one of four addresses: Three jump addresses are specified by *ADDR0*, *ADDR1*, and *ADDR2*, while the remaining address is the next address ($PC+1$) to the present one. Since it evaluates two variables at a time, the total evaluation time is reduced up to a half of a *B_BRANCH* instruction. Also, it can reduce the total number of instructions. We use four different *Q_BRANCH* instructions shown in Fig. 7. *SEL* in the *Q_BRANCH* specifies one of four combinations. Let i be the value of the variable specified by *INDEX*. If ($SEL=i$), then jump to $PC+1$, otherwise jump to $ADDR_i$. In addition, **unconditional jump instructions** are necessary to evaluate some QDDs. Example 2.2 illustrates this.

Example 2.2 *The program in Fig. 5 evaluates the MTBDD in Fig. 3. Consider the MTQDD shown in Fig. 4. Fig. 8 shows the MTQDD with address assignment for Q_BRANCH instructions, where SEL has the same meaning as Fig. 7. For A6, B_BRANCH instruction is used to perform an unconditional jump. The program in Fig. 6 evaluates the MTQDD.* *(End of Example)*

```
A0:  B_BRANCH  (A1,A7),x0
A1:  B_BRANCH  (A2,A3),x1
A2:  DATASET  01,0,A0
A3:  B_BRANCH  (A4,A5),x2
A4:  DATASET  10,0,A0
A5:  B_BRANCH  (A4,A6),x3
A6:  DATASET  00,0,A0
A7:  B_BRANCH  (A3,A8),x1
A8:  B_BRANCH  (A6,A5),x2
```

```
A0:  Q_BRANCH  (A2,A2,A5),X0,00
A1:  DATASET  01,0,A0
A2:  Q_BRANCH  (A3,A3,A4),X1,00
A3:  DATASET  10,0,A0
A4:  DATASET  00,0,A0
A5:  Q_BRANCH  (A4,A4,A4),X1,10
A6:  B_BRANCH  (A3,A3),--
```

Fig. 5. Program Code for the MTBDD in Fig. 3

Fig. 6. Program Code for the MTQDD in Fig. 8

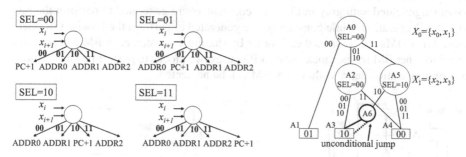

Fig. 7. Four Different Q_BRANCH Instructions

Fig. 8. MTQDD with 3-address Quaternary Branch Instructions

2.3 Branching Program Machine for a Sequential Circuit

Fig. 9 shows a branching program machine (BM) for a sequential circuit. It consists of the **instruction memory** that stores up to 256 words of 32 bits; the **instruction decoder**; the **program counter (PC)**; and the **register file**. In our implementation, two clocks are used to execute each instruction of the BM: A **Double-Rank Filp-Flop** is used to implement the state register and the output register [12]. Fig. 10 shows the Double-Rank Filp-Flop, where L_1 and L_2 are D-latches.

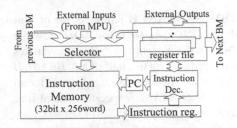

Fig. 9. BM for a Sequential Circuit

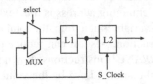

Fig. 10. Double-Rank Flip-Flop

In the BM, values of state register are feedbacked into its inputs. Thus, the BM can emulate a sequential circuit. A BM can load the external inputs, the state variables, and the outputs from other BMs by specifying the value of the input select register.

3   Parallel Branching Program Machine

3.1   8_BM

Fig. 11 shows the architecture of the **8_BM** consisting of 8 BMs. The output registers and the flag registers of BMs are connected in cascade through **programmable routing boxes**. Then, these values are stored into the common registers of the 8_BM. Also, the values of registers are feedbacked to the input of BM_0. Each BM can operate independently.

A programmable routing box implements either the bitwise AND, or the bitwise OR operation. Constant values can be also generated. In the programmable routing boxes (highlighted with gray in Fig. 11), constant 1s are generated to perform the bitwise AND operation, while constant 0s are generated to perform the bitwise OR operation. Since BMs are connected each other by sharing a register, each BM can send the signal to other BM in one clock. Since a BM uses two clocks to perform an instruction, the communication delay within an 8_BM can be neglected.

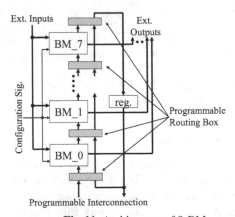

Fig. 11. Architecture of 8_BM

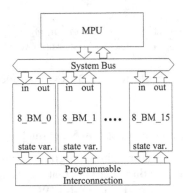

Fig. 12. Parallel Branching Program Machine (PBM128)

3.2 Parallel Branching Program Machine

Fig. 12 shows the **Parallel Branching program Machine (PBM128)** consisting of 128 BMs described in Section 2. Eight BM constitute an 8_BMs, and sixteen 8_BMs and a **programmable interconnection** constitute the PBM128. Primary inputs and configuration signals are sent to the 8_BMs. Each 8_BM has external outputs and state variables. The external outputs are connected to the system bus, while the state variables are sent to 8_BMs through the programmable interconnection. When the all 8_BMs finish the operation, the values of state variables of an 8_BM are sent to other 8_BMs through the programmable interconnection. These operations can be specified by the values of the flag register. In addition, MPU is used to control the whole system.

3.3 Programmable Interconnection

A multi-level circuit of multiplexers is used in the programmable interconnection. To increase the throughput, pipeline registers are inserted into the programmable interconnection. The insertion of pipeline registers increases the latency: Four clocks are used to connect the outputs of an 8_BM to other 8_BM. Since two clocks are used for an instruction of the BM, the PBM128 requires two instructions time to finish the connection between BMs in different 8_BMs. In the code generation, the wait time inserted.

4   Implementation and Experimental Results

4.1 Implementation of Parallel Branching Program Machine

We implemented the PBM128 on the Altera's FPGA (StratixII: EP2S130F1508C4). In our implementation, the maximum frequency is 132.73[MHz]. The PBM128 consumes 67817 ALUTs out of 106032 of available ALUTs. Each BM consumes 455 ALUTs (0.6% of used ALUTs), each 8_BM consumes 3778 ALUTs (5.6% of used ALUTs), sixteen 8_BMs consume 60764 ALUTs (89.6% of used ALUTs), and the programmable interconnection consumes 6307 ALUTs (9.3% of used ALUTs). As for the MPU, the embedded processor NiosII/f is used.

Table 1. Comparison of the Execution Code Size and the Execution Time

Name	In	Out	FF	Core2Duo		PBM128		Ratio(C2D/PBM)	
				Code	Time	Code	Time	Code	Time
s5378	35	49	164	74.6	12030	17.8	323	4.19	37.2
s9234	36	39	211	148.6	13450	33.4	352	4.44	38.2
dsip	229	197	224	112.1	17500	24.8	182	4.52	96.1
bigkey	263	197	224	149.5	19170	33.9	220	4.41	87.1
apex6	135	99		23.0	3700	4.8	163	4.79	22.6
cps	24	102		33.9	3468	8.3	162	4.08	21.4
des	256	245		123.1	16560	30.7	308	4.00	53.7
frg2	143	139		40.0	6390	9.2	215	4.34	29.7

4.2 Experimental Results

We selected benchmark functions [13], and compared the execution time and code size for the PBM128 with the Intel's general-purpose processor Core2Duo U7600 (1.2GHz, Cache L1 data 32KB, L1 instruction 32KB, and L2 2MB). The execution code was generated by gcc compiler with optimization option -O3. We partition the outputs into groups, then represent them by multiple MTQDDs, and finally convert them into the codes for the PBM128. We used a grouping method [10] that partitions outputs with similar inputs. As for the data structure, the MTQDD is used for the PBM128, while the MTBDD is used for the Core2Duo, since the MTBDD is faster than the MTQDD. We used the same partitions of the outputs in the Core2Duo and in the PBM128. To obtain the execution time per a vector, we generated random test vectors, and obtained the average time. The frequency for the PBM128 is 100[MHz], while that for the Core2Duo is 1.2[GHz]. Table 1 compares the code size and the execution time for the Core2Duo and the PBM128. In Table 1, *Name* denotes the name of benchmark function; *In* denotes the number of inputs; *Out* denotes the number of outputs; *FF* denotes the number of state variables; *Code* denotes the size of execution code [KBytes]; *Time* denotes the execution time [nsec]; and *Ratios* denote that for the code size and that of the execution time (Core2Duo/PBM128). Table 1 shows that the PBM128 requires approximately quarter of the memory for the Core2Duo, and is 21.4-96.1 times faster than the Core2Duo.

5 Conclusion

In this paper, we presented the PBM128 that consists of 128 BMs and a programmable interconnection. To represent logic functions on BMs, we used quaternary decision diagrams. To evaluate functions, we used 3-address quaternary branch instructions. We emulated many benchmark functions on the PBM128 and the Intel's Core2Duo microprocessor. The PBM128 requires approximately quarter of the memory of the Core2Duo, and is 21.4-96.1 times faster than the Core2Duo.

Acknowledgments

This research is supported in part by the Grants in Aid for Scientific Research of JSPS, and the grant of Innovative Cluster Project of MEXT (the second stage). Discussion with Mr.Hisashi Kajiwara was quite useful.

References

1. Ashar, P., Malik, S.: Fast functional simulation using branching programs. In: Proc. International Conference on Computer Aided Design, pp. 408–412 (November 1995)
2. Baracos, P.C., Hudson, R.D., Vroomen, L.J., Zsombor-Murray, P.J.A.: Advances in binary decision based programmable controllers. IEEE Transactions on Industrial Electronics 35(3), 417–425 (1988)

3. Boute, R.T.: The binary-decision machine as programmable controller. Euromicro Newsletter 1(2), 16–22 (1976)
4. Bryant, R.E.: Graph-based algorithms for boolean function manipulation. IEEE Trans. Compt. C-35(8), 677–691 (1986)
5. Butler, J.T., Sasao, T., Matsuura, M.: Average path length of binary decision diagrams. IEEE Trans. Compt. 54(9), 1041–1053 (2005)
6. Clare, C.H.: Designing Logic Systems Using State Machines. McGraw-Hill, New York (1973)
7. Davio, M., Deschamps, J.-P., Thayse, A.: Digital Systems with Algorithm Implementation, p. 368. John Wiley & Sons, New York (1983)
8. Iguchi, Y., Sasao, T., Matsuura, M.: Evaluation of multiple-output logic functions. In: Asia and South Pacific Design Automation Conference 2003, Kitakyushu, Japan, January 21-24, pp. 312–315 (2003)
9. Kam, T., Villa, T., Brayton, R.K., Sagiovanni-Vincentelli, A.L.: Multi-valued decision diagrams: Theory and Applications. Multiple-Valued Logic 4(1-2), 9–62 (1998)
10. Nakahara, H., Sasao, T., Matsuura, M.: A Design algorithm for sequential circuits using LUT rings. IEICE Transactions on Fundamentals of Electronics, Communications and Computer Sciences E88-A(12), 3342–3350 (2005)
11. McGeer, P.C., McMillan, K.L., Saldanha, A., Sangiovanni-Vincentelli, A.L., Scaglia, P.: Fast discrete function evaluation using decision diagrams. In: Proc. International Conference on Computer Aided Design, pp. 402–407 (November 1995)
12. Sasao, T., Nakahara, H., Matsuura, M., Iguchi, Y.: Realization of sequential circuits by look-up table ring. In: The 2004 IEEE International Midwest Symposium on Circuits and Systems, Hiroshima, July 25-28, pp. I:517–I:520 (2004)
13. Yang, S.: Logic synthesis and optimization benchmark user guide version 3.0. MCNC (January 1991)
14. Zsombor-Murray, P.J.A., Vroomen, L.J., Hudson, R.D., Tho, L.-N., Holck, P.H.: Binary-decision-based programmable controllers, Part I-III. IEEE Micro 3(4), 67–83 (Part I), (5), 16–26 (Part II), (6), 24–39 (Part III) (1983)

Memory Sharing Approach for TMR Softcore Processor

Yoshihiro Ichinomiya, Shiro Tanoue, Tomoyuki Ishida,
Motoki Amagasaki, Morihiro Kuga, and Toshinori Sueyoshi

Graduate School of Science and Technology, Kumamoto University,
2-39-1 Kurokami, Kumamoto, 860-8555 Japan

Abstract. SRAM-based field programmable gate arrays (FPGAs) are more susceptible to single event upsets compared to *ASIC*. We focus on triple modular redundancy (TMR) to ensure high reliability. Herein, we study the implementation of TMR on a softcore processor called "Base TMR" for considering design flexibility, and evaluate the resource usage and operating frequency. To resolve these problems , we propose two types of TMR designs: "Memory Shared TMR" and "Cache Enabled TMR." Memory Shared TMR achieved efficient memory usage, but it reduced the operating frequency to about 25% in comparison with Base TMR. Cache Enabled TMR improved the operating frequency to a value similar to that of the base processor in exchange for 125% of memory usage overhead. Consequently, when implementing the TMR processor, we need to adopt an adequate TMR design by considering the trade-offs.

1 Introduction

SRAM-based field programmable gate array (FPGA) is widely used, e.g., in industrial equipments, electronical devices, and embedded systems due to its reconfigurable feature, needlessness of non-refundable engineering cost, and fast time-to-market[1][2]. Although FPGA provides these great features, FPGA is vulnerable to radiation effects called single event upsets (SEU). If SEU occurs, the logic state of the memory element is changed. Therefore, FPGA is lesser reliable than ASIC when the factors reliability and continuous operation are considered[1][2]. Consequently, FPGA is unreliable when it is used in critical systems such as medical application, on-board electronics, and avionics.

To mitigate SEU effect, we focus on the triple modular redundancy (TMR) implementation[1][3]. However, it has large overhead, for example, there are logic resource and operating frequency degradation. In this paper, we study the dependability of digital systems implemented on Virtex-4 FPGA, which is manufactured by Xilinx. Additionally, we implement TMR on a softcore processor system considering the design availability. In our study, we propose two TMR structures: Memory Shared TMR that focuses on resource reduction and Cache Enabled TMR that focuses high performance.

The rest of the paper is organized as follows. Section 2 explains SEU effects on SRAM-based FPGA. Section 3 describes the TMR features, implementation

J. Becker et al. (Eds.): ARC 2009, LNCS 5453, pp. 268–274, 2009.
© Springer-Verlag Berlin Heidelberg 2009

method and prior evaluation. Section 4 explains the proposed TMR. Section 5 describes the implementation result. Conclusion is described in Section 6.

2   SEU Effects on SRAM-Based FPGA

When a charged particle attacks silicon chip, soft error called SEU is induced on circuit. SEU is a bit flip effect occurring in a memory or flip-flop (FF) . In the past, SEU were not very concerned at the ground level. However in recent years, SEU has become a problem. Because the threshold voltage decreases and the operating frequency increases with deep submicron process. These reasons mean SEU problem in FPGA becomes critical in a fine fabrication process[1].

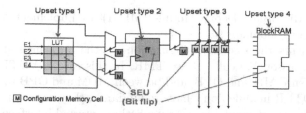

Fig. 1. SEU occurrence location

Fig.1 shows SEU occurring location. SEU effect in digital systems are classified into two types [1][2]: "permanent error" and "transient error". SEU occurs in the configuration memory of FPGA, such as look up table (LUT) or routing switch, and in a storage memory, e.g., "Upset types 1, 3, and 4" in Fig.1, it is classified as a permanent error. Permanent error makes a circuit operation faulty, and it requires correction processing to recover normal operation. In case where SEU in storage memory, the use of Error Correcting Code (ECC) can prevent SEU from acting on storage memory.

Otherwise if SEU occur in a FF or latch, e.g., "Upset type 2", it is classified as a transient error. Transient error corrupt the output, but its effect is temporal. Consequently reconfiguration process is not needed.

3   Dependable Softcore Processor Using TMR

3.1   TMR Architecture and Implementation

In this section, we explain the triple modular redundancy (TMR) feature. TMR is implemented by triplicating the module and employing majority voter (VOTER) at their output. Even if only one SEU occurs in the modules, VOTER can detect the occurrence of SEU and can continue correct output [1][3].

We use Virtex-4 FPGA manufactured by Xilinx to study the TMR design with a softcore processor[3]. Fig.2 represents the Base Processor design which is base structure for TMR implementation. Base Processor implements MicroBlaze v6.00.b softcore processor for design flexibility. Additionally, Block RAM

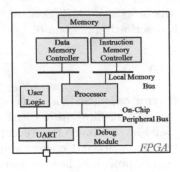

Fig. 2. Base Processor Design

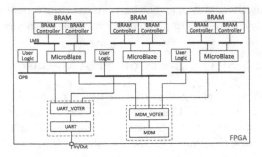

Fig. 3. Base TMR Architecture

(BRAM) and MicroBlaze Debug Module (MDM) are implemented for memory storage and debug module.

Fig.3 represents the system configuration on the implementation of TMR using Base Processor. We call it Base TMR. In this case, a VOTER module is inserted between UART and OPB, and between MDM and OPB too. As UART, MDM and VOTER module don't have redundancy, they cannot mitigate SEU. It is trade-off for the dependable system whether external interface modules are triplicated or not. For example, if VOTER are triplicated, we need to the triple number of I/O pins. It may confine implementable circuit.

3.2   Implementation of TMR Softcore Processor

In this study, we use Xilnx ML410 embedded development board with Virtex-4 XC4VFX60FF1152-10 and two Xilnx design tools, EDK9.1i (Embedded Development Kit) and ISE9.1i (Integrated Software Environment) . To simplify the system design, IP (Intellectual Property) based design is used. The TMR implementation process is explained as follows:

1. Design a VOTER module and import as a IP core.
2. Edit the Microprocessor Peripheral Definition (MPD) file to set the default setting for the imported IP core.
3. Edit the Microprocessor Hardware Specification (MHS) file to triplicate.

VOTER module has to be imported as an IP core so that it can be connected easily . When it is imported, VOTER and peripheral should be already connected as one module. In this instance , an input of the IP is shared with the three modules. When the IP core is imported, it has only one bus interface. The number of interfaces are able to be added editing MPD file. In addition, the MPD file defines the default parameter, address, etc[4]. Finally, triplicating a module, it need to edit MHS file. An MHS file defines the configuration of the embedded processor system and includes the processor, peripherals, connectivity, address space, etc. When circuit is triplicated, it is needed to copy the IP core, change the instance name, and edit the signal names in MHS file.

To check the system operation, we use the TOPPERS/JSP (Toyohashi OPen Platform for Embedded Real-time Systems/Just Standard Profile) kernel[5] which is open source RTOS kernel. We confirm that TMR circuit can output correct value and perform synchronous processing of external interrupt requests. At the same time, we inject the error input from external switch, and confirm only one error input is able to be mitigated on TMR.

3.3 Implementation Result

Table 1 shows the implementation result of Base Processor and Base TMR, they implementing JSP kernel. The percentage mention resource occupancy in the entire resource. Virtex-4 XC4VFX60 has 50,560 LUTs and 232 BRAM blocks.

Table 1. Implementation Result of Base TMR

	Number of LUTs	Number of BRAM blocks	Operating Frequency (MHz)
Base Processor	2,883 (5.7%)	32 (13.8%)	102.722
Base TMR	8,582 (17.0%)	96 (41.4%)	80.154

This table shows that the Base TMR requires about three times of LUT and BRAM resources as compared to the Base Processor, and the operating frequency of Base TMR is inferior to that of Base Processor by about 22%. When the number of BRAM blocks is scarce and limited, the memory block may be insufficient using it in another application. About reducing the operating frequency, we consider two reasons. First, signals are routed through the VOTER module. Second, the circuit is triplicated; routing lines become more complex and longer than those of the Base Processor. Consequently, wiring delay increases. To resolve these issues, we study two types of TMR designs. One reduces the memory resource, while the other offers high performance.

4 Proposed TMR Implementation

In this study, we propose two types of TMR— Memory Shared TMR and Cache Enabled TMR. They focuses area and performance overhead, respectively.

Fig.4 illustrates the Memory Shared TMR architecture. In this design, the VOTER circuit is inserted between the BRAM controller and the BRAM; consequently, access to BRAM is unified and the BRAM is shared by three processors. As a result of this approach, the redundancy of BRAM is disappeared; in other words, the BRAM can be used effectively.

Another thing, operating frequency is reduced by the implementation of TMR. If system requires to retain both performance and dependability, the implementation of Base TMR may cause problems. Therefore, we use the cache memory of each processor to maintain performance. Fig.5 represents Cache Enabled

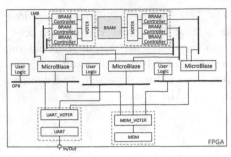 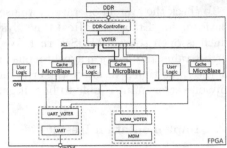

Fig. 4. Memory Shared TMR   **Fig. 5.** Cache Enabled TMR

TMR architecture that enables cache memory on MicroBlaze. We assign a 64-KB BRAM to the cache memory, which is the maximum cache size. As BRAM is used for the cache memory, DDR-SDRAM, which is implemented outside FPGA, is used for the main memory. The connection between MicroBlaze and DDR-SDRAM is through the Xilinx Cache Link (XCL) that connects the processor and DDR-controller via a cache, without passing through the OPB bus. As a result, it will provide fast data transfer. In this case, the DDR-SDRAM has to be shared by three MicroBlazes. However, the DDR-SDRAM operates at double the speed of FPGA's base clock; therefore, we cannot insert a VOTER between the DDR-SDRAM and its controller. For this reason, VOTER is inserted between MicroBlaze and DDR-controller.

As these approaches don't triplicate main memory, the reliability of stored data is concerned. We do not deal with this issue in this study, but we consider that it can be handled by using a dependable technique for memory such as error correction code (ECC).

5   Evaluation Result of Proposed TMR

In this section, we evaluate proposed two types TMR system. The implementation environment is the same as shown in section3.2. In this study, we evaluate about LUT and BRAM usages and operating frequency.

Table 2 represents the evaluation result of proposed TMR. First, we focus on Memory Shared TMR. The result shows BRAM block usage is saved as much

Table 2. Evaluation Result of Memory Shared TMR

	Number of LUTs	Number of BRAM blocks	Operating Frequency (MHz)
Base Processor	2,883 (5.7%)	32 (13.8%)	102.722
Base Processor with Cache	4,752 (9.4%)	72 (31.0%)	103.348
Base TMR	8,582 (17.0%)	96 (41.4%)	80.154
Memory Shared TMR	8,863 (17.5%)	32 (13.8%)	60.125
Cache Enabled TMR	11,962 (23.7%)	216 (93.1%)	100.200

as the case of Base Processor. On the other hand, the LUT resource consumption increases by only 3.3% (281 LUTs). These result signifies that the Memory Shared TMR achieves resource reduction of BRAMs. However, the operating frequency substantially decreased by 25.0% and 41.5% in comparison with Base TMR and Base Processor, respectively. If processors share BRAM blocks, all paths between the BRAM and the MicroBlaze have to be connected via the VOTER module. Additionally, as BRAM is a hard macro, which is distributed on FPGA, the interconnection around the BRAM blocks are complex and the wire length required may increase. As a result, its wiring delay becomes later than wiring delay of Base TMR. Thus, this implementation method facilitates effective memory usage, but reduces the operating frequency.

If a MicroBlaze cache is enabled, the use of BRAM and LUTs substantially increase in comparison to the case where the cache is disabled. As the MicroBlaze cache using BRAM and as the cache memory prepares each instruction cache and data cache, the consumption of BRAM resource is very large. In the case of the Cache Enabled TMR, the BRAM blocks consumption is 2.25 times that of the Base TMR, and 93.1% of the BRAM blocks implemented in Virtex-4 XC4VFX60 is used. These results suggest that the BRAM resource for other applications is restricted when a large-sized cache memory is used. Further, the resource consumption of LUT increases about 39% compared to the Base TMR. This is because if the cache memory is used, MicroBlaze has to be implemented using the cache control circuit. Another reason is that the DDR-Controller is larger than the BRAM-Controller. However, when comparing the Base Processor with cache, the LUT resources of Cache Enabled TMR are deserved to be less than three times of it because the DDR-Controller is shared by redundant processors. Operating frequency is improved by 25.0% comparing the operating frequency of Base TMR. Also, it get worse only 3.0% comparing the case of Base Processor with Cache. They are produced by direct connecting between MicroBlaze and DDR-Controller. This connection reduces the wiring delay. Therefore, the proposed TMR design can achieve a high operating frequency, in return for resource overhead.

6   Conclusion

Here in, we studied the implementation of TMR on a softcore processor system. At the beginning, we implemented the Base TMR that is triplicated except for the external interface , and we evaluated it to define the problems of TMR. Subsequently, considering the TMR trade-off, we proposed the Memory Shared TMR to improve the memory resource consumption and the Cache Enabled TMR for high performance. The Memory Shared TMR improved the memory resource consumption, but induced a reduction in the operating frequency. The Cache Enabled TMR showed high performance, but resulted in a substantial increase in resource consumption. As each TMR architecture has individual trade-offs, we need to adopt an adequate TMR design according to the trade-offs.

References

1. Kastensmidt, F.L., Carro, L., Reis, R.: Fault-Tolerance Techniques for SRAM-based FPGAs. Springer, Heidelberg (2006)
2. Asadi, G., Tahoori, M.B.: Soft Error Rate Estimation and Mitigation for SRAM-Based FPGAs. In: Proc. of the 2005 ACM/SIGDA 13th int'l symposium on Field-programmable gate arrays (FPGA 2005), pp.149–160 (February 2005)
3. Vasudevan, V., Waldeck, P., Mehta, H., Bergmann, N.: Implementation of a Triple Modular Redundant FPGA based Safety Critical System for reliable software execution. In: Proceedings of the 11th Australian workshop on Safety critical systems and software (SCS 2006), pp.113–119 (2006)
4. Xilinx Inc, Platform Specification Format Reference Manual (2007)
5. TOPPERS Project (2008), http://www.toppers.jp/jsp-kernel.html

The Need for Reconfigurable Routers in Networks-on-Chip

Debora Matos, Caroline Concatto, Luigi Carro,
Fernanda Kastensmidt, and Altamiro Susin

Federal University of Rio Grande do Sul – UFRGS
Informatics Institute, Electrical Engineering Dept.
Porto Alegre, Brazil
{debora.matos,cconcatto,carro,fglima,susin}@inf.ufrgs.br

Abstract. There are many examples in the literature of applications that show different communication needs within a MPSoC. Very often cores interconnected through a Network-on-Chip have routers containing different buffers size, with different clock speed requirements. In this context, we are proposing a dynamic reconfigurable router for a NoC. With the proposed architecture it is possible to reconfigure the depth of each FIFO of the channel inside the routers. It allows more reusability in the NoC since the FIFO depth in the channels can be defined in accordance with the application. Besides, a buffer that is not used by its own channel can be used by others channel, reducing the power consumption.

Keywords: heterogeneous NoC, reconfigurable router, FIFO, buffer.

1 Introduction

Multiprocessor System-on-Chip (MPSoC) is emerging as one of the technologies providing a way to support the growing design complexity of embedded systems, since it provides processor architectures adapted to selected problem classes, allied to programming flexibility.

To ensure flexibility and performance, future MPSoC will combine several types of processors cores and data memory units of widely different size, leading to a very heterogeneous architecture. The interconnection infrastructure must guarantee high throughput for certain communication patterns, the possibility of a very fast partial routing update for very dynamic applications, and scalability, all of these characteristics with low power, low energy and low area overhead.

The communication among cores of a MPSoC having reusable interconnections is being provided by Networks-on-Chip (NoC) [1]. Manferdelli et al. [2] assure that to guarantee the increase in performance of general purpose CPUs, one needs to use massive parallel computing. For this, more independent CPUs, bigger caches and more independent memory controllers have been used. One can find an example of this architecture on the Xbox360 [3]. Fig.1(a) shows a system block diagram of the Xbox, a platform with several cores, and each core having specific throughput and bandwidth. The communication rates are showed in the Fig. 1(a). The BIU/IO

J. Becker et al. (Eds.): ARC 2009, LNCS 5453, pp. 275–280, 2009.
© Springer-Verlag Berlin Heidelberg 2009

interface makes communication with the CPU, L2 Cache and with IO/Chip and all these communications have different throughputs. Therefore, a router must consider the possibility of different configurations to guarantee the QoS to every core, as well as the right bandwidth and throughput, while at the same time.

As another example of mixed communication behavior and requirement where there is a clear difference between cores in a SoC with out-of-order cores (OoCs) and in-order-cores (IoCs) is showed in the Fig. 1(b), [2]. OoCs are larger and have worse power performance than IoCs. Besides, there is more communication among IoCs than OoCs, thus the former need to have different interconnection characteristics among them, in order to guarantee a higher communication bandwidth among IoC devices, since their communication with OoCs occurs in a much smaller scale.

From the above MPSoC examples, one can see that, as in the microprocessor market, each NoC used in a MPSoC can have different communication performance and costs, depending on the target application. Designing the same NoC router to cover the whole spectre of applications would mean an oversized and expensive router, in terms of area and power.

In this work we characterize the need for a reconfigurable router and show the preliminary gains that could be achieved with such strategy. In this particular contribution, we focus on providing a reconfigurable router, since this is the basic block of any NoC, changing the amount of buffer utilization to ensure lower latency and QoS .

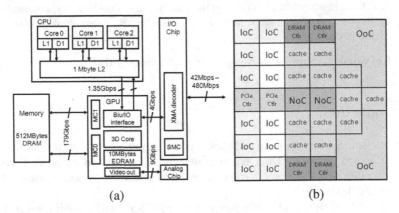

(a)   (b)

Fig. 1. (a) Xbox 360 block diagram. (b) Example of different cores used in a SoC.

2 Related Work

In an MPSoC it is usual to find different interconnection needs amongst processors, memories, peripherals and others elements. Due to this fact, it has been perceived the need for distinct bandwidth in each node of a NoC, as mentioned in the previous examples. In the literature some works present solutions that point in this direction, but generally with a static approach, used in the design phase only. In this section we did a study where several of these ideas demonstrate that in the same application there is the need to use routers with different features and communication needs.

Cardoso et al. [4] observed the need to have heterogeneous links in a network-on-chip, where for each application a link with appropriate size is used. A heterogeneous router was presented based on heterogeneous links with two wrappers for each router. These wrappers control the traffic between the heterogeneous channels and each channel works with the message compatible with its width. Following this path, Kreutz et al. [5] analyzed the architecture of three routers, each one having different characteristics. A heterogeneous NoC can be developed by an arrangement of these three routers in order to find an optimized configuration for each application, trading area for latency.

Ahmad et al. [6] proposed a network router designed with a bus like interface. An in-built wrapper is used, and thus any component compatible with a bus can be integrated into the NoC architecture. The interface of this router becomes a simple bus. The objective was to reduce the design time and to ease integration, since it is not necessary to known to the NoC architecture. When the network has a channel that requires high bandwidth, the NoC changes the switching, obtaining a dedicated path between the IPs.

Ahonen and Nurmi [7] proposed a hierarchical NoC, able to cope with inefficiencies obtained with a regular NoC. They used two types of on-chip network: the Global Network (NoC), and the Local Network (Bus-based). The Local Network is used to connect slaves to a master that together are called local clusters. The NoC is used to connect all local clusters, all of them having the same capabilities.

Eun Lee and Bagherzadeh [8] proposed the use of different clocks while sending flits in the NoC. Body flits operate faster than head flits. In accordance with them, as FIFOs work faster than the route decision, it is possible to use different clocks to body flits and head flits. While the head flit is analyzed to define the path of route, body flits can continue advancing along the reserved path already established, improving the performance of the router.

The problem of the proposals found in the literature is that all of them must be used at design time, hence causing problems to what regards scalability whenever the NoC is used for a new application in the same platform. Hence, product updates or even customization of a MPSOC for a different market, using the same components but with a different communication pattern is not possible without a costly redesign. Here it is clear that a dynamically reconfigurable router that can dynamically change, in accordance with the application needs, can potentially increase the performance of the NoC.

3 Reconfigurable Router

If a NoC has a larger FIFO, the throughput will be larger and the latency in the network smaller, since it will have fewer lost flits [9]. Nevertheless, there is a limit in the depth increase of the FIFO. Since each communication will have its peculiarities, sizing the FIFO for the worst case communication scenario will compromise not only the routing area, but power as well. However, if the NOC has a small FIFO depth, the latency will be larger, and QoS can be compromised.

A solution proposed is to have a heterogeneous router, in which each channel can have a different buffer size. In this situation, if a channel has a communication rate smaller than its neighbor, it may lend some of its buffer units that are not being used. In a different application or with a different communication pattern, the roles may be inverted or changed at runtime, without a redesign step.

The router architecture proposed was embedded in the SoCIN NoC. The router architecture used is the RASoC [5]. SoCIN uses packets composed of flits. The buffering is present only at the input channel. Each flit is stored in a FIFO buffer unit. Fig. 2 shows the two FIFO architectures for a single channel: the original FIFO architecture (Fig. 2(a)) and the proposed architecture (Fig. 2(b)). In Fig. 2(b) we are considering as example the South channel of a router. In a router, the FIFO proposed architecture is replied to four channels of the NoC.

In the new architecture it is possible to dynamically configure different buffer depths for different channels. If a channel is not using its own FIFO, it can lend its buffer to a neighbor channel, while buffers in this channel are not being used.

Each channel may only use the available buffers of its right and left neighbors. In such case each channel may have up to 3 times its buffer size. In order to reduce routing and extra multiplexers, we adopted the strategy of changing the control part of each channel. Hence, the borrow/lent process is coordinated only by simple finite state machines and pointer management for each FIFO storage unit. Each channel controls its storage flits, being these units stored on its own buffer or in the neighbor's channel buffers. In this manner, some signals of each channel must be sent for the neighboring channels in order to control its stored flits. The information about how many storage units of the buffer are used for each channel is sent by an external control (it is information received by an input pin of the NoC) and this information can be dynamically altered. In this design we are not considering the possibility of the *Local Channel* using neighbor FIFOs, only the *South*, *North*, *West* and *East Channel* of a router can make use of their adjacent neighbors. In order to guarantee the correct functioning of the arbiter we defined that a flit stored in a neighbor channel must be sent to its respective channel before it is passed to the next router. Each channel can receive three inputs. Let us consider the *South Channel* as an example, having the following inputs: the own input (*din_S*), the right neighbor input (*din_E*) and the left neighbor input (*din_W*).

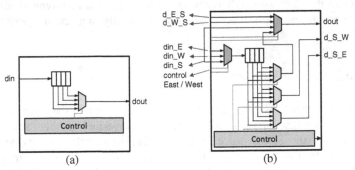

Fig. 2. Input FIFO (a) SoCIN. (b) Proposed.

When the *South Channel* has a flit stored in the East Channel and this flit is sent to the output, the flit is passed from the East Channel to the South Channel (*d_E_S*), and so this flit is directly sent to *dout_S* by a MUX. The South Channel has the following outputs: the own output (*dout_S*) and two more outputs (*d_S_E* and *d_S_W*) that sent flits stored in this channel but which belong to neighbor channels.

In the proposed router architecture each channel knows how much of its own FIFO is being used and how much is borrowed from neighbors. For illustration purposes, let us assume we are using a router with FIFO depth equal to 4, and there is a router that needs to be configured as follows: *South Channel* with FIFO depth equal to 9, *East Channel* with FIFO depth equal to 2, *West Channel* with FIFO depth equal to 1 and *North Channel* with FIFO depth equal to 4. In such case, the *South Channel* needs to borrow buffer units to its neighbors. As the *East Channel* occupies 2 units of 4, this channel can lend 2 units to its neighbor but even then, the *South Channel* still need more 3 buffer units. As the *West Channel* occupies only 1 unit, the 3 missing units can be lent to the *South Channel*. We consider that the buffer necessity among the channels will never exceed the available FIFO quantity.

4 Results

The proposed router is described in VHDL, and in order to verify the correct function of the new architecture, we simulated the code using the ModelSim tool. We verified that the flits are being written and read correctly in their neighbors. Table 1 presents the area and frequency results of the original and proposed router. Results were obtained to a CMOS 0.18um process technology using the Leonardo Spectrum 3 tool to the synthesis. To these results, we configured the channel width to 10 bits. As the intelligent router allows a channel to have until three times more buffer storage than the original router, we compared the proposed solution with a router designed with the same buffering possibilities.

In the proposed router there is a little gain in area, because one had to utilize more multiplexers and some registers to do the control. The gains in this proposal come from the possibility to reconfigure the NoC without wasting buffers. As the new router uses more multiplexers than flip-flops to store the flits, it is possible that the power consumption will be less than the original router with 3 times more buffer, since flip-flops have permanent power consumption due to the clock, what does not happen with the multiplexer. In real applications it is quite usual the sub utilization of the router, since not all of its channels are utilized. In such cases, the extra buffers on channels not used in the original router would be consuming power unnecessarily. The advantage in the use of the NoC with reconfigurable router instead of homogeneous router is that one can dynamically change the FIFO depth to each channel in accordance with the necessity of the application.

Thus, we can conclude that the obtained results emphasize the fact that the proposed NoC router does not degrade the system performance. With this architecture the FIFO depth can be dynamically reconfigurable, since in run time the depth of each channel can be changed.

Table 1. Area (in gates) and frequency (in MHz) results to the original and new router architecture

Proposed Router			Original Router		
FIFO Depth	Area	Frequency	FIFO Depth	Area	Frequency
2	4044	205	6	4087	227
3	5594	178	9	5616	195

5 Conclusions and Future Works

This paper presented new reconfigurable router architecture to be used within Networks-on-Chip. The reconfigurable router is required because each core can present different communication rates in an MPSoC. In such case, the connections among the cores cannot use a homogeneous NoC. Therefore, we propose a dynamic reconfigurable router where each channel can have until 3 times more FIFO space, dynamically reconfigured at run time. This increase in the buffer size is possible due to the lending of buffers among the channels. As future work, we are planning to measure the power consumption and quality of service of some applications using the NoC with the proposed reconfigurable router.

References

1. Benini, L., De Micheli, G.: Network on Chips: A new SoC Paradigm. IEEE Computer, 70–78 (2002)
2. Manferdelli, J., Govindaraju, N., Crall, C.: Challenges and Opportunities in Many-Core Computing. Proceeding of the IEEE 96(5), 808–815 (2008)
3. Andrews, J., Baker, N.: Xbox 360 System Architecture. IEEE Micro 26(2), 25–37 (2006)
4. Cardoso, R., Kreutz, M., Carro, S., Susin, A.: Design Space Exploration on Heterogeneous Network-on-chip. In: International Symposium on Circuits and Systems, vol. 1, pp. 428–431 (2005)
5. Kreutz, M., Marcon, C., Carro, L., Wagner, F., Susin, A.: Design Space Exploration Comparing Homogenous and Heterogeneous Network-on-Chip Architectures. In: Symposium on Integrated Circuits and Systems Design, SBCCI 2005, pp. 190–195 (2005)
6. Ahmad, B., Ahmadinia, A., Arslan, T.: Dynamically Reconfigurable NOC with Bus Based Interface for Ease of Integration and Reduced Designed Time. In: NASA/ESA Conference on Adaptive Hardware and Systems (AHS 2008), pp. 309–314 (2008)
7. Ahonen, T., Nurmi, J.: Hierarchically Heterogeneous Network-on-Chip. In: The International Conference on Computer as a Tool, EUROCON, pp. 2580–2586 (2007)
8. Eun Lee, S., Bagherzadeh, N.: Increasing the Throughput of an Adaptive Router in Network-on-Chip (NoC). In: International Conference on Hardware/ Software Codesign and System Synthesis, pp. 82–87 (2006)
9. Wu, C., Chi, H.: Design of a High-Performance Switch for Circuit-Switched On-Chip Networks. In: Asian Solid-State Circuits Conference, pp. 481–484 (2005)
10. Varatkar, G.V., Marculescu, R.: On-chip traffic modeling and synthesis for MPEG-2 video applications. IEEE Transactions on Very Large Scale Integration (VLSI) System, 108–119 (2004)

Transparent Dynamic Reconfiguration as a Service of a System-Level Middleware

Fernando Rincón[1], Jesús Barba, Francisco Moya, Juan Carlos López,
and Julio Dondo[2]

[1] Universidad de Castilla-La Mancha, Escuela Superior de Informática,
Ciudad Real, Spain
`fernando.rincon@uclm.es`
[2] Universidad Nacional de San Luis, San Luis, Argentina

Abstract. Designing reconfigurable applications is not an easy task, due
to the complex methodologies and the delegation of too many low level
details to the designer. The solution proposed in this paper [1]is based in
the distributed object model, where a transparent reconfigurable service
is built upon a Hw/Sw communications middleware.

1 Introduction

After two decades of research in dynamic reconfiguration, there is a good understanding on the reconfiguration mechanisms, architectures and implications
[6] [7], ... However, commercial reconfigurable systems are hard to find, and
reconfigurable devices have not reached the level of expectations that they were
supposed to: reconfiguration times are not negligible. Reconfiguration tools and
flows are hard to use, and design methodologies leave too many details of the
process exposed to the designer (structural consistency, state persistence, ...).

The solution we propose in this paper is based on the object-oriented approach as the unifying paradigm for both Hw and Sw worlds [2,5]. Everything
inside the system can be modelled after an object. Underneath, a system-level
middleware provides transparent communication between them. The middleware
(or OOCE [1][2] from now on) represents an intermediate layer in the System-On
a Chip that hides the inherent heterogeneity present in such kind of systems,
makes communication between the components of the system homogeneous and
provides the same programming interface for both HW and SW elements. OOCE
is based on the the distributed object paradigm.

The distributed object model also is well suited for partial dynamic reconfiguration, since it enforces a systematic way to deal with state, execution of operations and encapsulation. Reconfiguration can be provided as one more service of
the middleware. The main objective is to provide an extra degree of transparency

---

[1] This work has been funded by the Spanish Ministry of Science and Innovation under the project DAMA (TEC2008-06553/TEC), and by the Regional Goverment of
Castilla-La Mancha under project RGRID (PAI08-0234-8083).
[2] Object-Oriented Communication Engine.

J. Becker et al. (Eds.): ARC 2009, LNCS 5453, pp. 281–286, 2009.
© Springer-Verlag Berlin Heidelberg 2009

(reconfiguration transparency) which has two implications: (1) reconfigurable objects will offer exactly the same interface that their static counterparts, thus will make such capability transparent to the client; (2) reconfiguration management (creation, destruction and object persistence) will be performed automatically (implicitly), although that will not prevent from having a higher degree of control (explicit management).

2   The Reconfiguration Service

Reconfiguration management is a complex process mainly due to three aspects, all related to the dynamic behavior of reconfigurable systems. As it is briefly described in the following paragraphs, such management is better suited to the object model than to the traditional task-based [4] one. Therefore, the integration of reconfiguration as an additional service of OOCE is quite natural.

The first difficulty with reconfiguration is that it modifies the physical structure of the hardware. In order to keep the rest of the system unaffected, it is necessary to guarantee the isolation of the reconfigured area. This has some implications for the programming model used, since typically such isolation is provided keeping a constant physical interface. The advantage of the distributed object model, with respect to the traditional task-based [4] one, is that the adapters already exist (proxies and skeletons), they are systematic and they are automatically generated during the synthesis of the communication architecture. In fact, the reconfigurable entity (or core) is the sum of both the reconfigurable object plus the generated adapters, and they are indivisible. Those adapters, unlike objects, have a fixed interface: the one with the bus or network interface. So, any core (object + adapters), even those generated after the system deployment, can be instantiated into any reconfigurable area, with the only limitation of its size. When using tasks, such interface adaptation is usually a manual process completely delegated to the designer.

The second problem of dynamic reconfiguration is state consistency. It may be of interest to keep state information of dynamic circuitry, so it can be recovered at a later instantiation of the same piece of hardware, or even migrated to a software task. Here, the advantage of the object model is that it enforces a clear separation of state and operations. Then keeping state coherence is as simple as waiting for operations to complete before reconfiguration. Object state is consistent as far as there are no object operations in execution. In the task model state is not explicit, thus it is the designer who has to manually define a set of synchronization points where the state can be safely dumped or restored.

The third issue, state persistence, has already been introduced in the previous one, and refers to state transfer to and from any kind of memory, so it can be later restored or even migrated. And again, this concept is better suited to the object model, since state is explicitly defined in the object definition. Knowing the size and type of all state variables at design time leads to a systematic way to request allocation space, and to transfer state information to a persistent location, irrespective of what the concrete object is.

2.1 Reconfigurable Objects and Cores

Dynamically objects do not differ from static ones from the functional point of view. Both expose exactly the same functional interface to the client. The main difference lies in the way the object is created and destroyed, as well as how persistence is managed. Considering these two aspects, the first one only affects to reconfigurable adapters, while the second has also some implications on the object, since it must be able to import and export its internal state.

The skeleton [3] of a dynamically reconfigurable object includes extra logic for controlling the execution state of the object. A previous step for the eviction of the object from the reconfigurable area will be to issue a **stop** request. This will disable the reception of incoming method invocations, and wait for the completion of the pending ones, and thus guarantee state coherence. On the other side, after the instantiation of a new object (creation) an explicit **start** request will activate the object for incoming clients requests.

The skeleton also includes three special methods for state persistance management. They are the **getState** and **setState** methods for saving and downloading the state, respectively, and **initState** for initialization matters. The main difficulty with state management is that, although completely defined at design time, the designer can freely choose how to implement it. So attributes can be stored in special purpose registers, in memory blocks, or using any other storage resource. For that reason, and also due to implementation efficiency, the responsibility of state management is transfered to the designer, and those methods are redirected to the object. However, the middleware fixes how to code that state. Attribute order must follow the interface definition as well as the same marshalling rules than any other argument or return value of an operation.

2.2 Memory Allocation Service

Another problem with dynamically reconfigurable environments is that the need for memory may be difficult to predict at design time. Bitstreams for new object types may be deployed at any time, and extra unpredictable space is also needed for state storage of object instances with persistence capabilities. The solution adopted in this approach is to define a dynamic memory allocation service that will transparently provide basic primitives for memory management. The service is provided by an specialized object called the Allocator. The Allocator has two main characteristics. On one side it centralizes memory management for the whole system. On the other side it offers a well known interface, completely independent from a concrete implementation technology or memory hierarchy. The service interface is based on two methods. The **allocate** method requests the allocation of a certain memory block size, while the **release** method frees the memory block.

The return value for the **allocate** method is a proxy to memory. The Memory interface is a technology independent description of the capabilities of a memory:

---

[3] The adapter that translates bus read and write operations into object invocations.

read and write operations of a single or a sequence of words. Such description is a logical representation for real memories in the system. On the other side, proxies are references to remote objects, and since all objects inside the system-level are memory mapped, they are implemented as physical memory addresses. Then, any memory block in the system can be modelled with the Memory interface and used by means of its proxy, while from the implementation point of view, we are simply reading and writing to a certain address computed from a base (the proxy reference) plus an offset, the address specified in the methods.

There are several alternatives for the implementation of the allocator, depending on the speed, available size, and other requirements. As a last resort, when the scheduling must be performed in very few cycle clocks, the allocator can be fully implemented in hardware. However, reconfiguration latency is usually so high that a full software implementation would provide better memory use while still keeping an acceptable overhead.

2.3 Object Location Service

The main purpose of the system-level middleware is to provide transparency (for location, access, transport mechanism, ...). Location transparency allows clients to invoke methods from a remote object without any prior knowledge of their real location. This is of special interent in dynamic reconfiguration environments, since the reference (address assigned in the memory map) of a reconfigurable component can be deferred to the instantiation inside a certain reconfigurable area, at runtime. The location service, then is in charge of providing a valid endpoint (the address where the instantiated component is located) when a client requests the location of concrete object.

Two entities are involved in the location process. The proxy stores a reference for the locator object, instead of a static endpoint to the server hardcoded at design time. On the other side, the location service (or directory service), provides the valid endpoint from the requested object identity. When an invocation is received from the client object, the proxy will first request the current location of the remote object (using the object identifier). The location service contains a location table where object identities are linked with valid endpoints. Once the location is obtained, the object will perform a second request: the real invocation. However, indirection doesn't necessarily imply two requests per invocation. That can be easily avoided simply caching the obtained location.

The interface for the locator object has two kind of methods. The **locate** method provides the location functionality previously described. The rest of the methods are used for the administration of the location table inside the locator.

2.4 Object Factory

The factory service physically instantiates an object into a reconfigurable area. It is possible to create objects of any type at run time. It is only necessary to previously register (**registerClass**) the new object type or class (*classID*), with a reference to the memory location of the partial bitstream (*bitstreamRef*).

The factory keeps an internal table with the registered classes and it may be managed by using methods **deleteClass** and **updateClass** for entry deletion and updates respectively. New objects are created invoking the **createObject** method, supplying the object type (*classID*), the reconfigurable area in which it should be allocated, and the physical system address (*endpoint*) where requests from clients should be served. As a result of the invocation, the factory will transfer the partial bitstream from the memory to the reconfigurable area, and it will configure the skeleton with the corresponding *endpoint*. Once reconfiguration is done the object is ready to be activated and to serve invocations.

2.5   Reconfiguration Controller

The reconfiguration controller (RC) is the responsible for run-time object creation and destruction, including object state persistence management. The RC also updates with valid object endpoints the location information when necessary. This service is built upon the three basic ones described in previous sections (memory allocation, location and factory).

The RC holds an internal table where already known objects (those that have been used at any time even if they are not currently instantiated) are registered. For each entry the RC controls: the region within the reconfiguration fabric where the object was instantiated, and a pointer to the memory block where the object state was stored. That information can be inserted, removed, updated and looked up through a set of administrative methods.

Dynamic reconfiguration can be explicitly or implicitly triggered. In the former, the reconfiguration process is initiated through an invocation to the *allocate* method, while implicit reconfiguration starts when the RC detects that a required object is not instantiated. The invocation sequence for explicit reconfiguration is the following: (1) the RC looks up for the requested object identity in the known object table; (2) the Object Factory creates a new object; (3) if the object has persistent storage, the RC transfers the serialized state from the storage memory to the object invoking its *setState* method [4]; (4) the RC activates the object (*start* invocation); (5) the RC updates the object endpoint in the location service. Implicit activations follow a similar approach, but the reconfiguration process is initiated when the location service fails to provide a valid endpoint. The RC plays in this case the role of a secondary locator in the system. If the requested object has an entry in the known objects table, the reconfiguration process will continue as described in the explicit case. However, implicit reconfiguration has some other implications, such as selecting an active object as a candidate to be evicted when there is no free reconfiguration area.

3   Experimental Evidence

The reconfiguration service has been prototyped on the Xilinx XUP board, using a mixed hw and sw approach. The allocator service and the object factory are

---

[4] Not necessary for stateless or first instantiated objects.

both scheduled to a microblaze microprocessor. The locator and reconfiguration controller are implemented as hardware cores. A set of several types of objects (filters, counters, traffic generators) have been implemented to test the validity of the approach. The overhead in time due to reconfiguration management is almost negligible with respect to the huge configuration transfer times, while the cost of the reconfiguration system is mainly due to the size of the CAM memories in the locator and the logic for state management in persistent objects.

4   Conclusions

This work extends the heterogeneous distributed object model [1] to support partially dynamic reconfigurable systems. The distributed object model provides complete transparency from the client point of view. No modifications for the client code are required. From the hardware designer point of view, neither modifications are required for the object interface nor for the hardware design. The only exception is persistence support, since state management is totally implementation dependent. Thanks to the automatic generation of both reconfigurable services and reconfigurable adapters, the design of the reconfigurable system can also be tackled in an iterative way. A fully static system can be gradually transformed into a dynamic one, while studying the global impact of reconfiguration overhead.

References

1. OOCE, 2006 Object-Oriented Communication Engine for SoC Design, Object-Oriented Communication Engine for SoC Design (DSD), Lübeck, Germany (2007)
2. Paulin, P.G., et al.: Distributed Ojbect Models for Multiprocessor SoCs, With Applications to Low-Power Multimedia Wireless Systems. In: Design Automation and Test in Europe (DATE), Munich, Germany (March 2006)
3. Rezano, J., Mozos, D., Catthoor, F., Verkest, D.: A Reconfiguration Manager for Dynamically Reconfigurable Hardware. IEEE Design and Test of Computers, 452–460 (September-October 2005)
4. Mignolet, J.-Y., et al.: Infrastructure for Design and Management of Rlocatable Tasks in Heretogeneous Reconfigurable System-on-Chip. In: Design and Test in Europe (DATE) (2003)
5. Hecht, R., Kubisch, S., Michelsen, H., Zeeb, E., Timmermann, D.: A Distributed Object System Approach for Dynamic Reconfiguration. In: Reconfigurable Architecture Workshop (RAW) (2006)
6. Horta, E.L., Lockwood, J.W., Parlour, D.: Dynamic Hardware Plugins in an FPGA with Partial Run-Time Reconfiguration. In: Design Automation Conference (DAC) (2002)
7. Moore, N., Conti, A., Leeser, M., Smith King, L.: Writing Portable Applications that Dynamically Bind at Run Time to Reconfigurable Hardware. In: International Symposium on Field-Programmable Custom Computing Machines (FCCM) (2007)

Optimizing Memory Access Latencies on a Reconfigurable Multimedia Accelerator: A Case of a Turbo Product Codes Decoder

Samar Yazdani[1], Thierry Goubier[2], Bernard Pottier[1], and Catherine Dezan[1]

[1] Université de Bretagne Occidentale
Lab-STICC, UMR CNRS 3192,
Brest 29200, France
samar.yazdani@univ-brest.fr
[2] CEA, LIST
Embedded Real-Time System Foundations Laboratory
Mail Box 94 - F91191 Gif sur Yvette Cedex, France

Abstract. In this paper, we present an implementation of a turbo product codes (TPC) decoder achieved on a novel Reconfigurable Multimedia Accelerator (RMA). The RMA is based on the principle of hierarchical shared memory storage managed through a dedicated local controller favoring high data throughput, while squeezing round-trip memory latencies. The mapping methodology facilitates the characterization of the RMA for a TPC decoder in terms of the communication and computation resources.

1 Introduction

In this paper, we present the implementation of a Turbo Product Codes (TPC) decoder on a novel reconfigurable multimedia accelerator (RMA), weakly coupled to an application processor platform. RMA relies on explicit multithreading and streaming intrinsics [6,7] to mitigate the effects of memory latency and bandwidth in a unified manner. A mix of static and dynamic control reduces the overheads related to pure dynamic control. Several stream processors with differing characteristics have emerged including Cell Broadband Engine [4] and Merrimac[2]. On the other side, the Tera MTA[1] and Niagara[5] are multi-threaded architectures. RMA couples the explicit multithreading and streaming intrinsics through a local dedicated controller in a unified manner.

The dramatic increase of integrated circuit capacity makes on-chip sophisticated error control methods possible. Turbo product codes (TPC) have good error correction performance and are promising candidates for the FEC[1] scheme in 4G. We consider the implementation of the decoder algorithm presented in detail in [3].

The approach is based on achieving block-level parallelism by pipelining (prefetch/execute/poststore) stages in a modular Reconfigurable Multimedia Accelerator (RMA). The RMA associate a process-level execution to a set of local

---

[1] Forward Error Correction.

J. Becker et al. (Eds.): ARC 2009, LNCS 5453, pp. 287–292, 2009.
© Springer-Verlag Berlin Heidelberg 2009

memory banks fed from the off-chip storage. Multiple memory banks provide the bandwidth needed for the local computations. Given a set of communication and computation processes, shared data dependencies are managed using a synthesized local controller. This controller coordinates fine-grain atomic memory accesses, reducing computational latencies compared to the architectures in which data circulate through communication channels. Furthermore, a complete mapping methodology has been presented that facilitates the characterization of RMA for the TPC decoder in terms of communication and computation resources.

The outline of the paper is as follows: section 2 describes the SoC platform considered in this work. The target architecture RMA is explained in section 3. Section 4 describes the mapping of a parallel specification to the RMA. Section 5 is dedicated to the design space exploration and the results obtained.

2   System-on-Chip Architecture

The platform under consideration is a distributed multiprocessor architecture with shared memory and an interconnect network supporting out of order and split transactions. The host processor runs the operating system, and the subsystems attached to the host perform the compute intensive tasks of multimedia applications. Each sub-system has a DSP core with data and instruction cache, and a reconfigurable multimedia accelerator (RMA) coupled to the sub-system DSP by its internal bus, and to the system memory through a master port of the interconnect. There are two modes of communication with the RMA, one is memory to memory through interconnect, and the other is through shared memory with the host DSP. The RMA, once configured to run an application, performs stand-alone processing of blocks of data.

3   Reconfigurable Multimedia Accelerator - RMA

In RMA, the compute-intensive kernel is mapped spatially to the FPGA while the application control such as data sequencing and address generation logic is mapped to the data-transport engine. The streams of data that are consumed and eventually produced by the FPGA through its I/O primary ports are produced by a DMA attached to that port, which reads and writes from a local buffer memory. In a steady state, the FPGA can access a new data on each primary port at each clock cycle, and so the maximum throughput can be sustained to feed the FPGA. The streaming engine has been designed to meet this high throughput requirements. It is composed of a local memory and a set of address generation units to drive the DMAs attached to the FPGA ports. A multibanked, multiported memory block is used to store data prefetched from system memory, and to store temporary results of computations from the FPGA. This local buffer is useful to minimize traffic on the system interconnect, to mask bus latencies and keep a high compute efficiency for the RMA.

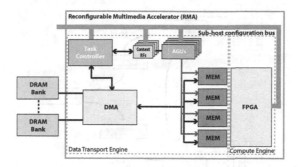

Fig. 1. An instance of Reconfigurable Multimedia Accelerator

The DMAs of the FPGA ports are under control of the address generation units (AGUs). It is their task to update the DMA burst descriptors. *Burst Descriptor* is a structure that contains the start address, increment and last address of the memory bank under access according to the application requirements. These processors are single-issue machines with an instruction memory and a data memory, and they communicate with each other through a set of shared registers that are read/write accessed by all the AGU, for instance to implement sync protocols.

[3] describes how to implement the Data Transport Engine in an interleaved scheme with the right number of pipeline stages and hardware duplication so as to allow one DTE pipelined to work at the same time on $block_i$ and $block_{i-1}$.

3.1 Execution Model

The execution model is composed of distinct pipeline stages. These pipeline stages are descibed as follows:

Prefetch (PF) a packet bus based transaction to transfer data from DRAM to local memory storage

Transmit (TX) a burst write access to feed compute nodes inside the compute engine

Receive (RX) a burst read access to rearrange processed data in the local memory storage

Poststore (PS) a packet bus transaction to write the processed data back to DRAM

4   Mapping Decoder Algorithm to the RMA

The decoding scheme used to map Mini-Maxi to the RMA is shown in figure 2. The architecture makes full use of a single block decoder, by interleaving the decoding of two blocks. While block i is being read from the input buffers and processed by the block decoder (one pair of decoded vector/received vector at a

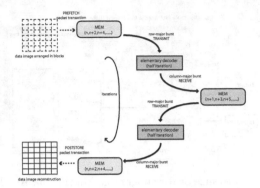

Fig. 2. Decoding scheme

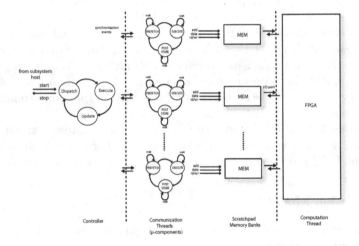

Fig. 3. Abstractions in the form of concurrent processes that are mapped to an RMA template

time) block i - 1 is being decoded and written to the output buffers (one pair of decoded vector/received vector at a time).

Once the decoding of a block is finished, the output buffers are exchanged with the input buffers, and the block decoder is ready to start the next half-iteration for this block (see figure 2). In this scheme, we maintain a full pipeline while copying with the necessary rebuild of the matrix between two half-iterations.

Figure 3 illustrates the virtualization of underlying hardware in terms of communication and computation threads. Each thread is abstracted as a component that has an exact mapping to the underlying architectural constituent. A communication thread is a set of 3 atomic tasks (prefetch, execute and poststore). Each communication thread is associated to a memory bank. The execution context of each communication thread is maintained by the controller that scoreboards the execution history. Furthermore, the controller program is synthesized automatically from a runtime system [6] that synchronizes the task dispatch hence data dependencies and allows concurrent shared memory accesses. The execution is traced for different data inputs, and architecture configurations are downloaded in the RMA at the time of boot phase.

5 Results - Design Space Exploration

Different implementation alternatives have been considered for the TPC decoder algorithm. As TPC decoder requires high-computational capacity and data bandwidth, a tradeoff between the use of different decoder instances and memory banks have been considered. A 2-bank, 1 elementary decoder, a 4-bank - 1 elementary decoder, a 4 bank - 2 elementary decoders and a 22 bank - 11 elementary decoder configurations have been studied.

Table 1 illustrates the application/architecture parameters used for the exploration while table 2 shows the results obtained for different architecture templates as previously explained. The performance is measured in terms of 3 criteria namely; execution latency, communication/computation overlap and throughput. Due to the iterative nature, the algorithm is not only demanding in memory bandwidth but also in terms of computational capacity. It could be seen from the results (see table 2 that the performance (throughput) increases significantly with the increase of memory banks and elementary decoders. The results are obtained for a reference algorithm explained in [3] for an $eBCH(32, 26)^2$ product codes. We exploit block level parallelism of an input data image having 16×16 blocks. Each block represents 32×32 symbols. A symbol is coded with 5

Table 1. Application and architecture reference parameters

Code	$eBCH(32, 26)^2$
Reference Algorithm	Mini-Maxi[3]
Quantization bits	5
Number of iterations	5
Memory block size	1024×5 bits
Clock frequency	100MHz

Table 2. Application and architecture reference parameters

	2-banks, 1 elementary decoder	4-banks, 1 elementary decoder	4-banks, 2 elementary decoders	22-banks, 11 elementary decoders
Execution Latency (cycles)	9014.6K	8992.2K	4512.2K	851.4K
Comm/Comp ratio	1.0626	1.06135	1.0602	1.0505
Throughput	14Mbits/sec	14Mbits/sec	29Mbits/sec	153Mbits/sec

bits. Each memory block used in the architecture has a 1024×5 bits granularity. The throughput is obtained for a clock frequency of 100MHz.

6   Conclusions

In this paper, we have shown that multiple shared memory buffers are useful to mask off-chip memory access latencies and to increase the data bandwidth. It is further shown, that concurrent memory accesses improve the application performance while relying on optimal synchronization i.e. one that follows the dataflow. To recall the case of Turbo Product Codes Decoder, it has been shown that by scaling memory banks from 2 to 22, processing bandwidth follow improvements from 14Mbits/sec to 153 MBits/sec. This scaling also demonstrates that the RMA mapping method provides a design space exploration capability to adapt the RMA dimensions to a set of target applications.

References

1. Callahan, D., Cummings, D., Koblenz, B., Porterfield, A., Alverson, R., Smith, B.: The tera computer system. In: Proceedings of the 4th international Conference on Supercomputing, ICS 1990, Amsterdam, The Netherlands, ACM, New York (1990)
2. Dally, W.J., Labonte, F., Das, A., Hanrahan, P., Ahn, J.-H., Gummaraju, J., Erez, M., Jayasena, N., Buck, I., Knight, T.J., Kapasi, U.J.: Merrimac: Supercomputing with streams. In: Supercomputing, 2003 ACM/IEEE Conference, pp. 35–35 (November 2003)
3. Goubier, T., Dezan, C., Pottier, B., Jégo, C.: Fine grain parallel decoding of turbo product codes: Algorithm and architecture. In: 5th International Symposium on Turbo Codes and Related Topics (September 2008)
4. Gschwind, M.: Chip multiprocessing and the cell broadband engine. In: CF 2006: Proceedings of the 3rd conference on Computing frontiers, pp. 1–8. ACM, New York (2006)
5. Kongetira, P., Aingaran, K., Olukotun, K.: Niagara: A 32-way multithreaded sparc processor. IEEE Micro 25(2), 21–29 (2005)
6. Yazdani, S., Cambonie, J., Pottier, B.: Coordinated concurrent shared memory access on a reconfigurable multimedia accelerator. ELSEVIER Journal of Microprocessors and Microsystems, Embedded Hardware Design (2008)
7. Yazdani, S., Cambonie, J., Pottier, B.: Reconfigurable multimedia accelerator for mobile systems. In: The proceedings of 21st IEEE International SoC Conference, pp. 287–291 (2008)

Tile-Based Fault Tolerant Approach
Using Partial Reconfiguration

Atsuhiro Kanamaru, Hiroyuki Kawai, Yoshiki Yamaguchi,
and Morisothi Yasunaga

Graduate School of Systems and Information Engineering
University of Tsukuba
1-1-1 Ten-ou-dai Tsukuba Ibaraki, 305-8573, Japan

Abstract. This paper deals with a dependable computing system using
a reconfigurable device. The work carried out for this purpose of this
study involved the proposition of a fault-tolerant approach which covers
microprocessors. TFT, which is short for tile-based fault tolerant approach, has the intermediate layer which makes the connection between
physical circuit layout and logical circuit layout for use in partial and
dynamic reconfiguration. The reconfiguration is effectively utilized for
online replacement of failed circuits. An advantage of TFT is that there
is no conflict with other fault-tolerant approaches, and therefore TFT is
freely available in the construction of dependable systems.

1 Introduction

A system failure surely occurs for a long operating time, and the higher failure rate is derived from extreme environmental conditions such as cosmic space,
desert, and the deep ocean. FPGAs have been attracting a great deal of attention
since an circuit configuration on an FPGA can be reconfigured after the estab-
lishment of a system. The use of FPGAs is spreading to dependable computing
[1] and particularly discussed in single event effects [2,3,4]. However, realizing
higher dependability of systems, fault tolerance is what need to be thrashed
out. Hardware fault, which is caused by hot electron [5,6], negative bias temperature instability [7] and gate oxide breakdown [8], sets up permanent failure
and requires fault tolerant techniques for long-term systems without any hand
maintenance. Here, we propose a tile-based fault tolerant (TFT) approach using
partial reconfiguration. TFT feature is high compatibility with any circuits and
to reduce the recovery time.

The article is explained as follows. Section 2 describes TFT approach how it
fixes circuit troubles using partial reconfiguration. In Section 3, we implement
simple TFT modules on the earlier and latest Xilinx FPGAs. To enhance the
experience, Section 4 shows an TFT implementation of a RISC processor, and
then, discusses the issues. Finally, Section 5 concludes this paper.

J. Becker et al. (Eds.): ARC 2009, LNCS 5453, pp. 293–299, 2009.
© Springer-Verlag Berlin Heidelberg 2009

2   Tile-Based Fault Tolerant (TFT) Approach

2.1   Triple Modular Redundancy (TMR) in Our System

TMR is one of well-known techniques for fault masking[9]. The concept of TMR is a majority voting on the outputs from the triplicate circuits. Many systems are based on TMR for achieving higher dependability against environmental disturbance. As for Xilinx FPGAs, TMR technique is presented in [10] and some examples are presented in [11]. We also adopt TMR as one of fault masking techniques and detect a failure part using its voting circuit.

Our voting circuit produces two outputs; a valid output is returned from a majority-voting function, and then, the error flag for identified damaged circuit is output by the comparison when an error is occurred. For instance, a comparison in the majority-voting function can identify what circuit has an error; the input of a function is "001", "010", "011", "100", "101" or "110". In our implementation, the identified results are merged in control circuits and it is utilized for a circuit swapping using a partial reconfiguration.

2.2   Overview of TFT Approach

TFT is an implementing rule for designing and constructing dependable computing systems. Fig.1 illustrates TFT overview.

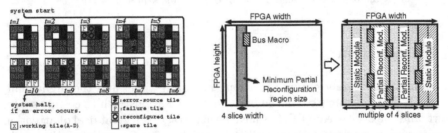

Fig. 1. TFT overview and its flowchart   **Fig. 2.** Xilinx PRM and its overview[12]

The t numbers in the Fig.1 correspond with the time step related to a repetition of tile failures and recoveries. The shaded tiles, which are inscribed from A to D, display a type of modules. The A, B, C, and D consist of 3, 4, 2 and 4 tiles respectively. No circuit is implemented on any spare tiles in the initial condition. When a working circuit on a tile has an error, the tile is replaced with a spare tile after the suitable reconfiguration.

For example, the device works well in the initial condition in Fig.1 ($t=1$). The system checks each tile using TMR and an error is found (Fig.1 (A at $t=2$)). The system replaces the wrong tile to a sparc tile (Fig.1 ($t=3$)). It repeats from $t=4$ to $t=10$. The system will halt when there is no spare tile for the reparation.

3 TFT Implementation on FPGAs

3.1 TFT Implementation on Earlier XILINX FPGAs

Modules can communicate with other modules using bus macros (BMs) [12][13]. BMs perform unchanged routing channels for keeping correct inter-module networks even if any partial reconfiguration modules (PRMs) are changed.

Standard BMs are composed of look-up tables and only support to connect between adjacent modules. TFT, however, requires to establish remote routing channels for communicating between distant modules. We therefore designed remote-channel BMs composed of tri-state buffers using XILINX ISE 6.3.03i[1]. The circuit relocation and remote-channel BMs are discussed by [14].

As a preliminary experiment of TFT implementation, a simplified model was evaluated regarding remote-channel communication. This model has six modules: one static module for I/O, three PRMs for computation, and two PRMs for spare modules. The intra-module network topology is a complete graph. For an intra-module network with n nodes, $2 \times {}_nC_2$ channels are totally required because each BM channel is unidirectional. The placement of modules is illustrated in Fig.3. Each PRM is 4 CLB width and FPGA device height. A static module is the rest of circuits, and however, we use only 5 CLB width. Each PRM is equivalent to a tile.

In our validation, PRM3 and PRM4 have no circuits except BM interfaces at the initial phase. These modules are applied to spare tiles; a circuit can be moved from PRM0 → PRM3 → PRM4, PRM2 → PRM4 followed by PRM1 → PRM3, et al.

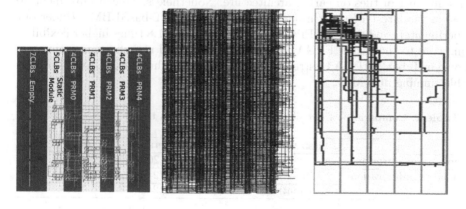

Fig. 3. TFT on 2V1000   **Fig. 4.** 5VLX50 overview   **Fig. 5.** 5VLX50 net diagram

---

[1] The handling is not supported by the latter versions of ISE 8.0. We have not tested any versions of ISE 7.x.

Table 1. Comparison of circuit size and reconfiguration time (XC2V1000 @333.3KHz)

	filesize (KB)	used LUTs/overall	time (sec)	ratio
whole reconfiguration	499	135/5,120	21.94	1
partial reconfiguration	(max.) 34	21/640	1.45	0.07
	(min.) 17	24/640	0.76	0.03

The whole and partial reconfiguration time are shown in Table 1. FPGA bitstreams were downloaded through XILINX platform cable.The time is actual measurement time observed by Agilent 54641D mixed-signal oscilloscope. The absolute reconfiguration speed is not so high, but it is improved when we use the maximum download frequency, 33.3 MHz. Consequently, we had higher flexibility and dependability of a system compared to common approaches.

3.2   TFT Implementation on the Latest XILINX FPGA

Following Section 3.1, we tested the latest FPGA, XC5VLX50. The latest architecture supports rectangle partial reconfiguration which is suitable for TFT, but not supporting remote-channel BMs with tri-state buffers. We therefore redesign remote-channel BM using LUTs. On the latest Xilinx architecture, it expands PRM commutative and circuit design flexibility because of higher flexibility and the increase in the number of remote-channel wires.

The size of a tile in Section 3.1 and this section is made as nearly equal as possible. It causes the increase in the use of BMs and the growth rate is calculated by $\frac{2\times_{30}C_2}{2\times_5 C_2}$, and therefore a whole circuit can not be divided into the large number of tiles on earlier architecture. Nonetheless, we can implement 30 tiles on the latest FPGA through the use of new LUT-based BMs. Under our experimental condition, the FPGA has approximately 1.8 times higher flexibility compared to the earlier FPGA. The whole and partial reconfiguration time are shown in Table 2. FPGA bitstreams were downloaded through XILINX Platform cable running at 6 MHz.

Table 2. Comparison of circuit size and reconfiguration time (5VLX50 @6MHz)

	filesize (KB)	used LUTs/overall	time (sec)	ratio
whole reconfiguration	1,533	1,792/7,200	4.41	1
partial reconfiguration	(max.) 36	62/240	0.28	0.06
	(min.) 24	60/240	0.18	0.04

4   RISC Processor Implementation on an FPGA

Using TFT, we have already achieved a positive result in regularly-structured circuits such as a cellular automata computation [15]. In this section, we introduce that TFT can be adopted to complex-structured circuits.

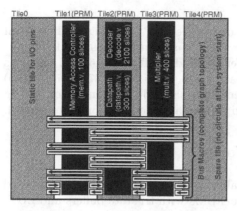

Fig. 6. SH core and its segmentation

Fig. 7. SH implementation (no TFT)

Table 3. Latency comparison of a whole (Fig.7) and TFT (Fig.8) implementations

	latency (ns)	speedup
a Whole implementation	29.471	1.00
TFT impllementation total time	33.437	0.88
except tri-state buffer (estimation)	(30.465)	(0.97)

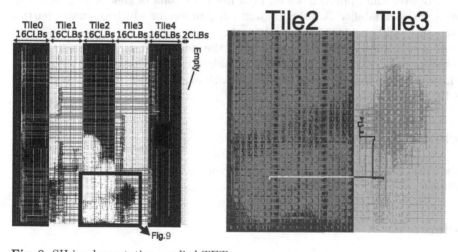

Fig. 8. SH implementation applied TFT

Fig. 9. Critical path in Fig.8

4.1 SuperH RISC Processor

SH, which is short for the SuperH RISC processor, is a name of microprocessor architecture produced by Hitachi Co.Ltd. [16], and is used in a large number of embedded systems. Aquarius is a SH compatible CPU core and freely available [17]. The main feature of Aquarius is the small circuit size required only about 2,900 slices on our implementation.

4.2   Implementation Results

Table 3 shows that the latency comparison between Fig.7 and Fig.8. The critical path in Fig.8 is a BM channel between tiles as shown in Fig.9. Its latency is 3.575ns and the time of a tri-state buffer induced by TFT is 0.603ns. It means that we can cut down on the critical path to 30.465ns (=33.437-(3.575-0.603)) through optimizing the circuit implementation based on the connection among tiles. This results show that TFT-related performance degradation is not critical.

5   Conclusion and Future Works

Aiming at the development of a dependable system with an FPGA, we proposed TFT in Section 2. We use remote-channel BMs with tri-state buffers and LUT-based BMs are used for a Virtex5 device in Section 3, and then Section 4 shows results from applying TFT to the implementation of a SuperH RISC processor core. Through our experiment, we reconfirm that PowerPC cores, BRAMs, and some hardware cores on an FPGA lead good performance for any other system but hinder its dependability because they make the circuit structure be much complicated than naive and old architechtures. In our current system environment, we can read out the content of distributed RAM and registers from partial bitstreams and implant its data directly into another-tile bitstream. In this regard, however, this approach is a bit poor from the point of view of its generation time and dependability. A no-redundant microprocessor which generates partial bitstreams will be serious bottleneck.

We note that, to solve these problems, the next stage is what an approach of circuits re-partition within a tile is considered on the basis of global routing architecture for circuit structure simplification. And then, other architecture [18,19] may be discussed.

Acknowledgments

This work was partially supported by Grant-in-Aid for Young Scientists (B) 20700044.

References

1. Cheatham, J.A., Emmert, J.M., Baumgart, S.: A survey of fault tolerant methodologies for FPGAs. ACM Trans. Des. Autom. Electron. Syst. 11(2), 501–533 (2006)
2. Swift, G.M.: Virtex-II Static SEU Characterization. XILINX Single Event Effects first Consortium Report (2004)
3. iRoC Technologies, Radiation results of the SER test of Actel, Xilinx and Altera FPGA instances (2004),
   http://www.actel.com/documents/OverviewRadResultsIROC.pdf
4. Quinn, H., Graham, P.: Terrestrial-Based Radiation Upsets: A Cautionary Tale. In: FCCM 2005, pp. 193–202 (2005)

5. Johnston, A.H., Swift, G.M., Shaw, D.C.: Impact of cmos scaling on single-event hard errors in space systems. In: Proc. of IEEE Symp. on Low Power Electronics, pp. 88–89 (October 1995)
6. White, M., Chen, Y.: Scaled cmos technology reliability users guide (March 2008)
7. Lesea, A., Percey, A.: Negative-bias temperature instability (nbti) effects in 90nm pmos, (November 2005),
   http://japan.xilinx.com/support/documentation/white_papers/wp224.pdf
8. Azizi, N., Yiannacouras, P.: Gate oxide breakdown (December 2003),
   http://citeseer.comp.nus.edu.sg/681500.html
9. Siewiorek, D.P., Swarz, R.S.: Theory and Practice of Reliable System Design. Digital Press, Bedford (1982)
10. Carmichael, C., Fuller, E., Fabula, J., Lima, F.D.: Proton testing of seu mitigation methods for the virtex fpga. In: Proc. of Int'l Conf. on Military and Aerospace Programmable Logic Devices (September 2001)
11. Lima, F., Carmichael, C., Fabula, J., Padovani, R., da Luz Reis, R.A.: A fault injection analysis of virtex fpga tmr design methodology. In: Proc. of Radiation and its Effects on Components and Systems, vol. 1, pp. 1–8 (2001)
12. XILINX Inc., XAPP290: Two Flows for Partial Reconfiguration: Module Based or Difference Based (September 2004)
13. XILINX Inc., XAPP290: Difference-Based Partial Reconfiguration (December 2007)
14. Kalte, H., Porrmann, M., Rückert, U.: System-on-programmable-chip approach enabling online fine-grained 1d-placement. In: Proc. of Int'l Symp. on Parallel and Distributed Processing, pp. 141–148 (April 2004)
15. Kawai, H., Yamaguchi, Y., Yasunaga, M.: Realization of the sound space environment for the radiation-tolerant space craft. In: ReConFig 2006, pp. 198–205 (September 2006)
16. SuperH RISC engine SH7040 series Sh7045, SH7044, SH7043, SH7042, SH7041, SH7040 Hardware Manual, 2nd edn., HITACHI, user Manual ADJ-602-128A (1997)
17. Aitch, T.: A Pipelined RISC CPU Aquarius (SuperH-2 ISA Compatible CPU Core) (July 2003), http://www.opencores.org/projects.cgi/web/aquarius/
18. Konishi, R., Ito, H., Nakada, H., Nagoya, A., Imlig, N., Shiozawa, T., Inamori, M., Nagami, K., Oguri, K.: PCA-1: A Fully Asynchronous, Self-Reconfigurable LSI. In: ASYNC 2001, Washington, DC, USA, p. 54 (2001)
19. Sugawara, T., Ide, K., Sato, T.: Dynamically Reconfigurable Processor Implemented with IPFlex's DAPDNA Technology. IEICE Transactions on Information and Systems 87(8), 1997–2003 (2004)

Regular Expression Pattern Matching Supporting Constrained Repetitions*

SangKyun Yun and KyuHee Lee

Department of Computer and Telecommunications Engineering,
Yonsei University, Wonju, Gangwon, 220-710, Korea
{skyun,powerpc}@yonsei.ac.kr

Abstract. In this paper we present regular expression pattern matching architecture supporting constrained repetitions. The proposed architecture can implement the constrained repetitions of a regular expression while previous works support only the constrained repetitions of a single character or a multi-cycle, fixed length pattern. The blocks for the constrained repetitions are simply implemented using a counter. The beginning constrained repetition blocks are implemented differently from the non-beginning blocks to support overlapped matching. The proposed architecture can implement all constrained repetitions used in Snort rule-sets with smaller resources.

1 Introduction

Regular expressions are widely used in the network intrusion detection system(NIDS) to represent attack patterns. Regular expressions can represent very large strings in compact forms. Signature-based NIDSs such as Snort rely on a multiple-pattern matching algorithm, where patterns may be represented as regular expressions. Regular expression pattern matching is a heavily computational task. Traditional software based NIDS fails to keep up with the throughput of high speed networks. To accelerate intrusion detection, there has been much work on hardware-based pattern matching, in particular, regular expression matching. Since the rule sets are continuously updated, FPGAs are commonly used for the hardware-based pattern matching.

Regular expressions can be implemented using NFA(non-deterministic finite automata) based compound blocks introduced by Sidhu and Prasanna [1]. However, they introduced only basic blocks such as concatenation, union(|), star(*). Regular expressions includes complex *constrained repetition* quantifiers such as Exactly($\{N\}$), AtLeast ($\{N,\}$), and Between ($\{N,M\}$) as well as simple quantifiers such as star(*), plus(+), question(?) [2]. Although there have been additional works about hardware-based regular pattern matching [3,4,5], there is no mention about constrained repetitions in their works.

Bispo et al. [6,7] introduced the implementation of constrained repetitions for the first time. However, their work implemented only constrained repetitions of single character using counters and Xilinx SRL16 shift registers They presented the synthesis of

---

* This work was supported by the Korea Research Foundation Grant funded by the Korean Government (KRF-2008-521-D00446).

J. Becker et al. (Eds.): ARC 2009, LNCS 5453, pp. 300–305, 2009.
© Springer-Verlag Berlin Heidelberg 2009

Table 1. Features of regular expressions

feature	description	feature	description
$RE_1 \mid RE_2$	(Union) RE_1 or RE_2	.	any character except new line
RE*	zero or more times RE	^	start of input
RE+	one or more times RE	$	end of input
RE?	zero of one times RE	[...]	character class
RE{N}	(Exactly) N times RE	[^...]	negate character class
RE{N,}	(AtLeast) N or more times RE	\d, \w,\s	shorthand character classes
RE{N,M}	(Between) between N and M times RE	\x$nn$	hexadecimal number nn

multi-cycle constrained repetitions as an open issues [8]. Recently, Bispo also proposed the solution for multi-cycle, fixed-length constrained repetitions [9]. However, they did not implement the constrained repetitions of a general regular expression.

In this paper, we propose the hardware solution which implements constrained repetitions of a regular expression. This paper is organized as follows. Section 2 describes related works and section 3 proposes the hardware solution of constrained repetitions. Section 4 evaluates the proposed architecture and section 5 presents the conclusion.

2 Related Work

A regular expression describes a set of strings without enumerating them explicitly. Table 1 lists the common features of regular expressions used in Snort rule sets [10]. There are three constrained repetition quantifiers such as Exactly, AtLeast, and Between in regular expressions. Although the recent rule-sets include many constrained repetitions, the hardware implementation of constrained repetitions has been proposed recently by Bispo and Sourdis et al. [6,7]. They implement the constrained repetition blocks using a counter and special shift registers SRL16 in Xilinx FPGAs.

However, their implementation has some drawbacks as follows. First, they implement only single-cycle repetitions such as $a\{5\}$ and $(a|b)\{20\}$. Multi-cycle repetitions such as $(abc)\{10\}$ and $(ab+)\{20\}$ must be implemented using full-unrolling, which may require large amount of hardware resources. Second, the required number of shift register SRL16s in Exactly and Between blocks is $\lceil N/17 \rceil$, which is proportional to N. Third, since they use a vendor-specific resource SRL16, we cannot use their architecture in other vendors' FPGAs

Bispo also proposed the hardware implementation of multi-cycle, fixed-length constrained repetitions [9]. However, multi-cycle, variable-length constrained repetitions are not supported.

Therefore, we need to develop the hardware architecture for the constrained repetition of a general regular expression without using vendor specific shift registers. In next section, we propose more efficient implementation method of constrained repetitions using only a counter and glue logic. Our method supports the constrained repetitions of general regular expressions including multi-cycle, variable length constrained repetitions.

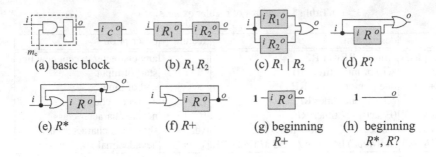

(a) basic block   (b) $R_1 R_2$ (c) $R_1 \mid R_2$ (d) $R?$

(e) $R*$ (f) $R+$ (g) beginning   (h) beginning
                                          $R+$ $R*, R?$

Fig. 1. Hardware blocks for basic regular expression primitives

3   Proposed Architecture

In this section, we present the regular expression pattern matching hardware architecture supporting constrained repetitions. The basic regular expression operators except constrained repetitions are implemented based on the previous works [1,6] as shown in Fig 1(a)-(f). Since patterns can start at any position of the input string, pattern matching is required to be evaluated in every position of the input string. This is called *overlapped matching*. To implement overlapped matching, the input of a beginning block remains high(1) during pattern matching. The beginning repetition blocks are reduced to Fig. 1 (g) and (h) since their inputs are 1. In other words, the beginning $R+$ is implemented as R and the beginning $R*$ and $R?$ are skipped.

The hardware architecture for constrained repetitions is also affected by their positions in regular expressions. So, we implement differently constrained repetition blocks in two cases: non-beginning blocks and beginning blocks.

Non-beginning constrained Repetition Blocks

Fig. 2 illustrates the hardware blocks of the constrained repetitions which are not at the beginning of a pattern. R is a regular expression and the constrained repetition blocks of R are implemented using a counter. The proposed architecture can implement the multi-cycle, variable length constrained repetitions since R is a regular expression, while previous works [6,9] cannot implement them.

The block R is first implemented, and then the constrained repetition of R is implemented. If R contains Δ characters or character classes, there are Δ flip-flops in the block R. In Fig. 2, the output z of the block R, denoted by R_z, is 1 when all the flip-flops in the block are zero, which means that there is no matched character in the block R. The input i and the output o of the block R are denoted by R_i and R_o, respectively.

The Exactly block $R\{N\}$ is illustrated in Fig. 2(a). It uses a modulo-N counter which requires $\log_2 N$ bits. The counter is initially zero and is incremented whenever R_o is 1. When R_o is 1, if the counter is $N - 1$, the output of the Exactly block is 1; otherwise, R_o gives feedback to R_i, which reactivates matching of subsequent R. When the output becomes 1, the feedback is stopped so that the hardware block cannot perform pattern matching for subsequent R. The counter is reset when R_z is 1.

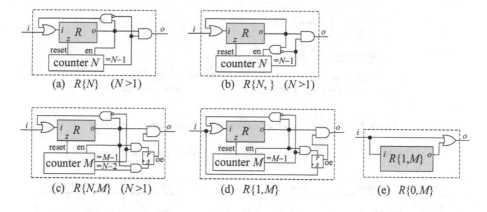

Fig. 2. Hardware blocks for constrained repetitions

The AtLeast block $R\{N,\}$ is illustrated in Fig. 2(b). It also uses a modulo-N counter. R_o always gives feedback to R_i since there is no upper bound in the number of repetitions. When R_o is 1, if the counter is $N - 1$, the output of the AtLeast block is 1; otherwise, the counter is incremented. If the counter is $N - 1$, the counter is not enable and remains $N - 1$ so that the output of the AtLeast block is 1 for subsequent Rs. The counter is reset when R_z is 1.

The Between block $R\{N,M\}$ is illustrated in Fig. 2(c)-(e). It uses a modulo-M counter and a flip-flop with synchronous reset and set. A flip-flop oe is 1 when the counter is between $N - 1$ and $M - 1$. The counter is incremented whenever R_o is 1. When R_o is 1, if the flip-flop oe is 1 (the counter is between $N - 1$ and $M - 1$), the output of the Between block is 1 and if the counter is not $M - 1$, R_o gives feedback to R_i. The counter is reset when R_z is 1. If N is 1, the input of the Between block is used as the set input of the flip-flop oe as shown in Fig. 2(d) and if N is 0, the Between block is implemented as shown in Fig. 2(e).

Beginning constrained Repetition Blocks

When the AtLeast repetition $R\{N,\}$ is at the beginning of a pattern, its block in Fig. 2(b) is reduced to Fig. 3(a) since its input is 1. However, the beginning $R\{N\}$ and $R\{N,M\}$ should be implemented as $R\{N,\}$ in order to support overlapped matching. For example, consider a pattern $a\{3\}bc$ and an input string "$aaaaabc\cdots$". The pattern $a\{3\}bc$ matches with the input string from the third input characters. This match is possible if the beginning $a\{3\}$ is implemented as $a\{3,\}$.

The beginning $R\{N,\}$ block in Fig. 3(a) may generate the wrong matching output if R is a pattern whose suffix and prefix are overlapped (called *SP-overlap*[9]). For example, consider a pattern $(aba)\{3\}$ and an input "$ababaaba\cdots$". The pattern aba is SP-overlapped pattern. The beginning block generates the match output at the third underlined a, but this is wrong. The wrong result occurs since R_z does not become 1 due to SP-overlap although the first repetition of aba is stopped at the fourth character b. If we implement $R\{N\}$ as $RR\{N - 1\}$ as shown in Fig. 3(b), this problem due to SP overlap is solved since the constrained repetition is not at the beginning of a pattern any longer.

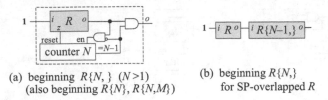

(a) beginning $R\{N, \}$ $(N > 1)$
(also beginning $R\{N\}, R\{N,M\}$)

(b) beginning $R\{N,\}$
for SP-overlapped R

Fig. 3. Hardware blocks for beginning constrained repetitions

Table 2. Comparison of the constrained repetition implementations

constraint repetitions	Bispo'06	Bispo'08	Our architecture
single-cycle	O	O	O
multi-cycle, fixed-length	×	O	O
multi-cycle, variable-length	×	×	O
Exactly block ($R\{N\}$)	$\lceil N/17 \rceil$ SRL16/FFs 4-bit counter	$\log_2 N$-bit counter $\log_2(\Delta \times N)$-bit counter* $\lceil \Delta \times N/17 \rceil$ SRL16/FFs*	$\log_2 N$-bit counter
AtLeast block ($R\{N,\}$)	$\log_2 N$-bit counter	unknown	$\log_2 N$-bit counter
Between block ($R\{N,M\}$)	$\lceil N/17 \rceil$ SRL16/FFs $\log_2 N$-bit counter $\log_2(M-N)$-bit counter	unknown	$\log_2 M$-bit counter a flip-flop(FF)

* Δ is the number of cycles of each repetition R and these resources are not used for beginning constraint repetitions.

4 Evaluation

Table 2 shows the comparison of the constrained repetition implementations among three architectures with respect to the supporting types of constrained repetitions and the required resources. The proposed architecture supports the implementation of all kinds of practical constrained repetitions. The required resource size in the proposed architecture is smaller than that in previous methods since our architecture requires only the counter and some glue logic. Our architecture does not use a SRL16 shift register which is vendor-specific and whose required size is proportional to N.

The proposed architecture cannot fully support overlapped matching for the following types of repeated patterns R although it can implement the constrained repetitions of almost all regular expressions.

1. A repeated regular expression R consists of the union of several patterns and one of them is prefix of another patterns. For example, consider a pattern $(R_1 R_2 | R_1)\{2\}$. For an input $R_1 R_2$, the block R $(= R_1 R_2 | R_1)$ generates its output twice and so, the constrained repetition block generates the match output. However, this is wrong.
2. A repeated regular expression R consists of the union of several patterns and one of them is the pattern preceding the constrained repetition of R. For example, consider a pattern $R_1(R_1 | R_2)\{2\}R_3$. Although an input $R_1 R_1 R_2 R_1 R_3$ matches with the given pattern, the proposed architecture does not generate the match output. This problem

can be solved by using additionally a $(N-1)$-bit shift register although the detailed block is not introduced in this paper.

However, these types of patterns are not found in Snort rule-sets. Thus, the proposed architecture can implement all the constrained repetitions in Snort rule-sets.

5   Conclusions

This paper proposed hardware architecture for the implementation of the constrained repetitions in a regular expression. The proposed architecture supports the implementation of constrained repetitions of almost all regular expressions. In particular, our architecture can implement all constrained repetitions in Snort rule-sets. The constrained repetition blocks are implemented using only a counter and some glue logic. The beginning constrained repetition block is implemented differently from the non-beginning one in order to support the overlapped matching. Thus, the proposed architecture is an efficient architecture that can implement the constrained repetitions of a general regular expression with smaller resources.

References

1. Sidhu, R., Prasanna, V.K.: Fast regular expression matching using FPGAs. In: IEEE Symp. Field Prog. Custom Comput. Machines (FCCM 2001), pp. 227–238 (2001)
2. PCRE: Perl compatible regular expressions, http://www.pcre.org
3. Hutchings, B.L., Franklin, R., Carver, D.: Assisting network intrusion detection with reconfigurable hardware. In: IEEE Symp. Field Prog. Custom Comput. Machines (FCCM 2002), pp. 111–120 (2002)
4. Sutton, P.: Partial character decoding for improved regular expression matching in fpgas. In: Int. Conf. Field-Programmable Logic and App (FPL 2006), pp. 25–32 (2004)
5. Lin, C.H., Huang, C.T., Jiang, C.P., Chang, S.C.: Optimization of regular expression pattern matching circuits on FPGA. In: Conf. Design, Automation and Test in Europe (DATE 2006), pp. 12–17 (2006)
6. Bispo, J.C., Sourdis, I., Cardoso, J.M., Vassiliadis, S.: Regular expression matching for reconfigurable packet inspection. In: IEEE Int. Conf. Field Programmable Technology (FPT 2006), pp. 119–126 (2006)
7. Sourdis, I., Vassiliadis, S., Bispo, J.C., Cardoso, J.M.: Regular expression matching in reconfigurable hardware. J. Signal Processing Systems 51(1), 99–121 (2008)
8. Bispo, J., Sourdis, I., Cardoso, J.M.P., Vassiliadis, S.: Synthesis of regular expressions targeting FPGAs: Current status and open issues. In: Diniz, P.C., Marques, E., Bertels, K., Fernandes, M.M., Cardoso, J.M.P. (eds.) ARCS 2007. LNCS, vol. 4419, pp. 179–190. Springer, Heidelberg (2007)
9. Bispo, J., Cardoso, J.M.: Synthesis of regular expressions for FPGAs. Int. J Electronics 95(7), 685–704 (2008)
10. Sourcefire: SNORT official web site, http://www.snort.org

Accelerating Calculations on the RASC Platform: A Case Study of the Exponential Function

Maciej Wielgosz, Ernest Jamro, and Kazimierz Wiatr

AGH University of Science and Technology,
al. Mickiewicza 30, 30-059 Krakow
ACK Cyfronet AGH
ul. Nawojki 11, 30-950 Krakow
{wielgosz,jamro,wiatr}@agh.edu.pl

Abstract. This paper presents results of the tests performed to determine high speed calculations capabilities of the SGI RASC platform. Different data transfer modes and memory management approaches were examined to choose the most effective combination of the Host and RASC memory adjustments. Obtained results of measurements revealed that Direct I/O mode together with DMA transfer provides the highest data throughput between the Host and RASC slice. Nevertheless, for some application multi-buffering may appear to be more suitable in terms of concurrent data transfer capabilities and FPGA algorithm execution. As an example of calculation to be accelerated the exponent function is taken for which computation speed is far beyond data transfer capability of the RASC platform.

Keywords: HPRC (High Performance Reconfigurable Computing), FPGA, exponent function.

1 Introduction

It has been investigated for a long time how to employ FPGA chips in HPC systems, not only as coprocessors, but also as a highly efficient computation module. It is worth enumerating several factors preventing FPGAs from being widely implemented in HPC solutions. The first one would be the need to increase effectiveness of the floating point calculations on FPGAs since this sort of computation is the predominant part of scientific applications run on HPC machines. SGI RASC RC100 [1] has been challenged on this issue by implementing double precision floating point modules as the test bench structure, results of which are presented in this paper. Another factor is GPUs [2] (Graphic Processor Unit) rising capabilities of high speed calculations, posing a challenge for FPGAs which are still struggling with interface issues within one system. Many vendors (e.g. SGI, SRC, DRC, Xtreme-Data) try to address these issues by releasing platforms which are equipped with multi-dimensional data transmission systems to keep up with the computational demands.

J. Becker et al. (Eds.): ARC 2009, LNCS 5453, pp. 306–311, 2009.
© Springer-Verlag Berlin Heidelberg 2009

The exponential function is commonly used in quantum chemistry algorithms. Therefore a question arise whether a single exp() function calculation can be accelerated on FPGAs; whether system overheads i.e. data transfers cause that employing FPGAs results in calculation speed-up. Consequently different data transfer modes have been tested both on the host and RASC side to provide the highest achievable data bandwidth. SGI provides RASC together with C-language software drivers. Nevertheless no implementation results (e.g. real data transfer throughput, latency) are provided. Therefore the main idea behind this article is to find out how FPGAs configuration time, data transfer influence the whole system speed-up. Both FPGAs configuration time on the host side was measured and possibility of concurrent software routines execution was tested. It should be noted that for both wavelet transform [5] and exponential function, the performance bottleneck is data transfer limit rather than FPGAs calculation speed.

2   SGI Altix 4700 with RASC

The Altix 4700 series is a family of multiprocessor distributed shared memory (DSM) computer systems that currently ranges from 8 to 512 CPU sockets (up to 1,024 processor cores) and can accommodate up to 6TB of globally shared memory in a single system while delivering a teraflop of performance in a small-footprint rack.

The RASC hardware blade contains two computational FPGAs, two TIO ASICs, and a loader FPGA for loading bitstreams into the FPGAs. The RASC blade has two Xilinx Virtx-4 LX200s on the board and memory resources with 10 synchronous static RAM modules (SSRAM DIMMs), which are grouped in three logical memory structures.

Two exp() functions have been implemented [4], each of which processes a 64-bit data chunk, so each clock cycle one 128 bit input word is fed into the implemented twin module structure and one result is obtained. SGI RASC v2.1 [1] device has four transmission/managing modes, two Host and two RASC settings. These options cover the huge spectrum of potential memory division and managing methods.

It is worth emphasizing that data transfer optimization is done on the Host side as well as on the RASC side. The method to apply the presented modes will be described later on in this paper.

3   RASC Memory Managing Modes

3.1   SRAM Buffering

This mode involves allocating data to the RASC SRAM memory. Input data must be transferred to one of the three SRAM banks, then user logic implemented in FPGA starts execution of the algorithm routine and calculations results are written back to memory. It is advisable to choose two different memory banks to make application execution more fluent.

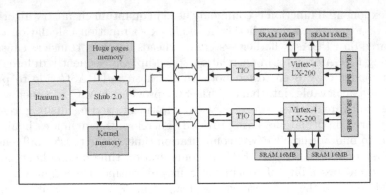

Fig. 1. Communication paths between host node and RASC slice

All the steps are conducted in sequence in contrast to multi-buffering mode. Implementation of the SRAM buffering mode leads to a three-stage data transfer operation for a single algorithm execution which in turn is time-consuming. However there is multi-buffering transfer mode which allows FPGA to concurrently transfer the data and perform calculations since Core services logic allows these two activities to be done simultaneously.

The RASC algorithm execution procedure, from processors perspective, is composed of several functions which reserve resources, queue commands and perform other preparation steps. It is noteworthy [Fig. 2] that the time consumed by the functions remains roughly the same value, independent of the algorithm being executed. The resource reservation procedure, once conducted, allows many runnings of the algorithm which amounts to huge time savings, since the procedure takes approximately 7.5 ms, which is roughly 99 % of overall execution time of the algorithm. Rasclib_algorithm_commit() and rasclib_algorithm_wait() calls are considered to be the key [Fig. 2] part of the RASC software execution routine. The first one activates FPGA algorithm, the second one waits for the completion flag. The period between these two commands is the transfer and algorithm execution time. All curves [Fig. 3] reflect overall processing time of the same amount of data, but differ in size of the single data chunk, which varies from 1024x64 bit = 8 kB to 1048576x64 bit = 8 MB. It has been observed that for the bigger chunk much better results are achieved in terms of effective execution time. However above 1 MB, a decrease of effective execution time seems to indicate saturation, therefore sending data in bigger portions may not improve the performance of the system so much. The most effective execution time of a single exp() function for SRAM buffering mode is 12 ns, so 9,5 ns is transport overhead due to bus delays. Theoretical calculation time of a single exp() function (data transfer is not taken into account) is 2.5 ns because two exp() are implemented on the RASC and clocked at 200 MHz[4].

It should be noted that the software drivers delivered by SGI are not optimized for multithreaded applications, i.e. a microprocessor is continually occupied by the SGI functions. Consequently a computation task cannot be divided into a

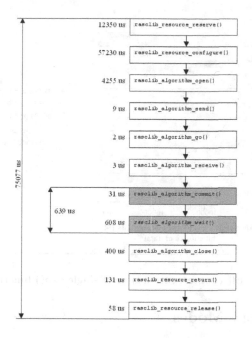

Fig. 2. Time estimations of rasclib function execution

microprocessors and FPGAs concurrent parts, e.g. the exp() function cannot be concurrently calculated on both microprocessor and FPGAs to further speed-up calculations. As a result, FPGAs should be employed only if the FPGAs solution together with data transfer and other system overheads offers a speed-up over a microprocessor solution. This holds even when a FPGAs is in an idle state. The above statement was practically proved by an insertion of an idle loop among the SGI functions. The total calculation time was increased by the loop calculation time. It is however possible to insert software routines between the commit() and wait() functions and run them concurrently with hardware accelerated procedures since wait() function does not absorb a processors computational power. Optimal structure of the hardware accelerated application should contain as few as possible initializations of the FPGA chips and also take advantage of processors lack of an activity between executions of commit() and wait() functions.

3.2   DMA Streaming

DMA streaming mode does not involve allocating SRAM memory to the RASC platform. Such an approach allows to save the time that would otherwise be consumed delivering data to onboard memory and then fetch the results from SRAM. Data is streaming directly through the Core Services logic to the algorithm block. Streaming DMA reduces effective time of single exp() execution to 7,8 ns.

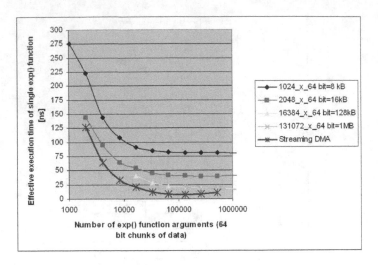

Fig. 3. Effective execution time of single exp() function

4   Host Memory Modes

Operating systems attempt to make the best use of the limited number of TLB (Translation Lookaside Buffer) resources. This optimization is more critical now as bigger and bigger physical memories (several GBs) are more readily available. A hugepage is a memory page of larger size than an ordinary page. They are usually available in multiple sizes, often up to several megabytes. Each hugepage occupies only one entry in the TLB, so the TLB coverage dramatically increases. This results in performance improvements of over 30% in many cases [1]. There are two memory modes available on the host, Buffered and Direct mode. The Direct mode takes advantage of hugepages to accelerate data transfers.

4.1   Buffered I/O Mode

Buffered I/O involves allocating memory for input and output data in the user space on the host. Unfortunately transferring the data to/from the SRAM on RC100 blade using buffered I/O involves an additional copy in the kernel memory space, thus lowering the maximum throughput.

4.2   Direct I/O Mode

Data to be processed by the algorithm is located on the *hugepages* by issuing dedicated API functions. The data is streamed from the *hugepages* memory on the host to the SRAM on the RC100 Blade, which results in significantly shorter transfer time in contrast to Buffered I/O mode.

Host memory management plays a crucial role, therefore it is advisable to take advantage of the hugepages by choosing the Direct I/O mode to achieve the highest acceleration. Switching between Buffered I/O and Direct I/O mode is quite a simple operation and requires only a change of the flag in rasclib_open function.

5 Summary

SGI RASC is the modern platform providing a handy tool to design HPRC applications. According to the results of the tests that were carried out to verify SGI transfer rate estimations, 3.2 GB/s as the top bandwidth has not been reached. Several measurements that have been conducted, applying different adjustments of the transfer parameters, have shown that DMA streaming together with Direct I/O is the most effective data transfer mode for the quantum chemistry application that we aim to accelerate.However the multi-buffering mode is also considered to be effective in terms of data transfer and algorithm execution time optimization.

For the quantum chemistry calculation perspective the following conclusion can be drawn from the implementation results: RASC calculation speed-up for a single exp() function calculated on a large vector is not obtained due to the data transfer overheads. In order to obtain calculation speed-up, some more functions must be incorporated into a single FPGAs to reduce transfer overheads.

References

1. Silicon Graphics, Inc. Reconfigurable Application-Specific Computing User's Guide, Ver. 005, SGI (January 2007)
2. Giles, M.: GPU's - the next big advance in HPC? In: Reconfigurable Supercomputing Conference (MRSC), Oxford University, Belfast, Northern Ireland, April 1-3 (2008)
3. Mazur, G., Makowski, M.: Development and Optimization of Computational Chemistry Algorithms. In: KDM 2008, Zakopane, Poland (March 2008)
4. Wielgosz, M., Jamro, E., Wiatr, K.: Highly Efficient Structure of 64-Bit Exponential Function Implemented in FPGAs. In: Woods, R., Compton, K., Bouganis, C., Diniz, P.C. (eds.) ARC 2008. LNCS, vol. 4943, pp. 274–279. Springer, Heidelberg (2008)
5. Mitra, A., Yao, G., Najjar, W.: Performance Analysis of SGI RASC RC100 Blade on 1-D DWT. In: Proceedings of the Third Annual Reconfigurable Systems Summer Institute (RSSI 2007), USA, Urbana, July 17-20 (2007)
6. Litke, A.G.: "'Turning the Page"'on Hugetlb Interfaces, IBM. In: Proceedings of the Linux Symposium, Ottawa, Ontario Canada, June 27th-30th (2007), agl@us.ibm.com

AES-Galois Counter Mode Encryption/Decryption FPGA Core for Industrial and Residential Gigabit Ethernet Communications

Jesús Lázaro, Armando Astarloa, Unai Bidarte,
Jaime Jiménez, and Aitzol Zuloaga

Escuela Superior de Ingenieros,
University of the Basque Country
Alameda Urquijo s/n
48013 Bilbao, Spain
{jesus.lazaro,armando.astarloa,unai.bidarte,
jaime.jimenez,aitzol.zuloaga}@.ehu.es
http://det.bi.ehu.es/~apert

Abstract. This paper presents an AES-GCM) core. This core has been designed and implemented taking into account two main aspects: It should provide a real throughput, capable of feeding a Gigabit Ethernet, and should be implemented in a commercial FPGA as part of a System-on-a-Chip (SoC). The AES-GCM encryption/authentication algorithm is of key importance as the fact of being introduced in four different standards, from Ethernet to mass storage devices, suggests. This algorithm is interesting because of two different reasons, first it provides authentication and encryption at the same time, and second its structure is highly parallelized. It is composed of two main blocks: an encryption core (AES in current standards) and a Galois Field multiplier.

1 Introduction

In the past few years several Calls for Algorithms have been made in the field of encryption and security. Some of these were looking for a new private key block cipher as with the Advanced Encryption Standard (AES) project [1]. Since both encryption and authentication are required in most applications, there are algorithms designed to perform both operations at the same time, the so called *Authenticated encryption*. Algorithms that fall into this category include CBC-MAC (CCM) [2], OCB mode [3], EAX [4] and Galois/Counter Mode (GCM) [5].

GCM mode combines the counter mode of encryption with the new Galois mode of authentication. GCM mode is used in the IEEE 802.1AE (MACsec) [6] Ethernet security, ANSI (INCITS) Fibre Channel Security Protocols (FC-SP) [7], IEEE P1619.1 tape storage [8], and IETF IPSec standards [9].

There exist several AES-GCM implementations in the literature [10, 11, 12]. They obtain a very high throughput, in excess of 30 Gbps depending on the

J. Becker et al. (Eds.): ARC 2009, LNCS 5453, pp. 312–317, 2009.
© Springer-Verlag Berlin Heidelberg 2009

implementation, but they are focused in an ASIC implementation, not an FPGA flexible implementation as the presented in this paper.

The rest of the paper is organized as follows. The first deals with the GCM algorithm and its structure, the next two sections are focused on the two main blocks of the GCM algorithm (multiplication in GF and AES). The following section explains the timing considerations for an optimal GCM core. The paper ends with the hardware results and final conclusions.

2   Overall Structure

The Galois/Counter Mode (GCM) of operation for block ciphers was designed to meet the need for an authenticated encryption mode that can efficiently achieve high speeds in hardware, can perform well in software, and is free of intellectual property restrictions. GCM has several useful features: it can accept IVs (Initial Vector) of arbitrary length, can act as a stand-alone message authentication code (MAC), and can be used as an incremental MAC [13]. Another useful feature is the ability to authenticate associated data that is not part of the message, such as packet headers.

2.1   Algorithm Structure

The GCM encryption operation is defined by several equations [5]. The first step is to calculate H, one of the factors of the GF128 product. To do so, a vector consisting of 128 zeroes is encrypted using the K key. The result is the H vector.

The second step is to calculate the initial value of the counter. This initial value (Y_0) can be calculated in two different ways depending on the length of the initial vector (IV). If the Initial vector is 96 bit wide, Y_0 is obtained appending 31 zeroes and a single '1'. Otherwise, Y_0 is the result of multiplying, in GF128, the H vector and IV.

This initial counter is incremented whenever a new word is encrypted and authenticated. This increment only affects the lower 32 bits of the counter. The encryption of the data (C) is done xoring the plaintext data (P) with the encrypted counter$(E(K, Y_i))$ using the initial key (K).

Data authentication is performed using a GF128 multiplier and multiplying the input data by the H vector. The value of the authenticating tag (T) is found using the last multiplication result and the encrypted value of the initial state of the counter.

Due to the internal structure of the algorithm, the decryption is done in the same way as encryption. The tag T' that is computed by the decryption operation is compared to the tag T associated with the message. If the two tags match (in both length and value), the message is returned as valid.

2.2   Hardware Structure

The implemented hardware follows the algorithm except in three points. First of all, the IV vector is always supposed to be 96 bit wide; second, the data (both A and P) must be an integer number of octets and finally the key must be 128 bit wide in order to use a standard AES block. These three points fulfil the requirements of the 802.1AE standard. The hardware is built around two main blocks, the GF128 multiplier and the AES encryption core. There is a third block that is in charge of controlling the whole design.

The GF128 multipliers accepts three different inputs: the data to be only authenticated (A), the encrypted data (C) and the combined length (L). The AES module accepts two inputs: the *all-zero* vector to calculate H and the counter value Y. The Y register is composed of two different parts, a register for the IV and an up counter with initial value '1'.

3   GF128 Multiplier

The GF128 multiplier is in charge of multiplying over the Galois Field $GF\ 2^{128}$ with generating polynomial $1+\alpha+\alpha^2+\alpha^7+\alpha^{128}$. The GF128 multiplier has two different elements: a non saturating multiplier and a normalizer. The multiplier is in charge of multiplying two inputs, one the H vector and the other one varies according to the data to be authenticated. The multiplication is identical to an arithmetic long multiplication except that the additions are substituted by the *xor* operation. The normalizer is in charge of converting the product into a valid GF128 number, this is done by dividing the result by the generating polynomial (changing subtractions for *xors*) and letting the remainder be the result.

3.1   Non Saturating Multiplier

The non saturating multiplier is a normal multiplier with the addition substituted by *xors*. In order to reduce the amount of resources required, the multiplier has been implemented in a sequential way thus the full product requires several clock cycles. In order to optimize the core, the Virtex5 6 input LUT has been used to full extent. A 6 input LUT is capable of calculating the product of a 3 by 3 number. Taking into account that there are no carries (no additions), each of the 3 by 3 products can be calculated independently. This basic structure is replicated to calculate a 128 by 3 product (3 lines of the long multiplication) to obtain a partial product. This line structure is replicated as many times as needed and the result is *xor*ed to obtain the result of the current cycle (partial result of the multiplication).

3.2   Normalizer

General considerations. In order to normalize the non saturated product (P), we must calculate an intermediate value, L, the most significant bit of every division step (see figure 1).

L values are calculated following the next equation. N is the number of bits of the original factors of the product. It must be noted that the most significant L bit is calculated first since lower bits depend on higher bits.

$$\frac{G_4 G_3 G_2 G_1 G_0 \big| L_2}{L_2 L_1 L_0} \equiv \begin{array}{ccccccc} P_6 & P_5 & P_4 & P_3 & P_2 & P_1 & P_0 \\ & & L_1 & X & X & X & P_1 \\ & & L_0 & X & X & X & P_0 \\ & & & M_3 & M_2 & M_1 & M_0 \end{array}$$

Fig. 1. Long division of the non saturated product (P) by the generating polynomial (G) to obtain the module (M) of the division. Instead of subtractions, *xors* are used. L is the most significant bit of every division step.

$$L_j = P_{N+j} \bigwedge \left(\bigoplus_{i=0}^{N-2-(j+1)} L_{j+i+1} \bigwedge G_{N-1-i} \right), \quad j = N-2 \ldots 0 \qquad (1)$$

Once the L values are known, the modulus can be calculated. This is because knowing the L values means knowing whether the P values must be *xored* with the generating polynomial G.

$$M_j = P_j \bigwedge \left(\bigoplus_{i=0}^{j} L(i) \bigwedge G_{j-i} \right), \quad j = 0 \ldots N-2 \qquad (2)$$

$$M_{N-1} = P_{N-1} \bigwedge \left(\bigoplus_{i=0}^{N-2} L_i \bigwedge G_{N-1-i} \right)$$

Particular considerations. Since each L value requires all the previous L values, this creates a combinational chain. This chain can be potentially very large, leading to high combinational times and thus, low operational frequency. In the case of a $GF\ 2^{128}$ multiplier, the polynomial is 129 bit wide ($N = 128$) leading to a L chain of 126 bits.

This could be a very limiting factor if it weren't for the low density in '1's of the generating polynomial and the fact that they are located in the lower part of the polynomial. The $GF\ 2^{128}$ only has 5 bits different to zero $(1+\alpha+\alpha^2+\alpha^7+\alpha^{128})$ leading to a very compact L representation. The first 120 bits of L are directly the P bits (the distance from α^{128} to α^7). The chain only appears in the lower 6 bits and even there it is only 3 elements deep (number of '1' in the first 126 bits of the generating polynomial).

A similar problem arises with the modulus itself (M). Each bit in the modulus requires all the L bits with index equal or smaller than the modulus index. This means that for the two most significant bits of the modulus, a function 127 bit wide could be necessary –the 126 bit L plus the corresponding product bit (P). This kind of functions are impractical but since the generating polynomial is sparse, the resulting equation is much simpler. Since in the generation of M the most significant bit of the polynomial is not present, the widest function is 5 bit wide (the P result plus 4 L bits).

4   AES Module

The AES module used in this design is an open source module from OPEN-CORES [14]. The AES cipher core consists of a key expansion module, an initial permutation module, a round permutation module and a final permutation module. The forward cipher block can perform a complete encrypt sequence in 12 clock cycles (10 cycles for the 10 rounds, plus one cycle for initial key expansion, and one cycle for the output stage). The forward cipher block accepts a key and the plain text at the beginning of each encrypt sequence. The beginning is always indicated by asserting a pin high.

5   Results

5.1   Timing Considerations

The number of cycles needed to obtain a valid data depends on the size of the data to be authenticated and encrypted but there is an inherent overhead. There are three unavoidable processes: H, E_0 and the final length multiplication. Since the encryption and multiplication time is almost the same and equal to approximately 26 cycles (25 of the product and an extra cycle for interfacing), we can express the throughput of the system as:

$$T = \frac{D \cdot F}{(\lfloor D/128 \rfloor + 6) \cdot 26} \tag{3}$$

Where T is the throughput in Mbits/s if D is the data size in bits and F is the clock frequency in MHz.

5.2   Hardware Results

In table 1 the area results (after place and route) for the proposed architecture in a Xilinx 5vlx50t FPGA can be found. This kind of FPGA has been selected since it has a hardware 10/100/1000 Ethernet MAC Block. As it can be seen, the core requires less than 10 % of the FPGA, leaving plenty of room to incorporate all the necessary cores to complete a SoC device. Focusing on the time results, the systems gives an overall frequency of 294 MHz leading to the required speed for successful Gigabit Ethernet performance. Without taking into account the overhead of the Ethernet, the core is capable of authenticating/encrypting with a throughput of 1.4 Gbps.

Table 1. Hardware area results when implemented in a Xilinx 5vlx50t FPGA

Number of RAMB18X2s	5	8%
Number of Slice Registers	2656	9%
Number of Slice LUTS	2506	8%
Number of DCM_ADVs	1	8%

6   Conclusions

This paper presents a FPGA core capable of encrypting and authenticating following the AES-GCM algorithm as described in the 802.1AE Secure MAC standard. The core is capable of delivering enough real throughput to be connected to a Gigabit Ethernet network, that is to say, taking into account the required inherent overhead of the Ethernet and the possible key change.

The design is focused on the use of an FPGA due to its configurable nature, that allows different designs to be implemented, depending on the requirements of area and speed. The core is flexible in terms of area/speed tradeoff and in terms of cryptographic modules. The circuit achieves the required area and speed through the use of an efficient Galois Field multiplier. The design is also area efficient using less than a 10 % of the selected FPGA.

The correctness of the algorithm has been tested using a simple comparison with software implementation.

Acknowledgment. This work has been supported by the project S-PE01UN1, a public research project funded by the Basque Government.

References

1. US NIST: Advanced Encryption Standard
2. Whiting, D., Housley, R., Ferguson, N.: Counter with CBC-MAC (CCM). RFC3610 (September 2003)
3. Rogaway, P., Bellare, M., Black, J.: OCB: A block-cipher mode of operation for efficient authenticated encryption. ACM Tr. Inf. Syst. Sec. 6(3), 365–403 (2003)
4. Bellare, M., Rogaway, P., Wagner, D.: The EAX Mode of Operation. In: Roy, B., Meier, W. (eds.) FSE 2004. LNCS, vol. 3017, pp. 389–407. Springer, Heidelberg (2004)
5. McGrew, D., Viega, J.: The Galois/Counter Mode of Operation, GCM (2004)
6. IEEE 802.1AE-2006 Media Access Control (MAC) Security. IEEE Standards Department (2006)
7. American National Standard for Information Technology: Fibre Channel Security Protocols (FC-SP). INCITS 1570-D
8. P1619.1: Standard for Authenticated Encryption with Length Expansion for Storage Devices. IEEE Standards Department (2006)
9. Viega, J., McGrew, D.: The Use of Galois/Counter Mode (GCM) in IPsec Encapsulating Security Payload (ESP). RFC4106 (June 2005)
10. Yang, B., Mishra, S., Karri, R.: A High Speed Architecture for Galois/Counter Mode of Operation (GCM). Cryptology ePrint Archive, Report 2005/146 (2005)
11. Satoh, A.: High-speed hardware architectures for authenticated encryption mode GCM. In: Proceedings. 2006 IEEE International Symposium on Circuits and Systems, 2006. ISCAS 2006, 4 p. (2006)
12. Lemsitzer, S., Wolkerstorfer, J., Felber, N., Braendli, M.: Multi-gigabit GCM-AES Architecture Optimized for FPGAs. In: Paillier, P., Verbauwhede, I. (eds.) CHES 2007. LNCS, vol. 4727, pp. 227–238. Springer, Heidelberg (2007)
13. Bellare, M., Goldreich, O., Goldwasser, S.: Incremental Cryptography: The Case of Hashing and Signing. In: Desmedt, Y.G. (ed.) CRYPTO 1994. LNCS, vol. 839, p. 216. Springer, Heidelberg (1994)
14. Usselmann, R.: AES (Rijndael) IP Core. Opencores (2004)

CCproc: A Custom VLIW Cryptography Co-processor for Symmetric-Key Ciphers

Dimitris Theodoropoulos[1,2], Alexandros Siskos[1], and Dionisis Pnevmatikatos[1]

[1] ECE Department, Technical University of Crete,
Chania, Greece, GR73100
gsiskos@electronics.tuc.gr, pnevmati@mhl.tuc.gr
[2] Computer Engineering Laboratory, EEMCS, TU Delft, P.O. Box 5031,
2600 GA Delft, the Netherlands
D.Theodoropoulos@tudelft.nl

Abstract. In this paper, we present CCProc, a flexible cryptography co-processor for symmetric-key algorithms. Based on an extensive analysis of many symmetric-key ciphers, including the five AES finalists, we designed an Instruction Set Architecture tailored to symmetric-key ciphers and built a hardware processor prototype by using the VHDL language. The design was mapped on FPGAs and ASIC. Results show a small-area design, while also supporting many ciphers. Besides flexibility, a 4-core FPGA design can achieve up to 615 Mbits/sec at 95 MHz for Rijndael.

Keywords: Cryptography, reconfigurable processors, VLIW.

1 Introduction

In this paper, we focus on the encryption and decryption processes for symmetric key cryptography ciphers, in order to identify common processing parts among them, and be able to design an ISA (Instruction Set Architecture) that efficiently supports them. These similarities were deeply analyzed and the result is a hardware VLIW co-processor called CCproc (Cryptography CoPROCessor). CCproc has its own symmetric-cipher-specific instruction set and an extended RISC datapath structure. Furthermore, it is capable of supporting many of today's symmetric key ciphers, plus new potential ones, while also functioning at very competitive speeds.

The main contributions of this work are:

- An extensive symmetric-key ciphers analysis, based on studying many cryptography algorithms;
- The design of an efficient and flexible cryptography co-processor (CCproc), based on the results of the aforementioned analysis.

The remainder of the paper is as follows: Section 2 discusses the main symmetric-ciphers properties and some related work, while Section 3 describes the CCproc architecture. Section 4 compares CCProc against other similar designs, while Section 5 concludes the paper.

J. Becker et al. (Eds.): ARC 2009, LNCS 5453, pp. 318–323, 2009.
© Springer-Verlag Berlin Heidelberg 2009

2   Symmetric-Key Ciphers Properties and Related Work

In order to make our analysis as complete as possible, the following algorithms were selected: Rijndael [10], MARS [5], Twofish [4], RC6 [15], Serpent [16], Blowfish [3], RC4, DES, RC5 [14] and International Data Encryption Standard (IDEA) [13]. We concluded that the most commonly used operations and structures are: 1) unsigned addition and subtraction modulo 2^{32}, 2) multiplication modulo (MM) 2^{32}, 3) 32-bit xor, 4) fixed shifts and rotations, 5) data dependent shifts and rotations, 6) finite field polynomial multiplication in the Galois Field 2^8 modulo an irreducible polynomial, 7) expansions and permutations (Xboxes), 8) substitution boxes (S-boxes) and 9) Feistel network structures [9].

In 32-bit processors, operations from 1 to 5 are implemented very fast. Finite Field polynomial Multiplication (FFM) modulo an irreducible polynomial does not have direct hardware support. Additions, subtractions and XORs are the simplest operations and are used just to scramble data, thus providing less security. Fixed rotations are mainly used to get specific data bits to places, from where they will be used by other operations. Data dependent rotations can be combined with arithmetic operations, thus protecting against linear cryptanalysis.

Besides arithmetic operations, there are common structures among ciphers. A symmetric cipher may have one or more different S-boxes (Look-Up-Tables) of arbitrary dimensions. Permutations and expansions are linear operations, and thus, not sufficient to guarantee security. However, when used with good non-linear S-boxes, they are vital for the security of a cipher, because they propagate the non-linearity uniformly over all bits. Finally, Feistel network is a common structure used by many symmetric ciphers and consists of all processing rounds along with their inner operations [9].

Regarding related work, Wu et al. in [11] introduce the *Cryptomaniac* cryptographic processor, a 4-wide 32-bit VLIW machine with no cache and a simple branch predictor, giving a throughput of 512 Mbits/sec for Rijndael. In [6], Oliva et al. describe the *Cryptonite*, a programmable processor. Its frequency is 400 MHz in TSMC 0.13 μm process. Results show a 700 Mbits/sec Rijndael performance. Elbirt et al. in [1] describe a design named COBRA, a specialized reconfigurable architecture optimized for the implementation of block ciphers, achieving a theoretical throughput of 3.9 Gbits/sec, 1.451 Gbits/sec and 2.306 Gbits/sec respectively.

3   CCproc Architecture

Design Considerations: Our initial motivation was a hardware design, flexible enough to support many of today's popular symmetric ciphers, and potential new ones [7]. As years go by, symmetric ciphers that use keys smaller than 128-bits are likely to be abandoned, because they will be vulnerable to brute-force attacks. *So, after a careful analysis, we concluded that some of their functional principles were not adopted by the newest ones.* A first example is bit permutation or expansion, which is primarily used by DES, however, none of the AES round 2 finalists used it. *Although different structures have been studied offering arbitrary bit permutations, they require a considerable amount of hardware [2], thus we decided not to use them.* Another characteristic not used by any of the AES round 2 finalists is the variable S-boxes. *Based on this, we decided to instantiate a few ROMs as cipher specific S-boxes and small RAMs for new S-boxes support, plus available data space during the key expansion process.*

Regarding the key expansion process, all AES round 2 finalists utilize rather simple ones, with the exception of MARS. *As a result, in order to explicitly support the key expansion process of a cipher, the only extra functional unit that we would add is a Key Register File (KRF) memory module, where all expanded keys will be stored. Furthermore, we employed an ISA expansion to support operations between Register File (RF) data and KRF data.* Another consideration was to record the instruction types and their frequency in symmetric ciphers. This research revealed a high frequency occurrence of 2 dependent back-to-back instructions, like add-add, add-sub and add-xor. *Thus, we decided that this type of double-instructions should be included in the CCproc ISA.*

We also noted that all AES round 2 finalists treat 128-bit plaintext as 4 32-bit words. Symmetric ciphers frequently require 64-bit, 96-bit or even 128-bit data values at the same time in order to proceed. *Having in mind a design that would achieve competitive performance, it was finally considered a VLIW processor that would consist of 4 32-bit clusters, capable of processing 4 32-bit instructions in 1 clock cycle.*

Another conclusion that came up from our cipher analysis was the small number of 32-bit registers utilization. In each cluster a maximum of 4 registers were used during out tests, ending up to a total of 16 32-bit registers among the 4 clusters. *However, it was decided an 8x32 RF in each cluster, in order to cover the case where a cipher, that was not tested, might need additional registers.* Furthermore, a fact that characterizes every symmetric cipher is the determined rounds number for the key expansion and encryption/decryption processes. Consequently, they can be implemented in a way that requires no branch tests. *Thus, we decided to support only a "loop" instruction that would add no stalls.*

A final consideration was cipher support. As we mentioned earlier in this section, every cipher that uses keys smaller than 128-bit are considered as non-secure. In addition, a cryptography co-processor should be able to support as many ciphers as possible, in order to provide a strong security level against various kinds of attacks [8]. *This fact led us to the decision to support all AES round 2 finalists, since these are the strongest ones, and to have an extended ISA efficient and general enough to cover future algorithms.*

Datapath Structure: As mentioned before, after a closer analysis of various symmetric ciphers, we concluded that a *loop* instruction was enough to handle all control hazards. In addition, ciphers processing required at most 4 32-bit registers per cluster for each of the AES round 2 finalists. As a result, RF in each cluster consists of 8 32-bit registers, to support not tested ciphers that might need more registers. The KRF is a special RAM in each cluster *decode* stage, where all expanded keys of a cipher are stored. Every KRF has 64 32-bit registers. *This size was chosen after observation of the expanded keys data size and finding that it did not exceed a total of 33 32-bit data values per cluster.* Since every cipher uses its expanded keys serially forwards or backwards, we decided to use a serial auto-increment KRF address generation approach.

As mentioned before, there are many double-instructions that require 3 operands. This fact led us to design an ALU with 3 32-bit inputs and 1 32-bit output. The ALU consists of 3 32-bit ASUs (Addition/Subtraction Units), 3 2-input 32-bit xors and 3 multiplexers. The ALU instructions have the specific format $Result \Leftarrow ((In1 \ op1 \ In2) \ op2 \ In3)$, where $In1$, $In2$ and $In3$ are the 3 ALU inputs and $op1$, $op2$ are the 2 operations that may be performed. The ALU has also 2 shift/rotate units. CCproc includes also multipliers modulo (MM) 2^{32} and Galois Field multipliers (GFM) modulo an irreducible polynomial over $GF(2^8)$. Our GFM is based on [12] and can perform 16 8x8 GF multiplications in 1 clock cycle.

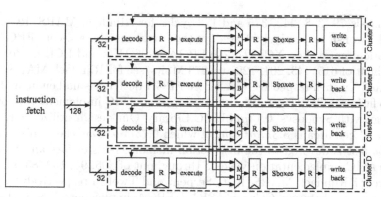

Fig. 1. CCproc schematic overview

Figure 1 illustrates the complete design. There is an *instruction fetch* unit for fetching a 128-bit instructions and passing them to the 4 clusters as 4 32-bit instructions. Each one of these instructions is forwarded to the *decode stage* of its corresponding cluster for further processing. The main unit in this stage is the *Decode controller*, which produces valid RF and KRF addresses, plus many other control signals that pass through the next stages. Next stage is the *execution stage*, where all logic and arithmetic operations are performed. The ALU, GFMs 16x8x8, MMs and shifters/rotators are all instantiated in this stage. Data from *execution stage* are used to access the appropriate cipher S-boxes or forwarded directly to the *write back stage* where data are written in RF. *MX* multiplexers (X=A, B, C, D) are used to efficiently exchange data among clusters in 1 clock cycle, while "R" represents a pipeline register.

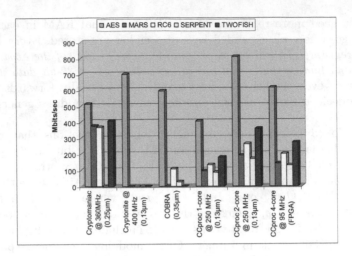

Fig. 2. Performance Comparison

4   Verification and Performance Evaluation

CCproc needs 79, 338, 242, 375 and 178 cycles for Rijndael, MARS, RC6, Serpent and Twofish respectively. Based on the above results, a 4-core FPGA implementation mapped on XC4VLX200 FPGA at 95 MHz and ECB mode yields a throughput of 615, 143, 201, 129 and 273 Mbits/sec for Rijndael, MARS, RC6, Serpent and Twofish respectively. A 1-core FPGA design is small enough (18045 slices) to fit in a XC4VLX40. We also developed an ASIC implementation of a 1-core design with Synopsys' $0.13\mu m$ UMC Library. Our design utilizes 93K cells, and its total cell area is $5.3mm^2$, out of which $0.73mm^2$ was the combinational logic. The rest is devoted to the instruction memory, register files and S-boxes. A 1-core ASIC implementation yields a throughput of 405, 95, 132, 85, and 180 Mbits/sec for Rijndael, MARS, RC6, Serpent and Twofish respectively.

A comparison between CCproc ASIC / FPGA implementations and other similar designs is shown in Figure 2. Cryptomaniac [11] is a flexible design, because it supports most of the current ciphers compared to the others. Cryptonite [6] supports only Rijndael from ciphers with 128-bit key. COBRA [14], according to the paper, currently supports 2 parallel atomic units running for Rijndael and RC6, and 1 atomic unit for Serpent. As it can be seen from Figure 2, CCproc is the only one that supports so far all AES round 2 finalists, while also mapped in FPGA and ASIC. A just 2-core CCproc ASIC implementation can deliver speeds of 810, 190, 264, 170, and 360 Mbits/sec for Rijndael, MARS, RC6, Serpent and Twofish respectively. Of course we should note that Cryptomaniac has the advantage of occupying smaller area than CCproc. Cryptonite yields better throughput than CCproc and Cryptomaniac where applicable, however it lacks of flexibility. However, today's cryptography co-processors should support multiple ciphers and have the capability to be reconfigured and upgraded in case a cipher is broken. [8].

5   Conclusions

In this paper, we analyzed many symmetric-key ciphers and designed from scratch a VLIW RISC-like co-processor, in order to efficiently support them in hardware level at very competitive speeds. It supports all AES round 2 finalists and can fit in small FPGAs. Furthermore, multiple CCproc cores can be placed in larger FPGAs to improve cipher performance.

References

1. Elbirt, A.J., et al.: An Instruction-Level Distributed Processor for Symmetric-Key Cryptography. IEEE Trans. on Parallel and Distributed Systems, 468–480 (2005)
2. Murat Fiskiran, A., et al.: Performance Impact of Addressing Modes on Encryption Algorithms. In: ICCD, pp. 542–545 (2001)
3. Schneier, B.: Description of a new variable-length key, 64-bit block cipher (Blowfish). In: Fast Software Encryption, Cambridge Security Workshop Proceedings, pp. 191–204
4. Scheier, B., et al.: Twofish: A 128-bit Block Cipher (1998)
5. Burwick, C., et al.: MARS - a candidate cipher for AES (1999)
6. Oliva, D., et al.: AES and the Cryptonite Crypto Processor. In: CASES, pp. 198–209 (2003)
7. Theodoropoulos, D., et al.: Cproc: An efficient Cryptographic Coprocessor. In: 16th IFIP/IEEE International Conference on Very Large Scale Integration (2008)
8. Huffmire, T.: Application of cryptographic primitives to computer architecture. Technical report, University of California (2005)
9. Smith, J.L.: Description of a new variable-length key, 64-bit block cipher (Blowfish). In: Fast Software Encryption, Cambridge Security Workshop Proceedings, pp. 191–204
10. Daemen, J., et al.: AES Proposal: Rijndael. Document Version 2 (1999)
11. Wu, L., et al.: Cryptomaniac: A Fast Flexible Architecture for Secure Communication. In: ISCA, pp. 110–119 (2001)
12. Jung, M., et al.: A Reconfigurable Coprocessor for Finite Field Multiplication in $GF(2^8)$. In: IEEE Workshop on Heterogeneous reconfigurable SoCs (2003)
13. MediaCrypt. International Data Encryption Algorithm. Technical report
14. Ronald, L.: Rivest. The RC5 Algorithm (1996)
15. Rivest, R.L., et al.: The RC6 Block Cipher (1998)
16. Anderson, R., et al.: A Proposal for the Advanced Encryption Standard. In: 5th workshop on Fast Software Encryption (1998)

Object Tracking and Motion Capturing in Hardware-Accelerated Multi-camera System

Sirisak Leephokhanon and Theerayod Wiangtong

Department of Electronic Engineering
Mahanakorn University of Technology
51 Cheumsampan Rd., Nongchok, Bangkok, Thailand 10530
theerayo@mut.ac.th

Abstract. This paper presents a multi-camera system where reconfigurable hardware and video codec are used to assist real-time video processing. Video inputs from all analog cameras are decoded and processed by FPGA to accelerate overall processing time. Two applications including multiple-object tracking and motion capturing are implemented in this system to verify real-time capability. In multiple-object tracking, video images are rearranged and combined into a single image that profits the tracking algorithm called multiple-CAMshift running in software. In motion capturing, every frame from all cameras, located in different angles, is processed to find the coordinates of 11 reference color-objects. Results are sent to a computer for constructing 3-D image in real-time.

1 Introduction

Most video processing algorithms are computational intensive however they need to process streaming video data in a limitation of time to achieve real-time manner. This becomes a major challenge for a system with high image resolution and video frame rate or a system with multiple video inputs from several cameras. Hardware such as video codec or FPGA (Field Programmable Gate Array) is unavoidably utilized in this type of system to speed up processing time.

For the last decade, object tracking has received considerable attention. Currently, the trend is moving towards applications that utilize multiple cameras such as surveillance [1] or traffic control and management systems. The well-known object tracking algorithm is the Continuously Adaptive Mean-shift (CAMshift) [2] algorithm, which is available in Intel OpenCV library [3]. Another interesting application is motion capturing. In robotic systems [4], encoder counters are used as sensors to track human motions. Nonetheless, in computer animation and video game industry, it traditionally uses difference frequency reflectors stuck all over a model in order to track its motions [5]. An expensive high speed camera, that can transmit different frequencies and then capture reflected picture more than 100 frames per second, is needed in such systems.

To achieve real-time capability, this paper presents the utilization of reconfigurable hardware for object tracking and motion capturing in multi-camera systems. A new algorithm, called multiple-CAMshift, is introduced for tracking

J. Becker et al. (Eds.): ARC 2009, LNCS 5453, pp. 324–329, 2009.
© Springer-Verlag Berlin Heidelberg 2009

multiple objects. In motion capturing, a pixel-wise comparison is used to find the positions of color objects from ordinary cameras located in different angles. Coordinates of all color objects will be sent to a computer for constructing 3-D image in real-time.

2   Hardware Accelerator Platform

The reconfigurable hardware accelerator platform used in this work is shown in Fig. 1. FPGA, memory and video codec chips are assembled as a PCI interface card (32bits 33MHz). It is capable to handle image data from 4 cameras, acquired by the video decoders (SAA7133). The output image format of the decoder is YUV 4:2:2 with the resolution of 720×576 pixels. Xilinx XC3S1000 FPGA is used as a core controlling and processing unit of this hardware platform. SDRAM memory (8Mbytes) working as video buffers operates at 100 MHz for real-time acquisition. In case of monitoring, data in the video buffer are read and rearranged to a video encoder (SAA7121) that complies with ITU-656 [6].

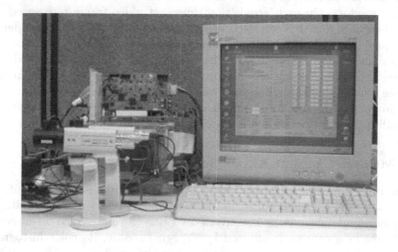

Fig. 1. A real development system

3   Implementation of Multiple Object Tracking

3.1   FPGA System Design

The hardware structure used to rearrange a new quad image is shown in Fig. 2(a) where video data from 4 cameras is acquired through the video decoders (SAA7133). Figure 2(b) exhibits the internal function blocks which are written in VHDL and implemented in FPGA. Streaming data from the video decoders is sent to video control blocks for preliminary re-sampling an image from NTSC/PAL size (720 pixels/line) to CIF size (360×288 pixels). The re-sampled

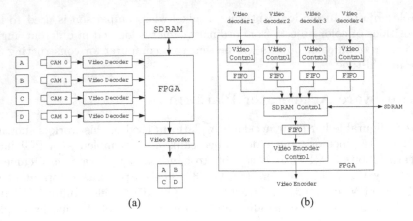

(a)   (b)

Fig. 2. (a) Hardware structure for quad image rearrangement (b) FPGA internal function blocks

data is buffered in 1KByte-FIFO (First-in-first-out) before being multiplexed to SDRAM memory. On each acquisition time – at video frame rate speed – the image data in SDRAM is retrieved to be rearranged by the video encoder, and a new quad image that consists of 4 images from 4 cameras is then obtained.

A new quad image, sending from the video encoder, is then processed by the tracking algorithm running on desktop PC. With this strategy to preliminarily combine multiple images using hardware, the algorithm can. work fast with a single image that represents all information from all cameras. This outperforms the traditional way that processes images on each camera individually.

3.2   Multiple-Camshift Algorithm

Our multiple-CAMshift algorithm extends the capability of the CAMshift algorithm to be able to track multiple objects in multi-camera systems. Initially, a new quad input image data is converted to HSV format. Once an interesting object area in a camera is selected by dragging mouse, its color histogram is calculated and stored as the i_{th} tracking object where $i = 1, 2, 3, .., n$. When a new object is selected, the algorithm will repeat the process as such. Then the algorithm utilizes CAMshift to determine the location of each selected object and display in the quad format picture.

4   Implementation of Motion Capturing

Instead of using an expensive high speed camera for motion capturing, commonly-used cameras connected to our reconfigurable hardware platform can be exploited in order to track color objects in different angles in real-time. The objects with different colors are attached to different proper locations on a human body where we can use the results of tracking coordinate data to recreate the movement of the human body. In our design, 11 different color objects (A-N) are exploited and located at positions as shown in Fig. 3. Multiple cameras at different video angles are necessary to avoid losing the appearance of some color objects when the body is moving.

FPGA is used to accelerate the pixel-wise comparison process to find objects which have the same colors as user-defined reference colors. Consequently, coordinates of all color positions will be sent to a computer through PCI bus for constructing 3-D image in real-time.

4.1 Pixel-Wise Comparison

For each pixel, a group of bits in YUV color components obtained from video decoders are selected and rearranged to obtain a new single 16-bit value, resulting in the linearity of color values that benefits pixel-wise comparison process as shown in Fig. 3. This value is then called a *linearized pixel value*.

Because FPGA resources are limited and comparison process of all 11 reference colors must be done concurrently to achieve real-time results, the simple pixel-wise comparison shown in Equation (1) is employed to evaluate the similarity between the linearized pixel values of video input frames ($input_{pix_i}$) and the linearized value of each reference color (ref) determined by users.

$$output_{pix_i} = \begin{cases} '1' & \text{if } |input_{pix_i} - ref| < threshold \\ '0' & \text{if } |input_{pix_i} - ref| \geq threshold \end{cases} \tag{1}$$

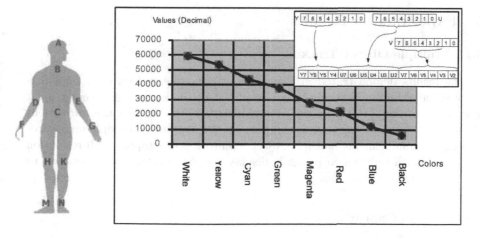

Fig. 3. Object locations and linearized pixel values used in comparison process

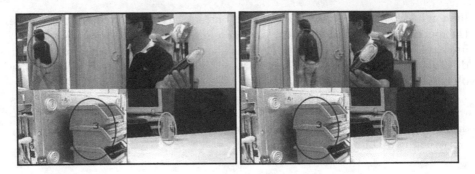

Fig. 4. Example of multiple object tracking result

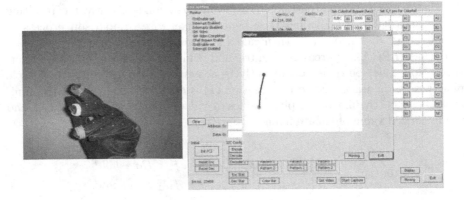

Fig. 5. Example of real-time motion capturing result

5   Experimental Results

5.1   Multiple Object Tracking

As the results demonstrated in Fig. 4, an object appeared on each camera is tracked individually. Tracking area is confined in single camera coverage area. The good aspects of this proposed system include a) the significant improvement of the tracking processing time as compared to the conventional single-image processing, b) simultaneous multiple-object monitoring c) support high-resolution mode, in which only video image is displayed d) straightforward extension to the system upto 32 cameras.

5.2   Motion Capturing

Two analog cameras are connected to the hardware accelerator platform. Video streaming from each camera is processed concurrently in FPGA to find every possible object positions. Moving color objects in both cameras can be detected and displayed smoothly at normal frame speed or 25frames/sec. However, some frames contain object positioning errors if lighting condition is changed or the linearized pixel values of reference colors are too close. The shape of the color objects, e.g. flat or sphere, also affects to light reflection when the body is moving. These troublesomes are the extensions of future work. More robust algorithms must be employed, as well as coordinates of the same color object obtained from different camera angles must be mapped to a single display space before using in 3-D recreation process.

6   Conclusions

In this paper, the real-time video applications of multiple-object tracking and motion capturing in multiple camera systems have been presented. The developed hardware accelerator platform utilizes FPGA for video image rearrangement to obtain a new quad image format that benefits tracking process. The tracking algorithm, namely multiple-CAMshift, has been developed based upon the existing CAMshift algorithm. In motion capturing, the pixel-wise comparison using the linearized pixel value is introduced in this work. Streaming video inputs from two cameras, located in diffent angles, can be processed to find the coordinates of color objects in real-time.

References

1. Nguyen, K., Yeung, G., Ghiasi, S., Sarrafzadeh, M.: A General Framework for Tracking Objects in a Multi-Camera Environment. In: Proceedings of IEEE International workshop on Digital and Computational Video, pp. 200–204 (2002)
2. Francois, A.R.J.: CAMSHIFT Tracker Design Experiments with Intel OpenCV and SAI. IRIS Technical Report IRIS-04-423, University of Southern California (2004)
3. Intel Corporation: Open Source Computer Vision Library Reference Manual (2001)
4. Lee, W.K., Jung, S.: FPGA Design for Controlling Humanoid Robot Arms by Exoskeleton Motion Capture System. In: IEEE International Conference on Robotics and Biomimetics, pp. 1378–1383 (2006)
5. Manache, A.: Understanding Motion Capture for Computer Animation and Video Games. Morgan Kaufmann Publishers, San Francisco (2000)
6. International Telecommunication Union ITU-656,
   http://www.itu.int/home/index.html

Implementation of the AES Algorithm for a Reconfigurable, Bit Serial, Fully Pipelined Architecture

Raphael Weber[1] and Achim Rettberg[2]

[1] University of Paderborn, C-Lab, Fürstenallee 11, 33102 Paderborn, Germany
[2] Carl von Ossietzky University Oldenburg, OFFIS, Escherweg 2, 26121 Oldenburg, Germany

Abstract. This paper describes the implementation of the Advanced Encryption Standard (AES) for a specific hardware architecture, which was developed based on the combination of different design paradigms. The architecture comprises synchronous and systematic bit–serial processing without a central controlling instance. To realize the AES cipher, we extended the architecture by designing specific elements. That means, we deeply analyzed the encryption algorithm and identified hardware characteristics leading to an optimal area and run–time efficient implementation. The implementation of AES is done with the developed synthesis tool of the hardware architecture in synthesizable VHDL code. For testing purposes, we simulated the generated VHDL code and ran some tests on an FPGA board.

1 Introduction

People's demand to keep secrets, only accessible to chosen people, is as old as mankind. In order to keep something secret one has to encrypt it, so that only trustworthy people can understand the contents. The most popular cipher algorithm is the Advanced Encryption Standard (AES) announced by the U.S. American National Institute of Standards and Technology (NIST) in late 2000.

In this paper we investigate an AES implementation for a special bit–serial, reconfigurable, fully pipelined, self–controlled architecture. Our goal is to design the complete AES encryption targeted for resource restricted environments.

Bit–serial architectures have the advantage of a low number of input and output lines leading to a low number of required pins. In synchronous design, however, the performance of these architectures is affected by the long wires, which are used to control the operators or the potential gated clocks. Nowadays, the wire delay in chip design is near to a break with the gate delay. Solutions to overcome this drawback are required. Basically, long control wires can be avoided by a local distribution of the control circuitry at the operator level. A similar approach is used for the architecture described in this work.

While the design of a fully interlocked asynchronous architecture is well understood, realizing a fully synchronous pipeline architecture still remains a difficult task. Through a one-hot implementation of the central control engine, its

J. Becker et al. (Eds.): ARC 2009, LNCS 5453, pp. 330–335, 2009.
© Springer-Verlag Berlin Heidelberg 2009

folding into the data path, and the use of a shift register, we realized a synchronous fully self–timed bit–serial and fully interlocked pipeline architecture called MACT (MACT = Mauro, Achim, Christophe and Tom).

The paper is organized as follows. In Section 2 we will shortly explain the AES cipher algorithm. The second part of that section contains the description of the MACT architecture. Section 3 features the description of our AES design for the MACT architecture. At the end of Section 3 we will give some synthesis results. Finally, Section 4 sums up with a conclusion and gives an outlook.

2 Basics

2.1 The Advanced Encryption Standard

AES is a block cipher algorithm which has a constant input/output block size of 128 bits. Data is encrypted in a differing number of loops in which four transformations are applied to the block, called *state*. The number of loops depends on the key size which can either be 128, 192, or 256 bits. In this work we will only consider the AES-128 with a 128-bit key and 10 loops (rounds).

Figure 1 displays how the cipher works, utilizing the transformations, described below. The RoundKey is generated from the key and changes each round. This procedure is called key expansion.

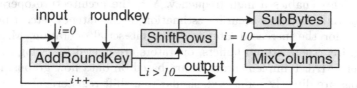

Fig. 1. AES-128 cipher

AddRoundKey XORs the state with the current round key in a byte–wise manner. The RoundKey applied before the loop is equal to the key. The byte–wise SubBytes transformation is the most costly operation in terms of hardware utilization. First, each byte is considered as an element in the Gallois Field (GF(2^8)) and the multiplicative inverse is calculated. Second, an affine transformation is applied to the byte. This results in a highly non linear mapping, which can be stored in a so–called S-Box. SubBytes can be implemented using combinational logic only using simple bit–wise XOR and AND operators [4,3]. Other implementations use a look–up–table [1]. ShiftRows cyclically shifts the bytes of a row over a differing number of offsets. MixColumns considers the bytes in each column of the state as coefficients in GF(2^8) and performs GF(2^8) multiplication and XOR operations to the bytes. A multiplication in GF(2^8) can be performed by a series of left shifts with a conditional XOR with the irreducible polynomial $m(x) = x^8 + x^4 + x^3 + x + 1 = \{01\}\{1b\}$.

2.2   The MACT Architecture

MACT is an architecture that breaks with classical design paradigms. Its development came in combination with a design paradigm shift to adapt to market requirements. The architecture is based on small and distributed local control units instead of a global control instance. MACT is a synchronous, de–centralized and self–controlling architecture. Data and control information is combined into one packet which is shifted through a network of operators using one single wire only (refer to Figure 2). To our knowledge, this is the second approach to implement a fully interlocked synchronous architecture after that of [2] and the first one which does not rely on gated clocks to realize the local control of operators.

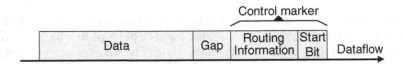

Fig. 2. Example data packet

The controlling operates locally, only based on arriving data. Thus, there are no long control wires, which would limit the operating speed due to wire delays [5]. This enables a high frequency. Yet, the architecture operates synchronously, thus enabling accurate estimation of the latency, etc. a priori. To compensate for the increased latency of the bit–serial operation, MACT uses pipelining, i. e., there are no buffers, operators are placed following each other immediately. MACT implementations are based on data flow graphs. Nodes of these graphs are directly connected, similar to a shift register.

We consider the flow of data through the operator network as processing in waves, i. e., valid data alternates with gaps. Additionally, we have to ensure that the control marker is not modified by an operator. This can be achieved by two additional signals, *open bypass* and *close bypass*. If *open bypass* is true the control marker and the gap of the data packet are routed around the operating unit inside the operator. If *close bypass* is true the data of the data packet is directed to the operating unit.

MACT is characterized by short and local control wires and no necessity to implement costly parallel/serial decoders or encoders. Thus, it may run with high speed, compensating the drawbacks of bit–serial processing. Furthermore, the local control structure avoids complex controllers. Additionally, the fully interlocked pipeline allows the architecture to support multiple applications within one implementation. The architecture is described in more detail in [7,6].

In order to realize reconfiguration within our architecture a component called router was developed. The router offers path selection, which can be controlled by the extension of the control marker in the data packet. That means, the control marker contains the routing information, see Figure 2. The realization of loops can also be achieved with routers.

3   AES Implementation for the MACT Architecture

The MACT architecture is a data flow oriented architecture, logic circuits can be generated from a data flow graph specification by a high level synthesis tool. We used this tool to draw our data flow graphs for all AES components including the key expansion. However, in order to achieve a prototype implementation we state some preliminary fixings, to simplify the design process: 1.) we use 16 separate bytes to represent the AES state, 2.) we will only use the key length of 128 bits, and 3.) we will not unroll the AES loop, to keep the design small.

First, we take a look at the four main transformations of the AES cipher specification. AddRoundKey only involves XORs and ShiftRows only reroutes wires. Some works on AES designs have implemented SubBytes as a look–up table [1]. For compact low–power designs of the S-Box most researchers used composite field logic implementations [3]. For this reason we have decided to do an arithmetic realization, since the MACT architecture is rather designed for a compact than a fast design. MixColumns is also most commonly implemented using composite field logic.

For a combinational S-Box we only need simple logic nodes like the XOR and the AND node, see [4] for a detailed description. However, the work of [4] is a bit–parallel design, simultaneously operating on each bit of the incoming byte. This is not possible in MACT, since it is a bit–serial architecture. Therefore we extended MACT by a so–called BitExtractor.

The BitExtractor processes n input packets and produces m output packets. The result are m output packets where the first output packet contains all LSBs of the n inputs, the second output packet contains all bits behind the LSB of the input packets, and so on. Hence, the number of inputs, n, is the new bitwidth of the outputs and the bitwidth of the inputs is the number of outputs, m.

Mathematically, our BitExtractor can be described as a matrix transposition: $y_j[n - i - 1] = x_i[j]$, for $0 \leq i < n$ and $0 \leq j < m$ with x_i as the ith input and $x_i[j]$ as the jth bit of x_i and y_j as the jth output and $y_j[n-i-1]$ as the $(n-i-1)^{th}$ bit of y_j. Figure 3 illustrates how the BitExtractor works ($n = m = 4$).

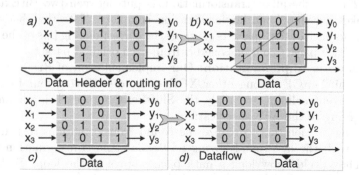

Fig. 3. A 4x4 BitExtractor in four states: *a)* passing through the header and routing information, *b)* transposition, *c)* start shifting through the data, and *d)* 2 cycles later

For `MixColumns` we need to do $GF(2^8)$ multiplications, which can be done by left shifts and conditional XORs, as mentioned above. The only problem is that the conditional XOR with $m(x)$ depends on the MSB after the left shift, but MACT operates LSB first. Our solution for that is a new ShiftLeftGF element that uses an additional sign tapping.

We extended the simple left shift operator. Figure 4 displays a ShiftLeftGF in a state, where it starts shifting the data. In order to determine the MSB we had to tap a new control signal to an earlier point in the data flow, where the register holds the MSB in the exact same moment the ShiftLeftGF starts to shift (when *close bypass* is high). This point is where the decision is made whether to XOR with {1b} or not.

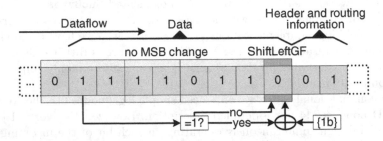

Fig. 4. An example of a ShiftLeftGF with a packet passing through it

For a correctly working ShiftLeftGF we have to ensure that no operators change the MSB. The easiest way to do this is to insert delay nodes.

AddRoundKey implementation: This transformation consists of 16 XOR operators with 16 state bytes and 16 round key bytes as input.

ShiftRows implementation: Since we work on the byte level we only need a rerouting of all 16 bytes of the state to implement this transformation.

SubBytes implementation: In [4] the implementation of a combinational S-Box is discussed and implemented on an FPGA. We derived our data flow graphs and hierarchy from this work. Then, the S-Box including multiplicative inversion over $GF(2^8)$ and the affine transformation, is put between two BitExtractors, which makes our `SubBytes` implementation complete. Note that between the BitExtractors each of the 8 packets contains the corresponding bits of the original packets, so each packet contains one bit from each original packet.

MixColumns implementation: Our implementation of `MixColumns` features our ShiftLeftGF among other XOR operators. Having four bytes input from the current column, we apply the ShiftLeftGF to each input and XOR them according to the AES specification.

Combining all elements to realize the round transformations to run exactly 10 rounds with the last round having no `MixColumns` transformation requires routers. They decide how long a data packet stays in the loop. To keep the design as small as possible, we included the tenth round into the loop. Firstly, we need routers to always route the packets through `MixColumns`, except for the last round. Secondly, we need routers to decide when a data packet leaves the loop. So a data packet passes two routers in each loop. For the routers to decide what path is used, they compare constants to the current routing information which is incremented in each round by a counter element. Thus, the structure of our data packets includes one start bit, four routing bits and eight data bits.

We synthesized our implementation for an inexpensive Xilinx Spartan 3 board, running at 50 MHz. One AES round takes 62 cycles, capable of processing two blocks at once. The packets are 13 bits long, so the minimum loop duration is 26 cycles (the minimum gap between packets is also 13). The logic (including an RS232 interface) utilizes 4,758 of the 4-input LUTs.

4   Conclusion

In this paper, we presented the implementation of the Advanced Encryption Standard (AES) for the MACT architecture. We extended MACT by specific elements for AES leading to a prototype implementation. This is done by a detailed mathematical analysis of the AES cipher algorithm. Finally, we used the MACT synthesis tool for implementation and a VHDL simulator for testing. In the future, we will take a closer look at the area optimization.

References

1. Fischer, V., Drutarovský, M.: Two Methods of Rijndael Implementation in Reconfigurable Hardware. In: Koç, Ç.K., Naccache, D., Paar, C. (eds.) CHES 2001. LNCS, vol. 2162, pp. 77–92. Springer, Heidelberg (2001)
2. Jacobson, H.M., Kudva, P.N., Bose, P., Cook, P.W., Schuster, S.E., Mercer, E.G., Myers, C.J.: Synchronous Interlocked Pipelines. In: 8th Intern. Symposium on Asynchronous Circuits and Systems (April 2002)
3. Järvinen, K.U., Tommiska, M.T., Skyttä, J.O.: A Fully Pipelined Memoryless 17.8 Gbps AES-128 Encryptor. In: FPGA 2003: Proceedings of the 2003 ACM/SIGDA eleventh international symposium on Field programmable gate arrays, pp. 207–215. ACM, New York (2003)
4. Mui, E.N.: Practical Implementation of Rijndael S-Box Using Combinational Logic (2007), http://www.xess.com/projects/Rijndael_SBox.pdf
5. Renshaw, D., Denyer, P.: VLSI Signal Processing: A Bit Serial Approach. Addison-Wesley, Reading (1985)
6. Rettberg, A., Dittmann, F., Zanella, M.C., Lehmann, T.: Towards a High-Level Synthesis of Reconfigurable Bit-Serial Architectures. In: Proceedings of the SBCCI 2003, Sao Paulo, Brazil, September 8-11 (2003)
7. Rettberg, A., Zanella, M.C., Bobda, C., Lehmann, T.: A Fully Self-Timed Bit-Serial Pipeline Architecture for Embedded Systems. In: Proceedings of the DATE 2003, Messe Munich, Munich, Germany, March 3-7 (2003)

A Hardware Accelerated Simulation Environment for Spiking Neural Networks

Brendan Glackin, Jim Harkin, Thomas M. McGinnity, and Liam P. Maguire

Intelligent Systems Research Centre
University of Ulster, Magee Campus,
Derry, Northern Ireland, BT48 7JL, UK
{b.glackin,jg.harkin,lp.maguire,tm.mcginnity}@ulster.ac.uk

Abstract. Spiking Neural Networks (SNNs) model the biological functions of the human brain enabling neuro/computer scientists to investigate how arrays of neurons can be used to solve computational tasks. However, as network models approach the biological scale with significantly large numbers of neurons, existing software simulation environments face the problem of scalability and increasing simulation times. Emulation in hardware offers a significant increase in the acceleration of simulations through the exploitation of parallelism and dedicated on-chip training. However, it is important that the configuration of SNNs for hardware emulation is abstracted from the novice end-user to allow flexible, high-level specification and execution. This paper presents a novel reconfigurable hardware architecture and internet-based configuration environment for the FPGA-based acceleration of SNNs with online training. Results are presented to demonstrate the acceleration performance.

Keywords: FPGAs, spiking neural networks, online training, reconfiguration.

1 Introduction

SNNs have emerged as a paradigm that more accurately model the biological functions of the human brain, offering the potential to re-create more biologically plausible computing systems [1]. SNNs differ from conventional artificial NN models as neurons communicate through pulses or spikes and use the timing of the pulses to transmit information and perform computations. One key area of SNN research is the exploration of network models to solve complex problems. Software-based simulation environments are often used as platforms for neuroscientists and computer scientists to investigate how arrays of neurons can be used to solve computational tasks [2]. However, the human brain is highly complex and it is estimated to have somewhere in the region of 10^{11} neurons operating in a parallel manner with an estimated 10^{14} connections between them [3]. Existing software simulation environments incur significant simulation times due to the distinct fundamental difference in how traditional sequential processing systems operate compared to biological systems [3]. This presents a significant challenge in the efficient computer modelling of SNNs as they approach the biological scale. The emulation of SNNs in hardware offers a significant increase in the acceleration of simulations

J. Becker et al. (Eds.): ARC 2009, LNCS 5453, pp. 336–341, 2009.
© Springer-Verlag Berlin Heidelberg 2009

times through the exploitation of parallelism [4]. Moreover, the use of programmable mixed signal [5-8] and Field Programmable Gate Array (FPGA) based [9-12] strategies provide varying acceleration platforms and levels of reconfiguration to accommodate the rapid exploration of SNN network configurations. Due to their highly reconfigurable nature, FPGAs are recognised as being a suitable platform for replicating to some degree the natural plasticity of biological neural networks [4]. However, due to the high computation costs involved, existing FPGA-based SNN approaches [9-12] do not currently provide on-chip support for localised training algorithms such as Spike Timing Dependent Plasticity (STDP) [13]. Consequently, current implementation approaches tend to offer offline training in software in an effort to minimise the hardware logic requirements. Moreover, the design or configuration of hardware tailored to a particular SNN network configuration requires significant hardware expertise and design time, something end-users such as neuroscientists find difficult to perform. Therefore, it is essential that the configuration and design of SNNs for hardware emulation are abstracted from the end users to allow flexible, high-level specification and execution. Whilst software simulation environments currently provide such levels of abstraction, the same cannot be said for existing SNN hardware emulation strategies.

This paper presents a novel integrated reconfigurable hardware architecture and configuration environment for the acceleration of SNNs with online training. The hardware architecture is primarily composed of scalable computing blocks realised on FPGA hardware. The architecture exploits both temporal and spatial parallelism of the SNN computing nodes to reduce area, and uses a register-based approach to support minimal runtime reconfiguration of SNN network configurations. The high level design environment integrates with the architecture to allow users to specify SNN networks and structures at an abstract level and rapidly re-configure computing blocks. Moreover, it is accessible via the internet permitting users to control the hardware emulation remotely. The key motivation and benefit of such an architecture and environment is the provision of an advanced acceleration platform to the computer science and neuroscience communities, allowing the rapid exploration and advancement of SNNs research. Section 2 of the paper presents the reconfigurable architecture and section 3 discusses the environment. Section 4 presents results on acceleration speed for an example SNN and section 5 provides conclusions and a summary of future work.

2   SNN Reconfigurable Architecture

The proposed reconfigurable architecture is presented in Fig.1, illustrating a generic SNN router, several SNN computing blocks and a PCI-X interface to a local microprocessor host. The neuron and synapse computations pertaining to a SNN network are mapped to each of the n computing blocks providing a method of parallelising the network. The SNN router provides local communication of spike events between nodes and also supports the communication of user data. For example, a fully interconnected layer of an SNN network containing 10^3 neurons, can be mapped to an architecture with $n=4$, whereby 250 neuron computations are performed by each of

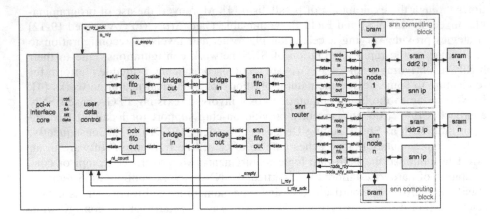

Fig. 1. Reconfigurable Architecture Overview

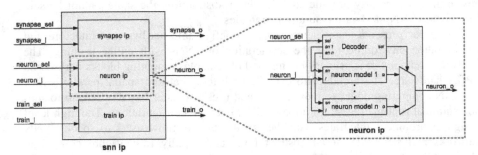

Fig. 2. SNN IP Block Diagram

the four computing nodes. This approach aims to avoid fully parallel implementations as the high fan-in/out requirements of the neurons prohibit large scale SNN implementations on FPGAs due to limited routing resources [6]. The proposed approach uses the SNN router and nodes to provide both temporal and spatial parallelism, allowing a balance between the level of speedup and the complexity of inter-neuron routing. Moreover, it aims to provide a configurable infrastructure whereby a number of SNN routers and nodes can be added to allow the system to scale in performance with area.

An individual SNN Intellectual Property (IP) block, as shown in Fig.2, can accommodate the acceleration of a range of SNN neuron models (e.g. conductance-based, spike response) and training algorithms as each block is reconfigurable. Each SNN node uses a Finite State Machine (FSM) to manage network data and control time-multiplexed access to the SNN IP, enabling large networks to be simulated. The network data for each node, such as the neuron membrane voltages and the synaptic conductance values, are stored in an individual external SRAM bank. Similarly, the parameters which define a network configuration (topology) and simulation parameters (simulation periods, neuron and synapse numbers) are stored in memory mapped simulation registers in on-chip memory (BRAM). Reconfiguration of the hardware architecture to realise new network simulations is achieved by updating the simulation registers via the FSM; removing the requirement to modify the configuration of the FPGA Bitstream. This update mechanism is controlled via the configuration environment making it possible for users to dynamically configure the nodes, and control the simulation at run time. A custom communication protocol that enables read/write Direct Memory Access (DMA) access to both the local and external memory of each node is implemented. In this manner, a highly configurable solution for simulating SNNs is provided that can be easily controlled from a software environment.

3 High-Level Configuration Environment

To support the hardware simulator architecture presented in section 2, a configuration environment is proposed which aims to abstract users from the process of creating SNN network structures, and provide an easy method of configuring and controlling simulations. A client/server based environment is proposed to support remote access to the reconfigurable hardware architecture for a wide user base of neuro/computer scientists, and also to explore the potential for remote collaboration on simulations. An overview of the client/server configuration environment is illustrated in Fig. 3.

The client side presents a Graphical User Interface (GUI) which removes the user from the hardware implementation details such that it appears to be directly equivalent to a software simulation environment. The proposed GUI will enable users to model highly complex SNN network topologies in a graphical drag and drop manner; selecting various neuron and synapse models from a library of available components, and connecting them together to create the desired network structure. To program the hardware simulation a user activates the download option and the SNN configuration is automatically translated into an Extensible Markup Language (XML) netlist file format and forwarded to the remote hardware services component of the server. The incoming XML file is parsed by the server application and the simulation starts once the required configuration parameters for the various SNN nodes are determined to efficiently partition the user network topology across the number of available SNN nodes in the hardware architecture. When a simulation is completed the results are packeted into an XML file which is forwarded to the services component of the client environment, and where a number of graphing and plotting tools are available to the end user to enable analysis of the results. A queue based system has also been included to accommodate multiple users and manage the order in which simulation jobs are processed. A database is currently used to log all submitted simulation requests and provide administration access.

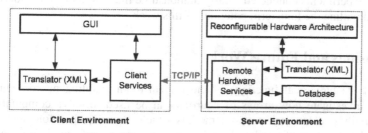

Fig. 3. Client/Server Configuration Environment

4 Experimental Results

The reconfigurable architecture presented in section 2 was specified in VHDL with the SNN IP created using the Xilinx System Generator tool, and implemented on the Nallatech BenNuey PCI-X FPGA development board. The PCI-X interface and user-data control were realised on the board's Xilinx XC4VFX60 device, while the SNN computing blocks were implemented on one of the six XCV4LX160 devices available. To demonstrate the acceleration performance of the reconfigurable architecture the example application of *co-ordinate transformation* was realised with a SNN and implemented in hardware [13]. This SNN consisted of 100 input and output spiking neurons, and 100 training neurons that used STDP to train the network for various input/output mappings. Significantly however, the number of neurons per layer and the number of synaptic connections can be updated remotely at runtime via the client interface. In terms of the reconfigurable architecture, four SNN computing blocks were deployed in this instance with each one clocked at 100 MHz. A software implementation of the same SNN was realised using the C language running on a 2.2 GHz Pentium 4 processor. An evaluation of both software and hardware SNN implementations exhibited execution times of 14 and 1.2175 seconds, respectively. Thus, a hardware acceleration speedup factor of 11.5 was achieved compared with the software equivalent; where only 8% of the available slices in the XCV4LX160 devices were used. This demonstrates the speed performance benefits in using the hardware accelerated architecture. In this early work only four computing nodes were realised however further additional nodes can be utilised providing the potential to significantly increase the speedup. Further work will investigate the optimisation of the architecture to increase clock speeds and also to incorporate scalable, efficient inter-FPGA communication using network-on-chip strategies [6].

The client and server applications of the configuration environment were developed using C++ with the wxWidgets GUI library used to provide cross platform support. While the long term objective of this work is the creation of an environment which can support arbitrary network topologies, the initial work reported placed a constraint on the types of networks supported. As opposed to a graphical 'drag and drop' interface, several predefined XML files for various network architectures were made available within the client GUI. While the outline topology was somewhat constrained in this manner, the end user was provided with the opportunity to control and manipulate the simulation by selecting parameters such as the number of neurons in each layer and the simulation time period. Whilst the authors acknowledge that the level of flexibility is somewhat limited during the early stages of this work, it is evident that the experiments conducted clearly demonstrate the validity of the underlying approach and outline the long term potential of this work.

5 Conclusions and Future Work

SNNs model the biological functions of the human brain enabling neuro/computer scientists to investigate how arrays of neurons can be used to solve computational tasks. To rapidly explore such network models which approach the biological scale requires the development of a tailored hardware acceleration platform. This paper has presented a reconfigurable architecture and a high level configuration environment for the hardware acceleration of SNNs. In particular, the architecture detailed the provision for low-level localised on-chip training algorithms in the form of STDP which is a fundamental characteristic of the human brain, and plays an essential role in underpinning the highly desirable properties of adaptation, reasoning and learning. Results were presented on the acceleration performance for an example application and benchmarked against a software equivalent. Future work will investigate the provision of a graphical drag and drop design interface for efficiently modelling complex network topologies and support for collaborative work within the environment. Whilst the current implementation supports the conductance based integrate and fire neuron model it is also planned to extend this to incorporate multiple alternative models, and explore memory and communication optimisations in the architecture for larger SNN simulations.

References

1. Maass, W.: Computation with Spiking Neurons: The Handbook of Brain Theory and Neural Networks. MIT Press, Cambridge (2001)
2. Hines, M.L., et al.: The NEURON Simulation Environment. In: The Handbook of Brain Theory and Neural Networks, 2nd edn., pp. 769–773. MIT Press, Cambridge (2003)
3. Furber, S., et al.: SpiNNaker: Mapping NNs onto a Massively-Parallel Chip Multiprocessor. In: IEEE World Congress on Computational Intelligence (2008)
4. Maguire, L.P., et al.: Challenges for Large-scale Implementations of SNNs on FPGAs. Neurocomputing 71(1-3), 13–29 (2007)
5. Vogelstein, R., et al.: Dynamically Reconfigurable Silicon Array of Spiking Neurons with Conductance-Based Synapses. IEEE Trans. Neural Nets 18(1), 253–265 (2007)
6. Harkin, J., et al.: Reconfigurable Platforms & the Challenges for Large-Scale Implementations of SNNs. In: IEEE Field Prog. Logic & Apps (FPL) Conf., pp. 483–486 (2008)
7. Rocke, P., et al.: Reconfigurable Hardware Evolution Platform for a Spiking Neural Network Robotics Controller. Applied Reconfigurable Computing, 373–378 (2007)
8. Merolla, P., Boahen, K.: Expandable Networks for Neuromorphic Chips. IEEE Trans Circuits and Systems I 54(2), 301–311 (2007)
9. Glackin, B., et al.: Novel Approach for the Implementation of Large-Scale SNNs on FPGAs. In: Artificial NNs Conference (2005)
10. Upegui, A., et al.: An FPGA platform for on-line topology exploration of SNNs. Microprocessors & Microsystems 29(5) (2005)
11. Pearson, M.P., et al.: Implementing SNNs for Real-Time Signal-Processing and Control Applications: A Model-Validated FPGA Approach. IEEE Trans. Neural Nets 18(5) (2007)
12. Torres-Huitzil, C., et al.: Hardware/Software Co-design for Embedded Implementation of Neural Networks. In: Applied Reconfigurable Computing Workshop, pp. 167–178 (2007)
13. Wu, Q.X., et al.: Adaptive Co-Ordinate Transformation Based on Spike Timing-Dependent Plasticity Learning Paradigm. In: Wang, L., Chen, K., S. Ong, Y. (eds.) ICNC 2005. LNCS, vol. 3610, pp. 420–428. Springer, Heidelberg (2005)

Survey of Advanced CABAC Accelerator Architectures for Future Multimedia

Yahya Jan and Lech Jozwiak

Faculty of Electrical Engineering
Eindhoven University of Technology, The Netherlands
{Y.Jan,L.Jozwiak}@tue.nl

Abstract. The future high quality multimedia systems require efficient video coding algorithms and corresponding adaptive high-performance computational platforms. In this paper, we survey the hardware accelerator architectures for Context-based Adaptive Binary Arithmetic Coding (CABAC) of H.264/AVC. The purpose of the survey is to deliver a critical insight in the proposed solutions, and this way facilitate further research on accelerator architectures, architecture development methods and supporting EDA tools. The architectures are analyzed, classified and compared based on the core hardware acceleration concepts, algorithmic characteristics, video resolution support and performance parameters, and some promising design directions are discussed.

Keywords: RC hardware architectures, accelerators, multimedia processing, UHDTV, video compression, H.264/AVC, CABAC.

1 Introduction

The real-time performance requirement of modern multimedia applications, like: video conferencing and telephony, medical imaging, and especially High Definition Television (HDTV) and new emerging Ultra HDTV (UHDTV) require highly efficient computational platforms. The problem is amplified by demands of higher and higher quality, particularly in the video broadcast domain, what results in a huge amount of data processing for the new standards of digital TV, like UHDTV that requires a resolution of (7680x4320)~33Megapixel with a data rate of 24Gbps. Additionally, the latest standards video coding algorithms are much more complex. The computational platforms for multimedia are also required to be (re-)configurable, to enable their adaptation to the various domains, accessing networks, standards and work modes. Hardware accelerators constitute the kernel of such (re-)configurable high-performance platforms.

The H.264/AVC [1] is the latest multi-domain video coding standard that provides the coding efficiency of almost 50% higher than former standards at the cost of almost four times increase in computational complexity. Context-based Adaptive Binary Arithmetic Coding (CABAC) [2], an entropy coding technique, covers Main and High profiles of H.264/AVC for high-end applications. Its purely software based implementation results in an unsatisfactory performance for High

J. Becker et al. (Eds.): ARC 2009, LNCS 5453, pp. 342–348, 2009.
© Springer-Verlag Berlin Heidelberg 2009

Definition (HD) video (e.g. 30-40 cycles are required on average for a single bin decoding on DSP [3]). CABAC is a bottleneck in the overall codec performance. Consequently, a sophisticated hardware accelerator for CABAC is an absolute necessity. However, the bitwise serial processing nature of CABAC, the strong dependencies among the different partial computations, a substantial number of memory accesses, and variable number of cycles per bin processing put a huge challenge on the design of such an effective and efficient hardware accelerator.

This paper surveys several most advanced recently proposed hardware accelerator architectures for CABAC. Its main purpose is to deliver a critical insight in the proposed solutions, and this way facilitate further research on accelerator architectures, development methods and supporting electronic design automation (EDA) tools. The architectures are analyzed, classified and compared based on the core hardware acceleration concepts, algorithmic characteristics, video resolution support and performance parameters in the hardware accelerator domain, like throughput, frequency, resource utilization and power consumption. Based on the architecture comparison some promising design directions are discussed in view of the requirements of current and future digital multimedia applications.

The rest of the paper is organized as follows. Section 2 introduces CABAC. Section 3 covers the main hardware accelerator concepts, implementation difficulties in CABAC and presents a critical review of advanced hardware accelerator architectures for CABAC in detail. Section 4 concludes the paper.

2   Introduction to CABAC

CABAC utilizes three elementary processes to encode a syntax element (SE), i.e. an element of data (motion data, quantized transform coefficients data, control data) represented in the bitstream to be encoded. The processes are: binarization, context modeling and binary arithmetic coding, as shown in Figure 1.

The *binarization* maps a non-binary valued SE to a unique binary representation referred to as bin string. Each bit of this binary representation is called a bin. The *context modeling* process estimates the probabilities of the bins in the form of context models, before they are encoded arithmetically. CABAC defines

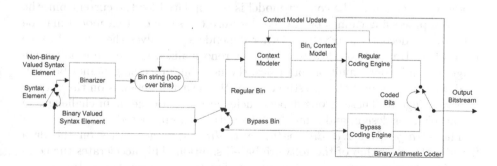

Fig. 1. Block Diagram of CABAC Encoder

460 unique context models, each of which corresponds to a certain bin or several bins of a SE, and are updated after bin encoding. Context model comprises of the probability state index (pStateIdx) and the most probable symbol (MPS) value of the bin. The *binary arithmetic coding engine* consists of two sub-engines: regular and bypass. The regular engine utilizes adaptive context models, but the bypass engine assumes a uniform context model to speed up encoding. To encode a bin, the regular coding engine requires the context model and the interval range (width) R and base (lower bound) L of the current code interval. The interval is then divided into two subintervals (R_{LPS}, R_{MPS}) according to the probability estimate (ρ_{LPS}) of the least probable symbol (LPS) [2]. Then one of the subintervals is chosen as the new interval based on whether the bin is equal to LPS or MPS. The context model is then updated, and the renormalization takes place to keep R and L within their legal ranges. The process repeats for the next bin.

3   Overview of Hardware Accelerators for CABAC

The main concepts of hardware acceleration can be summarized as follows: parallelism exploitation for execution of a particular computation instance due to availability of multiple application-specific operational resources working in parallel; parallelism exploitation for execution of several different computation instances at the same time due to pipelining; application-specific processing units with tailored processing and data granularity. More specifically these concepts can be oriented towards the data parallelism, functional parallelism and their mixture. In the past a number of different basic architecture types for hardware acceleration were proposed: parallel; pipeline; parallel pipeline; general purpose processor augmented by loosely coupled hardware accelerator; extensible/customizable application specific instruction set processor (ASIP) with basic accelerators in the form of instruction set extensions (ISE). These basic architectures will be used to categorize the CABAC accelerators.

Before considering the accelerators, we have to give a brief overview of the main implementation issues in CABAC. Five memory operations are involved in the en-/decoding of a single bin and two blocking dependencies that hamper the parallel and pipeline approaches. The first dependency is relevant to the context model update. Unless the context model is not updated for the current bin, the next bin processing cannot be started, because the same context model may be used to en-/decode the next bin. Other dependency involves the interval range R and base L update. Unless both are not renormalized in the renormalization stage, which involves multiple branches, the next bin processing cannot be initiated, because the probability estimation of the next bin depends on the current interval range R. These strong dependencies are some of the main challenges in the accelerator design, and a number of solutions are proposed.

The *straightforward datapath/controller* approach relies on the data flows in the algorithm of the software based solution. This accelerates the computations to some degree, but does not exploit the true (parallel) nature of the application algorithms. In CABAC accelerators, it takes as many as 14 cycles to process a single bin [4]. After further optimizations throughput of 0.2 bin/cycle is achieved in [4] for en-/decoding, and 0.33~0.50 bin/cycle in [5] for decoding.

The inefficiency of the straightforward approach for HD video motivated the research community to propose **parallel accelerators** to process more than 1 bin/cycle. However, in en-/decoding of even a single bin complex interdependencies have to be resolved as discussed before, and consequently, the algorithm can not be parallelized in its true basic nature. Utilizing the static and dynamic characteristics of the SEs that can be discovered through CABAC analysis for real video, the parallelism can be achieved up to some level for some SEs, what can result in processing of more than 1 bin/cycle. However, in parallel en-/decoding of two or more regular bins the context models have to be supplied to the coding engines. Due to the blocking dependencies, this cannot be performed in parallel.

In the first parallel architecture for CABAC decoding [3] the parallelism is achieved through a cascade of the arithmetic decoding engines: two regular ones and two bypass. This enables the decoding of 1 Regular Bin (1RB), 1RB with 1 Bypass Bin (1BB), 2RB with 1BB, and 2BB bins in parallel for frequently occurring SEs, like residual data and results in the throughput of 1~3 bins/cycle. The architectures [6][7][8][9] are based on the same concept, but after specific extensions are capable to en-/decode HD video. In [10] five different architectures for CABAC encoder were proposed. Two RB with BB architectures perform better for HD video than the others. A predictive approach is employed in [11]. Unlike [3][6][7][8][9], in which there is a latency due to the cascaded arithmetic engines, this architecture initiates decoding of two bins simultaneously by prediction.

The cascaded processing engines of the parallel accelerators increase the critical path delay and hardware resources. In addition, it accelerates only the processing of certain frequent SEs, and the number of bin(s)/cycle varies. Therefore, **pipeline accelerators** were proposed with the prime goal of achieving the real-time performance for HD video. However, the pipeline hazards appear as a byproduct of pipelining, due to the tight dependencies in the CABAC algorithm. There are two pipeline hazards in CABAC: data and structural. A data hazard occurs when the same context model is used for the next bin as for the current bin (read after write). A structural hazard occurs when the context memory is accessed at the same time due to the context model write for the current bin and context model read for the next bin. These hazards cause the pipeline stalls that decrease the throughput from the maximum of 1 bin/cycle to a lower value.

Zheng et al. [12] proposed a two-stage pipeline decoding architecture for residual data only. The stalls in the pipeline are eliminated using standard look ahead (SLA) technique, to determine the context model for the next bin using both possible values of the current bin. This SLA approach is also used in [13][14]. Yi et al. [15] proposed a two-stage pipeline decoding architecture, to reduce the pipeline latency and to increase the throughput. The data hazards are removed using the forwarding approach, and the structural hazards by using a context model reservoir. However, the stalls due to SE switching limit the throughput to an average of 0.25 bin/cycle. This problem is solved in [16] by using a SE predictor, that increases the throughput to 0.82 bin/cycle. Li et al. [17] proposed a three-stage dynamic pipeline codec architecture. The pipeline is dynamic as the pipeline latency varies between one and two cycles depending on the bin type. For data hazards removal a pipeline bypass scheme is used and for structural hazards a dual-port SRAM. Tian et al. [18] proposed a three-stage pipeline encoding architecture. Two pipeline buffers are introduced to resolve the pipeline hazards and the latency in [17]. This results in the throughput of exactly 1 bin/cycle.

The **parallel pipeline accelerators** combine the acceleration features of both approaches, what often results in a super fast accelerator. We could benefit from this approach, if we would be able to process multiple bins in a pipeline fashion without any stall. Although we can not fully utilize this approach, because it will make the accelerator architecture very complex or may even be impossible to design, its limited application is possible by utilizing the characteristics of SEs, like the processing of a single RB with one or more BB in parallel pipeline fashion. This approach drastically improves the throughput which is the requirement of future multimedia systems. Shi et al. [14] proposed a parallel pipeline approach for the real-time decoding of HD video with 4-stages that can decode 1RB or 2BB bin(s)/cycle without any stall. Due to the processing of multiple bypass bins in pipeline average throughput of 1.27 bins/cycle is achieved. The decoding rate of 254Mbins/s of this approach is much higher compared to ~45Mbins/s required for HD1080i video. Structural hazards are solved using two dual-port SRAMs and data hazards using forwarding technique and redundant circuitry.

The configurability and extensibility makes ASIP interesting option for the high-end adaptive applications. **ASIP-based accelerators** for CABAC were

Table 1. Comparison of Different Hardware Accelerator Architectures

Design Approach	Freq. MHz	Throughput Bin(s)/Cycle	VLSI Tech. TSMC(μm)	Circuit Area (gates)	Resolution Support
Datapath/Control					
[4] Codec	30	0.2	-	80,000(Inc.)*	SD480i
[5] Decoder	200	0.33~0.5	0.13	138,226(Inc.)	CIF
Parallel					
[3] Decoder	149	1~3	0.18	0.3mm^2+32x105reg	SD
[9] Encoder	186	1.9~2.3	0.35^{AMS}	19,426(Exc.)	CIF, HD
[11] Decoder	303	0.41	0.18	-	SD480i
Pipeline					
[12] Decoder	160	1	0.18	46.4K(Inc.)	HD1080i
[15] Decoder	225	0.25/0.82[16]	0.18	81,162+12.18KB	HD1080p
[17] Codec	230	0.60^{Enc}/0.50^{Dec}	0.18	0.496mm^2(Inc.)	HD1080i
[18] Encoder	186	1	0.35^{AMS}	19.1K(Exc.)	-
Parallel pipeline					
[14] Decoder	200	1.27	0.18	28,956+10.81KB	HD1080i
ASIP/ISE					
[20] Decoder	120	0.021/0.028**	-	-	-

*Context Memory included in the area calculation **LPS/MPS bins.

proposed in [19][20], but they do not satisfy the real-time requirements, e.g. in [20] 36 and 48 cycles are consumed in MPS and LPS bins decoding, respectively.

4 Conclusion

In this paper, we reviewed numerous approaches for the hardware accelerator architectures for CABAC from the viewpoint of the hardware acceleration concepts and performances. The straightforward architecture usually en-/decode from 0.2 to 0.5 bin/cycle, as shown in Table 1. Since the SEs are processed in a sequential manner, no substantial speed up is achieved. In the parallel approach the number of bins/cycle depends on the type of SE and fluctuates mostly between 1 and 4 bin(s)/cycle. In the purely pipeline approach the throughput never goes above 1 bin/cycle, but independent of SEs it remains at 1 or close to 1 bin/cycle. In the parallel pipeline approach, some extra performance is obtained from the characteristics of SEs, that enables to process some bins in parallel, and results in average throughput of more than 1 bin/cycle for HD video. This can be further improved, if the processing of one or more regular bin(s) and/or one or more bypass bin(s) is performed in parallel, but with steady and balanced pipeline, simple control and minimal area. From the analysis and comparison it follows that the parallel pipeline accelerator approach seems to be the most promising. However, the computational requirements of the current and future multimedia systems are increasing and require further research on accelerator architectures.

References

1. ITU-T: Recommendation and Final Draft International Standard of Joint Video Specification (ITU-T Rec. H. 264— ISO/IEC 14496-10 AVC) (May 2003)
2. Marpe, D.a.: Context-based adaptive binary arithmetic coding in the h.264/avc video compression standard. IEEE Transactions on CSVT, 620–636 (July 2003)
3. Yu, W., et al.: A high performance cabac decoding architecture. IEEE Transactions on Consumer Electronics, 1352–1359 (November 2005)
4. Ha, V., et al.: Real-time mpeg-4 avc/h.264 cabac entropy coder. In: 2005 Digest of Technical Papers. International Conference on ICCE, pp. 255–256 (January 2005)
5. Chen, J., et al.: A hardware accelerator for context-based adaptive binary arithmetic decoding in H. 264/AVC. In: ISCAS 2005, pp. 4525–4528 (2005)
6. Mei-hua, et al.: Optimizing design and fpga implementation for cabac decoder. In: International Symposium on HDP 2007, pp. 1–5 (June 2007)
7. Bingbo, L., et al.: A high-performance vlsi architecture for cabac decoding in h.264/avc. In: 7th International Conference on ASICON 2007, pp. 790–793 (October 2007)
8. Deprá, D.A., et al.: A novel hardware architecture design for binary arithmetic decoder engines based on bitstream flow analysis. In: SBCCI 2008, pp. 239–244 (2008)
9. Osorio, R.R., et al.: High-throughput architecture for h.264/avc cabac compression system. IEEE Transactions on CSVT, 1376–1384 (November 2006)
10. Pastuszak, G.: A high-performance architecture of the double-mode binary coder for h.264.avc. IEEE Transactions on CSVT, 949–960 (July 2008)

11. Kim, C., et al.: High speed decoding of context-based adaptive binary arithmetic codes using most probable symbol prediction. In: ISCAS 2006, p. 4 (2006)
12. Zheng, J., Wu, D., Xie, D., Gao, W.: A novel pipeline design for h.264 cabac decoding. In: Ip, H.H.-S., Au, O.C., Leung, H., Sun, M.-T., Ma, W.-Y., Hu, S.-M. (eds.) PCM 2007. LNCS, vol. 4810, pp. 559–568. Springer, Heidelberg (2007)
13. Eeckhaut, H., et al.: Optimizing the critical loop in the h.264/avc cabac decoder. In: IEEE International Conference on FPT 2006, pp. 113–118 (December 2006)
14. Shi, B., et al.: Pipelined architecture design of h.264/avc cabac real-time decoding. In: 4th IEEE International Conference on ICCSC 2008, pp. 492–496 (May 2008)
15. Yi, Y., et al.: High-speed h.264/avc cabac decoding. IEEE CSVT, 490–494 (2007)
16. Son, W., et al.: Prediction-based real-time cabac decoder for high definition h.264/avc. In: IEEE International Symposium on ISCAS 2008, pp. 33–36 (May 2008)
17. Li, L., et al.: A hardware architecture of cabac encoding and decoding with dynamic pipeline for h.264/avc. J. Signal Process. Syst., 81–95 (2008)
18. Tian, X.a.: Implementation strategies for statistical codec designs in h.264/avc standard. In: 19th IEEE International Symposium on RSP 2008, pp. 151–157 (June 2008)
19. Flordal, O., et al.: Accelerating cabac encoding for multi-standard media with configurability. In: 20th International IPDPS 2006, p. 8 (April 2006)
20. Rouvinen, J., et al.: Context adaptive binary arithmetic decoding on transport triggered architectures. In: SPIE Conference Series (March 2008)

Real Time Simulation in Floating Point Precision Using FPGA Computing

Beniamin Apopei, Andy Mills, Tony Dodd, and Haydn Thompson

Department of Automatic Control And Systems Engineering
Sheffield, UK
{B.Apopei,A.R.Mills,T.J.Dodd,H.Thompson,ACSE}@sheffield.ac.uk

Abstract. Real time simulations are indispensable for evaluation of new components, control system development, and system integration. There is a trade-off between model fidelity and the computational demands of the model; often lower fidelity models are chosen to speed development and to enable real time testing. FPGA technology offers an advantage over software simulation by exploiting bit and instruction level parallelism by default, but traditionally at the expense of coding effort and the need for experienced hardware engineers. The high cost of developing a model to execute on a FPGA is particularly prohibitive due to modifications occurring during system development. The work presents a process enabling an engineer to avoid hand-coded VHDL programming, yet take full advantage of the technology. The process described comes as a complete package: creating the model using pre-defined libraries, compilation and execution using specialized FPGA tools, simulation, co-simulation and interfacing with other technologies using in-house developed drivers.

1 Introduction

Execution of sequential code introduces major limitations in current computing technologies. As a model's complexity increases so does the effort required for testing or simulation. Despite often considerable efforts, it is frequently impossible to achieve the speed up required for high fidelity models. One solution to the problem is to develop physical prototypes for the systems in hardware [1] (e.g. engines, valve blocks, hydraulics, etc.) but sometimes results can be poor and the actual implementation expensive and complicated to achieve. Therefore there is a need for new technologies that can be manipulated, expanded, reconfigured and signal faults and errors injected in a model without damaging or putting the hardware equipment at risk.

FPGA technology can be reconfigured in order to simulate, emulate and replicate complex hardware models in real time. At the moment there is no simple process or feasible libraries of floating point control blocks that can be reused in a robust manner in order to speed up the execution of models. Available FPGA technologies offer solutions for fixed point implementations [2] but even so, the tools chain required is complicated to use. For floating point implementation, the available FPGA libraries require different pre-compilation stages, exporting and importing code from one

J. Becker et al. (Eds.): ARC 2009, LNCS 5453, pp. 349–354, 2009.
© Springer-Verlag Berlin Heidelberg 2009

software tool to another, additional hand written code without the use of visual interfaces or drag and drop features [3]. Therefore the work presented focuses on building
up a library of trusted and validated floating point VHDL blocks that can be reconfigured and reused in a drag and drop manner. Most of the blocks are hand coded VHDL
routines which are imported in MATLAB Simulink using System Generator, a visual
tool suite provided by Xilinx, one of the biggest FPGA manufacturers. The whole
process comes as a complete package where models are converted or created in a
MATLAB Simulink visual format, compiled into VHDL, exported into Xilinx ISE
and then loaded onto a FPGA platform as an end product.

In conventional software simulation this data flow is orchestrated by an operating
system [4]. The parallelism is limited, at best, to the number of processing cores
available and hence does not allow exploitation of multiple concurrent calculations as
discussed above. Most available VHDL blocks used in FPGA computing introduce
latencies [5] into the model and unwanted variations of sample time clocks. A significant contribution of the work presented in this paper is that all the blocks in the library of components output within the same clock cycle without introducing extra
latencies so there is no need for a sequential operating system or extra complicated
control signals to keep the multitude of blocks running at the same rate.

As the complexity of the models increases, the VHDL implementation cannot be
accommodated on a single FPGA chip therefore a new application was developed in
order to allow multi-chip inter-communication and spread the models across multiple
FPGA chips.

The work presented is undertaken within the DTI/TSB funded MOSAIC project
which started in the UK. The project is run by an industrial/academic consortium
including Rolls-Royce, Jaguar Cars and Land Rover, Goodrich and York University.
Our role was to develop a parallel processing platform for real-time simulations on
FPGA technology.

2 Tool Suite Used

The tool suite used allows integration with precompiled library components for which
the user does not require much FPGA experience to create and use. Virtually any
engineer with MATLAB Simulink knowledge should be able to use the tool suite and
explore the FPGA capabilities of this development platform.

Figure 1 shows the programming flow required for the whole process. It starts with
Core Generator [6], where some of the library components are developed. Subsequently, the components are imported into System Generator as black boxes. The
application is created here as a MATLAB Simulink model and then compiled into ISE
VHDL project format. Once the pin map is generated for the target application, ISE
[6] compiles the project and generates the configuration '.bit' files required by the
hardware. These files are downloaded to the FPGA platform via Impact and then
interfaced to MATLAB via Ethernet. The novelty of this process is that it allows
floating point, control blocks to be used and the compilation flow can be made transparent to the user by execution of predefined scripts.

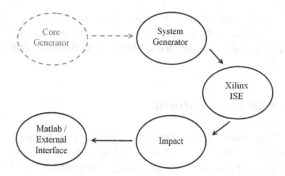

Fig. 1. Tool Suite programming flow: data is passed from one software tool to another, going through different compilation stages. The dashed grey line indicates an optional step.

3 Floating Point Block Library

In control systems, output precision is crucial. The models provided by Rolls-Royce and Jaguar Cars contained a multitude of feedback paths and a wide variation in the signals range. The work started by modeling the designs using fixed point implementation as the literature suggests that floating point operations typically require too much FPGA area to be practical on current devices [7]. Tests showed that in order to keep the modeling errors to an acceptable level compared to the single implementation, the width of the signals exceeded 64 bits in fixed point implementation and used more FPGA area.

All the basic floating point operations included in the library were generated using Core Generator [6]. The VHDL templates used contain all the information needed for replicating the operations in FPGA logic. The missing elements are the configuration script files required by Simulink and System Generator in order to integrate the components for use within MATLAB. These can easily be written using MATLAB Sfunctions. Therefore once the library is generated, the designer does not need to write any more scripts and the usage of black boxes becomes transparent to the user.

4 Multichip Interface Expansion

Most of the high fidelity models are very complex and the VHDL implementation requires that the application is spread across multiple FPGA chips. Our aim was to avoid using a processor to control the FPGA inter-chip communication as this would add a layer of complication and resource overhead to the design [8]. Therefore a new simpler communication algorithm suitable for FPGAs is proposed to make better use of the bandwidth available and significantly increase the performance of the system overall.

The data width uses 32 bits, representing single precision numbers and just 4 bits are used for control. This would allow 16 signals to be time-multiplexed transferred over a 36 bits channel. The implementation involves decomposing the FPGA clocking frequency 16-fold, to transmit one 32 bit wide message per clock.

Time multiplexing/de-multiplexing blocks were created in order to use with System Generator in Simulink and they are included in the interfacing library block set. These are configurable and reusable blocks that can be dragged and dropped into any System Generator design.

5 FPGA Development Platform

The multi-chip FPGA platform consists of 2 independent FPGA boards: a Virtex4 FPGA board used for the interface with the outside world and a Virtex5 FPGA board [9] used for the heavy computation and inter-chip communication. The Virtex4 board is designed for various interfaces (PCI express, analogue, optical fibre, parallel, pin to pin, fast serial, etc.). In the work presented it is mainly used for the Ethernet capabilities as most industry partners require Ethernet communication for both hardware in the loop [10] and desktop applications.

In real time systems any variation in the input sample time can produce false results. Clock synchronization is crucial and if the input sample time variation is relatively small this can be achieved by specialized integrated circuits like PLLs[1]. In order not to limit the capability of the FPGA platform to this constraint, a new interface design that resynchronizes itself was created. One of the Virtex5 chips is assigned as a master chip that is interfaced with the Virtex4 board and generates the synchronizations clocks.

The Virtex5 FPGA board waits until it receives a new input from the external interface. After the new data is received, the master FPGA asserts the model clocks for the different parts of the model running on different chips, computes the model results, de-asserts the model clock, sends the output results and then maintains the model clocks on stand-by until the next input arrives. This is another contribution of this paper: It allows the FPGA platform to run a system control model synchronously (e.g. models with discrete internal states like integrators, transfer functions) which receives inputs from an asynchronous interface without the use of a PowerPC or an operating system on the FPGA. Also, the results are all computed and transmitted during the same model clock cycle.

Figure 2 depicts the process: As the new data arrives in graph a), the master FPGA (FPGA1) asserts the model clock which runs the logic used for the model on the chip (model clock1). After T1 has elapsed, FPGA1 transmits data to FPGA2 using the inter-chip multiplexed communication described in the last chapter and temporary de-asserts model clock1. After Ti has elapsed, the FPGA1 asserts the model clock for FPGA2 (model clock2) which computes its part of the model. After T2 has elapsed, the FPGA1 de-asserts model clock2 on FPGA2 and holds it on standby. Data is sent back to FPGA1, model clock1 is re-asserted and used to compute the last part of the model. After T3 has elapsed, results are ready to be sent via Ethernet by FPGA1 and model clock1 is de-asserted. FPGA1 is clocked twice within the same sample period in order to allow data computed by FPGA2 to be used without introducing one sample period delay. All the blocks using internal states on FPGA1 are validated during T3 therefore the model is not oversampled by the use of T1 and T3.

---

[1] Phase Locked Loop.

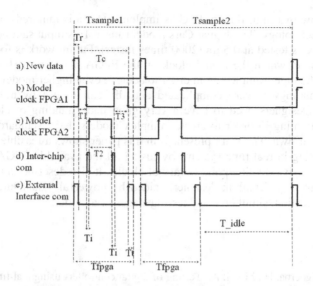

Fig. 2. FPGA platform integration with possible asynchronous systems. Graph a) represents the input sample timing. Graphs b) and c) represent the clock generated on FPGA 1 and FPGA 2 of the platform. Graph d) shows the timing for the inter-chip communications and graph e) the timing for the external interface.

Also, in Figure 2, Tfpga is always constant and does not depend on the input sample times. The parts of the model which are implemented on FPGA1 and FPGA2 do not have to be independent as intercommunication within the same sample rate is achievable. The FPGA platform is able to cope with any variations in the input sample time, provided that the sample time is not faster than the actual interface delays and FPGA computing time put together.

6 Results and Conclusion

The process described in this paper was tested using models provided by Jaguar Cars. Initial work showed that whole system could not be put onto a single FPGA chip. Therefore we partitioned the high frequency part of the model onto FPGA and the low frequency part onto COTS real-time operating system. The time multiplexed inter-chip interface described in Chapter 4 was used between 2 FPGA chips without affecting the sampling time of the model. The technique was successfully tested using Ethernet interface and connected to MATLAB Simulink using the UDP[1] packages library. The communication timing was monitored using Ethereal capture [11], a powerful Network Protocol Analyzer. Test benching was performed against the Simulink implementation of the models. In double point precision implementation, there were no errors on the output of the FPGA platform. Since Simulink cannot operate particular blocks in single precision (e.g. accumulation and internal states of integrators, etc.) exact test benching using only single precision was not achievable.

---

[1] User Datagram Protocol.

Results show that high fidelity FPGAs implementation is hundreds of times faster than current technology. The Jaguar Cars model runs at 1ms input sample rates yet the FPGA model was tested at 0.5 μs (2000 times faster). Future work is focused on creating a process in which the model clock on the FPGA platform performs runs as a multi-rate of the input sample rate in order to achieve even higher model fidelity.

FPGA technology is very complicated and difficult to use by non-experienced FPGA users. Designers need to have a very good understanding of electronics and VHDL programming in order to create complex models if the standard Xilinx tools are used on their own. The work presented in this paper shows a feasible way of using FPGA computing in real time systems by fusing all the available FPGA tools, creating a comprehensive floating point library of blocks. It also describes a process which is easy to follow by Simulink designers, aided by powerful visual interfaces which speed up the creation, simulation and testing stages of a model.

References

1. Wu, X., Figueroa, H., Monti, A.: Testing of digital controllers using real-time hardware in the loop simulation. In: Power Electronics Specialists Conference, 2004. PESC 2004. 2004 IEEE 35th Annual, Aachen, Germany, vol. 5, pp. 3622–3627 (2004)
2. Robert, D.T., Chris, D., David, B.P., James, H.: Modelling and Implementation of DSP FPGA Solutions. White Paper, 2000 - origin.xilinx.com (2004)
3. Zhi, G., Abhishek, M., Walid, N.: Automation of IP core interface generation for reconfigurable computing. In: 16th International Conference on Field Programmable Logic and Applications (FPL 2006), Madrid, Spain (2006)
4. Brian, S., Steve, C., Chen, C., Joe, C., Matt, F., Ivan, H., Tam, T., Terri, V.: Reconfigurable Architectures for Systems Level Applications of Adaptive Computing, University of Southern California Information Sciences Institute. Arlington, VA 22203 (2000)
5. Ho, C.H., Leong, M.P., Leong, P.H.W., Becker, J., Glesner, M.: Rapid Prototyping of FPGA based Floating Point DSP Systems. In: Rapid System Prototyping, 2002. Proceedings. 13th IEEE International Workshop, Hong Kong, Shatin, pp. 19–24 (2002)
6. Xilinx, http://www.xilinx.com
7. Ligon III, W.B., McMillan, S., Monn, G., Schoonover, K., Stivers, F., Underwood, K.D.: A re-evaluation of the practicality of floating-point operations on FPGAs. In: FPGAs for Custom Computing Machines, 1998. Proceedings. IEEE Symposium, Napa Valley, USA, pp. 206–215 (1998)
8. Vincent, K., Jörg, S., Günther, D.: Reusable Design of Inter-chip Communication Interfaces for Next Generation of Adaptive Computing Systems. In: Beigl, M., Lukowicz, P. (eds.) ARCS 2005. LNCS, vol. 3432, pp. 167–177. Springer, Heidelberg (2005)
9. Synplicity, http://www.synplicity.com/literature/haps/datasheets/haps-52-ds.pdf
10. Mark, K., Nariman, S.: Hardware-in-the-Loop Simulator for Research on Fault Tolerant Control of Electrohydraulic Flight Control Systems. In: Proceedings of the 2006 American Control Conference Minneapolis, USA (2006)
11. Ethereal, http://ethereal.brothersoft.com/

A Hardware Analysis of Twisted Edwards Curves for an Elliptic Curve Cryptosystem

Brian Baldwin[1,2], Richard Moloney[1,3], Andrew Byrne[2], Gary McGuire[1,3], and William P. Marnane[1,2]

[1] Claude Shannon Institute for Discrete Mathematics, Coding and Cryptography
[2] Dept. of Electrical & Electronic Engineering, University College Cork, Cork, Ireland
[3] Dept. of Mathematics, University College Dublin, Dublin, Ireland
{brianb,andrewb,liam}@eleceng.ucc.ie,
{richard.moloney,gary.mcguire}@ucd.ie

Abstract. This paper presents implementation results of a reconfigurable elliptic curve processor defined over prime fields $GF(p)$. We use this processor to compare a new algorithm for point addition and point doubling operations on the twisted Edwards curves, against a current standard algorithm in use, namely the Double-and-Add. Power analysis secure versions of both algorithms are also examined and compared. To the authors' knowledge, this work introduces the first documented FPGA implementation for computations on twisted Edwards curves over fields $GF(p)$.

1 Introduction

In this paper we present implementation results of a reconfigurable elliptic curve processor (ECP) for a generalisation of the Edwards curve [1], the twisted Edwards curve, recently proposed by Bernstein et. al. [2]. We examine both the implementation efficiency and implementation security of twisted Edwards curves and compare them against current standard curves and methods in use today. We examine firstly, in projective coordinates, the explicit formulas for point addition and point doubling of the standard twisted Edwards formulas [1] and compare against the widely used Double-and-Add method [3].We then examine the strongly unified formula, which is resistant to simple power analysis (SPA) [4], a form of side-channel analysis, and compare it to its equivalent, the Double-and-Add-Always method [5].

2 Elliptic Curves

We consider an elliptic curve over the field $GF(p)$ for some prime p. In Jacobian projective coordinates, this curve is given by the equation

$$Y^2 = X^3 + AXZ^4 + BZ^6 \tag{1}$$

[1] Explicit-formulas database. URL: http://hyperelliptic.org/EFD

J. Becker et al. (Eds.): ARC 2009, LNCS 5453, pp. 355–361, 2009.
© Springer-Verlag Berlin Heidelberg 2009

where the Jacobian projective point $(X_1 : Y_1 : Z_1)$ corresponds to the affine point $(X_1/Z_1^2, Y_1/Z_1^3)$ if $Z_1 \neq 0$, and $\mathcal{O}$ the point at infinity, if $Z_1 = 0$.

The basic operations of ECC are point scalar computations of the form $Q = [k]\,P$. Point scalar multiplication (PM) can be performed using algorithms such as the Double-and-Add method [3]. This method requires $m-1$ point doublings (PD) and $w-1$ point additions (PA), where m is the length and w is the Hamming weight of the binary expansion of k.

Each PA and PD is comprised of finite field additions, subtractions, multiplications and inversions. By representing each point on the curve in projective (X, Y, Z) rather than affine (x, y) coordinates, each PA and PD can be performed without the need for inversions, albeit at the cost of extra multiplications. This will improve efficiency since the cost of inversions is significantly more expensive than multiplications [6].

The equations governing PA and PD in projective coordinates using the Double-and-Add method, on a Weierstrass curve, are given in [3]. Each PA requires 16 multiplications and 7 additions/subtractions, with 10 multiplications and 4 additions/subtractions required for a PD.

2.1   Simple Power Analysis Resistance

Simple Power Analysis (SPA), makes use of side-channel analysis to monitor and measure the power emitted from a single execution of a cycle of a crypto processor [7]. Each PA and PD operation produces a different power trace when executed because of the different number of multiplications and additions involved in each, and as the execution of a point addition in the Double-and-Add is directly related to the current bit of the secret key (k_i), it is possible to retrieve the secret key by monitoring the power consumption of a single execution of a scalar multiplication.

The Double-and-Add-Always Algorithm [3], is a simplistic approach to solving the problem of the SPA susceptibility. It performs dummy point addition executions, so that every execution of the key k executes a point double and a point addition regardless of whether $k_i = 0$ or $k_i = 1$, with the key bit deciding where to write the result. This leads to an inefficient design as unnecessary operations are performed, but it does prevent the recognition of individual bits.

2.2   Edwards Curves

In [2], Bernstein et al. introduced the twisted Edwards curves

$$ax^2 + y^2 = 1 + dx^2 y^2 \tag{2}$$

where a, $d \in GF(p)$ are distinct and non-zero. If $a = 1$, the curve may be called an Edwards curve. They further showed that a significant number of elliptic curves over $GF(p)$ (roughly 1/4 of isomorphism classes of elliptic curves) are birationally equivalent to a twisted Edwards curve. Two curves are birationally equivalent if there is an invertible rational mapping between them (such as $(x, y) \mapsto (\frac{y}{x-1}, \frac{x}{y-1})$), which may be undefined at a finite number of points.

The chief advantage of Edwards and twisted Edwards curves over standard curves is that the addition laws defined on them can be made unified, i.e., a single addition formula can be used to add points and double points, with no exception for the identity. We use the projective twisted Edwards curve

$$aX^2Z^2 + Y^2Z^2 = Z^4 + dX^2Y^2 \tag{3}$$

so as to avoid inversions. The projective point $(X_1 : Y_1 : Z_1)$ corresponds to the affine point $(X_1/Z_1, Y_1/Z_1)$.

Algorithm 1 and 2 give the PD and PA for the non SPA resistant twisted Edwards algorithms, while Algorithm 3 gives the unified formula.

Algorithm 1: Point Doubling for twisted Edwards	**Algorithm 2**: Point Addition for twisted Edwards
input : $P(X_1, Y_1, Z_1) \in GF(p)$	**input** : $P(X_1, Y_1, Z_1)$;
output: $[2]P(X_3, Y_3, Z_3) \in$	$Q(X_2, Y_2, Z_2) \in GF(p)$
$E(GF(p))$	**output**: $P(X_3, Y_3, Z_3) \in E(GF(p))$
$B = (X_1 + Y_1)^2, C = X_1^2$	$A = Z_1Z_2, B = A^2$;
$C = X_1X_2, D = Y_1Y_2, E = aC$	$C = X_1X_2, D = Y_1Y_2$;
$F = E+D, H = Z_1^2, J = F-2H$	$E = dCD, F = B - E, G = B + E$;
$X_3 = (B - C - D)J,$	$X_3 = AF((X_1+Y_1)(X_2+Y_2)-C-D)$;
$Y_3 = F(E - D), Z_3 = FJ$	$Y_3 = AG(D - aC), Z_3 = FG$

Algorithm 3: Unified twisted Edwards point operation

input : $P(X_1, Y_1, Z_1); Q(X_2, Y_2, Z_2) \in GF(p)$
output: $P + Q(X_3, Y_3, Z_3) \in E(GF(p))$

$A = Z_1Z_2, B = A^2, C_1 = aX_1X_2, C_2 = X_1Y_2$;
$D_1 = Y_1Y_2, D_2 = X_2Y_1, E = dC_2D_2, F = B - E, G = B + E$;
$X_3 = AF(C_2 + D_2), Y_3 = AG(D_1 - C_1), Z_3 = FG$

Algorithm 2 requires 12 multiplications and 8 additions, Algorithm 1 requires 8 multiplications and 7 additions and Algorithm 3 processes the same formula for both PA and PD, thereby giving it the same power trace for either operation, at a cost of 14 multiplications and 5 additions per point operation.

3   FPGA Based Elliptic Curve Processor

A reconfigurable architecture for performing elliptic curve cryptography was designed [8] and ported onto an FPGA device. It consists of a controller, containing an instruction set stored in ROM and a finite state machine (FSM), a user definable number of arithmetic logic units (ALU's) for addition, subtraction and multiplication calculations in parallel, and BlockRAM for storage of results, as illustrated in Figure 1.

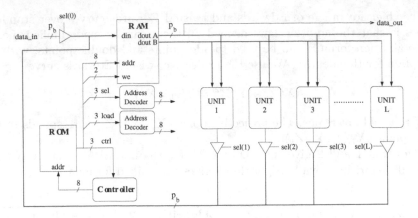

Fig. 1. Reconfigurable Elliptic Curve Processor

The ALUs perform the $GF(p)$ operations described in section 2, namely the modular multiplications, additions and subtractions. Mode bits are used to select between operations. Modular multiplication is achieved using the Montgomery multiplication algorithm [9] and is executed in $p_b + 2$ clock cycles, where p_b is the field size in bits, while modular additions and subtractions each take 2 clock cycles.

4   Performance Results of ECC Algorithms

The ECP can be programmed to run any number of ALUs in parallel to process an elliptic curve formula. This design is limited only by the size of the FPGA. For this paper, the architecture was evaluated on a Spartan3E XC3S500E, and used one to four ALUs operating in parallel. Table 1 shows the measured results for the FPGA.

Table 1 firstly details the post place and route (PPR) clock frequency (F_{max}). There is very little variation in clock frequency between the different algorithms. The clock frequency in fact depends on the number and type of ALUs used. The minimum PPR frequency reported for all the configurations and combinations was recorded when using four multipliers.

The circuit design also remains the same for each of the four formulae, differing only in the size of the instruction set in ROM. The area, therefore, approximately remains the same for each of the four different formulae, and increases equivalently with more ALUs.

The average power (Pwr) dissipation of the processor was measured at a frequency of 10 MHz. The current being drawn by the FPGA on its $VCCINT$ and $VCCAUX$ lines was measured. The voltage supplied to each line by the board's voltage regulator was also measured. These voltage and current measurements were then used to calculate the total average power consumed on both lines. The energy per average multiplication is also given. The energy is calculated using the

Table 1. Spartan3E XC3S500E-4fg320 FPGA Results

ALU	F_{max} (Mhz)	Area (slices)	Time (ms)	Pwr (mW)	Energy (mJ)	ATProd (Clk/Slic)
	Double-and-Add					
1	27.921	1703	30.704	88.04	2.703	60.831
2	28.333	2896	16.582	96.53	1.601	56.692
3	27.84	3988	12.917	109.58	1.415	59.756
4	26.438	4654	12.905	107.52	1.386	66.161
	Double-and-Add-Always					
1	28.539	1702	48.863	87.84	4.292	98.893
2	28.183	2897	25.935	100.56	2.608	88.231
3	27.808	3989	18.331	106.99	1.961	84.726
4	26.68	4654	17.012	105.73	1.798	92.205
	twisted Edwards					
1	28.245	1703	18.428	88.08	1.623	36.935
2	28.746	2898	10.565	98.67	1.042	36.144
3	28.01	4269	7.448	115.82	0.863	36.884
4	25.097	4654	7.836	105.93	0.83	40.173
	twisted Edwards Strongly Unified					
1	27.976	1700	27.247	88.09	2.4	55.08
2	27.852	3171	19.743	98.67	1.931	66.058
3	27.816	4553	18.041	115.82	1.926	73.868
4	25.052	4654	12.543	105.93	1.317	64.784

Table 2. Point Double and Point Addition Timing

ALU	Point Double			Point Addition		
	Mul	Add	Clks	Mul	Add	Clks
	Double-and-Add					
1	10	13	1948	26	20	5035
2	6	13	1178	13	20	2538
3	5	13	962	9	20	1770
4	5	13	962	8	20	1578
	Double-and-Add-Always					
1	25	20	4842	25	20	4842
2	13	20	2538	13	20	2538
3	9	20	1770	9	20	1770
4	8	20	1578	8	20	1578
	twisted Edwards					
1	8	7	1536	12	8	2322
2	4	7	770	8	6	1550
3	3	7	578	5	7	976
4	3	7	578	5	6	974
	twisted Edwards Strongly Unified					
1	14	5	2700	14	5	2700
2	9	4	1736	9	4	1736
3	7	4	1352	7	4	1352
4	6	4	1160	6	4	1160

average power value and the average time per point multiplication, as shown in Tables 1, based on the number of clock cycles and the 10 MHz clock frequency.

4.1   Computation Time

The scheduling of the point operations was examined, again with a variable number of ALUs, to review the timing of each algorithm. Using a key size of 192 and performing all multiplications and additions/subtractions for the Point Addition and Point Doubling Algorithms for the Double-and-Add, and the twisted Edwards Algorithms, 1, 2 and 3, defined in Section 2, the timing results in Table 2 were obtained. As can be seen from the table, the number of multiplication stages (Mul) required to process an algorithm decreases with an increase in parallelisation. We do not modify the number of addition stages Add as an addition is completed in only two clock cycles. Next we tested each of the formulae with a 192-bit value for the key (k) and a Hamming weight of $\frac{k}{2}$ to measure an iteration of the algorithms. Table 1 shows the timing results. The table shows that the standard twisted Edwards algorithm performs on average 60% faster than its equivalent Double-and-Add algorithm for all counts of ALUs.

The table also shows that the SPA resistant unified twisted Edwards performs comparably to the non SPA resistant Double-and-Add method and performs faster for one or four ALUs. However, neither the standard twisted Edwards nor Double-and-Add achieve any great increase in timing when increasing from

3 ALUs to 4 ALUs, due to the algorithms limitations of parallelism. From the table we can see that again the standard twisted Edwards gives the best value across the range of ALUs, with 3 ALUs giving the best performance. For the Unified twisted Edwards and both the Double-and-Add formulae 4 ALUs gives the fastest timing.

4.2   Area Time Product

The area-time (AT) product was calculated to get a representation of any speed increase against the increase in size, as shown in Table 1. This gives a more accurate representation of the cost that each increase in ALU has in relation to the overall system. The minimum AT value, i.e. the most efficient combination in an area time sense, is again the standard twisted Edwards, giving the best value across the range of ALUs, with 2 ALUs giving the best performance. For the Unified twisted Edwards, a single ALU gives the best performance, while the Double-and-Add formulae give best AT at 2 and 3 ALUs respectively.

5   Conclusions

In this paper, we presented implementation results of an ECP with a reconfigurable architecture and used it to compare the standard and strongly unified formulae that define the twisted Edwards curve, against the Double-and-Add and Double-and-Add-Always formulae. We showed that the twisted Edwards performs on average 60% faster and uses less area than the Double-and-Add, and that the performance of the SPA resistant strongly unified version of the twisted Edwards, far exceeded its Double-and-Add-Always equivalent. We also showed that by using one or four ALUs operating in parallel, the strongly unified twisted Edwards execution time exceeds the Double-and-Add for an equivalent number of ALUs. Future work could involve an examination of the cost of converting a Double-and-Add to a strongly unified twisted Edwards curve to gain SPA resistance at comparable speeds.

Acknowledgement

Supported by the Science Foundation Ireland under Grant No. 06/MI/006.

References

1. Edwards, H.M.: A normal form for elliptic curves. Bulletin of the American Mathematical Society 44(3), 393–422 (2007)
2. Bernstein, D., Birkner, P., Joye, M., Lange, T., Peters, C.: Twisted Edwards curves. In: Vaudenay, S. (ed.) AFRICACRYPT 2008. LNCS, vol. 5023, pp. 389–405. Springer, Heidelberg (2008)

3. Knuth, D.E.: The Art of Computer Programming, 3rd edn. Seminumerical Algorithms of Addison-Wesley series in computer science and information processing, vol. 2. Addison-Wiley, Chichester (2001)
4. Brier, E., Joye, M.: Weierstraß Elliptic Curves and Side-Channel Attacks. In: Naccache, D., Paillier, P. (eds.) PKC 2002. LNCS, vol. 2274, pp. 335–345. Springer, Heidelberg (2002)
5. Coron, J.S.: Resistance against differential power analysis for elliptic curve cryptosystems. In: Koç, Ç.K., Paar, C. (eds.) CHES 1999. LNCS, vol. 1717, pp. 292–302. Springer, Heidelberg (1999)
6. Orlando, G., Paar, C.: A scalable GF(p) elliptic curve processor architecture for programmable hardware. In: Koç, Ç.K., Naccache, D., Paar, C. (eds.) CHES 2001. LNCS, vol. 2162, pp. 356–371. Springer, Heidelberg (2001)
7. Örs, S.B., Oswald, E., Preneel, B.: Power-analysis attacks on an FPGA – first experimental results. In: Walter, C.D., Koç, Ç.K., Paar, C. (eds.) CHES 2003. LNCS, vol. 2779, pp. 35–50. Springer, Heidelberg (2003)
8. Byrne, A., Popovici, E., Marnane, W.P.: Versatile processor for GF(p) arithmetic for use in cryptographic applications. In: Computers & Digital Techniques, IET, vol. 2, pp. 253–264 (July 2008)
9. Montgomery, P.: Modular multiplication without trial division. In: Mathematics of Computation, vol. 44, pp. 519–521 (1985)

A Seamless Virtualization Approach for Transparent Dynamical Function Mapping Targeting Heterogeneous and Reconfigurable Systems

Rainer Buchty, David Kramer, Fabian Nowak, and Wolfgang Karl

Universität Karlsruhe (TH)
Institut für Technische Informatik, Lehrstuhl für Rechnerarchitektur
76128 Karlsruhe, Germany
{buchty,kramer,nowak,karl}@ira.uka.de

Abstract. Future systems are not only heading towards increased parallelism, but also embrace heterogeneity and reconfigurability. We therefore present an approach targeting comfortable program development and execution, enabling full exploitation of the underlying hardware without burdening the application programmer with the details of the underlying hardware infrastructure. The approach employs lightweight resource virtualization by means of on-demand function resolution. By carefully extending the existing system infrastructure, the approach comes at virtually no cost and with highest compatibility to existing legacy code. The approach is suitable for a wide range of architectures from embedded systems to high-performance computing platforms.

1 Introduction and Motivation

Heterogeneity has become a key characteristic of current and future MPSoCs within converging commodity, embedded, and high-performance computing markets. This trend towards heterogeneous parallel systems is illustrated by current forecasts [4] as well as vendor road-maps [1,6]. When maximizing silicon use, an increased use of reconfigurability will be seen, enabling on-demand configuration of required application-specific hardware units.

Key problem of such architectures is fully exploiting these platforms' potential. As of now, application programmers typically have to concentrate on hardware-aware programming as opposed to the plain application itself, therefore spending most of the time for tailoring the implementation towards the architecture, producing a non-scalable, architecture-bound implementation. Naturally, this approach is not suitable for upcoming reconfigurable systems.

We therefore propose an approach that frees the programmer from the burden of hardware-aware programming. This approach dissects into two major building blocks, an augmented application description suitable for execution on heterogeneous, reconfigurable platforms, and an according runtime system performing transparent mapping of desired application subroutines or functions to individual implementations to be processed on hardware and software implementations. With respect to the increasing computational demands in embedded real-time devices, we put special focus on addressing the specific requirements of embedded systems concerning compatibility and efficiency.

J. Becker et al. (Eds.): ARC 2009, LNCS 5453, pp. 362–367, 2009.
© Springer-Verlag Berlin Heidelberg 2009

By carefully using and extending the individual features of already existing system components, our approach was specifically designed towards low runtime overhead and high compatibility to existing legacy code and OS interfaces. It is therefore universally applicable to both high-performance computation platforms and embedded systems and offers significant benefits over existing approaches.

2 Related Work

One example of future heterogeneous systems is given by the *Cray XD1* [9] computing platform. It features AMD Opteron CPUs for general-purpose computation and dedicated, FPGA-based hardware accelerators as computation units or application-specific coprocessors. The system is interconnected using state-of-the-art communication buses.

Programming of such heterogeneous multicore systems can be a tedious task; as of now, several approaches of different complexity exist. The *RapidMind* [11] is able to parallelize applications written in C/C++ across multiple cores and manages application execution, freeing developers from low-level optimizations for performance tuning. It does, however, not specifically address the use of reconfigurable systems.

Dealing with reconfigurability requires the introduction of certain abstraction, e.g. by introducing multiple stages of hardware service and software layers as it is the case in the *NoTA* architecture [16]. An abstraction on lowest hardware level is demonstrated by the *MOLEN* reconfigurable processor [12], one of several approaches of processors featuring a reconfigurable instruction set. Similar abstraction techniques are also employed within dedicated programming models for parallel systems. Examples are *EXOCHI* [15] and the derived *Merge* [10] framework that both target complete dynamization of program execution on heterogeneous systems using a library-based approach. IBM's recent *Liquid Metal* (Lime) program [13] targets the creation of a single unified programming language and environment that allows potentially all portions of a system to move fluidly between hardware and software, dynamically and adaptively. The concept bases on transparent and dynamic compilation and HW synthesis of Java programs to be co-executed on general-purpose processors and reconfigurable hardware.

The benefit of our approach compared to the listed concepts lies in its seamless expansion of existing system and development infrastructures, not requiring additional software layers, hence enabling highest level of compatibility, lowest overhead, and therefore easy integration into and interoperability with existing system architectures.

3 Platform Overview

Core of our approach depicted in Figure 1 is a feedback system formed by the processing hardware and its according runtime system. On this system, an application binary is executed on a reconfigurable processing hardware with according mappings to library-provided alternative implementations taking place. Hence, our approach divides into 3 distinct layers that are code generation, runtime system, and reconfigurable hardware. An application, written in conventional programming environments, is augmented in two ways: parts of the application may be marked as reconfigurable, meaning that affected code parts may be mapped at runtime to individual implementations

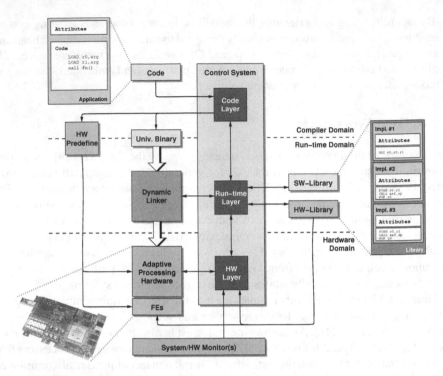

Fig. 1. Application Execution on Dynamically Reconfigurable Systems

with different properties, e.g. optimization for speed or for computational accuracy, and may require dedicated hardware to be executed on. Additional information is therefore provided defining the core requirements of affected code parts, such as hardware constraints, throughput, or computation accuracy. Using the possibilities of current binary file formats, this information is contained in each binary implementation, i.e. main program and linked libraries, and interpreted by the runtime system to guide mapping and configuration processes.

In order to adapt to to the heterogeneous system in the most adequate way, an application will typically consist of a static control part and dedicated, accelerable computing functions to be mapped to the current hardware configuration at runtime. The hardware configuration might be changed according to the requirements of the application or a dedicated computing function. To guide runtime configuration and mapping, we propose an **augmented binary** where an application will be enriched by according attributes, defining specific requirements of this application. Likewise, attributes are provided for implementation alternatives of accelerable functions. Within the generated binary, these functions point to a function stub which gets resolved by the runtime system according to the provided guidance information. That way, a smooth integration and upgrade path into existing program development infrastructures is ensured. On compiler side, only the extraction of attributes needs to be performed by a preprocessor and an according declaration of a function being changeable at runtime must be applied.

This can be done by exploiting the features of the *Executable and Linkable Format* (ELF) [14]: a single ELF file dissects into several segments carrying individual sections, hence enabling monolithic, multi-architecture binaries, or including additional segments required by a specific runtime system. This way, a uniform, self-contained binary file or library can be provided using the underlying structures and ideas of the ELF specification. Both, binary file and library, can be used with either traditional runtime environments, disregarding the guidance information, or a dedicated virtualization and mapping environment targeting reconfigurable and heterogeneous systems.

To permit execution of a uniform application binary on an adaptive, heterogeneous platform, we use a lightweight **virtualization layer**, dealing with function resolution and according hardware configuration. This virtualization layer is realized as an extension of existing dynamic linking methods as outlined in [2]. We therefore kindly direct the interested reader to that publication.

As an appropriate **hardware platform** for our virtualization layer, we implemented an adaptive heterogeneous multicore system. This system comprises an AMD Opteron 870 dual-core processor and an FPGA-based accelerator board [7] featuring a Xilinx Virtex4-FX100 FPGA and on-board memory. The FPGA's resources are partitioned in a way that up to six application accelerators can be integrated into the FPGA logic. The accelerator board is connected to the Opteron processor using HyperTransport [8], therefore enabling easy and low-latency memory access to and from the accelerator board.

4 Evaluation

In [2] we showed that no measurable overhead exists for the basic virtualization, which during normal execution, i.e. if no switching occurs, behaves identical to the native operation mode of the OS's runtime system for single- and multi-threaded (OpenMP) execution.

Verifying our hardware architecture und demonstrating its general applicability, we chose en- and decryption of arbitrary data using Triple DES (3DES); we used the TripleDES Core provided by OpenCores [3] for hardware, and the TripleDES implementation of the standard OpenSSL library [5], available on most modern Linux systems, as the software implementation. In our experimental setup, both function implementations are encapsulated in C functions and registered using the provided API. These functions are then extended by code counting the number of needed cycles.

For evaluation, we used 6 data files of different size with a maximum chunk size of 1MB each as input data to the 3DES unit, i.e. larger files were split accordingly. To avoid hard drive latencies, the files were stored in main memory both at the beginning and after decryption. The Opteron processor operated at a clock frequency of 2GHz, the application accelerators at 100MHz with a derived HT Link frequency of 200MHz. Table 1 shows the obtained results for single-thread/accelerator execution. For small file sizes, the software implementation is faster, as no overhead for initialization of the data transfer to the hardware accelerator or to main memory occurs. For medium or large file sizes, the hardware implementation should be used, as the data transfer overhead becomes insignificant compared to computation time.

Table 1. Runtime depending on the data size

File Size	Hardware Implementation (1 Core)			Software Implementation (1 Thread)		
	Cycles	Time [ms]	Thr.put [MB/s]	Cycles	Time [ms]	Thr.put [MB/s]
1 KByte	864023	0.4	2.50	88425	0.08	12.50
10 KByte	1290012	0.64	15.63	1419408	0.70	14.28
100 KByte	4994667	2.49	40.16	14074467	7.02	14.24
1 MByte	49980110	24.93	41.08	144060568	71.86	14.25
10 MByte	499340518	249.0	41.12	1424615045	710.7	14.41
100 MByte	4993356084	2491	41.12	14210768748	7089	14.45

5 Conclusion and Outlook

Future systems do not only feature massive parallelism, but furthermore expose a high degree of heterogeneity and will employ reconfigurability as a means to maximize silicon use. In order to foster adoption of such systems and ease the migration of conventional approaches, we developed an infrastructure targeting the full exploitation of the underlying hardware of heterogeneous, reconfigurable parallel systems without burdening the programmer with details of the underlying hardware.

Core of this framework is a lightweight runtime system performing function resolution according to the current system configuration and adhering to application requirements. This process is guided by an augmented application description, enabling declaration of implementation alternatives of individual functions and providing according meta-data such as required or provided performance data. This augmentation takes place by exploiting specific features of the ELF specification, providing compatibility with conventional systems. Embracing and extending the ELF's so-called lazy-linking technique, functions are resolved on-demand to be adjusted to changed software requirements or hardware environment. The runtime system offers a dedicated control interface to monitor both application execution and hardware. Furthermore, an interface for controlling hardware reconfiguration exists.

The core components of our framework were thoroughly evaluated, proving that the virtualization layer does not contribute a significant amount to the overall execution time, but furthermore does tightly integrate into the existing runtime layer.

Based on industry-standard components, a reconfigurable accelerator hardware was built and an application example was presented, concentrating on the control aspects, i.e. whether and when to migrate from software-based implementation to a hardware-accelerated version. This is an initial step towards a fully automated control daemon employing runtime profiling and evaluation to guide the function switching process and, at a later stage, driving binary transformation.

Currently, the virtualization layer is refined to further enhance compatibility aspects. A manually driven version of the control daemon exists, which is developed into an automated version. In addition, work is conducted with respect to code generation and augmenting the ELF format, containing attributed application and library binaries.

Overall, the concept has proven to be versatile in use while maintaining maximum compatibility, providing a smooth upgrade path from conventional, static parallel systems to future dynamically reconfigurable heterogeneous multicore systems.

References

1. Advanced Micro Devices. AMD Fusion Whitepaper, http://www.amd.com/us/MarketingDownloads/AMD_fusion_Whitepaper.pdf
2. Buchty, R., Kramer, D., Kicherer, M., Karl, W.: A Light-weight Approach to Dynamical Runtime Linking Supporting Heterogenous, Parallel, and Reconfigurable Architectures. In: The 2009 International Conference on Architecture of Computing Systems (ARCS 2008), Delft, The Netherlands (to appear) (March 2009)
3. Socek, D.: 3DES/DES VHDL Core (2006), http://opencores.org/projects.cgi/web/3des_vhdl/overview
4. De Bosschere, K., Luk, W., Martorell, X., Navarro, N., O'Boyle, M., Pnevmatikatos, D., Ramírez, A., Sainrat, P., Seznec, A., Stenström, P., Temam, O.: High-Performance Embedded Architecture and Compilation Roadmap. In: Stenström, P. (ed.) Transactions on High-Performance Embedded Architectures and Compilers I. LNCS, vol. 4050, pp. 5–29. Springer, Heidelberg (2007)
5. Ralf, S.: Engelschall and The OpenSSL Project. OpenSSL: The Open Source toolkit for SSL/TLS, http://www.openssl.org/
6. Held, J., Bautista, J., Koehl, S.: From a Few Cores to Many: A Tera-scale Computing Research Overview. Research at Intel Whitepaper (2006), http://download.intel.com/research/platform/terascale/terascale_overview_paper.pdf
7. Fröning, H., Nüssle, M., Slogsnat, D., Litz, H., Brüning, U.: HTX Board: A Rapid Prototyping Station. In: 3rd annual FPGAworld Conference (November 2006), http://ra.ziti.uni-heidelberg.de/pages/papers/2006/1.pdf
8. HyperTransport Consortium. HyperTransport: Low latency Chip-to-Chip and beyond Interconnect (2008), http://www.hypertransport.org
9. Cray Inc. Cray XD1 Supercomputer (2004), http://www.cray.com/downloads/Cray_XD1_Datasheet.pdf
10. Linderman, M.D., Collins, J.D., Wang, H., Meng, T.H.: Merge: a programming model for heterogeneous multi-core systems. In: ASPLOS XIII: Proceedings of the 13th international conference on Architectural support for programming languages and operating systems, pp. 287–296. ACM, New York (2008)
11. RapidMind, Inc. RapidMind Multi-Core Development Platform (2008), http://www.rapidmind.net/
12. Vassiliadis, S., Wong, S., Cotofana, S.D.: The MOLEN μ-coded Processor. In: Brebner, G., Woods, R. (eds.) FPL 2001. LNCS, vol. 2147, pp. 275–285. Springer, Heidelberg (2001)
13. Huang, S., Hormati, A., Bacon, D., Rabbah, R.: Liquid Metal: Object-Oriented Programming Across the Hardware/Software Boundary. In: Vitek, J. (ed.) ECOOP 2008. LNCS, vol. 5142, pp. 76–103. Springer, Heidelberg (2008)
14. The Santa Cruz Operation, Inc. System V Application Binary Interface, Edition 4.1 (1997), http://www.caldera.com/developers/devspecs/gabi41.pdf
15. Wang, P.H., Collins, J.D., Chinya, G.N., Jiang, H., Tian, X., Girkar, M., Yang, N.Y., Lueh, G.-Y., Wang, H.: EXOCHI: architecture and programming environment for a heterogeneous multi-core multithreaded system. SIGPLAN Not. 42(6), 156–166 (2007)
16. NoTA World. NoTA – Open Architecture Initiative (2008), http://www.notaworld.org/

Pipeline Scheduling with Input Port Constraints for an FPGA-Based Biochemical Simulator

Tomoya Ishimori[1], Hideki Yamada[1], Yuichiro Shibata[1], Yasunori Osana[2],
Masato Yoshimi[3], Yuri Nishikawa[3], Hideharu Amano[3], Akira Funahashi[4],
Noriko Hiroi[5], and Kiyoshi Oguri[1]

[1] Department of Computer and Information Sciences, Nagasaki University
[2] Department of Computer and Information Science, Seikei University
[3] Department of Information and Computer Science, Keio University
[4] Department of Biosciences and Informatics, Keio University
[5] EMBL-EBI
bio@pca.cis.nagasaki-u.ac.jp

Abstract. This paper discusses design methodology of high-throughput arithmetic pipeline modules for an FPGA-based biochemical simulator. Since limitation of data-input bandwidth caused by port constraints often has a negative impact on pipeline scheduling results, we propose a priority assignment method of input data which enables efficient arithmetic pipeline scheduling under given input port constraints. Evaluation results with frequently used rate-law functions in biochemical models revealed that the proposed method achieved shorter latency compared to ASAP and ALAP scheduling with random input orders, reducing hardware costs by 17.57 % and by 27.43 % on average, respectively.

1 Introduction

The importance of biochemical simulation is rising in the context of systems biology, which aims at understanding biological processes in a system level. While various biochemical simulators intended for whole-cell simulation have been developed[2,3], such large scale software simulators require both a fair amount of time and large computing resources. To overcome this problem, we have developed an FPGA-based biochemical simulator called ReCSiP (Reconfigurable Cell Simulation Platform)[1].

ReCSiP executes high-throughput simulation of biochemical model based on ordinary differential equations with custom hardware solvers tailored for given target models. The solvers are essentially deeply pipelined arithmetic function modules to calculate velocity of chemical reactions according to rate-law functions. While high-throughput design of solvers directly improves the overall performance of simulation, compact design allows higher degree of parallel execution with multiple solvers. So far, a wide range of research activities on high-level synthesis techniques that generate high throughput pipeline modules have been carried out [4,5,6,7,8,9]. However, the following two issues seem to be rarely addressed while they need to be taken into account in practical reconfigurable computing platforms like ReCSiP.

J. Becker et al. (Eds.): ARC 2009, LNCS 5453, pp. 368–373, 2009.
© Springer-Verlag Berlin Heidelberg 2009

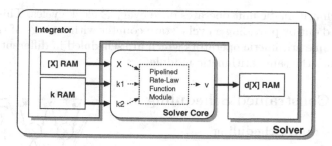

Fig. 1. Structure of a Solver

1. Due to data input bandwidth limitation for pipeline modules, all of input data required to calculate the arithmetic function cannot be fed at the same time.
2. The input data may not necessarily be able to be fed from any input ports. For example, each solver in ReCSiP has three input ports; one for variables conveying chemical concentration and two for variables of reaction rate coefficients. Any concentration variables can not be fed through ports for coefficients. Such architectural constraints effectively reduces switching costs, enabling high operational frequency.

Therefore, scheduling of the data input sequence also plays an important role in terms of the trade-off between performance and hardware costs of solvers.

2   ReCSiP Simulator and Solver Cores

An FPGA on ReCSiP contains ordinary differential equation *Solvers*, switch modules for inter-solver data communication, and PCI interface. Each Solver consists of a *Solver Core* module to calculate the change in concentrations of substances for each time step and an *Integrator* module to perform numerical integration and simulation control. Figure 1 shows the structure of a Solver.

A Solver Core, which is a statically scheduled pipeline module with single precision floating point arithmetic, calculates and outputs a reaction rate v using data from three input ports; one for concentrations of substances and two for reaction coefficients. The structure of Solver Core varies depending on the rate-law function to be calculated. An Integrator has three sets of memories for concentrations (corresponding to [X] RAM), for rate coefficients of each function (k RAM), and for concentration changes occurred by reactions (d[X] RAM). An Integrator performs numerical integration to calculate concentration changes for each time step using Solver Cores.

Since data-input bandwidth constraints to Solver Cores often prevent all the data required by the reaction from being initiated at once, those data should be ordered so as to mitigate arithmetic units' stalls by the inputs. Here, we define pipeline pitch P as the number of clock cycles to complete input. In the case that the value of P is 2 or more, idle clock cycles on arithmetic units might arise.

That is, each arithmetic unit operates once every P clock cycles. This control is easily carried out by providing a cyclic state counter with a range of the pipeline pitch. The same arithmetic operators which are scheduled in different states can be shared into the same arithmetic module.

3   Port Constrained Scheduling

3.1   Data-Input Scheduling

In our approach, we divide scheduling process into two tasks; we first assign a priority to each input data for a Solver Core based on structural information obtained by the corresponding DFG, then performs pipeline scheduling of minimize the conflicts of arithmetic units. We determine input timing of each data in the descending order of the following three priority metrics. Let us consider the following rate-law function:

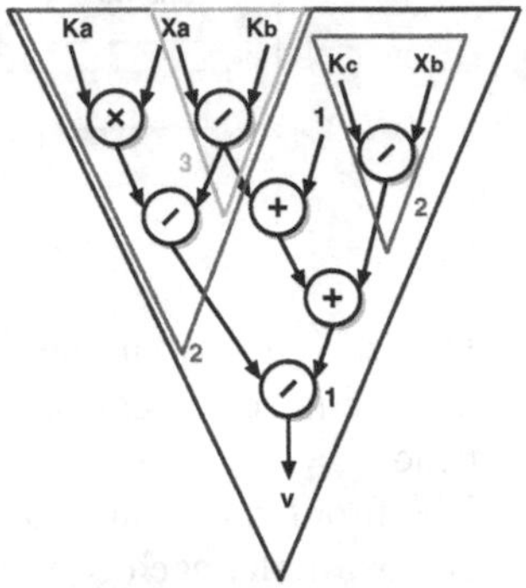

Fig. 2. DFG and subtrees for Function (1)

$$v = \frac{K_a X_a/(X_a/K_b)}{1 + X_a/K_b + K_c/X_b} \tag{1}$$

where X_a, X_b are input through the X port and K_a, K_b, K_c are fed by two K ports.

(1) Usage frequency: Assume that m arithmetic units need the same input data D_m, and n arithmetic units do D_n. When m is larger than n, it might be better to make the priority of D_m higher than that of D_n. To fill in the details, input of D_m allows m arithmetic units to be *half-ready*, in which a node waits for the other input data to initiate the operation, and the same holds true for D_n. Here, D_m could have the higher probability for the beginning of operations than D_n by the assumption, just $m \geq n$. Consequently, giving the higher priority to the input data used on more arithmetic units, might be preferable. Incidentally, usage frequency of input data corresponds directly to out-degree, or the number of edges leaving the node. Taking Function (1) for example, priorities come to be $\{\{X_a\}, \{X_b, K_a, K_b, K_c\}\}$.

(2) The number of successors: Obviously, making the data on the critical path of the DFG input first is better to minimize the latency. The precise critical path, however, can be changed by scheduling of the data input order itself. An easy way to predict the critical path is to use the sum of latencies of arithmetic units along the path, but this idea does not consider the stall time. Since each arithmetic unit may have different stall time, the path whose sum of latencies is small could be critical. Therefore, we propose to use the number of successors from primary input to primary output. The number of successors roughly corresponds to the number of operations performed until the primary output. Taking Function (1) for example, priorities come to be $\{\{X_a, K_b\}, \{X_b, K_a, K_c\}\}$.

(3) Divider subtrees: In general, dividers often have the largest latency among the basic arithmetic units. In fact, the latency of the divider is about 5 times larger than that of the add-subtractor and multiplier in the current ReCSiP design. Therefore, we propose to use the idea of subtrees headed by dividers as shown in Figure 2. To begin with the primary output v, its immediate predecessors are scanned to find dividers. Every time a divider is found, a new subtree is made toward the primary inputs. Finally, the priority of input data is assigned based on how many divider subtrees cover the corresponding the input data. Taking Function (1) for example, priorities come to be $\{\{X_a, K_b\}, \{X_b, K_a, K_c\}\}$.

3.2 Arithmetic Pipeline Scheduling

As a method for arithmetic scheduling, a wide varieties of algorithms such as the ASAP (As Soon As Possible) /ALAP (As Late As Possible) scheduling [4], heuristic optimal FDS (Force-Directed Scheduling) [5,6], a globally optimal ILP (Integer Linear Programming) [7], and List-based scheduling using DFG information [8,9] have been proposed. Our algorithm is based on the List-based scheduling and consists of the following steps:

1. Calculate the mobilities of each operation using the ASAP/ALAP schedule. The *mobility* is defined as the difference between the ASAP time and ALAP time of the operation. Make a *ready-list* (priority queue), which is always sorted with respect to a *priority function*. The operation with a smaller mobility has a higher priority.
2. Iterate Step 3 and 4 to complete the scheduling of all operations.
3. Determine the operation schedule according to the priority of a list, avoiding the same initiation states among operations.
4. Update a list and delete scheduled data from it. ASAP time and ALAP time of operations whose predecessors or successors have been scheduled, are changed. Then, these changed values are used to re-calculate the mobilities.

The hardware cost reduction is tried by using available information from the rate-law function of the corresponding DFG, keeping the latency of the Solver Core. The framework of this algorithm is similar to that of FDS, but complicated calculation process such as *force* is not necessary in our method.

4 Evaluation

The algorithm was implemented in C++ (gcc 4.0.0) and the steps from DFG generation to Verilog-HDL file generation are automated. To evaluate the quality of our method, it was applied on 18 rate-law functions of the 33 SBML (System Biology Markup Language) pre-defined functions. The generated Verilog files were mapped on a XC2VP70-6FF1517 FPGA, using the Xilinx ISE 8.2i tool. Latencies of adders, multipliers, and dividers used in this implementation are 5, 5, and 27 clock cycles, respectively.

Table 1. Implementation results and comparison to basic scheduling (N: operation count, L: latency, F: frequency, T: throughput, S: slice count)

Function	N	Basic ASAP				Basic ALAP				Proposed			
		L	F(MHz)	T(Mrps)	S	L	F(MHz)	T(Mrps)	S	L	F(MHz)	T(Mrps)	S
UCTR	15	71	123.9	41.3	2859	71	125.1	41.7	3605	71	124.3	41.4	2664
UMAR	15	71	123.9	41.3	2859	71	125.1	41.7	3605	71	124.3	41.4	2647
UMR	15	71	123.9	41.3	2858	71	125.1	41.7	3605	71	124.3	41.4	2647
UNIR	15	71	123.9	41.3	2858	71	125.1	41.7	3605	71	124.3	41.4	2663
UCTI	10	70	141.0	70.5	3356	70	141.0	70.5	2716	69	141.5	70.7	3285
UMAI	10	70	141.0	70.5	3356	70	141.0	70.5	2716	69	141.5	70.7	2570
UMI	10	70	141.0	70.5	3356	70	141.0	70.5	2716	69	141.5	70.7	2569
UNII	10	70	141.0	70.5	3356	70	141.0	70.5	2716	69	141.5	70.7	3285
UUCI	8	70	139.3	69.6	2513	70	139.3	69.6	2044	70	139.3	69.6	2028
UUCR	13	71	124.6	41.5	2842	71	126.0	42.0	3574	71	124.9	41.6	2090
UAII	7	64	138.1	69.0	2380	64	139.0	69.5	1728	64	138.1	69.0	2395
UAR	12	70	127.2	42.4	3309	70	124.9	41.6	2764	69	125.3	41.7	2623
UCII	7	64	138.1	69.0	2380	64	139.0	69.5	1728	64	138.8	69.4	2395
UCIR	12	70	127.2	42.4	3309	70	124.9	41.6	2764	69	125.1	41.7	2623
ORDBBR	34	93	108.1	21.6	9476	93	121.5	24.3	15664	90	119.8	31.9	6519
ORDBUR	18	82	122.0	30.5	3077	82	124.1	31.0	2501	79	122.3	30.5	2349
ORDUBR	18	76	124.5	31.1	2600	76	122.9	30.7	2420	74	123.9	30.9	2890
PPBR	25	83	115.7	23.1	6255	83	121.9	24.3	11085	79	113.1	22.6	3903

Table 2. Results with modified ASAP/ALAP scheduling (L: latency, F: frequency, T: throughput, S: slice count)

Function	Modified ASAP				Modified ALAP			
	L	F(MHz)	T(Mrps)	S	L	F(MHz)	T(Mrps)	S
UCTR	71	123.8	41.2	2780	71	125.1	41.7	3621
UMAR	71	123.8	41.2	2780	71	125.1	41.7	3621
UMR	71	123.8	41.2	2780	71	125.1	41.7	3621
UNIR	71	123.8	41.2	2780	71	125.1	41.7	3621
UCTI	69	141.0	70.5	3372	69	141.0	70.5	2716
UMAI	69	141.0	70.5	2569	69	141.0	70.5	2716
UMI	69	141.0	70.5	2569	69	141.0	70.5	2716
UNII	69	141.0	70.5	3372	69	141.0	70.5	2716
UUCI	70	139.3	69.6	2044	70	139.3	69.6	2060
UUCR	71	126.3	42.1	2175	71	126.0	42.0	3590
UAII	64	138.1	69.0	2380	64	139.0	69.5	1728
UAR	69	126.3	42.1	3409	69	124.9	41.6	2749
UCII	64	138.1	69.0	2380	64	139.0	69.5	1728
UCIR	69	126.6	42.2	2596	69	124.9	41.6	2749
ORDBBR	90	109.6	21.9	6928	90	121.5	24.3	15573
ORDBUR	79	124.5	31.1	5147	79	124.1	31.0	2453
ORDUBR	74	122.8	30.7	2588	74	122.9	30.7	2404
PPBR	79	109.5	21.9	5942	79	121.7	24.3	11041

Table 1 shows the implementation results of *basic* ASAP/ALAP scheduling and the proposed scheduling. Here, *basic* means data-input timing is determined in a random order. In determining data-input timing for the proposed scheduling, the highest priority is given to the number of successors, and then the number of divider subtrees gets preference over the usage frequency. Compared to the ASAP/ALAP, the proposed algorithm achieved the best latency for every function, reflecting the effectiveness of our data-input scheduling policy. In terms of the frequency and throughput (reactions per second), the achieved performance was almost same, while the required slice count was reduced by 17.57 % on average, showing considerable trade-off. The average hardware reduction rate of 27.43 % was achieved, affecting calculation throughput only by 0.5 %.

Furthermore, to evaluate the effect of arithmetic scheduling, we compared our algorithm to *modified* ASAP scheduling and *modified* ALAP scheduling. The results were summarized in Table 2. Here, *modified* means that data-input timing is determined in the same way as the proposed algorithm. Unlike the basic scheduling algorithms, any differences in latency were not observed for the modified algorithms and the proposed algorithm. This implies scheduling of data-input timing is quite important for achieving short latency. In terms of required slices, the proposed algorithm achieved the reduction rates of 11.37 % and 27.3 % on average compared to ASAP and ALAP, respectively. This reduction comes from arithmetic scheduling algorithm itself. In addition, the differences in the reduction rates between the basic and modified algorithms suggest that scheduling of data-input timing is also a significant factor to reduce the hardware costs.

5 Conclusion

In this paper, a priority assignment method for data-input to enable efficient arithmetic pipeline scheduling with input bandwidth constraints is proposed. Evaluation results with the SBML pre-defined functions revealed that the proposed method achieved shorter latency compared to randomly input ASAP and ALAP scheduling, reducing hardware costs by 17.57 % and by 27.43 % on average, respectively. Our future work includes further investigating of the trade-offs among the priority parameters with large scale graphs.

References

1. Osana, Y., et al.: ReCSiP: An FPGA-based general-purpose biochemical simulator. Elect. and Communications in Japan, Part 2, 90(7), 1–10 (2007)
2. Tomita, M., et al.: E-Cell: software environment for whole cell simulation. Bioinformatics 15(1), 72–84 (1999)
3. Moraru, I.I., et al.: The virtual cell: an integrated modeling environment for experimental for and computational cell biology. Annals of the New York Academy of Sciences, vol. 971, pp. 595–596 (2002)
4. Walker, R.A., Chaudhuri, S.: Introduction to the Scheduling Problem. IEEE Design and Test of Computers, 60–69 (Summer 1995)
5. Paulin, P.G., Knight, J.: Algorithm for High-Level Synthesis. IEEE Design & Test of Computers 6(6), 18–31 (1989)
6. Paulin, P.G., Knight, J.: Force-Directed Scheduling for the Behavioral Synthesis of ASICs. Trans. CAD 8(6), 661–679 (1989)
7. Hwang, C.-T., et al.: A Formal Approach to the Scheduling Problem in High Level Synthesis. IEEE Trans. CAD 10(4), 464–475 (1991)
8. Govindarajan, S., Vemuri, R.: Cone-Based Clustering Heuristic for List-Scheduling Algorithms. In: Proc. EDTC, Paris, France, pp. 456–462 (1997)
9. Sllame, A.M., Drabek, V.: An Efficient List-Based Scheduling Algorithm for High-Level Synthesis. In: Proc. DSD, pp. 316–323 (2002)

ACCFS – Operating System Integration of Computational Accelerators Using a VFS Approach

Andreas Heinig[1], Jochen Strunk[1], Wolfgang Rehm[1], and Heiko Schick[2,*]

[1] Chemnitz University of Technology,
Str. der Nationen 62, 09126 Chemnitz, Germany
{heandr,sjoc,rehm}@cs.tu-chemnitz.de
http://www.tu-chemnitz.de/cs/ra/projects/accfs/
[2] IBM Deutschland Research & Development GmbH
Schönaicher Str. 220, 71032 Böblingen, Germany
schickhj@de.ibm.com

Abstract. For a number of applications integrating specialized computational accelerators into a general-purpose computing environment yields more performance per watt and per dollar than a pure multi-core approach. In contrast to fully application-specific hybrid solutions we offer the advantage to maintain traditional programming models and development environments to a certain extent. In this paper we introduce an open generic operating system interface concept what we call Accelerator File System (ACCFS) for integrating application accelerators into Linux based platforms. By describing the proposed concepts and interface we contribute to a broader discussion of this challenging topic.

1 Introduction

The usage of reconfigurable hardware becomes more and more an important theme in research and industry. Especially FPGAs (e.g. Xilinx Virtex, Altera Stratix, DRC.) can speedup a variety of applications. Woods et al. [1] gained a speedup of more than 50 compared with a CPU when accelerating a Quasi-Monte Carlo Simulation.

An emerging type of computational accelerators are Programmable Graphic Processors. The leading vendors for graphic boards recently presented special techniques to accelerate applications with their chips. Massive parallel GPGPUs (General Purpose Graphics Processing Units), like the Nvidia Tesla or the AMD FireStream chips, enable huge speedups. For example, a "deformable image registration" calculation reaches a speedup by factor 34 [2].

Another platform is the IBM Cell/B.E. processor which was developed in a cooperation of IBM, Toshiba and Sony. On this processor multiple independent

---

* The ACCFS project is performed in collaboration with the Center of Advanced Study IBM Böblingen, Development and Research, Germany.

J. Becker et al. (Eds.): ARC 2009, LNCS 5453, pp. 374–379, 2009.
© Springer-Verlag Berlin Heidelberg 2009

vector processors called SPUs (Synergistic Processing Units) are built around a 64-bit PowerPC core (PPE).

One of the big challenges when using such "accelerators" is the efficient integration into a HPC system environment and the definition of appropriate programming models as well. In this paper we address the operating system integration by defining an open generalized interface. Therefore, we evolve basic concepts in Sections 3. The implementation called Accelerator File System (ACCFS) is described in Section 4. In Section 5 some accelerator examples are mentioned. Section 6 discusses further work and summarizes the results.

2   Related Work

To integrate a FPGA into the operating system several solutions exist. One is the extension of Linux with hardware processes (e.g. BORPH [3]) or hardware threads (e.g. ReconOS [4]). BORPH uses conventional UNIX IPC mechanisms to communicate. Inter-thread communication is mapped to FIFOs. The hardware threads introduced by ReconOS can use the normal operating system services to interact with the environment. However, both solutions only concentrate on FPGA integration without providing an open interface for easy integration of additional hardware by using clearly exported structures. Also, these models lack performance when they are implemented on platforms where the processor that is running the operating system is not an integral part of the FPGA itself. The main drawback is the deep modification of the Linux kernel. Thus porting to another kernel version becomes more complicated and sometimes impossible without patching when major kernel parts are changed in a new revision.

Another approach for FPGA integration is XVFS (Xilinx Virtual File System) presented by Donlin et al. [5]. Here a virtual file system is used to directly modify the low-level parts of the FPGA. XVFS represents all heterogeneous resources in a file system hierarchy. Thus, it is possible to use standard `read` or `write` system calls to get or manipulate the configuration of the FPGA. Furthermore, access to every LUT, BRAM and routing information is granted. However, we do not need such a detailed view as it is necessary for real-time or embedded system designers. In our scope the FPGA is a computational accelerator where we abstract the functionalities. Only the communication mechanisms message passing and direct memory access together with the (re)configuration are needed. This will enable us to establish a generalized accelerator model which is beneficial for library and application programmers. When accelerating an application, the same communication and usage models can be adopted even if different accelerator types are used.

If we look at graphic cards, we will see another integration approach named CUDA [6]. A C-like language is used to program Nvidia graphic chips. CUDA enforces a functional offload programming model where the compute kernels are off-loaded to the GPGPU. The graphic card is exported to the user-space via a character device. Data exchange is enabled through DMA transfers supported by a library. It is not possible to map the memory into the application address space. This restricts the achievable performance in a variety of communication patterns. A second drawback is the usage of the `ioctl` kernel interface. It is not possible to provide an open generic interface when using such `ioctl`s, because no standards exist how to define these.

A. Bergmann developed SPUFS (Synergistic Processing Unit File System) [7], which is used to integrate the SPUs of the Cell/B.E. processor into the Linux environment. The concepts of SPUFS are the virtualization of the SPU and the virtual file system context access. A context is mapped into a virtual file system such that it appears as a directory containing special files. File system operations on these files effect the communication with a SPU.

The main advantage of both, SPUFS and XVFS, is the clean interface without the usage of `ioctl`s. Additionally no modifications of existing kernel structures are necessary. Thus, we base our solution on these concepts.

3   Accelerator Integration Concepts

Virtualization. To virtualize the accelerators we abstract the *physical accelerator* with an *accelerator context*. The context is the operational data set of the accelerator. It includes all necessary information to describe the current hardware state in such a way that the operation can be interrupted and resumed later without data loss. In a multi-user/thread/process environment, like Linux, virtualization optimizes the resource usage of the accelerators. Contexts which do not make use of the hardware at a given time are not scheduled on the physical accelerator.

Generic Interface. We propose a virtual file system (VFS) to interface the accelerator. This offers the advantage of a complete `ioctl` free implementation because every functionality can be exported through a dedicated file. Each context can be bounded on a directory inside the VFS. The accelerator is accessible through a set of files supporting the POSIX file operations. To include reconfigurable hardware as well, this file set has to be dynamically exported.

Separation. The integration of new accelerators will be much easier when splitting the functionalities in a part which handles the common abstraction layers and a part managing the low-level hardware access.

Host initiated DMA (Direct Memory Access). To interact with the accelerator several methods are feasible. One is simple memory mapped IO with standard load/store machine instructions. In this memory access method the host is the active part who issues a read or write for every memory access. Another method is DMA-bulk transfer. Here the accelerator needs a DMA unit capable of moving the data. In cases where the accelerator is able to initiate these transfers by itself, the DMA unit has to handle virtual memory managing issues, too. However, not every accelerator supports virtual memory. For this reason we propose host initiated DMA, where the host setups the memory management unit and initialize the data transfer. The actual data movement is done asynchronously by the accelerator.

Asynchronous Context Execution. This concept eases the software development because multi-threading is not required when using multiple accelerator units. Every context runs asynchronously to the host system.

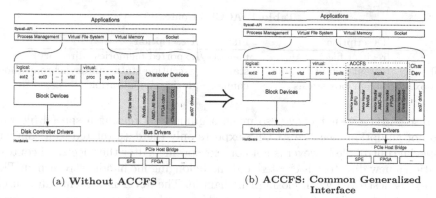

(a) **Without ACCFS**

(b) **ACCFS: Common Generalized Interface**

Fig. 1. ACCFS - Layered Structure

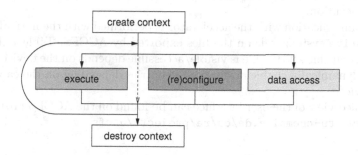

Fig. 2. Flow Diagram: ACCFS Interface Usage

4 ACCFS - Implementation

The concepts described in Section 3 are implemented in ACCFS (Accelerator File System). ACCFS is an open generic system interface based on SPUFS. It is designed to integrate different accelerator types into the Linux operating system. The goal of ACCFS is to replace the different character device based interfaces (cf. Figure 1a) with a generic file system based interface (cf. Figure 1b).

The whole dotted block in Figure 1b shows ACCFS which is divided into two parts. Part one, labeled "accfs", is the file system driver. Its task is to handle the common stuff equally belonging to all accelerators. Included are VFS management, context creation, setting up DMA transfers, and providing the user interface. Last but not least it handles the integration of the second part the "device handlers". Therefore, a special interface called "Vendor Interface" is implemented.

4.1 User Interface / VFS

ACCFS implements the flow diagram shown in Figure 2.

Before the application can use an accelerator a context has to be created by invoking the `acc_create` system call. The desired accelerator type is selected with the arguments *vendor_id* and *device_id*. We chose this extra system call

Table 1. ACCFS Context

File	Description	File	Description
regs	register file	memory/	exported memories (directory)
[io]box	in/out-bound mailbox	status	execution status and synchronization
[io]box_stat	in/out-box status	config	device configuration

because `mkdir` can not convey so much arguments. Creating a special file was also not an option, because ACCFS exports only the data related to a context. A special control file however is not context specific. After the successful context creation a new directory is created and the belonging file handle is returned. The context is destroyed when closing this handle. The `acc_run` system call is used to start the execution of the accelerator. The accelerator (program) is executed asynchronously, meaning that `acc_run` returns immediately without waiting for finished execution.

The communication with the accelerator is performed with the normal POSIX `read` or `write` system calls on the files exported by ACCFS. Table 1 shows an overview of the file set. If a file is visible/accessible depends on the device handler that can dynamically enable or disable the entries depending on the capabilities of the device.

A detailed view of the user interface can be found on the ACCFS project page `http://www.tu-chemnitz.de/cs/ra/projects/accfs`.

4.2   Vendor Interface

The vendor interface consists of a couple of functions exported by *accfs* and a structure called *accfs_vendor* which have to be registered by each device handler. This structure contains callback functions which are invoked by *accfs* instead of the generic routines. For example, if the vendor needs to constrain the register file access because the hardware can only write to 32bit boundaries, the device handler has to declare the `regs_write` function. Inside this function the correct alignment can be checked.

5   Accelerator Support

Currently we are working on Cell/B.E. integration. Hereby a QS21 Cell Blade is coupled with a Intel Xeon System via PCIe. We have already established a heterogeneous coupling over Ethernet. There the RSPUFS (Remote SPUFS)[8] implementation made the SPUs accessible on the AMD Opteron system.

As another proof of concept we have implemented an accelerator for arithmetic operations on a HyperTransport FPGA card [9] based on a Xilinx Virtex-4. An Iwill DK8-HTX motherboard with two Opteron processors is used as host system. To get the FPGA running as a HT cave device we replaced the pre-installed BIOS with a modified LinuxBIOS version. Our first test results looks promising. We are able to exchange reconfigurable modules (currently a pattern matcher and a Mersenne Twister) during run-time with the help of ACCFS. A detailed description of our solution will be published in a paper which is already submitted under the name "Run-Time Reconfiguration for HyperTransport coupled FPGAs using ACCFS".

The virtualization of the FPGA is currently not implemented. However, we plan to realize a cooperative scheduling model, where a module running on the FPGA is requested to step in a kind of a "stop" state. When reached, the module will be removed after saving the block RAM. This means all information inside the block RAM must be sufficient to continue the operation after restore.

6 Conclusion

In this paper we have presented aspects of the concepts and the implementation of ACCFS. These concepts build the grounding of our approach to establish an open generalized accelerator interface. We have analyzed both reconfigurable and non-reconfigurable hardware to define a common set of interface functions. This interface supports the direct access of an accelerator through register file, memory or via mail boxing. Those functionalities are reflected in files inside the VFS exported by ACCFS. The file system calls **open**, **close**, **read**, **write**, and **mmap** are building the user interface. With the exception of two new system calls we do not modify any parts of the Linux kernel. This enables us to provide ACCFS support also for future kernel releases.

Further research will focus on the complete integration of the Cell/B.E. and FPGAs. We are also planning to port ACCFS to host systems other than x86.

References

1. Woods, N.A., VanCourt, T.: FPGA Acceleration of Quasi-Monte Carlo in Finance. In: Proceedings of FPL, pp. 335–340. IEEE, Heidelberg (2008)
2. Samant, S.S., Xia, J., Muyan-Ozcelik, P., Owens, J.D.: High performance computing for deformable image registration: Towards a new paradigm in adaptive radiotherapy. Medical Physics 35(8), 3546–3553 (2008)
3. So, H.K.-H., Brodersen, R.: A unified hardware/software runtime environment for FPGAbased reconfigurable computers using BORPH. Trans. on Embedded Computing Systems 7(2), 1–28 (2008)
4. Lübbers, E., Planner, M.: ReconOS: An RTOS Supporting Hard-and Software Threads. In: Proceedings of FPL, pp. 441–446. IEEE, Amsterdam (2007)
5. Donlin, A., Lysaght, P., Blodget, B., Troeger, G.: A Virtual File System for Dynamically Reconfigurable FPGAs. In: Proceedings of FPL, pp. 1127–1129 (2004)
6. NVIDIA, NVIDIA CUDA Compute Unified Device Architecture Programming Guide. Santa Clara, CA, Tech. Rep, version 1.1 (November 2007)
7. Bergmann, A.: The Cell Processor Programming Model. IBM Corporation, Tech. Rep. (June 2005)
8. Heinig, A., Oertel, R., Strunk, J., Rehm, W., Schick, H.: Generalizing the SPUFS concept - a case study towards a common accelerator interface. In: Proceedings of MRSC, Belfast, April 1-3 (2008)
9. Nüssle, M., Fröning, H., Giese, A., Litz, H., Slogsnat, D., Brüning, U.: A Hypertransport based low-latency reconfigurable testbed for message-passing developments. In: Proceedings of KiCC 2007 (2007)

A Multithreaded Framework for Sequential Monte Carlo Methods on CPU/FPGA Platforms

Markus Happe, Enno Lübbers, and Marco Platzner

University of Paderborn, Germany
{cyclash,enno.luebbers,platzner}@upb.de

Abstract. Sequential Monte Carlo techniques are among the principal tools for the on-line estimation of the state of a non-linear dynamic system. We propose a framework for the multithreaded implementation of the widely popular *sampling importance resampling* (SIR) method on hybrid CPU/FPGA systems. The framework is based on the multithreaded reconfigurable operating system ReconOS which allows for an easy repartitioning of threads between hard- and software. We demonstrate the framework on a case study for visual object tracking and evaluate the performance of different hardware/software partitionings.

1 Introduction

Sequential Monte Carl (SMC) methods, also denoted as particle filters, have become a popular tool for on-line estimation of the state of a non-linear, dynamic system. Particle filters are iterative methods that track a number of possible state estimates, the so-called particles, across time and gauge their probability by comparing them to measurements. State estimation of non-linear dynamic systems is an important problem with applications in areas as diverse as object tracking, network packet processing, and sensor networks. Because the particles tracked by SMC methods are independent, many calculations can be parallelized and are, additionally, amenable to implementation in dedicated logic. For example, Athalye et al. [1] developed methods and architectures for accelerating the resampling stage of the SIR algorithm while at the same time reducing the memory requirements for hardware implementations. Our framework adapts their technique for parallelizing the resampling stage. At the same time, the sequential algorithm governing these computations is implemented more efficiently using general purpose CPUs. These facts make today's modern platform FPGAs, which integrate fine-grained reconfigurable logic with dedicated CPUs, a promising implementation target for particle filters in embedded systems.

The novel contribution of this paper is a framework for implementing SMC methods on hybrid CPU/FPGA platforms. The framework significantly simplifies the design of particle filters following the *sampling importance resampling* (SIR) algorithm. By building on top of our multithreaded reconfigurable operating system ReconOS [2] the framework handles the recurring tasks of particle data transfer and thread control, letting the designer focus on the application-specific details of an individual particle filter. Because the operating system

J. Becker et al. (Eds.): ARC 2009, LNCS 5453, pp. 380–385, 2009.
© Springer-Verlag Berlin Heidelberg 2009

transparently supports both software and hardware threads using one unifying programming model, the designer can quickly create different hardware/software partitionings to react to changing application and performance requirements. The work of Saha et al. [3], who developed a parameterizable framework for the hardware implementation of particle filters, bears some similarity to our approach in that it provides an interface for the model definition of a particle filter. However, their proposed framework targets a hardware-only implementation of the filter and thus significantly differs from our flexible, multithreaded hardware/software approach.

2   Sequential Monte Carlo Methods

We are considering a dynamic system with state x_t at a given time t. As there can be uncertainty in the state information, we model the initial system state by its probability distribution $p(X_0)$, where X_0 is a random variable describing the state at time $t = 0$. The *system model* is a Markov process of first order. Thus, $p(X_t|X_{t-1})$ denotes the probability distribution of the system's current state given the system's previous state. We assume that the system state can only be tracked by measurements y_t, which may be influenced by noise. The relation between measurements and system states is described by the *measurement model*. The distribution $p(Y_t = y_t|X_t)$ describes the probability of the current measurement given the system's current state.

To predict the current state based on past measurements, $p(X_t|y_1, \cdots, y_{t-1})$, our framework closely follows the *sampling importance resampling* (SIR) algorithm. SIR is one of the most widely used sequential Monte Carlo methods, which allow system state estimates to be computed on-line while the state changes, as it is the case for tracking algorithms. For a more thorough discussion of the theoretical foundations of SMC methods we refer to [4].

An SIR filter usually manages a fixed number of possible system state hypotheses x_t^i, also called particles. Ideally, these particles approximate the distribution of the system state, $p(X_t)$. The SIR algorithm distinct stages iterated over discrete time steps. Figure 1 graphically represents one iteration. The individual stages are:

- **Sampling:** To follow the state during subsequent iterations ($t \leftarrow t + 1$), the system model is used to obtain a possible new state for every particle $\tilde{x}_t^i$ based on its last state x_{t-1}^i. Formally, this corresponds to drawing or *sampling* the new particle state from the distribution $p(X_t|X_{t-1} = x_{t-1}^i)$. Now, the set of particles $\tilde{x}_t^i$ forms a prediction of the distribution of X_t.
- **Importance:** The measurement model is evaluated for every particle and the current measurement to determine the *likelihood* that the current measurement y_t matches the predicted state $\tilde{x}_t^i$ of the particle. Formally, this corresponds to evaluating $p(Y_t = y_t|X_t = \tilde{x}_t^i)$. The resulting likelihood is assigned as a weight w_t^i to the particle and indicates the relative quality of the state estimation. In Figure 1, particles with higher weights are drawn as larger circles.

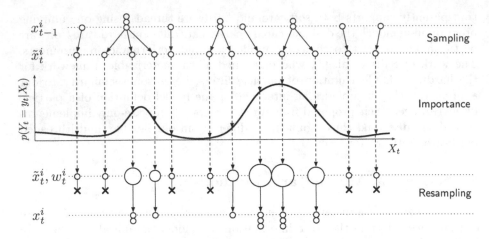

Fig. 1. Sampling importance resampling algorithm

- **Resampling:** Particles with comparatively high weights are duplicated and particles with low weights are eliminated. The distribution of the resulting particles x_t^i approximates the distribution of the weighted particles before resampling.

3   Particle Filter Framework

All particle filters using the SIR algorithm rely on the same underlying algorithmic structure. Hence, a substantial part of the functionality, code, and – in the case of hybrid CPU/FPGA systems – hardware circuitry can be re-used, allowing for a framework-based design approach. Our particle filter framework takes care of common tasks shared by all SIR implementations, such as data transfer and control flow, and lets the designer focus on the application-specific tasks, such as system and measurement modeling.

The distinctive feature of our particle filter framework is the use of multi-threaded programming across the hardware/software boundary. Because SIR filters are composed of a mixture of highly parallel, data-centric tasks and purely sequential, control-dominated tasks, hybrid CPU/FPGA systems appear as a natural choice for their implementation. Multithreading on such hybrid systems is enabled by the reconfigurable operating system ReconOS [2], which allows an application to be modularized into threads that are executed either in software on the system's CPU or in hardware in the FPGA's reconfigurable fabric. All threads communicate and synchronize using the same programming model primitives such as semaphores, message boxes, and shared memory.

Figure 2 shows the basic structure of an SIR implementation using our framework. The particles cycle through the three stages sampling, importance, and resampling. Each of these stages can have an arbitrary number of software and hardware threads. This execution structure is created and initialized by a software thread, which also sets the initial number of threads for each stage.

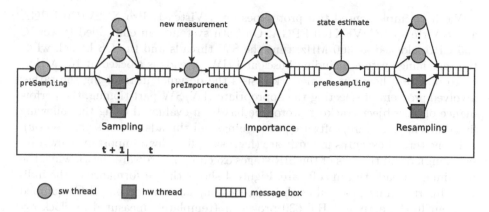

Fig. 2. Structure of an SIR filter implementation

Generally, the number of HW and SW threads for each of the stages will depend on the availability of computing resources, i.e. CPU utilization factors and logic area. The other threads of the framework are mainly control-dominated or show limited potential for parallelism and are therefore implemented in software. Access to the needed data, the control flow, as well as necessary operating system services for communication and synchronization are completely managed by the framework. Due to the fully transparent communication and synchronization across the hardware/software boundary provided by ReconOS, the designer can easily change the hardware/software partitioning by instantiating a different number of hardware and software threads in order to adapt to changing performance requirements and resource constraints.

4 Case Study

To demonstrate our framework, we have implemented a prototype system for visually tracking moving objects in a video sequence. The application uses the software implementation by Hess [5] as a template and reference. Given an initial tracking target, the particle filter estimates the object's position and size in each subsequent frame of the video sequence. An example of the desired tracking behavior can be seen in Figure 3.

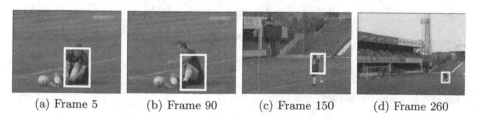

(a) Frame 5　　　　(b) Frame 90　　　　(c) Frame 150　　　　(d) Frame 260

Fig. 3. Object tracking in a video sequence (video sequence soccer)

We have implemented two prototypes on a Virtex-II Pro XC2VP30 FPGA and a Virtex-4 XC4VFX100 FPGA. On both systems, an embedded PowerPC 405 CPU, clocked at 300 MHz, runs the SW threads and the OS kernel, while the remaining system including buses and HW threads is clocked at 100 MHz.

To illustrate how our framework assists the designer in resolving the rather involved problem of selecting the appropriate HW/SW partitioning, the performance of our object tracking prototype has been evaluated using the following five different hardware/software partitionings: all threads run in software (sw), only one thread executes in hardware (hw_s: sampling, hw_i: importance, hw_r: resampling), or all threads of the SIR stages execute in hardware (hw_a), while the remaining threads run in software. Figure 4 shows the performance of the individual partitionings, as well as the reference implementation on a PC equipped with an Intel Pentium 4 HT 630 processor (template), measured in clock cycles per frame. The measurements were performed on the soccer video sequence displayed in Figure 3.

The overall drop of frame processing times in the first 250 frames of the sequence is due to the soccer player retreating into the background, which reduces the amount of image data to be considered per particle in the importance stage. Figure 4 also shows that partitionings which compute the importance stage in hardware, hw_i and hw_a, generally show the best performance. This indicates that, in our prototype, the importance stage is the computationally most expensive part of the application. However, the attainable speedup of any hardware-implemented stage is considerably data dependent – a partitioning that performs better than another during one part of the video can easily be worse during another part. This is demonstrated by the hw_r partitioning at frame 200 or 275. Also, computing more than one stage in hardware does not necessarily lead to better performance, as can be seen when comparing the hw_i and hw_a partitionings between frames 100 and 250.

Overall, the experimental results serve to highlight the advantage of a framework that allows for an easy HW/SW repartitioning. Using our framework, an application designer can quickly explore the design space to determine the

	Virtex2-Pro	Virtex-4
sw	5305	5355
hw_s	9449	9577
hw_i	8794	8955
hw_r	8314	8430
hw_a	—	15958

component	S	I	R
framework	1086	918	1227
user	1033	481(*)	-
OS	1353	1353	1353
total	3479	2873(*)	2580

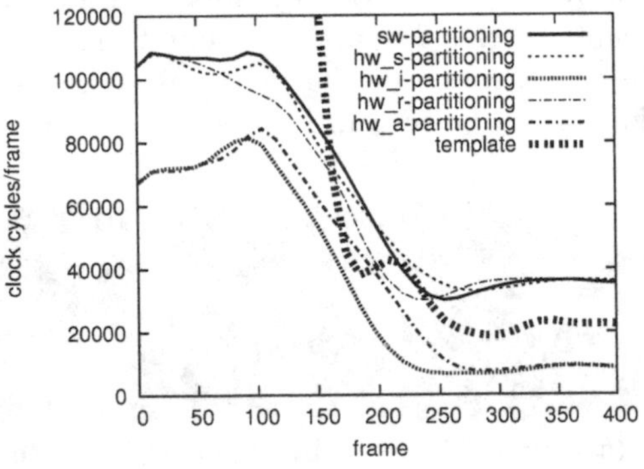

Fig. 4. Resource usage (slices) and performance ($\frac{cycles}{frame}$) of different partitionings

suitable partitioning. The framework even allows for changing the partitioning during runtime driven by characteristics of the input data. Adaptive repartitioning approaches are part of our ongoing research.

The resource requirements of the object tracking prototype as implemented on both target FPGAs are given in slices in the top table of Figure 4. It can be seen that the area used for the different partitionings is about the same on both target FPGAs. The most resource-consuming partitioning, hw_a, could only be mapped to the Virtex-4 board. The bottom table of Figure 4 shows FPGA resource utilization after synthesis for the three hardware threads of the framework, divided into slices for the functions provided by the framework, the user functions, and the ReconOS interface core.

5 Conclusion

In this work, we have presented a multithreaded framework for the implementation of SIR filters on hybrid CPU/FPGA systems, and demonstrated it using a case study for visual object tracking which uses the repartitioning capabilities of the framework to quickly explore the design space with regard to hardware/software partitioning of the filter's threads.

Our ongoing research focuses on two areas. First, we are working on refining and optimizing the structure of the framework to allow for a more efficient usage of hardware resources. Second, we are working on approaches to adapt the partitioning during runtime. Here, we are trying to exploit the target FPGA's partial reconfiguration capabilities for better utilization of the logic resources.

Acknowledgement

This work was supported by the German Research Foundation under project number PL471/2-1.

References

1. Athalye, A., Bolić, M., Hong, S., Djuric, P.M.: Generic Hardware Architectures for Sampling and Resampling in Particle Filters. EURASIP Journal on Applied Signal Processing (2005)
2. Lüubbers, E., Platzner, M.: ReconOS: An RTOS supporting Hard- and Software Threads. In: IEEE Int. Conf. on Field Programmable Logic and Applications (2007)
3. Saha, S., Bambha, N.K., Bhattacharyya, S.S.: A Parameterized Design Framework for Hardware Implementation of Particle Filters. In: IEEE Int. Conf. on Acoustics, Speech and Signal Processing (2008)
4. Doucet, A., de Freitas, N., Gordon, N.: Sequential Monte Carlo Methods in Practice. Springer, Heidelberg (2001)
5. Hess, R.: Particle Filter Object Tracking (2006),
   http://web.engr.oregonstate.edu/~hess

Author Index